DEDICATION

To the gallant and courageous men, past and present, who have come to the world's most famous brickyard over the years and made the Indianapolis "500" truly "The Greatest Spectacle in Automobile Racing."

THE INDIANAPOLIS 500

THE
INDIANAPOLIS
500

JACK C. FOX

THE WORLD PUBLISHING COMPANY

CLEVELAND AND NEW YORK

Published by The World Publishing Company
2231 West 110th Street, Cleveland, Ohio 44102

Published simultaneously in Canada by Nelson, Foster & Scott Ltd.

Library of Congress Catalog Card Number: 67 — 18019

ACKNOWLEDGMENTS

The author would like to take this opportunity to thank many of the people who have contributed so much toward making this book a reality. To complete a research project of this scope has required the cooperative efforts of the Indianapolis Motor Speedway Staff, racing historians, photographers and photo collectors, artists and production specialists as well as a number of people whose recollections of the cars, drivers and races helped to fill many of the blank spaces in the statistical tables.

Albert W. Bloemker, Indianapolis Motor Speedway Director of Publicity, gave his assistance in making the official Speedway photos and records available, offered guidance regarding the location of supplemental sources of information, and made valuable suggestions relative to the marketing problems of the book.

J. H. "Bud" Jones, Official Speedway Photographer, undertook the task of supervising the printing of over 1,600 photographs from the Speedway files. These photos constitute the majority of the car and driver photographs as well as many of the informal scenes, action photos, and driver portraits.

J. Robert "Bob" Laycock has been of invaluable assistance in two ways. He contributed most of the "History of the '500'" and checked the facts, entries, times and finishes with the official Speedway records, of which he is custodian in his capacity as Indianapolis Motor Speedway Historian.

Donald Davidson, who knows almost everything about the "500", was responsible for much of the research on the early-day relief drivers, officials, and pace cars. He also helped with the selection of a number of pictures and checked copy and statistics for factual errors.

Without the cooperation and assistance of racing's foremost historian and photo collector, Charles Lytle, this book might never have gone beyond the planning stages. No other person can come close to matching Charles' collection of historic "500" photos and, as the owner of the original glass plate negatives taken between 1913 and 1922 by Harry H. Coburn, he holds the key to any publication showing the cars and drivers of that era. His personal knowledge of the contestants and his entertaining recollections of past "500's" have been most helpful in the preparation of this book.

A. E. "Scotty" Brubaker and Mike Connor, of the Firestone Tire and Rubber Company, have been especially cooperative in furnishing, and allowing me to reproduce, nearly a hundred historic photos from the Firestone archives. They have also given me access to Firestone's racing files for the purpose of additional research.

Either recently, or in past years, the following people have contributed anecdotes, pictures or information about the cars, their builders or their color combinations which have been used in this volume.   I am grateful to: J. C. Agajanian, Ronnie Allyn, Clay Ballinger, Henry Banks, Lloyd M. "Shorty" Barnes, Bear Manufacturing Corporation, Cliff Bergere, Paul Bost, Frank Brisko, Walter Bull, Anthony F. "Tony" Caccia, Jack Carmody, Floyd Clymer, George Connor, Dany Day, Peter DePaolo, S. T. "Pinkie" Donaldson, Richard G. "Dick" Doyle, Denny Duesenberg, William Enoch, Jr., Harlan Fengler, the late Earl B. Gilmore, Anthony "Tony" Gulotta, Harry Hartz, Luther Johnson, Paul Johnson, David J. Koetzla, Joe Lencki, the late A. B. "Deacon" Litz, Charles Marant, Carl Marchese, Cyrus Marshall, Ivan Mikan, Ralph Mulford, Dennis "Duke" Nalon, Joe Petrali, Ron Plew, Charles Saylor, Gordon Schroeder, Phil "Red" Shafer, Russell Snowberger, "Babe" Stapp, William Ray Stearns, Myron Stevens, The Studebaker Corporation, Perc C. Swartz, Ira Vail, Cornelius W. Van Ranst, Richard G. Webber, and Louis "Curly" Wetteroth.

I express sincere appreciation also to the staff of the H. M. Gousha Company for untiring efforts in design and technical preparation of the book. Above all, I give full measure of credit to Eugene F. Pisha for his devotion to publication of a complete, illustrated history of the "500" and his abiding faith that it could be done.

PREFACE

You hold in your hands a most unusual book.

It stands both as a fitting tribute to the thousands of people associated with the Indianapolis "500" Race in its first fifty presentations and as an enduring record of the evolution in racing machines which took place during the same period.

Thirty years of collecting elusive facts and figures, as well as thousands of photographs of winners and losers, are brought together in this work. It represents over sixteen years of my own personal observations as a photographer and writer covering the "500" for the Illustrated Speedway News.

As part of the historical research required to document this book, information otherwise unavailable from official sources was sought from drivers, car owners, builders, mechanics, photographers, historians and statisticians. Information obtained in this manner and reported herein as fact, may be subject to slight variation depending on the observer's memory and point of view.

Race statistics — times, speeds and finishing positions — were obtained from official Speedway records and are presumed to be accurate. Engine specifications were taken from official entry blanks and may differ somewhat from actual engine specifications at the start of the race.

Since the Speedway did not keep records of relief drivers prior to 1925, newspaper, periodical accounts, and personal recollections were relied on in compiling these data for the years 1911 through 1924. In this task, valuable assistance was rendered by Donald C. Davidson, Statistician of the United States Auto Club.

To veteran "railbirds" as well as to initiates in the fraternity of automobile racing fans, it is my sincere wish that some of the drama, spectacle, color, and sportsmanship attendant with each "500" race has been captured in the following pages. If this book also aids in focusing attention on the debt of gratitude owed to racing by motorists the world over, who daily benefit from lessons learned at the Speedway, then my efforts will have been well rewarded.

San Jose, California
February 9, 1967   Jack C. Fox

HISTORY OF THE "500"

Carl Fisher was a man of vision. He was also an astute businessman endowed with an aggressiveness which enabled him to turn his visions into practical realities.

When the "horseless carriage" made its appearance, Fisher, a former bicycle racer and dealer, immediately realized the vast possibilities of this revolutionary invention and bought the first automobile in Indianapolis. Soon he was selling curved-dash Oldsmobiles and barnstorming the Midwest in one of Alexander Winton's pioneer race cars.

In 1908, Fisher and a fellow automotive enthusiast, Jim Allison, were partners in the Prest-O-Lite Co., manufacturing carbide gas headlamps, when Fisher hit upon the idea of building a large speedway near Indianapolis. This speedway, when not holding competitive events, could be used by the automobile manufacturers of the area for testing their products.

After asking Lem Trotter, who was in charge of Fisher's real estate interests, to find a suitable piece of land for the construction of such a Speedway, Fisher set about contacting influential friends who, he felt, would be interested in helping him finance this ambitious project.

The Indianapolis Motor Speedway was incorporated on February 9, 1909, and capitalized at $250,000.00. The original officers were: Carl Fisher, President; Arthur Newby of National Motor Vehicle Company, First Vice-President; Frank Wheeler of Wheeler-Schebler Carburetor Company, Second Vice-President; and Jim Allison,

Secretary-Treasurer. Three hundred and twenty acres of level ground northwest of Indianapolis were purchased and plans for the World's Greatest Race Course were put in motion.

Construction started immediately on a rectangular track of crushed stone and asphaltum, two and a half miles in length, with four turns each a quarter of a mile in length. These turns were joined by two long straightaways of five-eighths of a mile and by two shorter straightaways each one-eighth of a mile.

While work on the race course was still in progress, the first competitive event, a balloon race, took place at the Speedway on June 5, 1909. The event drew a crowd of approximately 3,500 to the Speedway grounds and a throng of 40,000 watched from outside the gates, causing a king-sized traffic jam.

The track was completed in time for an inaugural series of auto races on August 19, 1909, but it broke up badly during the afternoon, causing the deaths of one driver, two riding mechanics, and two spectators. The Speedway management quickly decided that the only solution was to pave the track with brick, the finest material available at the time. More than three million bricks, each weighing ten pounds, were used and the monumental task was completed in sixty-three days.

Exhibition races were scheduled for December 17 and 18, and although it was bitter cold, Lewis Strang drove his 200-horsepower Fiat to a new American speedway five-mile record of 91.81 miles per hour. He also ran a quarter mile on the main straightaway at 111.86.

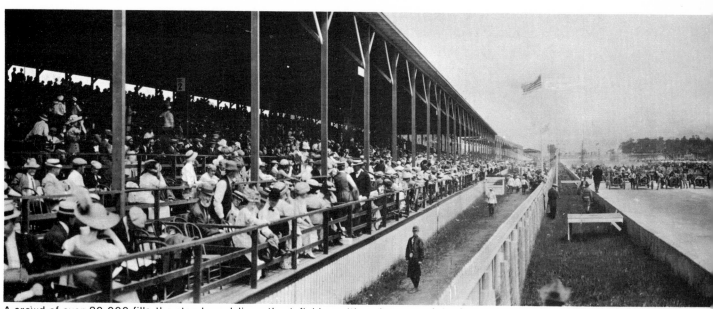

A crowd of over 80,000 fills the stands and lines the infield awaiting the start of the first Indianapolis "500" on May 30, 1911.

Starting on May 27, 1910, 42 events ranging from 5 to 200 miles in length were run, and the only serious injury was a broken leg sustained by driver Herb Lytle. A crowd of about 60,000 attended the events which lasted three days. Similar programs were run on the July 4th and Labor Day weekends.

The management soon agreed that one major event each year would be better, and they decided on a 500-mile race to be run on Memorial Day of 1911 for the then unheard-of purse of $25,000. T. E. "Pop" Myers was made general manager and Eloise "Dolly" Dallenbach became his secretary — a most popular team. Car numbers and starting positions were assigned according to the order of entry and the only qualification requirement was that each car must run a quarter of a mile at better than 75 miles an hour. Piston displacement was limited to 500 cubic inches. Forty cars took the starting flag and Ray Harroun in the Marmon Wasp, Number 32, won the first "500" at an average speed of 74.59.

For 1912 it was decided to reduce the number of starters to 33, and make riding mechanics mandatory. The car numbers and starting positions again were assigned according to date of entry and the qualification distance was increased to one lap at better than 75 miles an hour. Teddy Tetzlaff led the first two laps of the race before Ralph DePalma took over for the next 196. On the 199th lap a broken connecting rod forced his Mercedes out of the race and Joe Dawson passed him to win at a record speed of 78.72. The 196 laps that DePalma led were the most of any non-winner and the two that Dawson led are the least of any winner. It was necessary to go the full 500 miles to be eligible for any prize money and Ralph Mulford, in the last car running, took 8 hours and 53 minutes to complete the 500 miles at an average speed of 56.29 miles an hour. He won tenth place and

$1,200, recording the lowest speed of any finisher in the track's long history.

For 1913, piston displacement was lowered to 450 cubic inches in an effort to interest entries from Europe. Minimum qualification speed remained at 75 miles per hour, but for this event drivers drew for starting positions the night before the race. A five-story Japanese-type pagoda was built at the starting line to house officials and the press and a second tunnel was added under the main straightaway. Several European factories entered cars and Jules Goux, driving a French Peugeot, finished 13 minutes and 8 seconds ahead of second place driver Spencer Wishart. This margin is the greatest in the race's history and was accomplished in spite of Goux's six pit stops and quite possibly because of the six chilled bottles of champagne which the little Frenchman drank while his Peugeot was being serviced.

Stands E and F were constructed for the 1914 race and a third tunnel was added, this one under the second (SE) turn. Again drivers drew for starting positions the night before the race, but this year only 30 cars were permitted to start. The Europeans, led by Rene Thomas with a new 500-mile record of 82.47 miles an hour, swept the first four places. First American car to finish was a Stutz driven by Barney Oldfield, and it was over twenty minutes behind Thomas' Delage.

1915 saw the addition of Grandstand G, as well as a new garage with space for thirty cars which graced the infield. Piston displacement was lowered to 300 cubic inches and the starting lineup was determined by one-lap qualifying runs. Cars were numbered according to their qualifying speeds with #1 starting on the pole. Minimum qualifying speed was raised to 80 and the 33 fastest cars were allowed to start, though no more than three cars of the same make were permitted in the

Carl G. Fisher's Stoddard-Dayton roadster, with Jim Allison as a passenger, will shortly lead the forty-car field on the pace lap.

starting field. The race was originally scheduled for Saturday, May 29, but heavy rains and flood conditions on May 27 forced it to be delayed until Monday, May 31st. This is the only time that the race has been postponed on account of rain. Ralph DePalma drove his Mercedes to a new 500-mile record of 89.84, and for the third year in a row a European-built car had won at Indianapolis.

Because of war in Europe and the shortage of new cars it was decided to limit the 1916 race to 300 miles. Dario Resta took over the lead on the 18th lap in his Peugeot and led the rest of the way for the fourth straight triumph by a European car.

The Harvest Auto Racing classic, consisting of one 20-mile race, one 50-mile and one 100-mile race, was run on September 9th. Johnny Aitken, driving one of the Speedway-owned Peugeots, won all three events from a short field of cars before a disappointing crowd of 10,000.

When the United States entered World War I it became necessary to suspend the "500" for the duration. The Speedway transformed quickly into an aviation depot and many of the participants took jobs to further the war effort. After the Armistice on November 11, 1918, a quick survey was taken and it was decided that plenty of cars would be available for the 1919 race. To avoid any unpleasant publicity, the race was scheduled for Saturday, May 31st, instead of on Memorial Day. A full field of 33 cars qualified and Rene Thomas won the pole with a new record one-lap speed of 104.7. Howdy Wilcox averaged 88.05 miles per hour to win the race, in one of the Speedway-owned Peugeots, making the fifth straight time a European car was victorious.

The displacement was lowered to 183 cubic inches in 1920 to conform with the new International Formula and for the first time, four-lap qualification attempts were made. The cars lined up according to their quali-

fying day, a system still in use today. Grandstand H was constructed at the north end of the main straightaway and a lap prize fund of $20,000 ($100 a lap) served as an added inducement. Ralph DePalma, in a new French Ballot, was leading when he experienced magneto trouble and stalled on the backstretch. Gaston Chevrolet in a Monroe took over and an American-built car won the race for the first time since 1912. Chevrolet averaged 88.62 miles an hour and for the first time the winning car went the entire 500 miles without a tire change. He used Firestone-built Oldfield tires and since then every winning car has been equipped with Firestone's tires.

Steve Hannagan took over as publicity director for the 1921 race and soon became one of the best known press agents in the country. Ralph DePalma, first driver to start on the pole two years in a row, qualified his Ballot at 100.75. The popular Italian-American, in his French car, led all except one of the first 110 laps, but dropped out of the race at that point with bearing failure. Tommy Milton then took charge, in his Frontenac, and led the rest of the way to win by a two-lap edge over second place Roscoe Sarles.

Jimmy Murphy, fresh from a Grand Prix triumph at Le Mans the previous summer, won the pole position for the 1922 race in his Murphy Special at a speed of 100.50. He became the first driver to start on the pole and win the race as he set a new record speed of 94.48.

The rule forcing cars to carry riding mechanics had been rescinded by AAA for the 1923 race, and the piston displacement was lowered to 122 cubic inches. Ethyl gasoline was used for the first time and this assisted Tommy Milton as he raised the track record by 7.42 miles per hour as he won the pole position with a speed of 108.17. Howdy Wilcox made one of the most unusual qualifying runs in Speedway history when he went out the first day in a driving rainstorm and qualified at a

Contestants line up for the official picture before the start of the 1919 "500". The pace car is a Packard.

speed at 81.00 miles per hour. This was just one mile an hour faster than the minimum qualifying speed, and 5.65 miles an hour slower than the next slowest qualifier, but it enabled him to start the race in 8th position. The early stages of this race were highly competitive and the lead changed hands fourteen times between Milton, Wilcox, Jimmy Murphy and Cliff Durant during the first 67 laps. Milton finally took over and led the rest of the way except for 6 laps when he made his second pit stop.

Due to other business interests, Carl Fisher turned over the presidency of the Speedway to Jim Allison for the 1924 race. The prize money was boosted to $60,000 and for the first time centrifugal superchargers were used. Joe Boyer led the first two laps in his Duesenberg, but he sheared a key off the supercharger gears and dropped out of contention. He took over L. L. Corum's Duesenberg on the 110th lap and won the race at an average speed of 98.23 — exceptionally fast when you consider Corum's qualifying speed was 93.333.

The new Firestone balloon (low pressure) tire was introduced for the 1925 race and the pole winning speed went up to 113.196. Peter DePaolo, with relief from Norman Batten while having his blistered hands bandaged, won the race at the new 500-mile record speed of 101.13. For the second straight year a new track record was set for every distance in the race. The pagoda burned the morning after the race.

The Speedway management decided to lower the piston displacement to 91½ cubic inches and raise the minimum qualifying speed to 90 miles per hour for the 1926 race. A rookie, Frank Lockhart, set a new one-lap track record of 115.488 on his first qualifying attempt, but he shredded a right rear tire after his second lap and was forced to come in. He finally qualified on his third and last attempt at 95.870 and started the race in 20th position. He moved up steadily through the field, took over the lead on the 60th lap, was in front on the 71st lap, when a sudden rainstorm forced the starter to halt the race. After an hour and 15 minute delay, the cars resumed competition in single file, in the same order they had been running. Harry Hartz trailed Lockhart by over two laps when a downpour made it necessary to stop again at the completion of 400 miles. This time officials declared the race finished and Lockhart became the first rookie to win since Rene Thomas in 1914. This is the only time that the "500" has been stopped and restarted on account of rain. For the second year the winner's average speed (95.885) was faster than his qualifying speed (95.780).

Frank Lockhart set a new record when he qualified for the 1927 race at 120.100. The blond Californian started on the pole and led for the first 81 laps, but a broken connecting rod put him out of the race at the 300 mile mark. George Souders, the only driver to go the full distance without relief, won the race by a margin of 12 minutes and 2 seconds over Earl DeVore.

On August 15, 1927, World War air ace and former driver Eddie Rickenbacker bought the Speedway from the original owners and assumed the presidency. Leon Duray joined Ralph DePalma and Jimmy Murphy as two-time pole winners when he qualified for the 1928 "500" with a new four-lap record of 122.391. He led for the first 64 laps until a 3-minute pit stop dropped him to 13th place and he went out of the contest with an overheated engine after 132 laps. Louie Meyer, who had driven relief for Wilbur Shaw the year before, won the race in the Miller Special to which Wilbur originally had been assigned, but which had been sold out from under him. Henry Kohlert was the slowest qualifier at 93.545 and the 28.8 miles per hour difference between fast and slow time is the greatest in any field.

1929 was to be the last year for the 91½ cubic inch engines. It was also the last time that an alternate starter would be found in the starting lineup. Phil Pardee wrecked his Miller on May 29th and Billy Lindau was permitted to start in his place. Louis Meyer was again leading, but killed his engine on his last pit stop. It was 7 minutes before he got it started again

Carl G. Fisher, first president of the Speedway

Benson Ford, Henry Ford II, Edsel Ford, Henry Ford and Eddie Rickenbacker with driver Tony Gulotta.

and he finished 6 minutes and 14 seconds behind Ray Keech, who was driving a car Frank Lockhart had designed and built.

Rickenbacker announced a big change in specifications for the 1930 event, presumably brought about by the 1929 Depression which was gripping the country and making money very scarce. The piston displacement was raised to 366 cubic inches to make many of the cheaper semi-stock engines eligible for competition, while superchargers were barred on all four-cycle engines and a minimum weight of either 1,750 pounds or 7½ pounds per cubic inch of piston displacement (whichever was larger) became effective. Riding mechanics again were mandatory and the limit on starting positions was raised to 40, although only 38 took the green flag. Billy Arnold put the front-wheel-drive car of Harry Hartz on the pole and, after Louis Meyer held the lead for the first two laps, took over for the last 198 to win by more than 7 minutes over Shorty Cantlon. Arnold became the first driver to average over 100 miles per hour without relief and when the Champion 100-Mile-an-Hour Club was formed several years later, he was the first driver eligible. His 198 leading laps were also a record number.

For 1931 the minimum qualifying speed was raised to 95 miles an hour and forty cars started the race for the first time since 1911. Rain forced the start to be delayed and the green flag fell at 12:03 p.m. Billy Arnold had missed the opening day of qualifications and although his four lap speed was 3.5 miles per hour faster than any other car in the race, he started in 18th position. He worked his way to the front on the 7th lap and led through the 161st when the right rear axle broke. He was hit by Luther Johnson's car and went over the outside wall coming out of the northwest (No. 4) turn. He was leading by over four laps at the time.

Louie Schneider then took over in his Bowes Seal Fast Special and went on to victory. Dave Evans became the first driver to go 500 miles without a pit stop when he drove his Cummins Diesel to 13th place.

The minimum qualification speed was raised to 100 miles per hour for the 1932 race and forty cars started the race with Lou Moore on the pole. Billy Arnold took over the lead on the second lap and led until the 59th lap when he was forced to spin to miss a car that was spinning in front of him; he went over the wall in the northeast (No. 3) turn. Fred Frame drove Harry Hartz's other entry to victory despite having to make six pit stops to add water to the radiator. His winning speed of 104.144 was a new record for the 500 miles.

The purse dropped from $70,000 to $40,200 for the 1933 race, while the lap prize fund hit an all time low of $3,150. The number of starters was increased to 42 and, for the only time, qualification attempts on the first two days were eligible for the pole position. The qualification distance was raised to 10 laps (25 miles), and a maximum fuel tank capacity was set at 15 gallons. Bill Cummings qualified his Boyle Products Special at 118.350 to win the pole. The race was delayed for about 20 minutes when the drivers threatened to strike if Howdy Wilcox II, who had failed to pass the race-day physical examination, was not permitted to start. It was finally agreed to move his car to the rear of the field and put rookie Mauri Rose in the cockpit. This was the first of fifteen consecutive races that Mauri was to start, a record unequalled by any other driver. Two accidents resulted in the deaths of drivers Mark Billman and Les Spangler and mechanic G. L. Jordan. Louis Meyer won at a new record speed of 104.162, joining Tommy Milton as a two-time winner.

Because of 1933's high accident rate, the 1934 starting lineup again was set at 33 cars. A car could carry

only 6 gallons of oil and fuel was limited to 45 gallons. The Champion 100-Mile-an-Hour Club held its first meeting with 12 charter members. Joe Copps succeeded Steve Hannagan as Speedway Publicity Director. Kelly Petillo set his Red Lion Special on the pole with a ten-lap average speed of 119.329. Bill Cummings won by a 27-second margin over Mauri Rose and set a new record of 104.863 for the 500 miles.

In 1935 green and yellow traffic lights were installed and crash helmets were required, while the fuel allotment was cut to 42½ gallons with fuel limits also in force for the time trials. Kelly Petillo set a new ten-lap record of 121.687 on the first day of qualifications but it was disallowed because he had used more fuel than the rules permitted. He blew an engine on his second attempt and finally made it on his third try at 115.095, good for 22nd starting position. Kelly took over the lead on the 68th lap and although Rex Mays and Wilbur Shaw each led for a brief period afterwards, he won the race by a 40-second margin over Shaw and raised the 500-mile record speed to 106.240. Due to a drizzle, a number of laps were run under the caution flag.

The fuel allotment was cut to 37½ gallons in 1936 and a new outside wall, at a 90-degree angle to the bank of the track, was constructed. The inside retaining wall was removed and safety aprons installed so that a car could spin harmlessly into the infield instead of bounding back into the middle of the track, a hazard that had caused several serious accidents in previous years. It also was decided that each new driver at the Speedway would have to take a driver's test of five phases of ten laps each at 80, 90, 100, 105 and 110 miles per hour, with the final phase under the observation of a committee of veteran drivers. Henry Banks, now Director of Competition for the United States Auto Club, was the first rookie to complete his test. Rex Mays joined Ralph DePalma, Jimmy Murphy and Leon Duray as two-time pole winners when he qualified Paul Weirick's Gilmore Special at 119.644. He led for the first twelve

Three-time winner Lou Meyer with mechanic Lawson Harris.

laps but made a long pit stop to repair throttle linkage and fell out of contention. Wilbur Shaw was leading by 80 seconds at 200 miles when a loose hood forced him into the pits for a 17-minute repair job. Louie Meyer in his red and white Ring Free Special won the race to become the "500's" first three-time winner. He started in 28th position and thus tied Ray Harroun for the distinction of winning from farthest back in the starting field. Shaw's actual running time was 4 minutes and 15 seconds faster than Meyers, although Louie set a new 500-mile record of 109.069 miles an hour. For the first time the pace car, a Packard, was presented to the winner and this policy has been followed in every succeeding "500".

The minimum qualifying speed was raised to 105 miles an hour for the 1937 race and, while the restriction on the amount of fuel was lifted, it was limited to commercial pump gasoline. For the first time magna-fluxing of vital parts was required, and the turns and short straightaways were resurfaced with asphalt. During practice, the Duesenberg driven by Overton Phillips spun and crashed into the Ray 8 Special, which was standing in the pits. Otto Rhode, Chief Engineer for the Champion Spark Plug Company, who was servicing the car in the pits, and George Warford — a fireman — were killed. Both cars caught fire and were badly damaged. Bill Cummings became the fifth two-time pole winner when he qualified his Boyle Products Special at 123.343, a new track record. In the race Wilbur Shaw was running over a lap ahead of second place driver, Ralph Hepburn, with only 20 laps to go when he began to lose his oil pressure. Shaw slowed down to preserve his engine and beat Hepburn to the finish line by only 2.16 seconds, the closest finish in Speedway history. His winning speed of 113.580 beat the old record by 4.5 miles per hour.

In 1938, all practice session pitwork was done behind the inside retaining wall to avoid another incident like the one that happened the previous year. During the race, however, the cars were serviced on the track side of the wall as before. The approaches in and out of the turns were resurfaced with asphalt, the piston displacement was lowered to 274 cubic inches and riding mechanics again were ruled unnecessary. There were no restrictions on oil or fuel with one exception: no oil could be added after the start of the race. Floyd Roberts set his Burd Piston Ring Special on the pole with a ten-lap record speed of 125.681 and became the third race winner to start on the pole when he set a new 500-mile record of 117.200. Wilbur Shaw was second again but this time he was 3 minutes and 35 seconds behind the flying Roberts.

The 1939 race saw a new 4-lap qualification minimum of 115 miles per hour which was to last through the 1956 race. Louie Meyer became the first driver to qualify at over 130 miles per hour when he ran four

laps in his Bowes Seal Fast Special at 130.067, although later in the day his speed was bettered by Jimmy Snyder who earned the pole with a speed of 130.138 miles per hour. The race was marred by the death of Floyd Roberts who was the first Speedway winner to be killed at Indianapolis. Roberts, Bob Swanson and Chet Miller figured in a spectacular flaming crash going into the backstretch. Wilbur Shaw drove Mike Boyle's Maserati to victory, the first time a foreign-made car had won the race since 1919.

The track was all asphalt now except for the main straightaway, which remained brick for sentimental reasons. Shaw again drove his maroon Boyle Maserati to victory in the 1940 race, joined Louis Meyer as the only three-time winners, and became the first man to win two races in a row. Rex Mays was the first driver to win the pole position three times and the front row finished in the first three positions, the only time this has been accomplished. The last fifty laps were run under the yellow flag because of a light rain.

The driver's test speeds were raised to 85, 95, 105, 110 and 115 miles per hour in 1941 and early arrivals were treated to an unscheduled bit of excitement when the south garages caught fire about 6 o'clock race day morning. Two cars were destroyed and much valuable equipment was damaged. Wilbur Shaw was well

Tony Hulman and Wilbur Shaw.

on his way to his third straight victory when a right rear wheel collapsed on the 151st lap and put him into the wall in the southwest (No. 1) turn. Only 31 cars took the green flag as George Barringer's rear-engined Miller was a fire victim and the one qualified by Sam Hanks was wrecked on May 29th. Mauri Rose started on the pole in his Elgin Piston Pin Special and led for the first 38 laps. After this car retired to the pits with magneto trouble at 60 laps, he jumped into teammate Floyd Davis' car when Floyd made his first pit stop after 71 laps while running in 12th position. Mauri moved up through the field rapidly and won by a minute and a half margin over Rex Mays.

No races were held during World War II, and on November 14, 1945, Tony Hulman purchased the Speedway from Rickenbacker. Wilbur Shaw, who originally interested Hulman in the purchase, became President and General Manager and the beloved "Pop" Myers was named Vice-President. Grandstand G and the Paddock, both steel and concrete, were built while the Pagoda and remaining wooden stands were refurbished. There was a gigantic traffic jam on race day and many fans were still coming in when the race was half completed. Cliff Bergere earned the pole but the biggest news prior to race day was made by Ralph Hepburn in the rebuilt Novi when he raised the qualifying record to 133.944. Though Hepburn started 19th, he roared into the lead on the 12th lap and led through the 55th lap when he was forced to make a nine-minute pit stop to repair his hydraulic brakes. George Robson took over the lead from rookie Jimmy Jackson on the 93rd lap and led the rest of the way.

New gates and roads were constructed for 1947 so that 21 lanes of traffic could be accommodated. The American Society of Professional Automobile Racing (ASPAR) was formed before the season got underway, and the members refused to turn in their entries unless the Speedway guaranteed to pay a purse amounting to 40% of the gate. The Speedway refused and only 35 entries were on file by the April 15 deadline. Owners of the 16 ASPAR cars held out until after the first weekend of qualifications, and then agreed to compete under the provisions of the original entry form. The lack of practice was costly to the post entries and a total of only 30 cars were able to qualify at better than the 115-mile minimum speed. Lou Moore, his two front-drive Blue Crown Specials running first and second late in the race, gave both of his drivers the "E-Z" sign. Bill Holland, who was leading, slowed down thinking he had a lap lead over Mauri Rose, who was running second. He waved as Mauri passed him on the 192nd lap and Rose went on to win his second "500".

In 1948 the driver's test was shortened to 100 miles with the slowest phase of 85 miles per hour being dropped. It is hard to believe that Rex Mays, again on the pole, won that position four times and yet never

held the one-lap or four-lap track record. This was to be the last race for Ted Horn who also had an almost unbelievable "500" record. He drove 1799 out of a possible 1800 laps between 1936 and 1948. He was flagged in the rain in 1940 while running 4th on his 199th lap. He finished 2nd, 3rd or 4th each of those nine races and is second in the all-time point leaders, though he never won the race. The 1947 finish was duplicated in '48 with Mauri Rose first and Bill Holland second, but this time there was no controversy. Rose joined Louie Meyer and Wilbur Shaw as the only three-time winners and also became the second driver to win two in a row. His speed of 119.814 was a new 500-mile record.

Tommy Milton took over as chief steward for 1949 and served in that capacity through 1952. WFBM-TV televised the race and the first section of Grandstand E was constructed. Duke Nalon and Rex Mays handled driving chores in the Novis and started in the first two positions. Nalon led for the first 23 laps until the left rear axle broke and he lost the wheel, causing him to crash into the wall coming out of the northeast (No. 3) turn. The car burst into flame and burned fiercely, but Duke was able to get out of the cockpit and over the wall in time to escape with serious burns about the neck and face. Rex then led until the 35th lap, but a bad magneto put him out 13 laps later. Bill Holland took the lead from Lee Wallard on the 55th lap and led the rest of the way, setting a new track record of 121.327, making the third victory in a row for Lou Moore's front-drive Blue Crown Specials.

The second section of Stand E was completed for the 1950 race. Walt Faulkner passed his driver's test and astounded the "railbirds" when he qualified for the pole with a new four-lap record of 134.343 and a one-lap record of 136.013. Johnnie Parsons won the race, called on account of rain after 345 miles.

Grandstand A was replaced for the 1951 race, and the driver test speeds were increased to 100, 110, 115 and 120 miles per hour. The front-drive enthusiasts refused to give up as Duke Nalon set new one and four-lap track records to place the Novi on the pole, making Duke the sixth driver to win the pole position a second time. Lee Wallard led the first two laps in the little Belanger 99, then regained the lead on the 81st lap to win the first 500-mile race completed in less than four hours. Wallard's new track record was 126.244.

The final section of Grandstand E was completed in time for the 1952 race, and the first Frank Kurtis-constructed Kurtis-Kraft 500A "roadster" took the track. A new Cummins Diesel made its appearance with the engine mounted in a horizontal position to reduce frontal area. Alberto Ascari of Italy, who was to win the World Championship in 1952, drove a 12-cylinder Ferrari and qualified well at 134.308 with a difference of only .08 of a second between his fastest and slowest lap.

The opening day of qualifications saw the track record broken twice, first by Andy Linden, in a supercharged Offy, and later by Freddie Agabashian when he won the pole in the Cummins Diesel with a speed of 138.010. The next weekend Bill Vukovich in the Fuel Injection roadster boosted it to 138.312, and finally Chet Miller in the Novi raised the record to 139.034. Vukovich was leading Troy Ruttman by 20 seconds with eight laps to go when a pivot pin on the steering assembly broke and he hit the wall coming out of the northeast (No. 3) turn. Troy went on to win at a record speed of 128.922. This was to be the last win at Indianapolis for a dirt track chassis and the roadster was destined to dominate the winner's circle until 1965 when the rear-engine cars took over. The Stark and Wetzel Rookie of the Year Award was given for the first time; Art Cross, who finished fifth in his Bowes Seal Fast Special, was the recipient.

Former driver Harry McQuinn replaced Tommy Milton as chief steward for the 1953 race and the driver test speeds were raised to 105, 115, 120 and 125 miles per hour. Vuky put the same Howard Keck roadster on the pole in front of the most evenly balanced starting field in history with only 3.1 miles per hour separating the fastest and slowest car. It had started to rain as Bill was on his last qualification lap and he took the checkered flag with a big rooster tail of spray coming from behind his car. Vuky became the fifth driver to win from the pole position and he dominated the race in the most convincing manner of anyone since 1930 when Billy Arnold led for all but the first two laps. Bill led all but five laps, finishing over three laps ahead of runner-up Art Cross.

A new Grandstand B was among the improvements made for the 1954 race. Sam Hanks, the defending National Champion, ran the most consistent qualifying laps in the history of the track with only .04 of a second difference between his fastest and slowest laps. His times were 1:05.24, 1:05.21, 1:05.20 and 1:05.23. His total time was 4:20.88, or a one-lap average of 1:05.22, the

Bill Vukovich was fatally injured seeking his third straight win.

only figure missing in the individual lap times. Jack McGrath became the first driver to qualify at better than 140 miles an hour when he put his Hinkle Special on the pole with a four-lap speed of 141.033 miles an hour. Car trouble on the first weekend of qualification forced Bill Vukovich to start the race in 19th position, but he took the lead on the 61st lap and won the race by a margin of more than a lap over Jimmy Bryan. Vuky set a new 500-mile record of 130.840 and joined Wilbur Shaw and Mauri Rose as the only drivers to win two races in a row. The first car out of the race was Bill Homeier, who hit the pit wall as he was going back out on the track after his first pit stop on the 75th lap. 1954 saw the most total laps of any race with 33 starters when the field completed 5,592 out of a possible 6,600 laps. Compare this with the 1966 race when a total of only 2,647 laps were run.

The racing fraternity was still mourning the beloved "Pop" Myers, who passed away on March 13, 1954, when they were shocked and saddened by the death of Wilbur Shaw in an airplane crash on October 30th.

The driver test speeds were raised to 110, 115, 120 and 125 for the 1955 race and the old tunnel at the starting line was rebuilt. Jack McGrath was again the fastest qualifier with a new track record of 142.580 but he started outside in the front row as Jerry Hoyt had won the pole on a windy opening day. Vuky started in the middle of the second row and the stage was set for probably the most exciting opening laps in Speedway history. Jack led for the first 3 before Vuky took over for the next 11. Jack led the 15th and then Vuky took charge again for the next 9. Jack led the 25th and 26th and then Vuky charged back into the lead until his fatal accident on the 57th lap. This was the second time the previous year's winner had been killed in the race and the only time the race leader was fatally injured. McGrath died in a crash at Phoenix later in the year

and so the battle between two of the Speedway's greatest stars was ended. Vuky led the 1952, '53, '54 and '55 races for a total of 485 laps and is still in third place on the list of all-time lap leaders at the Speedway. Probably no other driver has dominated a four year span as did Vukovich. With several of the early leaders sidelined, Bob Sweikert drove his John Zink roadster to victory in the last 500-mile race to be sanctioned by the American Automobile Association.

On August 3, 1955, AAA abolished its Contest Board and automobile racing was left without a governing body. A few days later an open forum of all interested racing people was arranged by Tony Hulman and presided over by Judge George M. Ober. As a result, on September 16, 1955, the United States Auto Club was incorporated with Duane Carter named Director of Competition. The Speedway was repaved with Kentucky Rock Asphalt except for the main straightaway. and a combination office-museum was erected at the main entrance to the grounds. The supercharged Novi engines were mounted in new rear-drive cars and A. J. Watson built the first of his famous roadsters. Pat Flaherty put his new Watson on the pole with a four-lap track record of 145.596. During the race Paul Russo in the Novi passed both Pat O'Connor and Pat Flaherty at the end of the main straightaway to take over the lead on the 11th lap. Ten laps later he blew a tire and crashed into the first turn wall. Flaherty led for the last 124 laps of the race and became the sixth winner to have started the race on the pole.

Enormous changes were made to the Speedway in 1957. A new three-lane tunnel was constructed under the backstretch and the golfer's foot bridge was taken down. The old pagoda and the entire pit parquet section was demolished and a new safety pit area, control tower and Tower Terrace section was constructed. The piston displacement was lowered to 256 cubic inches and the driver test speeds were changed to 115, 120, 125 and 130 miles an hour. George Salih brought a new race car to the track with its Offenhauser engine mounted only 18 degrees from horizontal and with the top of the hood only 21 inches above the track. Sam Hanks was the driver but due to new car "bugs" the car missed the first day of qualification, causing Sam to start in 13th position, although his car was the sixth fastest. For the first time the cars lined up in single file order on the new safety pit area, but a crash between Elmer George and Eddie Russo as they were moving into three-abreast formation on the backstretch on the parade lap eliminated two cars and only 31 cars took the green flag. Sam charged by Paul Russo, in the Novi, on the backstretch on the 37th lap to take over the lead and, except for pit stops, led the rest of the way. Sam announced his retirement from racing in Victory Lane, the first driver to do so since Ray Harroun in 1911. His winning speed of 135.601 was a new record.

Historic race cars highlight the Speedway Museum.

Harlan Fengler replaced Harry McQuinn as chief steward for the 1958 race. For the first time crash helmets were required to pass USAC inspection and safety belts were mandatory. Dick Rathmann and Ed Elisian waged a terrific duel during the practice session for high-speed honors, and on the first qualifying day it was the same thing, Elisian qualifying first with a new one-lap record of 146.508 and a new four-lap record of 145.926. Dick then went out and won the pole position from Ed with a four-lap average of 145.974 though he couldn't beat Elisian's one-lap record. On race day the cars were again lined up in single file order on the pit apron. The three front-row cars got away ahead of the pace car and it was necessary to run an embarrassing extra lap to get all of the cars in line. The three leaders caught the others in time to take the green flag in their proper position and everyone got through the first two turns without incident, although neither Rathmann or Elisian would slow first at the end of the backstretch. Elisian got into the turn ahead of Rathmann but lost control and took Rathmann into the wall, breaking Dick's car in half. In the ensuing confusion Pat O'Connor went over the top of Jimmy Reece's car, which had been hit by Bob Veith, and landed upside down on the track, resulting in fatal injuries to the popular Hoosier. Jerry Unser used Paul Goldsmith's car for a ramp and cartwheeled spectacularly over the wall, luckily suffering only a dislocated shoulder. In all, seventeen cars were involved, with eight being eliminated and nine able to continue after pit stops for repairs. When the green flag was again displayed at the start of the 19th lap, a tremendous battle broke out between Jimmy Bryan, Tony Bettenhausen, Eddie Sachs and rookie George Amick. The lead changed hands thirteen times between them before their first pit stops settled things down a bit. Bryan won the race in the same car that Sam Hanks had driven to victory in 1957.

Roll bars were mandatory in 1959, and driver's uniforms were required to be of one-piece design, dipped in a fire-resistant solution. The first section of Stand K was built and the pit area electric scoreboard was installed. Johnny Thomson set a new one-lap record of 146.532 as he qualified his "lay-down"-engined car for the pole. Rodger Ward won the race in a new upright-engined Watson roadster at a record speed of 135.857, with Jim Rathmann second in another new Watson roadster and Thomson third, despite having to make four pit stops because of uneven tire wear.

The second section of Stand K was completed for the 1960 race and the minimum qualification speed was raised to 130 miles per hour. Eddie Sachs put his Dean Van Lines Special on the pole with a record breaking 146.592, though the big surprise came on the second weekend when rookie Jim Hurtubise qualified his Travelon Trailer roadster at the remarkable speed of 149.056, including one lap at 149.601. The race was one of the best. The lead changed hands 29 times and

Jim Rathmann took over for the last time on the 197th lap when Rodger Ward was forced to slow down because of a badly worn tire. Few people realized, however, that Rathmann's 197th lap was the fastest leading lap in the race and was turned at 146.128 miles an hour. Jim's 500-mile speed of 138.767 beat the old record by almost 3 miles an hour.

A new Paddock Stand was constructed for the 1961 race with a press box suspended from the penthouse, while a new concrete outside retaining wall was built along the backstretch and an inside concrete wall was installed coming out of the northwest (No. 4) turn. The driver test speeds were raised to 120, 125, 130 and 135 and minimum qualification speed was set at 135. Eddie Sachs became the third driver to win the pole two years in a row when he qualified at 147.481. The race again was very competitive with the lead changing 20 times. A. J. Foyt had the race apparently won when he had to make an extra pit stop after the 183rd lap because of a refueling failure on his previous pit stop which he had thought would be his last. Eddie Sachs then seemed to have the race in his pocket until he too had to make an unscheduled pit stop to replace a badly worn tire on the 198th lap and Foyt cruised the last two laps to win at a record speed of 139.130, truly one of the Speedway's most exciting finishes. For the first time there were co-winners of the Rookie of the Year award. Parnelli Jones and Bobby Marshman received an equal number of votes and the sponsors, Stark and Wetzel, made duplicate awards.

For the 1962 race the home stretch was paved with asphalt except for a strip of brick a yard wide at the starting line, so that, for sentimental reasons, the Speedway may still be referred to as the "brickyard". Other improvements included Stand M and the first unit of Stand J. Parnelli Jones became the first man to turn the Speedway officially in less than a minute when he put his Agajanian-Willard Battery Special on the pole with a new four-lap average speed of 150.370. He led all but five of the first 125 laps of the race but a worn-through brake line caused him to slow his speed and he was

Parnelli Jones was the first driver to officially break 150 mph.

forced to finish in seventh position without any brakes. Rodger Ward took over from Parnelli and won his second "500" with a new record speed of 140.293. Len Sutton was second, Eddie Sachs third and Don Davis fourth. This was the only time the first four finishers were on the same lap at the end of the race.

1963 saw a new 600-foot addition made to the Paddock, a new Stand C installed, and the construction of the long-awaited new Golf Clubhouse, together with the 96-unit Speedway Motel. Parnelli Jones became the fourth driver to start on the pole two years in a row when he qualified his trusty roadster "Calhoun" at a record speed of 151.153, to lead the closest field in Speedway history timewise, as Parnelli was only 5:35 seconds faster than Dempsey Wilson, the slowest qualifier. Jim Hurtubise led the first lap in the Novi and then gave way to Parnelli who led until he made his first pit stop. When Jim Clark, in his gasoline burning rear-engine Ford Lotus, made his only pit stop after 95 laps, Parnelli went back into the lead and slithered his way on an oily track to become the seventh winner to start the race in the pole position. His average speed of 143.137 beat the old track record by almost three miles an hour. Jim Clark drove a terrific race to finish second and the days of the Offy roadsters were numbered.

The second section of Stand J was finished and Grandstand L was constructed for 1964 with the northeast (No. 3) turn resurfaced and a new three-lane tunnel put under the north end of the track near another welcome addition, a new electric scoreboard in the north center of the infield. Closed circuit television was also offered for the first time. The entire front row of starting lineup was composed of rear-engined Fords with Jim Clark on the pole boasting a new four-lap record speed of 158.828. The race was marred by a fiery crash on the second lap that claimed the lives of rookie Dave MacDonald and veteran Eddie Sachs. For the first time the race was halted because of an accident. Shortly after the restart Bobby Marshman took a commanding lead, but got too low in the southeast (No. 2) turn while passing a slower car, knocked off an oil plug, and was forced out of the race. Jim Clark then regained the lead, but a broken left rear suspension caused when a large chunk of rubber from a faulty tire wrapped itself around the spinning axle put him out of running. This put Parnelli Jones in charge but his fuel tank exploded as he was leaving his pit and though Parnelli was not seriously injured, his car was out of action. With Clark and Jones sidelined, A. J. Foyt took command in his Sheraton-Thompson roadster and won the race with a new 500-mile record of 147.350. He finished a lap and a half ahead of Rodger Ward in his rear-engine Watson Ford which experienced fueling problems and made five pit stops. New track records were set at every period of the race for the first time since 1925.

Grandstand J was completed for the 1965 race, and fire-wary officials made sweeping rule changes regarding the highly volatile fuels. Pressurized refueling tanks were ruled out and, to avoid possible trouble in the pit area, only gravity feed tanks were permitted. The fuel tanks of the race cars were limited to 75 gallon capacity, and no tanks were permitted in front of the cockpit. Rubber inserts or liners were required in the tanks and to discourage large fuel loads, two pit stops during the race became mandatory. The driver test speeds were raised to 130, 135, 140 and 145 and no minimum qualifying speed was required. For the first time the rear-engined cars outnumbered the roadsters and most of the "hot dogs" had "back up" cars entered. Three first-day qualifiers in a row broke the track record and the third one, A. J. Foyt in an Americanized Lotus, won the pole position with the amazing speed of 161.233. The only contest for the lead was between Foyt and Jim Clark and when A. J. went out of the race after 115 laps, Clark "coasted home" with almost a two-lap lead over Parnelli Jones whose car stalled with an empty fuel tank in the northwest (No. 4) turn just after taking the checkered flag. Mario Andretti was only 6 seconds behind Parnelli and was chosen Rookie of the Year. Clark's winning average speed of 150.686 beat the old track record by 3.3 miles an hour.

1966 fans found a new South Vista Stand in the southwest (No. 1) turn, Stand H replaced and the tunnel at the north end of the main straightaway enlarged to accommodate three traffic lanes. Mario Andretti was speed leader during practice sessions and he put his Dean Van Lines Hawk on the pole with a new four-lap record of 165.899. For the first time an accident just after the cars took the green flag threatened to wipe out a significant part of the starting lineup and the race had to be red flagged at the end of the first lap. Eleven cars were damaged too badly to restart, but luckily none of the drivers was injured though it was all "hustle bustle" along the south end of the main straightaway for a minute. Only seven cars were running at the finish of the race and former World Road Racing Champion Graham Hill of England became the first rookie to win the "500" since 1927. There was only one roadster in the starting lineup and it was wrecked in the first-lap accident. Jackie Stewart of Scotland, who dropped out of the race with no oil pressure while leading on the 191st lap, was elected Rookie of the Year for his tremendous performances in practice, qualifying, and during the race. The race had the fewest total laps of any race with 33 starters, with only 2,647 out of a possible 6,600 being completed.

Could Carl Fisher come back today and see the old Pressley farm which he and Lem Trotter first visited in 1908, he would find a modern, multi-million-dollar racing plant with concrete and steel grandstands which can seat more than twice the entire attendance of the first "500". He would see radical, rear-engined race cars

The 1966 start was marred by a spectacular frontstretch accident which eliminated almost a third of the field.

turning the track at more than twice the speeds the track was originally designed to accommodate. The creaking, rickety Pagoda has been replaced by a glass and steel tower equipped with every modern facility for timing, scoring and communication. The megaphones which once amplified the heroic names "Harroun, Goux, Thomas, DePalma, Cooper and Milton" have been replaced with a fine public address system to proclaim the equally heroic feats of "Andretti, Clark, Foyt, Jones, Ruby and Hill". Near where the ancient Westcott crashed into the pits and demolished the hapless Apperson and unsuspecting Fiat, a black column rises, its orange lights proclaiming the positions of all 33 cars, as well as the speed and laps completed by the leader. The lumbering Marmons, Duesenbergs, and Millers are now relegated to the modern museum at the track's entrance while the 4-cam Fords and super-

charged Offys scream their challenge to the electric eye which records their triumphs or failures. The more than 300,000 race fans who annually press through the gates to personally view the "500" are but a small part of the millions who follow the progress of the race. Throughout the country closed circuit TV showings provide front row seats for hundreds of thousands, while literally millions in almost every corner of the world listen to Sid Collins reporting the thrills and action on the Indianapolis Speedway Network.

One thing, however, would Carl Fisher find basically unchanged. The fascination of speed and the love of competition burns just as strongly today in the hearts of the gallant drivers who slip into their sleek, rear-engined creations as they did in the hearts of their predecessors. It is this common bond which has made the "500" such a great event.

OFFICIALS AND PACE CARS

YEAR	HONORARY REFEREE	STARTER	PACE CAR	PACEMAKER	YEAR	HONORARY REFEREE	STARTER	PACE CAR	PACEMAKER
1911	R.P. Hooper	Fred J. Wagner	Stoddard-Dayton	Carl G. Fisher	1938	Harvey S. Firestone	Seth Klein	Hudson	Stuart Baits
1912	R.P. Hooper	Fred J. Wagner	Stutz	Carl G. Fisher	1939	Roscoe Turner	Seth Klein	Buick	Charles Chayne
1913	Laurens Enos	Charles P. Root	Stoddard-Dayton	Carl G. Fisher	1940	Paul G. Hoffman	Seth Klein	Studebaker	Harry Hartz
1914	John A. Wilson	Thomas J. Hay	Stoddard-Dayton	Carl G. Fisher	1941	Guy Vaughn	Seth Klein	Chrysler Newport	A.B. Couture
1915	A.R. Pardington	Thomas J. Hay	Packard "6"	Carl G. Fisher	1946	Jack Dempsey	Seth Klein	Lincoln	Henry Ford, II
1916	Howard Marmon	George M. Dickson	Premier "6"	Frank E. Smith	1947	Ralph Gates	Seth Klein	Nash	George W. Mason
1919	E.V. Rickenbacker	E.C. Patterson	Packard V-12	Col. J.G. Vincent	1948	Al Feeney	Seth Klein	Chevrolet	Wilbur Shaw
1920	Clifford Ireland	E.C. Patterson	Marmon V-16	Barney Oldfield	1949	J.E. McManamon	Seth Klein	Oldsmobile	Wilbur Shaw
1921	David Beecroft	Thomas J. Hay	H.C.S. "6"	Harry C. Stutz	1950	Clarence Beesmyer	Seth Klein	Mercury	Benson Ford
1922	Richard Kennerdell	E.V. Rickenbacker	National "8"	Barney Oldfield	1951	Clarence Beesmyer	Seth Klein	Chrysler	Dave Wallace
1923	John O. La Gorce	E.V. Rickenbacker	Duesenberg "8"	Fred S. Duesenberg	1952	Raymond Firestone	Seth Klein	Studebaker	P.O. Peterson
1924	Henry Ford	W.S. Gilbreath	Cole V-8	Lew Pettijohn	1953	Henry Ford II	Seth Klein	Ford	William Clay Ford
1925	Charles Schwab	Seth Klein	Rickenbacker "8"	E.V. Rickenbacker	1954	Ralph DePalma	W.H. Vandewater	Dodge	William C. Newberg
1926	Arthur Brisbane	Seth Klein	Chrysler "8"	Louis Chevrolet	1955	R.A. Stranahan, Jr.	W.H. Vandewater	Chevrolet	T.H. Keating
1927	Charles Kettering	George Townsend	LaSalle V-8	Willard Rader	1956	Herman Teetor	W.H. Vandewater	DeSoto	L.I. Woolson
1928	Larry P. Fisher	Chester Maitland	Marmon "78"	Joe Dawson	1957	Louis Schwitzer, Sr.	W.H. Vandewater	Mercury	F.C. Reith
1929	Harvey S. Firestone	Larry P. Fisher	Studebaker	George Hunt	1958	R.A. Stranahan, Jr.	W.H. Vandewater	Pontiac	Sam Hanks
1930	Vincent Bendix	Grantland Rice	Cord	E.L. Cord	1959	Vernon A. Bellman	W.H. Vandewater	Buick	Sam Hanks
1931	William S. Knudsen	Barney Oldfield	Cadillac	Willard Rader	1960	Vernon A. Bellman	W.H. Vandewater	Oldsmobile	Sam Hanks
1932	Edsel Ford	Gar Wood	Lincoln	Edsel Ford	1961	Raymond Firestone	W.H. Vandewater	Ford Thunderbird	Sam Hanks
1933	Larry P. Fisher	Roscoe Turner	Chrysler	Byron Foy	1962	R.A. Stranahan, Jr.	Pat Vidan	Studebaker Lark	Sam Hanks
1934	Roy D. Chapin	Seth Klein	LaSalle	Willard Rader	1963	Baxter F. Ball	Pat Vidan	Chrysler 300	Sam Hanks
1935	Amelia Earhart	Seth Klein	Ford V-8	Harry Mack	1964	Raymond Firestone	Pat Vidan	Ford Mustang	Benson Ford
1936	Ralph DePalma	Seth Klein	Packard	Tommy Milton	1965	Raymond Firestone	Pat Vidan	Plymouth Fury	P.N. Buckminster
1937	William S. Knudsen	Seth Klein	LaSalle	Ralph DePalma	1966	Raymond Firestone	Pat Vidan	Mercury Comet	Benson Ford

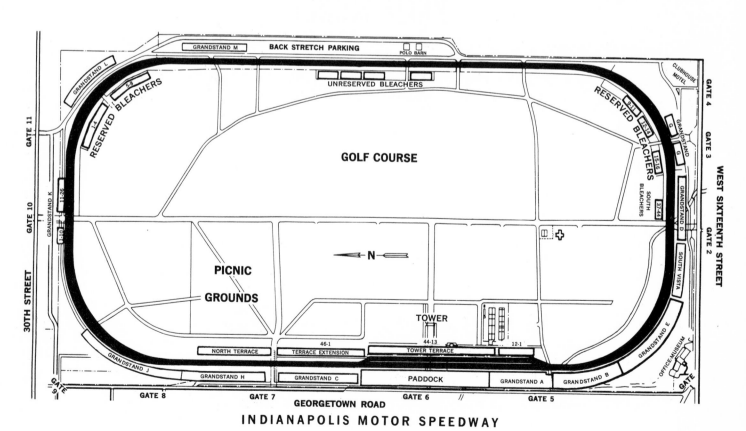

INDIANAPOLIS MOTOR SPEEDWAY

TRACK RECORDS

DISTANCE	DATE	DRIVER	CAR	TIME	SPEED
1 Lap*	5/14/66	Mario Andretti	Dean Van Lines Special	54.11	166.328
4 Laps*	5/14/66	Mario Andretti	Dean Van Lines Special	3:37.00	165.899
1 Lap	5/31/65	Jim Clark	Lotus Powered by Ford	59.45	151.388
2 Laps	5/31/65	A. J. Foyt	Sheraton-Thompson Special	1:58.20	152.284
25 Miles	5/31/65	Jim Clark	Lotus Powered by Ford	9:42.81	154.424
50 Miles	5/30/64	Bobby Marshman	Pure Oil Firebird Special	19:24.29	154.601
75 Miles	5/30/64	Bobby Marshman	Pure Oil Firebird Special	29:05.20	154.710
100 Miles	5/31/65	Jim Clark	Lotus Powered by Ford	39:34.31	151.623
125 Miles	5/31/65	Jim Clark	Lotus Powered by Ford	49:17.55	152.153
150 Miles	5/31/65	Jim Clark	Lotus Powered by Ford	59:01.25	152.489
175 Miles	5/31/65	A. J. Foyt	Sheraton-Thompson Special	1:08:51.57	152.484
200 Miles	5/31/65	Jim Clark	Lotus Powered by Ford	1:19:10.17	151.574
225 Miles	5/31/65	Jim Clark	Lotus Powered by Ford	1:28:51.89	151.916
250 Miles	5/31/65	Jim Clark	Lotus Powered by Ford	1:38:33.85	152.185
275 Miles	5/31/65	Jim Clark	Lotus Powered by Ford	1:48:16.44	152.391
300 Miles	5/31/65	Jim Clark	Lotus Powered by Ford	1:58:11.21	152.301
325 Miles	5/31/65	Jim Clark	Lotus Powered by Ford	2:08:28.90	151.773
350 Miles	5/31/65	Jim Clark	Lotus Powered by Ford	2:18:58.83	151.100
375 Miles	5/31/65	Jim Clark	Lotus Powered by Ford	2:28:52.21	151.138
400 Miles	5/31/65	Jim Clark	Lotus Powered by Ford	2:38:47:25	151.145
425 Miles	5/31/65	Jim Clark	Lotus Powered by Ford	2:48:46.29	151.092
450 Miles	5/31/65	Jim Clark	Lotus Powered by Ford	2:58:48.79	150.996
475 Miles	5/31/65	Jim Clark	Lotus Powered by Ford	3:08:54.52	150.867
500 Miles	5/31/65	Jim Clark	Lotus Powered by Ford	3:19:05.34	150.686

*record established in qualifications

PRIZE MONEY

YEAR	SPEEDWAY PRIZES	ACCESSORY PRIZES	LAP PRIZES	TOTAL PRIZES	YEAR	SPEEDWAY PRIZES	ACCESSORY PRIZES	LAP PRIZES	TOTAL PRIZES
1911	$25,100	$ 2,450		$27,550	1938	$63,100	$21,875	$6,100	$91,075
1912	50,000	5,225		55,255	1939	63,100	17,550	6,400	87,050
1913	50,000	5,875		55,875	1940	63,100	14,825	7,600	85,525
1914	50,000	1,675		51,675	1941	63,100	18,425	9,400	90,925
1915	50,000	1,200		51,200	1946	75,350	20,100	20,000	115,450
1916	30,000	1,350		31,350	1947	98,350	19,075	20,000	137,425
1919	50,000	5,275		55,275	1948	123,900	27,175	20,000	171,075
1920	50,000	23,550	$20,000	93,550	1949	136,300	22,750	20,000	179,050
1921	50,000	19,300	17,350	86,650	1950	154,900	26,125	20,010	201,135
1922	50,000	12,550	8,025	70,575	1951	154,700	32,950	20,000	207,650
1923	50,000	21,325	12,100	83,425	1952	169,300	40,800	20,000	230,100
1924	60,000	20,600	6,250	86,850	1953	176,900	39,400	30,000	246,300
1925	60,000	12,750	15,000	87,750	1954	199,200	40,175	30,000	269,375
1926	60,000	12,100	16,000	88,100	1955	199,900	40,500	30,000	270,400
1927	60,000	9,850	20,000	89,850	1956	205,002	47,050	30,000	282,052
1928	60,000	15,750	15,000	90,750	1957	218,052	52,200	30,000	300,252
1929	60,000	15,150	20,000	95,150	1958	221,667	53,550	30,000	305,217
1930	60,000	27,600	17,000	97,600	1959	250,500	57,600	30,000	338,100
1931	60,000	10,650	11,150	81,800	1960	274,850	64,300	30,000	369,150
1932	70,000	13,200	10,700	93,900	1961	301,675	68,325	30,000	400,000
1933	40,200	11,100	3,150	54,450	1962	320,428	75,724	30,000	426,152
1934	60,000	19,550	4,225	83,775	1963	382,300	81,731	30,000	494,031
1935	60,000	14,425	4,150	78,575	1964	397,150	79,475	30,000	506,625
1936	60,000	17,025	5,500	82,525	1965	500,493	97,906	30,000	628,399
1937	60,000	23,635	8,500	92,135	1966	545,293	116,516	30,000	691,809
					Total	$7,014,338	$1,574,986	$833,610	$9,416,034

1911

A cool, partly cloudy afternoon greeted the impressive crowd of 80,000 on hand for the first running of the "greatest spectacle in racing". Promptly at 10:00 a.m., pacemaker Carl Fisher, in his Stoddard-Dayton roadster led the parade lap and then Fred Wagner flagged the forty cars on their way. Johnny Aitken led the first few laps in his National before Spencer Wishart passed him only to give way shortly to Fred Belcher in the Knox. David Bruce-Brown then worked his big red Fiat into the lead and started pulling away. Early in the race Louis Disbrow and Teddy Tetzlaff tangled on the frontstretch and wrecked their cars. On his 12th lap, Arthur Greiner hit the wall going into the backstretch and his mechanic, Sam Dickson, was thrown to the track and fatally injured. Nearing the halfway mark Joe Jagersberger's Case broke a steering knuckle and swerved, throwing his mechanic, C. L. Anderson, to the track. Harry Knight turned left to miss him and crashed into the pits, demolishing Herb Lytle's Apperson and Caleb Bragg's Fiat. Fortunately, there were no serious injuries. Ray Harroun finally passed Bruce-Brown and won with some relief help from Cyrus Patschke. Harroun, who had designed the sleek "Wasp", announced his retirement from racing.

Ray Harroun

NO.	DRIVER	CAR	ENTRANT	ENGINE	CYL.	DISP.	CHASSIS	COLOR	QUAL. SPEED	ST.	FIN.	LAPS/SPEED/REASON OUT
32	Ray Harroun	Marmon "Wasp"	Nordyke & Marmon Co.	Marmon	6	477	Marmon	yellow, black		28	1	200-74.59
33	Ralph Mulford	Lozier	Lozier Motor Co.	Lozier	4	544	Lozier	white		29	2	200-74.29
28	David Bruce-Brown	Fiat	E. E. Hewlett	Fiat	4	589	Fiat	maroon, white		25	3	200-72.73
11	Spencer Wishart	Mercedes	Spencer Wishart	Mercedes	4	583	Mercedes	gray		11	4	200-72.65
31	Joe Dawson	Marmon	Nordyke & Marmon Co.	Marmon	4	495	Marmon	yellow, black		27	5	200-72.34
2	Ralph DePalma	Simplex	Simplex Automobile Co.	Simplex	4	597	Simplex	red, white		2	6	200-71.13
20	Charlie Merz	National	National Motor Vehicle Co.	National	4	447	National	blue, white		18	7	200-70.37
12	W. H. "Jack" Turner	Amplex	Simplex Automobile Co.	Amplex	4	443	Amplex	red		12	8	200-68.82
15	Fred Belcher	Knox	Knox Automobile Co.	Knox	6	432	Knox	brown		13	9	200-68.63
25	Harry Cobe	Jackson	Jackson Automobile Co.	Jackson	4	559	Jackson	dark maroon, white		22	10	200-67.90
10	Gil Anderson	Stutz	Ideal Motor Car Co.	Stutz	4	390	Stutz	battleship gray, white		10	11	200-67.73
36	Hughie Hughes	Mercer	Mercer Motors Co.	Mercer	4	300	Mercer	yellow, blue		32	12	200-67.73
30	Lee Frayer	Firestone-Columbus	Columbus Buggy Co.	Firestone Col.	4	432	Firestone Col.	scarlet, gray		26	13	flagged
21	Howdy Wilcox	National	National Motor Vehicle Co.	National	4	589	National	blue, white		19	14	flagged
37	Charles Bigelow	Mercer	Mercer Motors Co.	Mercer	4	300	Mercer	yellow, blue		33	15	flagged
3	Harry Endicott	Inter-State	Inter-State Automobile Co.	Inter-State	4	390	Interstate	gray, black		3	16	flagged
41	Howard Hall	Velie	Velie Motors Corp.	Velie	4	334	Velie	battleship gray		36	17	flagged
46	Billy Knipper	Benz	E. A. Moross	Benz	4	444	Benz	white		40	18	flagged
45	Bob Burman	Benz	E. A. Moross	Benz	4	520	Benz	white		39	19	flagged
38	Ralph Beardsley	Simplex	Simplex Automobile Co.	Simplex	4	597	Simplex	red		34	20	flagged
18	Eddie Hearne	Fiat	Edward A. Hearne	Fiat	4	487	Fiat	red, white		16	21	flagged
6	Frank Fox	Pope-Hartford	Pope Manufacturing Co.	Pope-Hartford	4	390	Pope-Hartford	red, white		6	22	flagged
27	Ernest Delaney	Cutting	Clark-Carter Auto Co.	Cutting	4	390	Cutting	gray, black, white		24	23	flagged
26	Jack Tower	Jackson	Jackson Automobile Co.	Jackson	4	432	Jackson	dark maroon, white		23	24	flagged
23	Bert Adams	McFarlan	Speed Motors Co.	McFarlan	6	377	McFarlan	lead, white		20	25	flagged
42	Bill Endicott	Cole	Cole Motor Car Co.	Cole	4	471	Cole	green		37	26	flagged
4	Johnny Aitken	National	National Motor Vehicle Co.	National	4	589	National	blue, white		4	27	125-con. rod
9	Will Jones	Case	J. I. Case T. M. Co.	Case	4	284	Case	red, gray		9	28	122-steering
1	Lewis Strang	Case	J. I. Case T. M. Co.	Case	4	284	Case	red, gray		1	29	109-steering
7	Harry Knight	Westcott	Westcott Motor Car Co.	Westcott	6	421	Westcott	battleship gray		7	30	90-wrecked FS
8	Joe Jagersberger	Case	J. I. Case T. M. Co.	Case	4	284	Case	red, gray		8	31	87-wrecked FS
35	Hervert Lytle	Apperson	Apperson Bros. Automobile Co.	Apperson	4	546	Apperson	vermillion, white		31	32	82-wrecked in pits
19	Harry Grant	Alco	American Locomotive Co.	Alco	6	580	Alco	black		17	33	51-bearings
17	Charles Basle	Buick	Buick Motor Co.	Buick	4	594	Buick	white, red		15	34	46-mechanical tbl.
5	Louis Disbrow	Pope-Hartford	Pope Manufacturing Co.	Pope-Hartford	4	390	Pope-Hartford	red, black		5	35	45-wrecked FS
16	Arthur Chevrolet	Buick	Buick Motor Co.	Buick	4	594	Buick	white, red		14	36	30-mechanical tbl.
39	Caleb Bragg	Fiat	Caleb S. Bragg	Fiat	4	487	Fiat	maroon		5	37	24-wrecked in pits
24	Fred Ellis	Jackson	Jackson Automobile Co.	Jackson	4	355	Jackson	dark maroon, white		14	38	22-withdrawn
34	Teddy Tetzlaff	Lozier	Lozier Motor Co.	Lozier	4	544	Lozier	white, red		35	39	20-wrecked FS
44	Arthur Greiner	Amplex	Simplex Motor Car Co.	Amplex	4	443	Amplex	red, white		21	40	12-wrecked BS

Ralph Mulford

David Bruce-Brown

Spencer Wishart

Joe Dawson

Ralph DePalma

Charlie Merz

W. H. "Jack" Turner

Fred Belcher

Harry Cobe

Gil Anderson

Hughie Hughes

Lee Frayer

Howdy Wilcox

Charles Bigelow

Harry Endicott

Howard Hall

Billy Knipper

Bob Burman

Ralph Beardsley

Eddie Hearne

Frank Fox

Ernest Delaney

Jack Tower

Mel Marquette (relief driver)

Bill Endicott

Johnny Aitken

Will Jones

Lewis Strang

Harry Knight

Joe Jagersberger

Herbert Lytle

Harry Grant

Charles Basle

Louis Disbrow

Arthur Chevrolet

Caleb Bragg

Fred Ellis

Teddy Tetzlaff

Arthur Greiner

Below, left: Ray Harroun, who retired after winning the 1910 National Championship, returned for one final race and won the first "500" at the wheel of the Marmon "Wasp" which he had designed. Below, right: Bob Burman after breaking the track record for one mile in the time of 35.25 (102.127 mph) the day before the first "500". Burman's Blitzen Benz was too large to be eligible for the race and the record run was merely a publicity stunt planned by Carl Fisher. Burman broke a record formerly held by Barney Oldfield. Bottom: Howdy Wilcox is shown in action with his National.

Above: Partially obscured by smoke, the field of cars hits the first turn. Louis Disbrow is driving the No. 5 Pope Hartford, Joe Jagersberger, the No. 8 Case and Will Jones is Jagersberger's teammate in the No. 9 Case. Center: Pacemaker Carl Fisher's Stoddard-Dayton roadster stands at the head of the 40-car field just before the pace lap. Fisher's passenger is Jim Allison, his business partner and Secretary-Treasurer of the Speedway Corporation. Lewis Strang is on the pole followed by Ralph DePalma, Harry Endicott and Johnny Aitken. Bottom: the two cars of the Benz Team line up beside their pits prior to taking their places in the starting lineup. No. 45 was driven by Bob Burman and No. 46 by Billy Knipper.

1912

Twenty-four cars faced Starter Fred Wagner's flag and Teddy Tetzlaff went out in front as they hit the first turn. On the third lap, a determined Ralph DePalma nosed his Mercedes by Tetzlaff and immediately began building up a commanding lead. As Mel Marquette was entering the frontstretch on the 64th lap, the rear wheels of his McFarlan collapsed and he hit the inside wall. Neil Whalen, driving relief for Eddie Hearne, blew a tire going into the backstretch. Whalen regained control and thereby averted a serious accident. "Wild Bob" Burman had the misfortune to throw two rear tires as he entered the backstretch on his 157th lap causing his car to skid and turn over. Burman was cut and bruised but not seriously injured. De-Palma had things his own way until his 197th lap when his engine began sputtering. Although he was several laps in front of Joe Dawson, he was unable to nurse the faltering car the final few miles. A lap and a half from the checkered flag, the Mercedes ground to a halt, a connecting rod through the crankcase. Aided by mechanic Rupert Jeffkins and encouraged by the cheers of the crowd, DePalma pushed the heavy car around to the pits. Exhausted, he watched Joe Dawson sweep by to an unexpected victory.

Joe Dawson

NO.	DRIVER	CAR	ENTRANT	ENGINE	CYL.	DISP.	CHASSIS	COLOR	QUAL. SPEED	ST.	FIN.	LAPS/SPEED/REASON OUT
8	Joe Dawson	National	National Motor Vehicle Co.	National	4	491	National	blue, white	86.13	7	1	200-78.72
3	Teddy Tetzlaff	Fiat	E. E. Hewlett	Fiat	4	589	Fiat	red	84.24	3	2	200-76.75
21	Hughie Hughes	Mercer	Mercer Motors Co.	Mercer	4	301	Mercer	yellow	81.81	17	3	200-76.13
28	Charlie Merz	Stutz	Ideal Motor Car Co.	Stutz	4	390	Stutz	gray	78.88	22	4	200-76.00
18	Bill Endicott	Schacht	Schacht Motor Car Co.	Stutz	4	390	Schacht	red	80.57	15	5	200-74.25
2	Len Zengel	Stutz	Ideal Motor Car Co.	Stutz	4	390	Stutz	gray	78.85	2	6	200-73.83
14	Johnny Jenkins	White	White Indianapolis Co.	White	6	490	White	white	80.82	11	7	200-73.25
22	Joe Horan	Lozier	Dr. W. H. Chambers	Lozier	4	545	Lozier	white, red	80.48	18	8	200-71.50
9	Howdy Wilcox	National	National Motor Vehicle Co.	National	4	590	National	blue, white	87.20	8	9	200-69.30
19	Ralph Mulford	Knox	Ralph Mulford	Knox	6	597	Knox	white, red	87.88	16	10	200-56.29
4	Ralph DePalma	Mercedes	E. J. Schroeder	Mercedes	4	583	Mercedes	white	86.02	4	11	198-con. rod
15	Bob Burman	Cutting	Clark-Carter Auto Co.	Cutting	4	598	Cutting	white, red	84.11	12	12	157-wrecked SE
12	Bert Dingley	Simplex	Bert Dingley	Simplex	4	597	Simplex	red, white	80.77	10	13	116-con. rod
25	Joe Matson	Lozier	O. Applegate	Lozier	4	545	Lozier	white, red	79.90	21	14	110-crankshaft
7	Spencer Wishart	Mercedes	Spencer Wishart	Mercedes	4	583	Mercedes	gray, black, red	83.95	6	15	82-water connection
1	Gil Anderson	Stutz	Ideal Motor Car Co.	Stutz	4	390	Stutz	gray, white	80.93	1	16	80-wrecked NE
17	Billy Liesaw	Marquette-Buick	Will Thomson	Buick	4	594	Marquette	tan, red	77.51	14	17	72-caught fire
5	Louis Disbrow	Case	J. I. Case T. M. Co.	Case	6	450	Case	white, red	76.54	24	18	67-differential pin
23	Mel Marquette	McFarlan	Speed Motors Co.	McFarlan	6	425	McFarlan	gray	78.08	19	19	63-broken wheels
6	Eddie Hearne	Case	J. I. Case T. M. Co.	Case	6	450	Case	white, red	81.85	5	20	55-burned bearing
16	Lee Frayer	Firestone-Columbus	Columbus Buggy Co.	Firestone-Col.	4	345	Firestone-Col.	crimson, black	77.30	13	21	43-intake valve
29	David Bruce-Brown	National	National Motor Vehicle Co.	National	4	590	National	blue, white	88.45	23	22	25-valve trouble
10	Harry Knight	Lexington	Lexington Motor Car Co.	Lexington	6	422	Lexington	brown, white	75.92	9	23	6-engine trouble
24	Len Ormsby	Opel	I. C. Stern & B. C. Noble	Opel	4	450	Opel	gray, red	84.09	20	24	5-con. rod

Teddy Tetzlaff

Hughie Hughes

Charlie Merz

Bill Endicott

Len Zengel

Johnny Jenkins

Joe Horan

Howdy Wilcox

Ralph Mulford

Ralph DePalma

Bob Burman

Bert Dingley

Joe Matson

Spencer Wishart

Gil Anderson

Billy Liesaw

Louis Disbrow

Mel Marquette

Eddie Hearne

Lee Frayer

David Bruce-Brown

Harry Knight

Len Ormsby

Below, left: Len Zengel in action through the first turn in a Stutz. Below, right: Joe Dawson receives the checkered flag from Starter Fred J. Wagner. It was a surprise win for Dawson who led only two laps of the race after Ralph DePalma was forced out with engine trouble on his 199th lap. This was the last "500" started by Wagner who resigned after several disputes with Carl Fisher. Wagner remained as Starter for most major AAA events until his retirement in the 1930's. Bottom: The frontstretch and first turn as seen from the front gate of the track. Georgetown Road is in the upper left hand corner and the garage area is in the upper right.

Second Annual
International 500-Mile Race
Indianapolis Motor Speedway
Photo by
H. H. COBURN CO., Indianapolis

Above, left: The Stutz Team awaits the start. Above right: Eddie Rickenbacker at the wheel of Lee Frayer's Firestone-Columbus. Rickenbacker, who one day would own the Speedway, drove relief in this car both in 1911 and 1912. Middle left: Eddie Hearne in action driving the radically streamlined Case. Middle right: Johnny Jenkins prepares to leave the starting line in the White. Below: Ralph DePalma, a smile hiding his crushing misfortune, pushes his disabled Mercedes down the frontstretch to the pits after the car broke a connecting rod a few miles from the finish.

1913

The odd combination of a blistering sun, a voluble little French-man, a bobtailed blue race car and six pints of champagne proved to be the winning combination in the third "500." Jules Goux, driving under the instructions of a track-wise American, Johnny Aitken, easily won in his blue Peugeot while his adversaries were spending valuable time in the pits changing shredded tires and making mechanical repairs. Cooled and refreshed by the wine which he requested during his first pit stop, Goux ran just fast enough to stay in front and watched as other drivers were repeatedly forced to the pits with tire trouble caused by the ninety degree heat. Bob Burman, his most serious competition in the early stages of the race, lost too much time changing a faulty carburetor to be of any further threat and Gil Anderson's Stutz suffered a broken camshaft while battling for the lead in the latter laps. Jack Tower received a broken leg and his mechanic some broken ribs when their Mason turned over on the south stretch. These were the only injuries in the race. Harry Martin, mechanic for third place finisher Charlie Merz, thrilled the crowd as he crawled on to the hood to beat out flames as their blazing Stutz took the checkered flag.

Jules Goux

NO.	DRIVER	CAR	ENTRANT	ENGINE	CYL.	DISP.	CHASSIS	COLOR	QUAL. SPEED	ST.	FIN.	LAPS/SPEED/REASON OUT
16	Jules Goux	Peugeot	Peugeot	Peugeot	4	448	Peugeot	blue, white	86.03	7	1	200-75.933
22	Spencer Wishart	Mercer	Mercer Motors Co.	Mercer	4	300	Mercer	yellow	81.99	19	2	200-73.49
2	Charlie Merz	Stutz	Ideal Motor Car Co.	Stutz	4	400	Stutz	white, red	84.46	16	3	200-73.38
9	Albert Guyot	Sunbeam	Sunbeam Motor Car Co.	Sunbeam	6	368	Sunbeam	battleship gray	80.75	2	4	200-70.92
23	Theodore Pilette	Mercedes-Knight	E. C. Patterson	Knight	4	251	Mercedes	gray, white	75.52	13	5	200-68.15
12	Howdy Wilcox	Gray Fox	Frank Fox	Pope-Hartford	4	390	Pope-Hartford	gray	81.46	20	6	200-67.65
29	Ralph Mulford	Mercedes	E. J. Schroeder	Mercedes	4	449	Mercedes	gray	80.79	22	7	200-66.95
31	Louis Disbrow	Case	J. I. Case T. M. Co.	Case	4	449	Case	gray, red	82.76	23	8	200-66.80
35	Willie Haupt	Mason	Mason Motor Co.	Duesenberg	4	350	Duesenberg	dark tan	80.72	15	9	200-63.48
25	George Clark	Tulsa	Tulsa Auto Manufacturing Co.	Tulsa	4	340	Tulsa	red, black	75.91	27	10	200-62.99
4	Bob Burman	Keeton	Keeton Motor Co.	Keeton	4	449	Keeton	green, white	84.17	21	11	200-flagged
3	Gil Anderson	Stutz	Ideal Motor Car Co.	Stutz	4	400	Stutz	white, red	82.63	14	12	187-camshaft gears
5	Robert Evans	Mason	Mason Motor Co.	Duesenberg	4	350	Duesenberg	dark tan	82.01	4	13	158-clutch
17	Billy Liesaw	Anel	Will Tompson	Buick	4	318	Buick	orange, black	78.02	3	14	148-loose rods
19	Caleb Bragg	Mercer	Mercer Motors Co.	Mercer	4	424	Mercer	yellow	87.34	1	15	128-pump shaft
10	Billy Knipper	Henderson	Henderson Motor Car Co.	Duesenberg	4	350	Knipper	azure blue	80.26	11	16	125-clutch
27	Teddy Tetzlaff	Isotta	Isotta	Isotta	4	444	Isotta	red, green	81.30	8	17	118-drive chain
32	Joe Nikrent	Case	J. I. Case T. M. Co.	Case	4	449	Case	gray, red	78.89	24	18	67-burned bearing
6	Jack Tower	Mason	Mason Motor Co.	Duesenberg	4	350	Duesenberg	dark tan	88.23	25	19	51-wrecked SW
28	Vincenzo Trucco	Isotta	Isotta	Isotta	4	444	Isotta	red, green	81.94	18	20	39-loose gas tank
1	Harry Endicott	Nyberg	Nyberg Auto Co.	Nyberg	6	377	Nyberg	red	76.35	10	21	23-transmission
15	Paul Zuccarelli	Peugeot	Peugeot	Peugeot	4	448	Peugeot	blue, white	85.83	26	22	18-main bearing
21	Ralph DePalma	Mercer	Mercer Motors Co.	Mercer	4	340	Mercer	yellow	76.30	12	23	15-burned bearing
26	Harry Grant	Isotta	Isotta	Isotta	4	444	Isotta	red, green	75.96	6	24	14-gas tank
18	Johnny Jenkins	Schacht	Schacht Motor Car Co.	Schacht	4	299	Schacht	red, white	82.84	17	25	13-crankshaft
8	Don Herr	Stutz	Ideal Motor Car Co.	Stutz	4	400	Stutz	white, red	82.84	5	26	7-clutch shaft
33	Bill Endicott	Case	J. I. Case T. M. Co.	Case	6	448	Case	gray, red	85.70	9	27	1-drive shaft

Spencer Wishart

Charlie Merz

Albert Guyot

Theodore Pillette

Howdy Wilcox

Ralph Mulford

Louis Disbrow

Willie Haupt

George Clark

Bob Burman

Gil Anderson

Robert Evans

Billy Liesaw

Caleb Bragg

Billy Knipper

Teddy Tetzlaff

Joe Nikrent

Jack Tower

Vincenzo Trucco

Harry Endicott

Paul Zuccarelli

Ralph DePalma

Harry Grant

Johnny Jenkins

Don Herr

Bill Endicott

Below: The Stutz Team lines up on the pit apron. In No. 2 is Charles Merz, who placed third in the race. Gil Anderson is the driver in No. 3 which broke a camshaft after completing 187 laps and No. 8 is driven by Don Herr, who completed only 7 laps before a clutch shaft broke. Bottom: Ralph DePalma stands by as his Mercer is weighed.

Above: Willie Haupt watches as his pit crew changes a rear tire on his Mason. The Masons were actually built by the Duesenberg Brothers and gave a good account of themselves. Jack Tower's Mason was the fastest qualifier of the twenty-seven-car starting field and Haupt finished in ninth place. This was Duesenberg's first of many "500" appearances. Bottom: Led by Carl Fisher, the cars roar down the frontstretch to take the red starting flag.

1914

For the second year, France dominated the finish of the "500" as Rene Thomas piloted his Delage home in front of fellow countrymen Arthur Duray, Albert Guyot and Jules Goux. The only ray of light in an otherwise gloomy afternoon for American race fans was the fifth place scored by the barnstorming immortal, Barney Oldfield, in his white Stutz. Trailing Barney were Josef Christiaens in the Belgian Excelsior and Harry Grant in a British Sunbeam. The race, whose lead changed hands many times, proved that America was far behind her overseas neighbors when it came to preparing really competitive race cars. This was, however, the most complete European domination in the history of the race. Added incentive prizes and trophies for the leader at the 100, 200, 300, and 400 mile marks were all won by Frenchmen as Arthur Duray won the first two and Thomas, the remainder. Two accidents marred the race: Jean Chassagne turned over in the northwest turn on his 20th lap but was not seriously injured and Ray Gilhooley flipped his Isotta coming out of the southeast turn on his 44th. Joe Dawson was forced to crash his Marmon to avoid Gilhooley's mechanic who crawled into his path. Both drivers and their mechanics were seriously injured.

Rene Thomas

NO.	DRIVER	CAR	ENTRANT	ENGINE	CYL.	DISP.	CHASSIS	COLOR	QUAL. SPEED	ST.	FIN.	LAPS/SPEED/REASON OUT
16	Rene Thomas	Delage	L. Delage Co.	Delage	4	380	Delage	blue, white	94.54	15	1	200-82.47
14	Arthur Duray	Peugeot	Jacques Munier	Peugeot	4	183	Peugeot	blue, white	90.00	10	2	200-80.99
10	Albert Guyot	Delage	Albert Guyot	Delage	4	380	Delage	blue, white	89.15	11	3	200-80.20
6	Jules Goux	Peugeot	Jules Goux	Peugeot	4	345	Peugeot	blue, white	98.13	19	4	200-79.49
3	Barney Oldfield	Stutz	Stutz Motor Car Co.	Stutz	4	434	Stutz	white, red	87.25	30	5	200-78.15
9	Josef Christiaens	Excelsior	Josef Christiaens	Excelsior	6	446	Excelsior	Belgian yellow	91.21	7	6	200-77.44
27	Harry Grant	Sunbeam	Sunbeam Motor Car Co.	Sunbeam	6	273	Sunbeam	black, red, white	86.46	26	7	200-75.69
5	Charles Keene	Beaver Bullet	Charles Keene	Case	4	449	Keene	robin's egg blue	86.87	27	8	200-74.82
25	Billy Carlson	Maxwell	United States Motor Co.	Maxwell	4	445	Maxwell	black, white	93.36	5	9	200-70.97
42	E. Rickenbacker	Duesenberg	Duesenberg Bros.	Duesenberg	4	361	Duesenberg	red, white, blue	88.14	23	10	200-70.83
23	Ralph Mulford	Mercedes	E. J. Schroeder	Peugeot	4	448	Mercedes	white, blue	88.21	6	11	200-69.55
43	Willie Haupt	Duesenberg	Duesenberg	Duesenberg	4	361	Duesenberg	red, white, blue	89.39	28	12	200-66.66
31	Billy Knipper	Keeton	Keeton Motor Co.	Case	4	449	Keeton	red	89.57	12	13	200-65.79
7	Georges Boillot	Peugeot	Georges Boillot	Peugeot	4	345	Peugeot	blue, white	99.86	29	14	141-broken frame
34	Ernst Friedrich	Bugatti	Ettore Bugatti	Bugatti	4	390	Bugatti	white	87.73	18	15	134-drive pinion
1	Louis Disbrow	Burman	Bob Burman	Case	4	449	Burman	Burman blue, white	86.79	24	16	128-con. rod
19	Spencer Wishart	Mercer	Mercer Motors Co.	Mercer	4	445	Mercer	yellow	92.69	25	17	122-camshaft
2	Earl Cooper	Stutz	Stutz Motor Car Co.	Stutz	4	343	Stutz	white, red	88.02	14	18	118-broken wheel
21	Caleb Bragg	Mercer	Mercer Motors Co.	Mercer	4	445	Mercer	yellow	92.97	9	19	117-camshaft
15	Art Klein	King	Arthur H. Klein	Case	4	449	King	yellow, blue	86.87	8	20	87-valve
38	William Chandler	Braender Bulldog	Braender Rubber Co.	Duesenberg	4	449	Duesenberg	white, black	87.54	7	21	69-con. rod
4	Howdy Wilcox	Gray Fox	Frank Fox	Pope-Hartford	4	432	Fox	gray	90.76	3	22	67-valve
13	George Mason	Mason	Mason Motor Co.	Duesenberg	4	361	Duesenberg	green, red	87.10	13	23	66-piston
17	Bob Burman	Burman	Bob Burman	Case	4	449	Burman	Burman blue	90.41	22	24	47-con. rod
26	Joe Dawson	Marmon	Charles E. Erbstein	Marmon	4	445	Marmon	yellow, black	93.55	17	25	45-wrecked BS
24	Gil Anderson	Stutz	Stutz Motor Car Co.	Stutz	4	416	Stutz	white, red	90.49	16	26	42-loose cylinder bolts
49	Ray Gilhooley	Isotta	G. M. Heckschew	Isotta	4	375	Isotta	Italian green	84.20	20	27	41-wrecked BS
8	Teddy Tetzlaff	Maxwell	United States Motor Co.	Maxwell	4	445	Maxwell	black	96.36	2	28	33-rocker arm
12	Jean Chassagne	Sunbeam	Sunbeam Motor Car Co.	Sunbeam	6	273	Sunbeam	green	88.31	1	29	20-wrecked NW
48	S. F. Brock	Ray		Case	4	449	Ray	gray, red	87.83	21	30	5-camshaft

Arthur Duray

Albert Guyot

Jules Goux

Barney Oldfield

Josef Christiaens

Harry Grant

Charles Keene

Billy Carlson

Eddie Rickenbacker

Ralph Mulford

Willie Haupt

Billy Knipper

Georges Boillot

Ernst Friedrich

Louis Disbrow

Spencer Wishart

Earl Cooper

Caleb Bragg

Art Klein

William Chandler

Howdy Wilcox

George Mason

Bob Burman

Joe Dawson

Gil Anderson

Ray Gilhoolie

Teddy Tetzlaff

Jean Chassagne

S. F. Brock

Above: Bob Burman qualifies with an average speed of 90.41 in his blue Burman Special. Right: Georges Boillot, in the No. 7 Peugeot, goes down the frontstretch during a pre-race practice session.

Below: Not a group of visiting politicians but four of the best drivers in international competition. Left to right are Arthur Duray, Rene Thomas, Josef Christiaens, and Albert Guyot. Bottom: The Peugeot Team in its garage. Second from left is Georges Boillot who later gained fame as a French aviator in World War I. He was shot down by the Germans after destroying a number of enemy aircraft. On his right, with the moustache, is 1913 "500" winner, Jules Goux.

1915

Ralph DePalma, whose 1912 victory was snatched from his grasp when almost in sight of the checkered flag, was not to be denied this year. Although the same mechanical trouble happened at the same stage of the race, the intrepid DePalma was able to nurse his ailing Mercedes through those last two laps to beat Dario Resta's Peugeot. For many laps it was a close battle between the big cream-colored Mercedes and the blue Peugeot with the Mercedes having the best of it in the turns while the Peugeot displayed higher straightaway speeds. Gil Anderson, in a Stutz, finished third after leading the first part of the race and doing an excellent job all afternoon. At one point Resta was a lap in front of DePalma, but a blown tire and resulting skid caused him to lose this advantage. It was a safe race, the only accident being Joe Cooper's crash into the wall on his 155th lap. With three laps to go, DePalma's Mercedes broke a connecting rod which punched two holes in the block. Although he slowed down considerably, he was able to complete the final seven miles and win the race almost four minutes in front of Resta. As soon as the flag fell, DePalma drove his crippled car directly to his garage. Soon, however, he emerged to receive the crowd's plaudits.

Ralph DePalma

NO.	DRIVER	CAR	ENTRANT	ENGINE	CYL.	DISP.	CHASSIS	COLOR	QUAL. SPEED	ST.	FIN.	LAPS/SPEED/REASON OUT
2	Ralph DePalma	Mercedes	E. C. Patterson	Mercedes	4	274	Mercedes	cream, red, black	98.58	2	1	200-89.84
3	Dario Resta	Peugeot	Peugeot Auto Import Co.	Peugeot	4	274	Peugeot	blue, white	98.47	3	2	200-88.91
5	Gil Anderson	Stutz	Stutz Motor Car Co.	Stutz	4	296	Stutz	white, red	95.14	5	3	200-87.60
4	Earl Cooper	Stutz	Stutz Motor Car Co.	Stutz	4	296	Stutz	white, red	96.77	4	4	200-87.11
15	Eddie O'Donnell	Duesenberg	Duesenberg Bros.	Duesenberg	4	299	Duesenberg	white, red	88.93	11	5	200-81.47
8	Bob Burman	Peugeot	Bob Burman	Peugeot	4	296	Peugeot	blue, white	92.40	7	6	200-80.36
1	Howdy Wilcox	Stutz	Stutz Motor Car Co.	Stutz	4	296	Stutz	white, red	98.90	1	7	200-80.11
10	Tom Alley	Duesenberg	Duesenberg Bros.	Duesenberg	4	299	Duesenberg	white. red	90.00	9	8	200-79.33
19	Billy Carlson	Maxwell	United States Motor Co.	Maxwell	4	298	Maxwell	black, white, red	84.11	16	9	200-78.96
7	Noel Van Raalte	Sunbeam	Sunbeam Motor Car Co.	Sunbeam	4	271	Sunbeam	green, white	86.87	14	10	200-75.87
28	Willie Haupt	Emden	R. E. Donaldson	Emden	4	298	Emden	red, white	80.36	24	11	200-70.75
14	Harry Grant	Sunbeam	Fortuna Racing Team, Inc.	Sunbeam	6	278	Sunbeam	maroon, green	89.29	10	12	184-loose mud apron
21	Tom Orr	Maxwell	United States Motor Co.	Maxwell	4	298	Maxwell	black, white, red	83.55	17	13	168-axle bearing
6	Jean Porporato	Sunbeam	Sunbeam Motor Car Co.	Sunbeam	4	271	Sunbeam	green, red	94.74	6	14	164-piston
18	Joe Cooper	Sebring	E. E. Miles & J. W. Gwin	Duesenberg	4	299	Duesenberg	white, red	85.55	15	15	154-wrecked SS
22	Ralph Mulford	Duesenberg	Duesenberg Bros.	Duesenberg	4	299	Duesenberg	white, red	82.72	18	16	124-con. rod
12	George C. Babcock	Peugeot	Peugeot Auto Import Co.	Peugeot	4	188	Peugeot	blue, white	89.46	12	17	117-broken cylinder
9	Art Klein	Kleinart	Art Klein	Duesenberg	4	299	Duesenberg	white, red	90.45	8	18	111-disqualified, smoking
23	E. Rickenbacker	Maxwell	United States Motors Co.	Maxwell	4	298	Maxwell	black, white, red	81.97	19	19	103-con. rod
27	Louis Chevrolet	Cornelian	Louis Chevrolet	Cornelian	4	103	Cornelian	white, red	81.01	23	20	76-valve
17	John DePalma	Delage	James E. Wilson	Delage	4	299	Delage	blue, red, white	87.04	13	21	41-loose flywheel
24	John A. Mais	Mais	John A. Mais	Mercer	4	298	Mais	white, red	81.97	20	22	23-left course
26	George Hill	Bugatti	C. W. Fuller	Bugatti	4	300	Bugatti	white, black	81.52	22	23	20-water pump gear
25	G. C. Cox	Cino-Purcell	Edward D. McNay	Mercer	4	299	Cino	white, red	81.52	21	24	12-timing gears

Dario Resta

Gil Anderson

Earl Cooper

Eddie O'Donnell

Bob Burman

Howdy Wilcox

Tom Alley

Billy Carlson

Noel Van Raalte

Willie Haupt

Harry Grant

Tom Orr

Jean Porporato

Joe Cooper

Jack LeCain, (relief driver)

Art Klein

Eddie Rickenbacker

Louis Chevrolet

John DePalma

John A. Mais

George Hill

G. C. Cox

Ralph Mulford—no picture available

Above: Ralph DePalma, after several heartbreaking mishaps, finally takes the checkered flag in a "500". Though his Mercedes again had engine trouble near the finish, he was able to nurse it over the finish line in record-breaking time. Middle: Noel Van Raalte makes a pit stop in his English Sunbeam. Bottom: Winner Ralph DePalma poses in his big cream-colored Mercedes.

Below left: John DePalma's wrecked car after he hit the inside wall during a practice session. DePalma was able to repair the Delage in time to qualify for a starting position in the race, although he failed to finish because of a loose flywheel. Below right: Winner Ralph DePalma. Bottom: The Sebring, which was driven by Joe Cooper, is quartered next door to Eddie O'Donnell's Duesenberg (right) in the Speedway garage area. This row of garages, now refurbished and enlarged, is still standing and makes up the northern half of "Gasoline Alley".

1916

Because of the World War raging in Europe and the withdrawal of foreign racing teams, the Speedway management decided to shorten the 1916 race to 300 miles. That this decision was not especially popular was seen by a drop in attendance. The absence of Ralph DePalma from the starting field undoubtedly contributed even more to this drop. DePalma's post entry was refused after a dispute with the Speedway over the payment of appearance money. Dario Resta, one of the few foreign entries, didn't have too much trouble taking the lead in the early stages of the race and holding on to score a reasonably easy win. Wilbur D'Alene was second in a Duesenberg and Ralph Mulford was third in a Peugeot. The Duesenberg's performance was the best of any American car since 1913 and it foretold the later successes of the financially harassed German born brothers. Only two serious accident took place — both early in the race. Tom Rooney hit the wall in the first turn, breaking his hip and seriously injuring Thane Houser, his riding mechanic. At almost the same time and near the same place, Jack LeCain, driving relief for Jules DeVigne, had a similar accident and received serious head injuries. Bob Moore, his mechanic, was unhurt.

Dario Resta

NO.	DRIVER	CAR	ENTRANT	ENGINE	CYL.	DISP.	CHASSIS	COLOR	QUAL. SPEED	ST.	FIN.	LAPS/SPEED/REASON OUT
17	Dario Resta	Peugeot	Peugeot Auto Racing Co.	Peugeot	4	274	Peugeot	blue, white	94.40	4	1	120-83.26
1	Wilbur D'Alene	Duesenberg	Duesenberg Bros.	Duesenberg	4	299	Duesenberg	white	90.87	10	2	120-83.15
10	Ralph Mulford	Peugeot	Ralph Mulford	Peugeot	4	274	Peugeot	blue, white	91.09	20	3	120-82.60
14	Josef Christiaens	Sunbeam	Sunbeam Motor Car Co.	Sunbeam	6	299	Sunbeam	silver-gray	86.08	14	4	120-79.96
15	Barney Oldfield	Delage	Barney Oldfield	Delage	4	275	Delage	blue	94.33	5	5	120-79.20
4	Pete Henderson	Maxwell	Prest-O-Lite Racing Team	Maxwell	4	298	Maxwell	white	91.33	9	6	120-78.30
29	Howdy Wilcox	Premier	Indianapolis Speedway Team Co.	Premier	4	274	Premier	green, white	93.81	6	7	120-76.80
26	Art Johnson	Crawford	William Chandler	Duesenberg	4	298	Crawford	orange, black	83.69	17	8	120-74.40
24	William Chandler	Crawford	William Chandler	Duesenberg	4	298	Crawford	orange, black	84.84	15	9	120-74.20
9	Ora Haibe	Osteweg	S. Osteweg	Wisconsin	4	296	Osteweg	white	87.08	13	10	120-74.00
12	Tom Alley	Ogren	Ogren Motor Car Co.	Duesenberg	4	299	Duesenberg	blue	82.04	19	11	120-73.55
8	Louis Chevrolet	Frontenac	Chevrolet Bros.	Frontenac	4	300	Frontenac	maroon, white	87.69	21	12	82-con. rod
28	Gil Anderson	Premier	Indianapolis Speedway Team Co.	Premier	4	274	Premier	green, white	95.94	3	13	75-oil line
25	Dave Lewis	Crawford	William Chandler	Duesenberg	4	298	Crawford	orange, black	83.12	18	14	71-loose gas tank
18	Johnny Aitken	Peugeot	Indianapolis Speedway Team Co.	Peugeot	4	274	Peugeot	blue, white	96.69	1	15	69-valve
21	Jules DeVigne	Delage	Harry Harkness	Delage	4	274	Delage	blue	87.17	12	16	61-wrecked NS
27	Tom Rooney	Premier	Indianapolis Speedway Team Co.	Premier	4	274	Premier	green, white	93.39	7	17	48-wrecked SS
7	Arthur Chevrolet	Frontenac	Chevrolet Bros.	Frontenac	4	300	Frontenac	maroon	87.74	11	18	35-magneto
19	Charles Merz	Peugeot	Indianapolis Speedway Team Co.	Peugeot	4	274	Peugeot	blue, white	93.33	8	19	25-lubrication
5	E. Rickenbacker	Maxwell	Prest-O-Lite Racing Team	Maxwell	4	298	Maxwell	white	96.44	2	20	9-steering
23	Aldo Franchi	Peusun	Aldo Franchi	Sunbeam	4	299	Peugeot	orange, black	84.12	16	21	9-engine trouble

Wilbur D'Alene

Ralph Mulford

Josef Christiaens

Barney Oldfield

Pete Henderson

Howdy Wilcox

Art Johnson

William Chandler

Ora Haibe

Tom Alley

Louis Chevrolet

Gil Anderson

Dave Lewis

Johnny Aitken

Jules DeVigne

Tom Rooney

Arthur Chevrolet

Charlie Merz

Eddie Rickenbacker

Aldo Franchi

Above: Winner Dario Resta and his Peugeot are surrounded by well-wishers when they return to their garage. Right: Howdy Wilcox during his qualifying run. Wilcox is driving one of the Speedway-owned Premiers which were built to insure an adequate starting field after World War I caused a serious shortage of foreign entries. The Premiers were virtual copies of the successful Peugeots.

Below: The front row lines up for the start. Johnny Aitken's Peugeot is on the pole followed by Eddie Rickenbacker's Maxwell, Gil Anderson's Premier, and Dario Resta's Peugeot. Bottom: Barney Oldfield makes a pit stop during a practice session. Behind Oldfield's Delage is one of the three cars from the Crawford Team.

1919

Howdy Wilcox plugged along in a Speedway-owned Peugeot to win the first post-war "500" which proved to be a race of tragedy. Three men died in accidents while two others were critically injured, one from a freak injury which happened in full view of the frontstretch patrons. The starting lineup consisted of 33 cars and while Wilcox wasn't one of the early leaders he stayed within striking distance until the halfway mark when he took over the lead from Louis Chevrolet. At the finish he was almost four minutes in front of Eddie Hearne. On his 45th lap, Arthur Thurman overturned on the northeast turn and received fatal injuries. His mechanic, Nicholas Molinero, was injured critically. In front of Grandstand G, on its 97th lap, the Roamer, driven by Louis LeCocq, had its gas tank explode and overturned. Both LeCocq and Robert Bandini, his mechanic, were killed instantly. Late in the race Louis Chevrolet threw a wheel on the frontstretch and his hub cut the timing wire. The wire snapped back and caught Elmer Shannon across the throat, cutting it badly. He almost bled to death before he reached the pits. His mechanic took over the wheel and finished 12th. Jean Chassagne, relieving Bablot, and Andre Boillot also crashed but were uninjured.

Howdy Wilcox

NO.	DRIVER	CAR	ENTRANT	ENGINE	CYL.	DISP.	CHASSIS	COLOR	QUAL. SPEED	ST.	FIN.	LAPS/SPEED/REASON OUT
3	Howdy Wilcox	Peugeot	Indianapolis Motor Speedway	Peugeot	4	275	Peugeot	blue, white	100.01	2	1	200-88.05
14	Eddie Hearne	Durant	R. Cliff Durant	Stutz	4	299	Stutz	gray	94.50	8	2	200-87.09
6	Jules Goux	Peugeot	Indianapolis Motor Speedway	Premier	4	275	Peugeot	blue, white	95.00	22	3	200-85.93
32	Albert Guyot	Ballot	Ernest Ballot	Ballot	8	296	Ballot	blue, white	98.30	3	4	200-84.44
26	Tom Alley	Bender	Ahlberg Bearing Co.	Bender	4	289	Bender		92.20	28	5	200-82.18
4	Ralph DePalma	Packard	Packard Motor Car Co.	Packard	12	299	Packard	cream	98.20	4	6	200-81.04
7	Louis Chevrolet	Frontenac	Frontenac Motors	Frontenac	4	300	Frontenac	maroon	103.10	12	7	200-81.03
27	Ira Vail	Hudson	Hudson Motor Car Co.	Hudson	6	289	Hudson	blue, white	94.10	10	8	200-80.49
21	Denny Hickey	Stickle	A. C. Stickle	Hudson	6	289	Hudson	blue, white	92.50	27	9	200-80.22
41	Gaston Chevrolet	Frontenac	Frontenac Motors	Frontenac	4	300	Frontenac	maroon, white	100.40	16	10	200-79.50
31	Rene Thomas	Ballot	Ernest Ballot	Ballot	8	296	Ballot	blue, white	104.70	1	11	200-78.75
8	Earl Cooper	Stutz	Earl Cooper	Stutz	4	299	Stutz	white, red	94.25	9	12	200-78.60
23	Elmer T. Shannon	Shannon	Elmer T. Shannon	Duesenberg	4	299	Duesenberg	white	91.70	29	13	200-76.75
17	Ora Haibe	Hudson	Hudson Motor Car Co.	Hudson	6	289	Hudson	blue	92.80	26	14	200-
37	Andre Boillot	Baby Peugeot	Jules Goux	Peugeot	4	275	Peugeot	blue, white	89.50	32	15	195-wrecked BS
48	Ray Howard	Peugeot	A. G. Kaufman	Peugeot	4	275	Peugeot	blue, white	95.00	21	16	130-lost oil pressure
22	Wilbur D'Alene	Duesenberg	Duesenberg Bros.	Duesenberg	4	299	Duesenberg	white	94.20	23	17	120-axle
15	Louis LeCocq	Roamer	Roscoe Sarles	Duesenberg	4	299	Duesenberg	gray, blue	92.90	25	18	96-wrecked SE
29	Art Klein	Peugeot	Arthur H. Klein	Peugeot	4	275	Peugeot	blue, white	94.90	7	19	70-oil line
19	Chas. Kirkpatrick	Detroit	Frank P. Book	Mercedes copy	4	274	Mercedes copy	silver	90.00	11	20	69-con. rod
33	Paul Bablot	Ballot	Ernest Ballot	Ballot	8	296	Ballot	blue, white	94.90	6	21	63-wrecked
10	Eddie O'Donnell	Duesenberg	Duesenberg Bros.	Duesenberg	4	299	Duesenberg	brown	97.30	5	22	60-piston
12	Kurt Hitke	Roamer	Roscoe Sarles	Duesenberg	4	299	Duesenberg	gray, blue	93.50	24	23	56-rod bearing
1	Cliff Durant	Chevrolet	R. Cliff Durant	Stutz	4	299	Stutz	tan	96.50	20	24	54-steering
9	Tommy Milton	Duesenberg	Duesenberg Bros.	Duesenberg	4	299	Duesenberg	brown	89.90	31	25	50-con. rod
34	Louis Wagner	Ballot	Ernest Ballot	Ballot	8	296	Ballot	blue, white	101.70	13	26	44-broken wheel
18	Arthur Thurman	Thurman	Arthur Thurman	Duesenberg	4	299	Duesenberg		98.00	18	27	44-wrecked NE
43	Omar Toft	Toft	Omar Toft	Miller	4		Miller	white	91.50	30	28	44-con. rod
2	Ralph Mulford	Frontenac	Ralph Mulford	Frontenac	4	300	Frontenac	maroon	100.50	15	29	37-driveshaft
36	J. J. McCoy	McCoy	J. J. McCoy		4			white, red	86.50	33	30	36-oil line
39	Joe Boyer	Frontenac	Frontenac Motors	Frontenac	4	300	Frontenac	maroon	100.90	14	31	30-rear axle
5	W. W. Brown	Richards	C. L. Richards	Brown-Brett	6		Brown	yellow	99.80	17	32	14-con. rod
28	Roscoe Sarles	Oldfield	Barney Oldfield	Miller	4		Miller	gold	97.70	19	33	8-rocker arm

Eddie Hearne

Jules Goux

Albert Guyot

Tom Alley

Ralph DePalma

Louis Chevrolet

Ira Vail

Denny Hickey

Gaston Chevrolet

Rene Thomas

Earl Cooper

Elmer T. Shannon

Ora Haibe

Andre Boillot

Ray Howard

Wilbur D'Alene

Louis LeCocq

Art Klein

Charles Kirkpatrick

Paul Bablot

Eddie O'Donnell

Kurt Hitke

Cliff Durant

Tommy Milton

Louis Wagner

Arthur Thurman

Omar Toft

Ralph Mulford

J. J. McCoy

Joe Boyer

Roscoe Sarles

W. W. Brown-no picture available

Below left: Jean Chassagne poses beside the Ballot shortly after crashing over the wall. He was driving relief for Paul Bablot when the accident happened. Below, right: The two Packards driven by Ralph DePalma. No. 4 is the 300-cubic-inch car that DePalma drove in the "500" and the un-numbered car is the 905-cubic-inch car in which DePalma broke the World's Mile Speed Record at Daytona Beach on February 12, 1919 with a speed of 149.875 mph. Bottom: Another view of the Ballot which was wrecked by Jean Chassagne.

Above: Rene Thomas leads the field on the pace lap in his No. 31 Ballot. No. 3 is the eventual winner, Howdy Wilcox, in one of the Speedway-owned Peugeots. Left: The wreckage of Louis LeCocq's Roamer remains in front of Grandstand G after its gas tank exploded and killed LeCocq and his riding mechanic.

1920

Once again in his "500" career, Ralph DePalma had trouble near the end of the race and this robbed him, for the second time, of a victory. After trailing Joe Boyer for the first 39 laps, DePalma's Ballot took the lead and began piling up a margin of two laps over Gaston Chevrolet's Monroe. On the 187th lap, the Ballot sputtered and caught fire. With the car still moving at a fast clip, mechanic Pete DePaolo crawled over the hood and put out the fire. Despite DePaolo's efforts, the car came to a halt and, thinking the Ballot was out of gas, DePaolo ran to the pits to get some. He was met on his return trip by DePalma who once again had the Ballot running. Instead of being out of gas, one magneto had quit and, while Chevrolet roared to victory, DePalma limped home on four of the car's eight cylinders. Chevrolet also had a close call as he was forced to stop for fuel three laps from the finish. Four cars were involved in accidents although there were no serious injuries. Art Klein crashed on his 41st lap and Roscoe Sarles hit the northeast wall on his 59th and later, while relieving Bennett Hill, Sarles did the same thing in the same turn. Ira Vail, driving relief for Joe Boyer, hit the northeast wall and turned over on his 192nd lap.

Gaston Chevrolet

NO.	DRIVER	CAR	ENTRANT	ENGINE	CYL.	DISP.	CHASSIS	COLOR	QUAL. SPEED	ST.	FIN.	LAPS/SPEED/REASON OUT
4	Gaston Chevrolet	Monroe	William Small Co.	Frontenac	4	183	Frontenac	green, white	91.55	6	1	200- 88.16
25	Rene Thomas	Ballot	Ernest Ballot	Ballot	8	181	Ballot	blue, white	93.95	18	2	200- 87.47
10	Tommy Milton	Duesenberg	Duesenberg Bros.	Duesenberg	8	181	Duesenberg	yellow	90.20	11	3	200- 86.52
12	Jimmy Murphy	Duesenberg	Duesenberg Bros.	Duesenberg	8	181	Duesenberg	yellow	88.70	15	4	200- 85.10
2	Ralph DePalma	Ballot	Ralph DePalma	Ballot	8	181	Ballot	cream	99.15	1	5	200- 82.12
31	Eddie Hearne	Duesenberg	Duesenberg Bros.	Duesenberg	8	182	Duesenberg	yellow	88.05	9	6	200- 80.15
26	Jean Chassagne	Ballot	Ernest Ballot	Ballot	8	181	Ballot	blue, white	95.45	4	7	200- 79.94
28	Joe Thomas	Monroe	William Small Co.	Frontenac	4	181	Frontenac	green	92.80	19	8	200- 78.60
33	Ralph Mulford	Mulford	Ralph Mulford	Duesenberg	8	182	Mulford	brown	......@	23	9	200- 68.33
15	Pete Henderson	Revere	Revere Motor Car Corp.	Duesenberg	4	181	Duesenberg	white, red	81.15	17	10	200- 67.93
32	John Boling	Richards	C. L. Richards	Brett	6	179	Brett	yellow	81.85	14	11	199-flagged
6	Joe Boyer	Frontenac	Frontenac Motor Co.	Frontenac	4	183	Frontenac	red	96.90	2	12	192-wrecked NE
9	Ray Howard	Peugeot	Peugeot Auto Racing Co.	Peugeot	4	182	Peugeot	blue, white	84.60	10	13	150-camshaft
29	Eddie O'Donnell	Duesenberg	Duesenberg Bros.	Duesenberg	8	182	Duesenberg	yellow	88.20	12	14	149-oil line
16	Jules Goux	Peugeot	Jules Goux	Peugeot	4	182	Peugeot	blue, white	84.30	21	15	148-engine trouble
34	Willie Haupt	Meteor	Meteor Motors Co.	Duesenberg	8	182	Duesenberg		85.48	13	16	146-con. rod
7	Bennett Hill	Frontenac	Frontenac Motor Co.	Frontenac	4	183	Frontenac	red	90.55	8	17	115-wrecked NW
3	Louis Chevrolet	Monroe	William Small Co.	Frontenac	4	183	Frontenac	green	96.30	3	18	94-steering
18	Howdy Wilcox	Peugeot	Jules Goux	Peugeot	4	182	Peugeot	blue, white	88.82	20	19	65-engine trouble
5	Roscoe Sarles	Monroe	William Small Co.	Frontenac	4	183	Frontenac	green	90.75	7	20	58-wrecked NW
8	Art Klein	Frontenac	Frontenac Motor Co.	Frontenac	4	183	Frontenac	red, white	92.70	5	21	40-wrecked
19	Jean Porporato	Gregoire	Jean Porporato	Gregoire	4	182	Gregoire	blue, white	79.98@	22	22	23-car fell apart
17	Andre Boillot	Peugeot	Jules Goux	Peugeot	4	182	Peugeot	blue, white	85.40	16	23	16-engine trouble

@Did not qualify under rules, but allowed to start with official permission

Rene Thomas

Tommy Milton

Jimmy Murphy

Ralph DePalma

Eddie Hearne

Jean Chassagne

Joe Thomas

Ralph Mulford

Pete Henderson

John Boling

Joe Boyer

Ray Howard

Eddie O'Donnell

Jules Goux

Willie Haupt

Bennett Hill

Louis Chevrolet

Howdy Wilcox

Roscoe Sarles

Art Klein

Jean Porporato

Andre Boillot

Less than seven months after he won the 1920 "500" Gaston Chevrolet (below, left) was fatally injured in an accident on the board speedway in Beverly Hills, California. Below, right: Tommy Milton, in a Duesenberg, and Jean Chassagne, in the No. 26 Ballot, wait in the pits prior to taking practice runs. Bottom: Tommy Milton's huge Duesenberg, in which he set a world's record for the mile (156.046 mph) on the Florida sands, is a popular visitor to the Speedway.

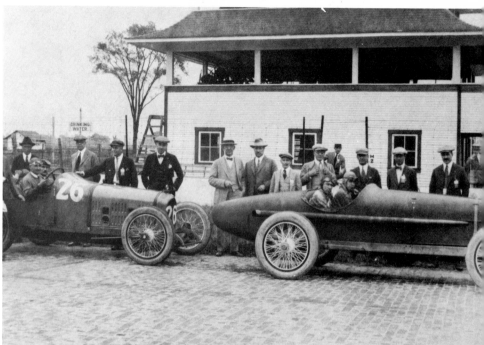

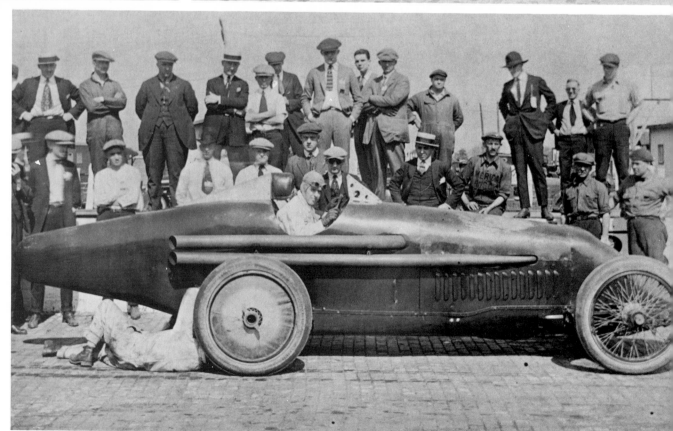

Gaston Chevrolet, Winner 1920

Above: Gaston Chevrolet in the Monroe which was designed by Cornelius W. Van Ranst and built by the Chevrolet Brothers. The Monroes and the Frontenacs were identical cars built by the Chevrolets, their only difference being their colors. The Frontenacs were red and the Monroes, green. Left: The wreck of Arthur Chevrolet's Frontenac after it was side-swiped by Rene Thomas' Ballot in practice. Despite the accident, the car was repaired in 24 hours and driven in the race by Bennett Hill. Chevrolet was seriously injured.

1921

Tommy Milton, who filled the vacancy on the Frontenac Team caused by Gaston Chevrolet's death at Beverly Hills, drove a masterful race to defeat Roscoe Sarles, in a Duesenberg, by over two laps. Once again it was a heartbreaker for Ralph DePalma who led until the 112th lap only to break a connecting rod in his Ballot. Sarles was in contention all afternoon but he couldn't beat the smooth, steady performance of Milton who drove Louis Chevrolet's plum-colored straight-eight. It was a great day for Louis' cars as they finished first, third and ninth. Tom Alley, another team member, was running an excellent race near the head of the pack when he broke a rod on his 133rd lap. It was an injury-free race although there were some thrilling spins and crashes. On its 25th lap, Eddie Pullen's car, with Joe Thomas driving relief, broke a steering knuckle and hit the wall in the southwest turn. A few laps later Louis Fontaine spun off the track and climbed the outside wall coming into the frontstretch when his brakes locked. The rear wheels were almost in the front row of the box seats and gave the spectators a good scare. Just after the halfway mark, Jimmy Murphy also had steering trouble and spun coming out of the northwest turn.

Tommy Milton

NO.	DRIVER	CAR	ENTRANT	ENGINE	CYL.	DISP.	CHASSIS	COLOR	QUAL. SPEED	ST.	FIN.	LAPS/SPEED/REASON OUT
2	Tommy Milton	Frontenac	Louis Chevrolet	Frontenac	8	178	Frontenac	Plum, white	93.05	20	1	200-89.62
6	Roscoe Sarles	Duesenberg Straight 8	Duesenberg Bros.	Duesenberg	8	184	Duesenberg	Confederate gray	98.35	2	2	200-88.61
23	Percy Ford	Chicago Frontenac	Stanley Kandul	Frontenac	4	182	Frontenac	red, white	87.00	8	3	200-85.02
5	Eddie Miller	Duesenberg Straight 8	Duesenberg Bros.	Duesenberg	8	184	Duesenberg	Confederate gray	83.85	9	4	200-84.65
16	Ora Haibe	Sunbeam	Sunbeam Motor Car Co.	Sunbeam	8	182	Sunbeam	silver	93.50	13	5	200-84.28
9	Albert Guyot	Duesenberg Straight 8	Duesenberg Bros.	Duesenberg	8	183	Duesenberg	Confederate gray	87.78	14	6	200-83.03
3	Ira Vail	Leach	Ira Vail	Miller	8	181	Leach	unpainted	82.35	10	7	200-80.15
21	Bennett Hill	Duesenberg Straight 8	John Thiele	Duesenberg	8	183	Duesenberg	Confederate gray	87.75	15	8	200-79.13
8	Ralph Mulford	Frontenac	Louis Chevrolet	Frontenac	8	183	Frontenac	red, white	91.70	21	9	177-flagged
15	Rene Thomas	Sunbeam	Sunbeam Motor Car Co.	Sunbeam	8	181	Sunbeam	silver	83.75	17	10	144-water connection
27	Tom Alley	Frontenac	L. L. Corum	Frontenac	4	182	Frontenac	red, white	80.50	18	11	133-con. rod
4	Ralph DePalma	Ballot	Ralph DePalma	Ballot	8	176	Ballot	cream	100.75	1	12	112-con. rod
1	Eddie Hearne	Revere	E. A. Hearne	Duesenberg	8	182	Duesenberg	white	96.18	4	13	111-oil line
24	Jimmy Murphy	Duesenberg Straight 8	Duesenberg Bros.	Duesenberg	8	184	Duesenberg	Confederate gray	93.60	19	14	107-hit wall, damaged
17	Riley J. Brett	Junior	George L. Wade	Brett	6	179	Brett	cream	87.70	16	15	91-hit wall, damaged
28	C. W. Van Ranst	Frontenac	C. W. Van Ranst	Frontenac	4	183	Frontenac	green, white	88.35	23	16	87-water connection
7	Joe Boyer	Duesenberg Straight 8	Duesenberg Bros.	Duesenberg	8	184	Duesenberg	Confederate gray	96.65	3	17	74-rear axle
19	Jean Chassagne	Peugeot	Jean Chassagne	Peugeot	4	182	Peugeot	blue	91.00	6	18	65-lost hood
22	Jules Ellingboe	Frontenac	Jules Ellingboe	Frontenac	4	182	Frontenac	red, white	95.40	5	19	49-steering
14	Andre Boillot	Talbot-Darracq	Louis Coatalen	Sunbeam	8	181	Sunbeam	silver	97.60	11	20	41-con. rod
18	Louis Fontaine	Junior	George L. Wade	Brett	6	179	Brett	blue	88.30	7	21	33-wrecked FS
25	Joe Thomas	Duesenberg Straight 8	Duesenberg Bros.	Duesenberg	8	184	Duesenberg	Confederate gray	96.25	22	22	25-steering
10	Howdy Wilcox	Peugeot	Jules Goux	Peugeot	4	176	Peugeot	blue	96.00	12	23	22-con. rod

Roscoe Sarles

Percy Ford

Eddie Miller

Ora Haibe

Albert Guyot

Ira Vail

Bennett Hill

Ralph Mulford

Rene Thomas

Tom Alley

Ralph DePalma

Eddie Hearne

Jimmy Murphy

Riley J. Brett

C. W. Van Ranst

Joe Boyer

Jean Chassagne

Jules Ellingboe

Andre Boillot

Joe Thomas (qualifier)

Eddie Pullen (qualifier)

Howdy Wilcox

Below, left: The winner, Tommy Milton. Below, right: Louis Fontaine's Junior Special after it crashed coming into the frontstretch and almost found a seat in the grandstand. Fontaine wasn't seriously injured and by the time the picture was taken the spectators had returned to their seats to watch the remainder of the race. Bottom: The Sunbeam Team with their drivers (left to right) Andre Boillot, Ora Haibe and Rene Thomas. Of this group, Haibe was the most successful, finishing fifth.

Above: A victory celebration after the race: Arthur Chevrolet (white shirt and cap), riding mechanic Harry Frank with glass, winner Tommy Milton, Louis Chevrolet in straw hat, AAA Representative W. D. "Eddie" Edenburn in checkered coat and Barney Oldfield with his ever present cigar. Famous speedboat racer, Gar Wood, is between Edenburn and Oldfield. Left: Eddie Miller qualifies his Duesenberg Straight 8. Bottom: Roscoe Sarles in the Duesenberg he drove to second place.

1922

The Duesenberg Brothers made an almost clean sweep of the first ten positions as their fast, reliable cars captured all but third and ninth. San Francisco's Jimmy Murphy, fresh from his impressive win in the 1921 French Grand Prix, dominated the field and led 154 laps to win by a two-lap margin over rookie Harry Hartz. Though Murphy's chassis was a Duesenberg, he had installed a new Miller engine under the hood and the combination proved to be a winner. The only non-Duesenbergs in the first ten were the Ballot, driven by Eddie Hearne to third, and Tom Alley's Monroe which finished ninth. Peter DePaolo, who had led the race for a short time, hit the wall in the northeast turn while he was trying to catch Murphy on the 110th lap. His Frontenac was too badly damaged to continue but he finished the race driving relief for Joe Thomas in a Duesenberg. The only Duesenberg not in the first ten was driven by Jules Ellingboe who spun three times and hit the wall, breaking a rear wheel and putting the car out of the race on its 26th lap. Murphy's time of 5:17:30.79 was a new record for the distance, breaking Ralph DePalma's 1915 mark. Two interesting additions to the field were the Fronty-Fords, racing versions of the famed Model T.

Jimmy Murphy

NO.	DRIVER	CAR	ENTRANT	ENGINE	CYL.	DISP.	CHASSIS	COLOR	QUAL. SPEED	ST.	FIN.	LAPS/SPEED/REASON OUT
35	Jimmy Murphy	Murphy	Jimmy Murphy	Miller	8	181	Duesenberg	white	100.50	1	1	200-94.48
12	Harry Hartz	Duesenberg Straight 8	Duesenberg Bros.	Duesenberg	8	182	Duesenberg	white	99.97	2	2	200-93.53
15	Eddie Hearne	Ballot	Jules Goux	Ballot	8	180	Ballot	blue	95.60	23	3	200-93.04
17	Ralph DePalma	Duesenberg Straight 8	Ralph DePalma	Duesenberg	8	181	Duesenberg	cream	99.55	3	4	200-90.61
31	Ora Haibe	Duesenberg Straight 8	Duesenberg Bros	Duesenberg	8	177	Duesenberg	gray	92.90	14	5	200-90.58
24	Jerry Wonderlich	Duesenberg Straight 8	Duesenberg Bros.	Duesenberg	8	182	Duesenberg	buff, red	97.76	7	6	200-88.79
21	I. P. Fetterman	Duesenberg Straight 8	Duesenberg Bros.	Duesenberg	8	180	Duesenberg	gray	93.28	13	7	200-87.99
1	Ira Vail	Disteel Duesenberg	Disteel Flyers, Inc.	Duesenberg	8	183	Duesenberg	white	96.75	9	8	200-86.15
26	Tom Alley	Monroe	William Small Co.	Frontenac	4	182	Frontenac	green, white	94.05	12	9	200-84.20
10	Joe Thomas	Duesenberg Straight 8	Duesenberg Bros.	Duesenberg	8	181	Duesenberg	gray	88.80	17	10	200-82.50
3	"Cannonball" Baker	Frontenac	Louis Chevrolet	Frontenac	8	183	Frontenac	red	89.60	16	11	200-79.25
34	Cliff Durant	Durant	R. Cliff Durant	Miller	8	181	Miller	blue	95.85	11	12	200-77.75
22	W. Douglas Hawkes	Bentley	Bentley	Bentley	4	182	Bentley	silver	81.90	19	13	200-74.95
18	Jack Curtner	Fronty-Ford	Jack Curtner	Fronty-Ford	4	181	Ford T	red	@	21	14	160-flagged
25	Wilbur D'Alene	Monroe	William Small Co.	Frontenac	4	182	Frontenac	green, white	87.80	18	15	160-flagged
9	Frank Elliott	Leach	Ira Vail	Miller	8	181	Miller	green, white, yellow	97.75	8	16	195-axle
27	L. L. Corum	Monroe	William Small Co.	Frontenac	4	183	Frontenac	green, white	89.65	15	17	169-engine trouble
19	C. Glenn Howard	Fronty-Ford	Chevrolet Bros. Mfg. Co.	Fronty-Ford	4	181	Ford T	red	83.90	27	18	165-engine trouble
5	Ralph Mulford	Frontenac	Louis Chevrolet	Frontenac	4	182	Frontenac	red	99.20	5	19	161-con. rod
7	Peter DePaolo	Frontenac	Louis Chevrolet	Frontenac	8	183	Frontenac	red	96.20	10	20	110-wrecked NE
6	Art Klein	Frontenac	Louis Chevrolet	Frontenac	4	183	Frontenac	black	87.15	25	21	105-con. rod
4	Leon Duray	Frontenac	Louis Chevrolet	Frontenac	4	183	Frontenac	red, white	99.25	4	22	94-broken axle
2	Roscoe Sarles	Frontenac	Louis Chevrolet	Frontenac	4	183	Frontenac	red	98.00	6	23	88-con. rod
8	Tommy Milton	Leach	Tommy Milton	Miller	8	181	Milton	red	94.40	24	24	44-loose gas tank
14	Jules Goux	Ballot	Jules Goux	Ballot	8	180	Ballot	blue	96.95	22	25	25-broken axle
23	Jules Ellingboe	Duesenberg Straight 8	Duesenberg Bros.	Duesenberg	8	182	Duesenberg	gray	95.50	20	26	25-wrecked
16	Howdy Wilcox	Peugot	Howard Wilcox	Peugeot	8	177	Peugeot	blue	86.10	26	27	7-valve spring

@Did not qualify

Harry Hartz

Eddie Hearne

Ralph DePalma

Ora Haibe

Jerry Wonderlich

I. P. Fetterman

Ira Vail

Tom Alley

Joe Thomas

'Cannonball" Baker

Cliff Durant

W. Douglas Hawkes

Jack Curtner

Wilbur D'Alene

Frank Elliott

L. L. Corum

C. Glenn Howard

Ralph Mulford

Peter DePaolo

Art Klein

Leon Duray

Roscoe Sarles

Tommy Milton

Jules Goux

Jules Ellingboe

Howdy Wilcox

Above: An early aerial view of the Speedway with the cars lined up awaiting the start. Right: The Ballot, assigned to Jules Goux, arrives from France. Tires were removed to facilitate shipping. Bottom: Ralph Mulford beside the Frontenac he was to drive in the race.

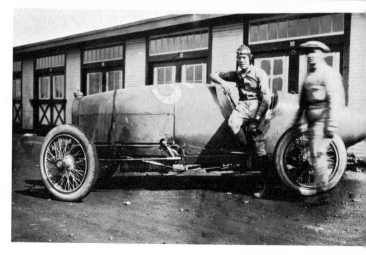

Below, left: Jerry Wonderlich working on the Duesenberg Straight 8 he was to drive to sixth place. Below, right: I. P. Fetterman in his Duesenberg. During the race, Fetterman was relieved by Phil "Red" Shafer. It was the first of many races for Shafer whose career as a driver and owner would extend to the late 1930's. Bottom: Leon Duray, second from left, with his crew and the No. 4 Frontenac.

1923

Tommy Milton became the first driver to win the "500" twice when he scored an easy and impressive victory in his Miller-powered H. C. S. Special. Milton's only real problem came from badly blistered hands resulting from a tight pair of white gloves which were replaced while Howdy Wilcox, Milton's teammate, was driving relief after his own car was forced out with clutch trouble. With his hands taped, Milton regained the lead after changing a faulty gas filler cap for which a tape-covered orange had been only a mediocre replacement. Harry Hartz, who had led briefly while Milton was resting, settled back to protect his second place position from a determined Jimmy Murphy and Milton, no longer pressed, drove his usual consistent race to win by three-and-a-quarter minutes. It was not a race without tragedy as, on lap 23, Tom Alley, driving relief for Earl Cooper, crashed off the track on the backstretch and went through the outside fence after striking three youths watching the race through a knothole. Teenager Bert Schoup was killed and his two companions injured. Earlier in the race Christian Lautenschlager, driving a Mercedes, hit the southwest wall but escaped injury. The Mercedes and Bugatti teams made up the European contingent.

Tommy Milton

NO.	DRIVER	CAR	ENTRANT	ENGINE	CYL.	DISP.	CHASSIS	COLOR	QUAL. SPEED	ST.	FIN.	LAPS/SPEED/REASON OUT
1	Tommy Milton	H.C.S.	H.C.S. Motor Co.	Miller	8	121	Miller	white, red	108.17	1	1	200-90.95
7	Harry Hartz	Durant	R. Cliff Durant	Miller	8	121	Miller	yellow, black	103.70	2	2	200-90.06
5	Jimmy Murphy	Durant	R. Cliff Durant	Miller	8	121	Miller	yellow, black	104.05	9	3	200-88.08
6	Eddie Hearne	Durant	R. Cliff Durant	Miller	8	121	Miller	yellow, black	97.30	14	4	200-86.65
23	L. L. Corum	Barber-Warnock Ford	Barber-Warnock	Fronty-Ford	4	122	Ford T	orange	86.65	7	5	200-82.58
31	Frank Elliott	Durant	R. Cliff Durant	Miller	8	121	Miller	yellow, black	93.25	16	6	200-82.22
8	Cliff Durant	Durant	R. Cliff Durant	Miller	8	121	Miller	yellow, black	102.65	10	7	200-82.17
15	Max Sailer	Mercedes	Daimler Motoren Gesellschaft	Mercedes	4	121	Mercedes	white	90.55	20	8	200-80.68
19	Prince deCystria	Bugatti	Prince deCystria	Bugatti	8	122	Bugatti	blue	88.90	22	9	200-77.64
34	Phil Shafer	Duesenberg	Duesenberg Bros.	Duesenberg	8	121	Duesenberg	gray	88.00	24	10	200-74.98
16	Christian Werner	Mercedes	Daimler Motoren Gesellschaft	Mercedes	4	121	Mercedes	white	95.20	15	11	200-74.65
18	Pierre de Viscaya	Bugatti	Martin de Alsaga	Bugatti	8	122	Bugatti	blue	90.30	6	12	166-con. rod
28	Leon Duray	Durant	R. Cliff Durant	Miller	8	121	Miller	yellow, black	89.90	21	13	136-con. rod
4	Dario Resta	Packard	Packard Motor Car Co.	Packard	6	122	Packard	blue	98.02	3	14	88-head gasket
2	Ralph DePalma	Packard	Packard Motor Car Co.	Packard	6	122	Packard	blue	100.42	11	15	69-head gasket
26	Harlan Fengler	Durant	R. Cliff Durant	Miller	8	121	Miller	yellow, black	90.75	19	16	69-gas tank
25	Howdy Wilcox	H.C.S.	H.C.S. Motor Co.	Miller	8	121	Miller	white, red	81.00	8	17	60-clutch
3	Joe Boyer	Packard	Packard Motor Car Co.	Packard	6	122	Packard	blue	98.80	13	18	59-differential
35	Bennett Hill	Miller	Harry A. Miller	Miller	8	120	Miller		91.20	18	19	44-crankshaft
27	Count L. Zbrowski	Bugatti	Count L. Zbrowski	Bugatti	8	122	Bugatti	blue	91.80	5	20	41-con. rod
29	Earl Cooper	Durant	R. Cliff Durant	Miller	8	121	Miller	yellow, black	99.40	12	21	21-wrecked BS
22	Raul Riganti	Bugatti	Martin de Alsaga	Bugatti	8	122	Bugatti	blue	95.30	23	22	19-gas leak
14	C. Lautenschlager	Mercedes	Daimler Motoren Gesellschaft	Mercedes	4	121	Mercedes	white	93.20	17	23	14-wrecked SW
21	Martin de Alsaga	Bugatti	Martin de Alsaga	Bugatti	8	122	Bugatti	blue	92.90	4	24	6-con. rod

Harry Hartz

Jimmy Murphy

Eddie Hearne

L. L. Corum

Frank Elliott

Cliff Durant

Max Sailer

Prince de Cystria

Phil "Red" Shafer

Christian Werner

Pierre de Viscaya

Leon Duray

Dario Resta

Ralph DePalma

Harlan Fengler

Howdy Wilcox

Joe Boyer

Bennett Hill

Count L. Zbrowski

Earl Cooper

Raul Riganti

Christian Lautenschlager

Martin de Alsaga

FENGLER'S MOTOR
DURANT SPECIAL

Top, left: Prince de Cystria vaults from the cockpit of his Bugatti during a pit stop. Top, right: The engine of one of the three Mercedes entries. Middle, left: Louis Chevrolet inspects the Fronty-Ford which is being driven by L. L. "Slim" Corum. This entry marked, unofficially, Ford's debut in the "500" as most of the car's parts were Model T components. Middle, right: The Miller engine in Harlan Fengler's Durant Special. This is similar to the Miller that powered Jimmy Murphy's winning car in 1922. Bottom: A Durant Special with the body removed. The car was built under the direction of Harry A. Miller.

INDIANAPOLIS MOTOR SPEEDWAY
ANNUAL 500 MILE RACE 1924
HARRY HARTZ DURANT CHASSIS
KIRKPATRICK-PHOTO # 6605

Below; left: Winner Tommy Milton smokes a cigarette while sponsor Harry C. Stutz is congratulated by a well-wisher. Below, right: Jimmy Murphy, 1922 winner, immediately after his third place finish. Bottom: Fred Duesenberg gets set to lead the pace lap in a Duesenberg 8 passenger car. On the pole is Tommy Milton in the H.C.S. Special which carried him to his second victory.

JIMMY MURPHY - THIRD - AT THE FINISH

1924

A slim field of 22 cars faced W. S. Gilbreath's red starting flag (green wasn't used until 1930) but the action soon made up for the lack of cars. Jimmy Murphy took the lead, hotly pursued by Bennett Hill, Harry Hartz, and Earl Cooper. Joe Boyer, favorite of the Duesenberg team, began having trouble almost immediately in the maroon No. 9, one of the first three American cars to use a supercharger in the "500". His teammate, Ernie Ansterberg, crashed on the third lap when a steering knuckle broke as the car was entering the backstretch. He hit the wall but was uninjured. Lora L. Corum, with whom the Duesenberg fortunes now rested, was running well but seemed to lack the ability to move up to battle the flying Murphy. On the 109th lap, Fred Duesenberg called Corum in and replaced him with the leadfooted Boyer who immediately started a drive toward the front. Cooper and Murphy had been alternating in the lead until tire trouble forced Murphy back to third. Boyer then set his sights on Cooper. On the 178th lap, Cooper had to make a pit stop, and Boyer took a lead which he never lost. Boyer's original car came to grief on its 177th lap as Thane Houser hit the wall in the first turn. Pete DePaolo in the fourth Duesey finished sixth.

L. L. Corum

NO.	DRIVER	CAR	ENTRANT	ENGINE	CYL.	DISP.	CHASSIS	COLOR	QUAL. SPEED	ST.	FIN.	LAPS/SPEED/REASON OUT
15	L. L. Corum-J. Boyer	Duesenberg	Duesenberg	Duesenberg	8	121	Duesenberg	maroon	93.333	21	1	200-98.23
8	Earl Cooper	Studebaker	Earl Cooper	Miller	8	121	Miller	green	103.900	6	2	200-97.79
2	Jimmy Murphy	Miller	Jimmy Murphy	Miller	8	121	Miller	yellow	108.037	1	3	200-97.27
4	Harry Hartz	Durant	R. Cliff Durant	Miller	8	121	Miller	French gray, blue	107.130	2	4	200-96.55
3	Bennett Hill	Miller	Harry A. Miller	Miller	8	121	Miller	red	104.840	5	5	200-96.46
12	Peter DePaolo	Duesenberg	Duesenberg Bros.	Duesenberg	8	121	Duesenberg	maroon	99.280	13	6	200-94.30
14	Fred Comer	Durant	R. Cliff Durant	Miller	8	121	Miller	French gray, blue	92.880	16	7	200-93.43
6	Ira Vail	Ira Vail	Ira Vail	Miller	8	121	Miller	yellow	96.400	15	8	200-92.45
32	Antoine Mourre	Mourre	Antoine Mourre	Miller	8	121	Miller	red	99.490	9	9	200-91.76
19	Bob McDonough	Miller	Harry A. Miller	Miller	8	121	Miller	red	91.550	18	10	200-90.51
18	Jules Ellingboe	Miller	Harry A. Miller	Miller	8	121	Miller	silver	102.600	7	11	200-90.47
7	Jerry Wonderlich	Durant	R. Cliff Durant	Miller	8	121	Miller	yellow	99.360	11	12	200-85.48
16	Cliff Durant	Durant	R. Cliff Durant	Miller	8	121	Miller	silver	101.610	8	13	199-out of gas
26	Bill Hunt	Barber-Warnock Ford	Barber-Warnock	Fronty-Ford	4	122	Ford T	red	85.040	19	14	191-flagged
31	Ora Haibe	Schmidt	Albert Schmidt	Mercedes	4	120	Mercedes	red	92.810	17	15	182-flagged
28	Alfred E. Moss	Barber-Warnock Ford	Barber-Warnock	Fronty-Ford	4	122	Ford T	red	85.270	20	16	177-flagged
27	Fred Harder	Barber-Warnock Ford	Barber-Warnock	Fronty-Ford	4	122	Ford T	red	82.770	22	17	177-flagged
9	Joe Boyer, T. Houser	Duesenberg	Duesenberg Bros.	Duesenberg	8	121	Duesenberg	maroon	104.840	4	18	176-hit wall SW
1	Eddie Hearne	Durant	R. Cliff Durant	Miller	8	121	Miller	silver	99.230	14	19	151-fuel line
21	Frank Elliott	Miller	Frank R. Elliott	Miller	8	121	Miller	silver	99.310	12	20	149-gas tank
5	Tommy Milton	Miller	Tommy Milton	Miller	8	121	Miller	red, blue	105.200	3	21	110-gas tank
10	Ernie Ansterberg	Duesenberg	Duesenberg	Duesenberg	8	121	Duesenberg	maroon	99.400	10	22	2-wrecked BS

Earl Cooper

Jimmy Murphy

Harry Hartz

Bennett Hill

Peter DePaolo

Fred Comer

Ira Vail

Antoine Mourre

Bob McDonough

Jules Ellingboe

Jerry Wonderlich

Cliff Durant

Bill Hunt

Ora Haibe

Alfred E. Moss

Fred Harder

Joe Boyer

Eddie Hearne

Frank Elliott

Tommy Milton

Ernie Ansterberg

INDIANAPOLIS MOTOR SPEEDWAY
ANNUAL 500 MILE RACE 1924
HARRY HARTZ DURANT CHASSIS
KIRKPATRICK-PHOTO # 6613.

INDIANAPOLIS MOTOR SPEEDWAY
ANNUAL 500 MILE RACE 1924
Driver JIMMY MURPHY Car MILLER SPECIAL.

Top: Joe Boyer, co-winner with L. L. Corum, took over the wheel of Corum's trailing Duesenberg and charged up through the field to a well-earned victory. Middle, left: The chassis of the Durant Special driven by Harry Hartz. Middle, right: Jimmy Murphy's Miller in which the San Francisco leadfoot finished third and in which he crashed to his death three months later at Syracuse, N. Y. Bottom: The well-dressed drivers were seen in caps and coveralls. Left to right are Ira Vail, Jimmy Murphy and Eddie Hearne.

Left: AAA Contest Board Representative W. D. "Eddie" Edenburn, who served as a "500" official for many years. Below, left: One of the double overhead camshaft heads on a Model T Ford engine which powered the Barber-Warnock Specials. This particular car was driven by Fred Harder. Below, middle: Salvatore Barbarino, slated to be Joe Boyer's relief driver, poses in Boyer's Duesenberg while Joe stands at right. Thane Houser finally got the relief assignment after Boyer replaced L. L. Corum and, near the end of the race, crashed into the wall at the end of the frontstretch. Below, right: Earl Cooper, who finished second in his Miller-powered Studebaker Special.

Above, left: Harlan Fengler leans on the cockpit of the Wade Special which he rebuilt from the car wrecked in 1923 by Tom Alley. Fengler crashed in practice and did not again qualify for a "500" although he returned in 1958 to assume the duties of Chief Steward, a position he still holds. Second from right is Bennett Hill and far right is Jimmy Murphy. Above, right: The Miller with four up-draft carburetors which powered the Durant Special driven by Harry Hartz. Bottom: Peter DePaolo, who took sixth in the only unsupercharged Duesenberg in the race.

1925

Paced by World War I flying ace Eddie Rickenbacker, driving the passenger car bearing his name, 16 Millers, including a much heralded front-drive creation, four Duesenbergs, a Fiat and a sleeved down Model T Ford hit the first turn with Pete DePaolo in his banana colored "Duesey" taking the lead. It was obvious from the start that it would be a fast race and DePaolo was hard pressed to keep in front of the hot Millers. Except for ten laps when teammate Phil "Red" Shafer took over for a small slice of the lap prize money, DePaolo led commandingly until he made his first scheduled pit stop shortly after the halfway mark. His blistered hands were taped while Norman Batten relieved him for 21 laps. The two stops dropped DePaolo to fifth but he regained the lead when an exhausted Dave Lewis stopped on the 173rd lap. Benny Hill took over for Lewis in the little front-drive Miller but by then he was a lap behind. DePaolo drove the last few laps at a reduced pace to finish a half-lap in front. Again there were no injuries although there were several crashes. Herb Jones hit the wall on the south chute and caught fire. Cooper, while leading, hit the south turn wall and Jimmy Gleason, relieving Morton, hit the wall on the backstretch.

Peter DePaolo

NO.	DRIVER	CAR	ENTRANT	ENGINE	CYL.	DISP.	CHASSIS	COLOR	QUAL. SPEED	ST.	FIN.	LAPS/SPEED/REASON OUT
12	Peter DePaolo	Duesenberg	Duesenberg Bros.	Duesenberg*	8	122	Duesenberg	banana, black	113.083	2	1	200-101.13
1	Dave Lewis	Junior 8	R. Cliff Durant	Miller*¢	8	121	Miller	light blue	109.061	5	2	200-100.82
9	Phil Shafer	Duesenberg	Duesenberg Bros.	Duesenberg*	8	122	Duesenberg	green	103.523	22	3	200-100.18
6	Harry Hartz	Miller	Harry Hartz	Miller*	8	121	Miller	French gray	112.433	3	4	200- 98.89
4	Tommy Milton	Miller	Tommy Milton	Miller*	8	121	Miller	red, blue	104.366	11	5	200- 97.26
28	Leon Duray	Miller	Harry Hartz	Miller*	8	121	Miller	maroon, gold	113.196	1	6	200- 96.91
8	Ralph DePalma	Miller	Ralph DePalma	Miller*	8	122	Miller	cream	108.607	18	7	200- 96.85
35	Peter Kreis	Duesenberg	Duesenberg Bros.	Duesenberg*	8	122	Duesenberg	maroon	106.338	9	8	200- 96.32
15	Dr. W. E. Shattuc	Miller	Dr. W. E. Shattuc, M.D.	Miller*	8	121	Miller	red	102.070	14	9	200- 95.74
22	Pietro Bordino	Fiat	Peitro Bordino	Fiat*	8	121	Fiat	red	107.661	8	10	200- 94.75
5	Fred Comer	Miller	Harry Hartz	Miller*	8	121	Miller	lilac	104.296	12	11	200- 93.67
27	Frank Elliott	Miller	Richard G. Doyle	Miller*	8	121	Miller	green, yellow	104.910	10	12	200- 92.23
24	Earl DeVore	Miller	Bancroft & Pope	Miller*	8	121	Miller	silver	97.799	15	13	198-flagged
14	Bob McDonough	Miller	Tommy Milton	Miller*	8	121	Miller	red, blue	101.931	20	14	188-truss rod
23	Wade Morton	Duesenberg	Duesenberg Bros.	Duesenberg*	8	122	Duesenberg	blue	95.821	16	15	156-wrecked NW
17	Ralph Hepburn	Miller	Earl Cooper	Miller	8	121	Miller	apple green, jade	108.489	6	16	144-gas tank
2	Earl Cooper	Miller	R. Cliff Durant	Miller	8	121	Miller	green, lt. green	110.487	4	17	127-wrecked SW
3	Bennett Hill	Miller	Harry A. Miller	Miller*	8	121	Miller	red, silver	104.167	13	18	69-rear spring
29	Herbert Jones	Jones	Herbert Jones	Miller	8	121	Miller	white	89.401	17	19	69-wrecked SS
19	Ira Vail	R. J.	R. J. Johnson	Miller	8	121	Miller	light blue	104.785	19	20	63-con. rod
7	M. C. Jones	Skelly	H. J. Skelly	Fronty-Ford	4	122	Ford T	unpainted	88.478	21	21	33-transmission
10	Jules Ellingboe	Miller	Jerry Wonderlich	Miller	8	121	Miller	Mojave brown	107.832	7	22	24-steering key

*Supercharged   ¢Front Drive

Dave Lewis

Phil "Red" Shafer

Harry Hartz

Tommy Milton

Leon Duray

Ralph DePalma

Peter Kreis

Dr. W. E. Shattuc

Pietro Bordino

Fred Comer

Frank Elliott

Earl DeVore

Bob McDonough

Norman Batten (relief driver)

Ralph Hepburn

Earl Cooper

Bennett Hill

Herbert Jones

Ira Vail

H. J. Skelly (car owner)

Jules Ellingboe

Below, left: Winner Peter DePaolo. Below, right: Peter DePaolo in his Duesenberg. Behind DePaolo is driver Antoine Mourre, wearing cap, and the distinguished gentleman with the beard is Dr. Moss, the engineer who designed the supercharger used on the Duesenbergs. This was the first car to win the "500" using balloon tires. Bottom: Dave Lewis in the Junior 8 Special, one of the two front-drive Millers. The first front-drive car to compete in the "500" had been originally designed for the late Jimmy Murphy. Its success set a trend that would last until the 1950's.

WINNER.
13th Annual 500 Mile Race
Indianapolis Motor Speedway
MAY-30-th 1925.

Photo # 980

DAVE LEWIS IN JUNIOR 8
2ND PLACE

Above: Eddie Rickenbacker, who was to purchase the Speedway in 1927, takes a group of officials for a ride in the pace car which bears his name. Middle, left: Harry Hartz works on the Miller which was to carry him to fourth place. Middle, right: The engine and transmission of the Junior 8 showing the excellent workmanship which characterized the cars built under the direction of Harry A. Miller. Bottom: Tommy Milton in his Miller Special.

1926

Frank Lockhart, a young Californian with some dirt track experience but no time on the famed bricks, substituted for Peter Kreis when Kreis was stricken with flu and proceeded to win the race, shortened to 400 miles due to rain. The blond garage mechanic from Los Angeles came to Indianapolis as Kreis' relief driver but stayed to collect the $20,000 first prize. Following Lockhart was Harry Hartz, who trailed closely until his last pit stop when he forgot to turn on the ignition switch and lost valuable seconds as Lockhart extended his lead. The race had been suspended over an hour on Lockhart's 72nd lap due to a heavy sprinkle and when it appeared that a storm was coming, officials decided to stop the grind at the 400 mile mark. Despite the damp track, only one accident took place and that caused by a broken axle. On his 55th lap, Ben Jones, in the two-cycle Duesenberg, hit the wall but wasn't injured. In qualifying trials, Herb Jones wrecked the Elcar Special in the northwest turn and died of injuries. The car was repaired, however, and driven to ninth place by John Duff. This was the first year for the little 91.5 cubic inch cars and they performed well though a bit slower than the larger jobs. All of the cars in the race were supercharged.

Winner
Frank Lockhart-Miller Special

Frank Lockhart

NO.	DRIVER	CAR	ENTRANT	ENGINE	CYL.	DISP.	CHASSIS	COLOR	QUAL. SPEED	ST.	FIN.	LAPS/SPEED/REASON OUT
15	Frank Lockhart	Miller	Peter Kreis	Miller*	8	90	Miller	white	95.780	20	1	160-95.885
3	Harry Hartz	Miller	Harry Hartz	Miller*	8	90	Miller	lt. gray	109.542	2	2	158-94.481
36	Cliff Woodbury	Boyle	Cliff R. Woodbury	Miller*	8	90	Miller	red, silver	105.109	14	3	158-94.131
8	Fred Comer	Miller	Harry Hartz	Miller*	8	90	Miller	lt. gray	100.612	13	4	155-92.323
12	Peter DePaolo	Duesenberg	Duesenberg Bros.	Duesenberg*	8	90	Duesenberg	cream	96.709	27	5	153-91.544
6	Frank Elliott	Miller	Frank Elliott	Miller*	8	91	Miller	green, white, yellow	105.873	8	6	152-90.917
14	Norman Batten	Miller	Norman Batten	Miller*	8	91	Miller	cream	101.428	16	7	151-90.275
19	Ralph Hepburn	Miller	Ralph Hepburn	Miller*	8	91	Miller	brown	102.517	15	8	151-89.882
18	John Duff	Elcar	Al Cotey	Miller*	8	91	Miller		95.546	28	9	147-87.551
4	Phil Shafer	Miller	Phil Shafer	Miller*	8	90	Miller	yellow, red	106.647	5	10	146-87.096
31	Tony Gulotta	Miller	Harry Hartz	Miller*	8	91	Miller	lt. gray	102.789	12	11	142-flagged
16	Bennett Hill	Miller	Harry A. Miller	Miller*	8	90	Miller	maroon, red, white	105.876	7	12	136-flagged
33	Thane Houser	Abell	George G. Abell	Miller*	8	90	Miller	maroon, gold	93.672	21	13	102-flagged
27	W. Douglas Hawkes	Eldridge	E. A. D. Eldridge	Eldridge*	4	91	Eldridge	silver	94.977	17	14	91-frozen camshaft
1	Dave Lewis	Front Drive Miller	Harry A. Miller	Miller*¢	8	90	Miller¢	red, white	107.009	4	15	91-broken valve
5	Earl Cooper	Front Drive Miller	Harry A. Miller	Miller*¢	8	90	Miller¢	green	111.735	1	16	73-transmission
9	Cliff Durant	Locomobile Junior 8	R. Cliff Durant	Locomobile*	8	90	Fengler	steel green, white	104.855	11	17	60-gas tank leak
29	Ben Jones	Duesenberg Two-Cycle	Duesenberg Bros.	Duesenberg*	8	90	Duesenberg	maroon, cream, black	92.142	18	18	54-wrecked
26	E. A. D. Eldridge	Eldridge	E. A. D. Eldridge	Eldridge*	4	91	Eldridge	green	89.777	23	19	45-tie rod
23	L. L. Corum	Schmidt	Albert Schmidt	Argyle*	6	90	Schmidt	light blue	88.849	24	20	44-shock absorbers
24	Steve Nemish	Schmidt	Albert Schmidt	Argyle*	6	91	Schmidt	light blue	92.937	22	21	41-transmission
7	Jules Ellingboe	Miller	F. P. Cramer	Miller*	8	90	Miller	maroon, red, cream	106.376	6	22	39-supercharger
10	Leon Duray	Locomobile Junior 8	R. Cliff Durant	Locomobile*	8	90	Fengler	steel green, white	109.186	3	23	33-broken axle
17	Fred Lecklider	Nickel Plate	Earl DeVore	Miller*	8	91	Miller	silver	100.398	26	24	24-con. rod
28	Jack McCarver	Hamlin Front Drive	Chevrolet Bros.	Fronty-Ford*	4	90	Ford T	red, white	86.418	25	25	23-con. rod
34	Bon McDougall	Miller	R. G. McDougall	Miller*	8	91	Miller	Mojave brown	105.180	9	26	19-valve
22	Dr. W. E. Shattuc	Miller	Dr. W. E. Shattuc, M.D.	Miller*	8	91	Miller	red	104.977	10	27	15-valve
39	Albert Guyot	Guyot	Albert Guyot	Argyle*	6	91	Schmidt	light blue	88.580	19	28	8-steering knuckle

*Supercharged   ¢Front drive

Harry Hartz

Cliff Woodbury

Fred Comer

Peter DePaolo

Frank Elliott

Norman Batten

Ralph Hepburn

John Duff

Phil "Red" Shafer

Tony Gulotta

Bennett Hill

Thane Houser

W. Douglas Hawkes

Dave Lewis

Earl Cooper

Cliff Durant

Ben Jones

E. A. D. Eldridge

L. L. Corum

Steve Nemish

Jules Ellingboe

Leon Duray

Fred Lecklider

Jack McCarver

R. G. "Bon" McDougall

Dr. W. E. Shattuc

Albert Guyot

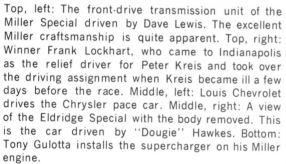

Top, left: The front-drive transmission unit of the Miller Special driven by Dave Lewis. The excellent Miller craftsmanship is quite apparent. Top, right: Winner Frank Lockhart, who came to Indianapolis as the relief driver for Peter Kreis and took over the driving assignment when Kreis became ill a few days before the race. Middle, left: Louis Chevrolet drives the Chrysler pace car. Middle, right: A view of the Eldridge Special with the body removed. This is the car driven by "Dougie" Hawkes. Bottom: Tony Gulotta installs the supercharger on his Miller engine.

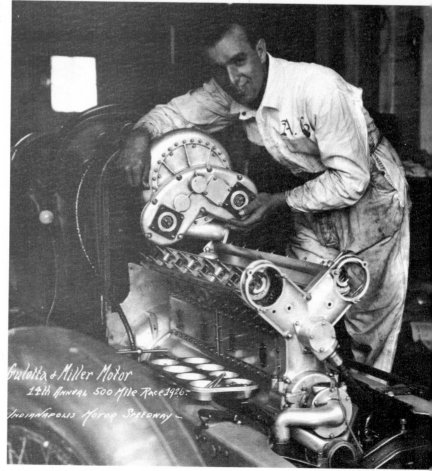

Below, left: Ben Jones at the wheel of the two-cycle Duesenberg. Below, right: Bennett Hill with the two cylinder blocks from his 91-cubic-inch Miller. Bottom: Peter DePaolo and his son Tommy, whose baby shoes were usually attached to Pete's car as a good luck token, pose with Phil "Red" Shafer's Miller. The car, actually owned by the A-C Spark Plug Company, was purchased by Alden Sampson in 1928 and carried Lou Meyer to victory.

1927

It looked like a repeat of the 1926 race as Frank Lockhart took an early lead in his white Miller. He outbattled the field until his first pit stop when Charles "Dutch" Bauman replaced him as the leader only to drop out with differential failure. Early in the race, front-stretch fans were treated to one of the most thrilling sights in "500" history as Norman Batten's Miller burst into flames. Batten guided the blazing car off the track away from his fellow drivers, but was not seriously burned. A few minutes later, Jules Ellingboe hit the northwest wall and was badly injured. A short time after this accident, Henry Kohlert tangled with Cliff Bergere and hit the wall in the first turn, severely injuring Kohlert. After completing its 120th lap, Lockhart's Miller broke a connecting rod and was out of the race. Rookie George Souders, driving DePaolo's winning Duesenberg owned by Bill White, assumed the lead after DePaolo, driving relief for Bob McDonough, ran into trouble shortly after Lockhart dropped out. Babe Stapp, running second in Benny Shoaff's car, had rear end trouble with but three laps to go. Souders won by eight laps from Earl DeVore who, in turn, was three laps in front of Tony Gulotta and rookie Wilbur Shaw.

George Souders

NO.	DRIVER	CAR	ENTRANT	ENGINE	CYL.	DISP.	CHASSIS	COLOR	QUAL. SPEED	ST.	FIN.	LAPS/SPEED/REASON OUT
32	George Souders	Duesenberg	William S. White	Duesenberg*	8	90	Duesenberg	gray, black	111.551	22	1	200-97.545
10	Earl DeVore	Miller	F. P. Cramer	Miller*	8	90	Miller	red, white, black	107.497	15	2	200-93.868
27	Tony Gulotta	Miller	Anthony Gulotta	Miller*	8	90	Miller	blue, white	107.765	27	3	200-93.139
29	Wilbur Shaw	Jynx	Fred Clemons	Miller*	8	90	Miller	gold	104.465	19	4	200-93.110
21	Dave Evans	Duesenberg	David E. Evans	Duesenberg*	8	91	Duesenberg	red, blue, white	107.360	28	5	200-90.782
14	Bob McDonough	Cooper	Cooper Engineering Co.	Miller*¢	8	90	Cooper	yellow, black	113.175	7	6	200-90.410
16	Eddie Hearne	Miller	Harry Hartz	Miller*	8	90	Miller	lt. gray, blue	105.115	18	7	200-90.064
6	Tommy Milton	Detroit	Tommy Milton	Miller*¢	8	90	Detroit	gray, silver	108.758	25	8	200-85.081
25	Cliff Bergere	Miller	Muller Bros.	Miller*	8	91	Miller	green	108.820	14	9	200-79.929
5	Frank Elliott	Junior 8	Frank Elliott	Miller*¢	8	91	Miller	red, white	109.682	13	10	200-78.244
31	Fred Frame	Miller	O. B. Dolfinger	Miller*	8	90	Miller	cream	106.859	33	11	199-flagged
42	Jim Hill	Nickel Plate	Earl DeVore	Miller*	8	90	Miller	silver	107.392	32	12	197-flagged
24	Benny Shoaff	Perfect Circle Duesenberg	Duesenberg Bros.	Duesenberg*	8	91	Duesenberg	red, blue	110.152	31	13	198-rear end gears
41	Wade Morton	Thompson Valve	Duesenberg Bros.	Duesenberg*	8	91	Duesenberg	red, blue	108.075	26	14	152-wrecked (Winnai)
44	Al Melcher	Miller	Charles Haase	Miller*	8	90	Miller	green	102.918	20	15	144-supercharger
43	Louis Schneider	Miller	Fred Lecklider	Miller*	8	91	Miller	tan	109.910	23	16	137-timing gears
9	Peter Kreis	Cooper	Cooper Engineering Co.	Miller*¢	8	90	Cooper	yellow, black	109.900	12	17	123-bent front axle
2	Frank Lockhart	Perfect Circle Miller	Frank S. Lockhart	Miller*	8	90	Miller	white	120.100	1	18	120-con. rod
15	Cliff Woodbury	Boyle Valve	Cliff Woodbury	Miller*	8	90	Miller	white, blue, red	113.200	6	19	108-supercharger
26	"Dutch" Bauman	Miller	Harry S. Miller	Miller*	8	90	Miller	yellow	106.078	17	20	90-pinion shaft
35	Al Cotey	Elcar	Al Cotey	Miller*	8	91	Miller		106.295	29	21	87-universal joint
17	Dr. W. E. Shattuc	Miller	Dr. W. E. Shattuc, M.D.	Miller*	8	91	Miller	red, white	107.060	16	22	83-valve
23	Fred Lecklider	Elgin Piston Pin	Henry Kohlert	Miller*	8	91	Miller	black, white	105.729	30	23	49-wrecked SW (Kohlert)
19	Ralph Hepburn	Boyle Valve	Cliff Woodbury	Miller*	8	91	Miller	white	114.209	5	24	39-leaking fuel tank
1	Harry Hartz	Erskine Miller	Harry Hartz	Miller*¢	8	90	Miller	lt. gray, blue	116.739	4	25	38-crankshaft
3	Peter DePaolo	Perfect Circle Miller	Peter DePaolo	Miller*¢	8	90	Miller	banana, black	119.510	2	26	31-supercharger gears
12	Leon Duray	Miller Front Drive	Leon Duray	Miller*¢	8	90	Miller	black, white	118.788	3	27	26-leaking fuel tank
4	Bennett Hill	Cooper	Cooper Engineering Co.	Miller*¢	8	90	Miller	yellow, black	112.013	9	28	26-rear spring shackle bolt
18	Jules Ellingboe	Cooper	Earl Cooper	Miller*¢	8	90	Miller	yellow, black	113.239	21	29	25-wrecked
8	Norman Batten	Miller	Norman K. Batten	Miller*	8	90	Fengler	red, silver	111.940	10	30	24-caught fire
38	Babe Stapp	Duesenberg	Duesenberg Bros.	Duesenberg*	8	91	Duesenberg	brown, white	109.555	24	31	24-universal joint
22	Jack Petticord	Boyle Valve	Cliff Woodbury	Miller*	8	91	Miller	white, blue, red	109.920	11	32	22-supercharger
7	Dave Lewis	Miller Front Drive	Dave Lewis	Miller*¢	8	90	Miller	white, red	112.275	8	33	21-front spring pad

*Supercharged   ¢Front Drive

Earl DeVore

Tony Gulotta

Wilbur Shaw

Dave Evans

Bob McDonough

Eddie Hearne

Tommy Milton

Cliff Bergere

Frank Elliott

Fred Frame

Jim Hill

Benny Shoaff

Wade Morton

Al Melcher

Louis Schneider

Peter Kreis

Frank Lockhart

Cliff Woodbury

Chas. "Dutch" Bauman

Al Cotey

Dr. W. E. Shattuc

Henry Kohlert (relief driver)

Ralph Hepburn

Harry Hartz

Peter DePaolo

Leon Duray

Bennett Hill

Jules Ellingboe

Norman Batten

Babe Stapp

Jack Petticord

Dave Lewis

Below, left: George Souders, who gained fame on the Texas dirt tracks, drove his first ''500'' at the wheel of Bill White's Duesenberg and finished eight laps in front of his nearest competitor, Earl DeVore. Below, right: The engine, supercharger and intercooler on the Detroit Special designed and built by Tommy Milton. The engine is a Miller with many of Milton's modifications. The intercooler was designed to cool the highly compressed air from the supercharger before it entered the cylinder chambers. Bottom: George Souders in Bill White's Duesenberg, the same car that carried Pete DePaolo to victory in 1925.

Norman Batten's Car on Fire.

As it was approaching the pits, Norman Batten's Miller Special burst into flames. Batten guided his blazing car away from the pits and the other cars on the track, finally reaching a safe spot at the end of the frontstretch. Not until then did he jump off. He was not seriously burned and his heroic action undoubtedly saved others from injury. In 1928, Batten and Earl DeVore died at sea when the S. S. Vestris went down on the way to Argentina.

1928

Pre-race favorite was Leon Duray in his black front-drive Miller in which he had set a phenomenal new track record of 122.391. As predicted, Duray took the lead at the start and stayed in front until the 200 mile mark when several long pit stops dropped him out of contention, Jimmy Gleason taking over in a Duesenberg. Gleason was sailing along in no apparent trouble at 400 miles, but a pit stop for water was his downfall. One of the pitmen, in his hurry to refill the radiator, poured a large portion of the water over the magneto and Gleason's threat was ended. Tony Gulotta then took the lead and he, too, appeared to be a sure winner but his fuel line became clogged on the 181st lap and he dropped to tenth place before it was cleared. Lou Meyer, driving a very consistent race in Alden Sampson's gold Miller, found himself in front of Lou Schneider who was relieving Lou Moore, and won the race without further incident. There were no injuries though Ira Hall, Benny Shoaff and Earl DeVore all hit the wall. DeVore's accident and his recovery inspired an ovation from the crowd as he brought his damaged car around to the pits after bashing the tail into the south turn wall. The race was run under the yellow flag for several laps due to a light rain.

Lou Meyer

NO.	DRIVER	CAR	ENTRANT	ENGINE	CYL.	DISP.	CHASSIS	COLOR	QUAL. SPEED	ST.	FIN.	LAPS/SPEED/REASON OUT
14	Lou Meyer	Miller	Alden Sampson, II	Miller*	8	90	Miller	gold, black	111.352	13	1	200-99.482
28	Lou Moore	Miller	Charles Haase	Miller*	8	90	Miller	green, white	113.826	8	2	200-99.241
3	George Souders	State Auto Insurance	William S. White	Miller*	8	90	Miller	lt. blue, white	111.444	12	3	200-98.034
15	Ray Keech	Simplex Piston Ring	M. A. Yagle	Miller*	8	90	Miller	white, blue	113.421	10	4	200-93.320
22	Norman Batten	Miller	Norman K. Batten	Miller*	8	90	Fengler	red, silver	106.585	15	5	200-93.228
7	Babe Stapp	Miller	Phil Shafer	Miller*¢	8	90	Miller	gold, black, white	116.887	5	6	200-92.638
43	Billy Arnold	Boyle Valve	Boyle Valve Co.	Miller*	8	90	Miller	white, blue, red	111.926	20	7	200-91.111
27	Fred Frame	State Auto Insurance	William S. White	Duesenberg*	8	91	Duesenberg	lt. blue, white	107.501	14	8	200-90.079
25	Fred Comer	Boyle Valve	Boyle Valve Co.	Miller*¢	8	90	Miller	white, blue, red	113.690	9	9	200-88.889
8	Tony Gulotta	Stutz Blackhawk	J. R. Burgamy	Miller*	8	90	Miller	white, black	117.031	4	10	200-88.888
24	Louis Schneider	Armacost Miller	Louis F. Schneider	Miller*	8	91	Miller	red, silver	114.036	7	11	200-87.964
12	Dave Evans	Boyle Valve	Boyle Valve Co.	Miller*	8	90	Miller	white, blue, red	108.264	23	12	200-87.401
29	Henry Kohlert	Elgin Piston Pin	Elgin Piston Pin Co.	Miller*	8	91	Miller	red, white	93.545	28	13	180-flagged
23	Deacon Litz	Miller	A. B. Litz	Miller*	8	91	Miller	cream, black	106.213	17	14	161-flagged
39	Jimmy Gleason	Duesenberg	H. C. Henning	Duesenberg*	8	91	Duesenberg	maroon	111.708	21	15	195-magneto
5	Cliff Durant	Detroit	Tommy Milton	Miller*¢	8	90	Detroit	black, red, white	99.990	18	16	175-supercharger
33	Johnny Seymour	Marmon	Cooper Engineering Co.	Miller*¢	8	90	Cooper	yellow, black	111.673	11	17	170-supercharger
6	Earl DeVore	Chromolite	Metals Protection Co.	Miller*	8	90	Miller	chrome, red	109.810	24	18	161-wrecked SW
4	Leon Duray	Miller	Leon Duray	Miller*¢	8	90	Miller	black, white	122.391	1	19	133-overheating
38	Sam Ross	Aranem	Reed & Mulligan	Miller*¢	8	90	Miller	red, black	106.572	16	20	132-timing gears
26	Ira Hall	Duesenberg	Henry Maley	Duesenberg*	8	91	Duesenberg	lt. blue, red	96.886	27	21	115-wrecked SW
32	Peter Kreis	Marmon	Cooper Engineering Co.	Miller*¢	8	90	Cooper	yellow, black	112.906	19	22	73-rod bearings
10	Cliff Woodbury	Boyle Valve	Boyle Valve Co.	Miller*¢	8	90	Miller	white, red, blue	120.418	2	23	55-timing gears
16	Ralph Hepburn	Miller	Harry A. Miller	Miller*¢	8	90	Miller	dark blue, white	116.354	6	24	48-timing gears
1	Wilbur Shaw	Flying Cloud	Peter DePaolo	Miller*¢	8	90	Miller	banana, black	100.956	29	25	42-timing gears
18	Benny Shoaff	Duesenberg	Duesenberg Bros.	Duesenberg*	8	91	Duesenberg	lt. blue, red	102.409	26	26	35-wrecked SW
41	C. W. Belt	Green	Green Engineering Co.	Green*	8	91	Green		96.026	25	27	32-valve
21	Cliff Bergere	Miller	Cliff Bergere	Miller*¢	8	90	Miller	red, white	119.956	3	28	7-supercharger
34	Russ Snowberger	Cooper	Cooper Engineering Co.	Miller*¢	8	90	Cooper	yellow, black	111.618	22	29	4-supercharger

*Supercharged   ¢Front drive

Lou Moore

George Souders

Ray Keech

Norman Batten

Babe Stapp

Billy Arnold

Fred Frame

Fred Comer

Tony Gulotta

Louis Schneider

Dave Evans

Henry Kohlert

Deacon Litz

Jimmy Gleason

Cliff Durant

Johnny Seymour

Earl DeVore

Leon Duray

Sam Ross

Ira Hall

Peter Kreis

Cliff Woodbury

Ralph Hepburn

Wilbur Shaw

Benny Shoaff

C. W. Belt

Cliff Bergere

Russell Snowberger

Below, left: Henry "Cotton" Henning, perhaps the most beloved and respected mechanic in "500" history, at work on the supercharger of Johnny Seymour's Cooper Special. Below, right: Lou Meyer shortly after winning his first "500". Bottom: The lineup for the race with record-breaker Leon Duray on the pole.

Top, left: The supercharger and intercooler on Benny Shoaff's Duesenberg. Top, right: The "Largest Band in the World" entertains before the start of the race. Middle, left: Pete DePaolo's wrecked Flying Cloud Special in the northeast turn. He was seriously injured but the car was repaired and driven in the race by Wilbur Shaw. On race day, DePaolo was taken back to the track and watched the "500" on a stretcher. Cliff Bergere, behind the car's tail, is discussing the accident with officials. Middle, right: 1912 winner Joe Dawson in the Marmon "78" pace car. Bottom: The men seem to be enjoying the race a bit more than their wives. Possibly the ladies don't like being photographed sitting on a beer truck during prohibition. Note spectators in tree.

1929

Ray Keech, driving a Miller originally built by the late Frank Lockhart, drove a steady, consistent race to outlast a fast field of cars and win after it looked like 1928 winner Lou Meyer would make it two in a row. Fast qualifier and pole driver Cliff Woodbury was eliminated on his fourth lap when he hit the wall in the northwest turn, escaping injury. Not so lucky was Bill Spence who hit the southeast wall and overturned on his 10th lap. Spence died on the way to the hospital from a fractured skull. A short while later Frenchman Jules Moriceau wrecked his Amilcar near the spot of Woodbury's accident but emerged uninjured. While battling Duray and Hepburn for the lead early in the race, Deacon Litz reached for his hand brake and found it had fallen off. Unable to slow down, he shot by both drivers to take first place which he held until a rod let go on the 56th lap. With Litz out, Lou Meyer and Lou Moore began alternating in the lead, with Keech and Fred Frame also getting a little lap money while Moore and Meyer were in the pits. It began to look like Meyer's race when he made his last pit stop but his engine stalled and it was seven minutes before he could get it started again. By that time Keech was well in front.

Ray Keech

NO.	DRIVER	CAR	ENTRANT	ENGINE	CYL.	DISP.	CHASSIS	COLOR	QUAL. SPEED	ST.	FIN.	LAPS/SPEED/REASON OUT
2	Ray Keech	Simplex Piston Ring	M. A. Yagle	Miller*	8	90	Miller	white, blue	114.905	6	1	200-97.585
1	Lou Meyer	Miller	Alden Sampson, II	Miller*	8	90	Miller	white, black	114.704	8	2	200-95.596
53	Jimmy Gleason	Duesenberg	A. S. Duesenberg	Duesenberg*	8	91	Duesenberg	lt. blue, red	110.345	23	3	200-93.699
43	Carl Marchese	Marchese	Marchese Bros.	Miller*	8	92	Miller	white	108.440	25	4	200-93.541
42	Freddy Winnai	Duesenberg	A. S. Duesenberg	Duesenberg*	8	91	Duesenberg	maroon	113.892	21	5	200-88.792
48	"Speed" Gardner	Chromolite	F. P. Cramer	Miller*	8	90	Miller	black	105.985	28	6	200-88.390
6	Louis Chiron	Delage	Louis Chiron	Delage*	8	90	Delage	lt. blue	107.351	14	7	200-87.728
9	Billy Arnold	Boyle Valve	Cliff R. Woodbury	Miller*	8	90	Miller	white, red	114.752	7	8	200-83.909
25	Cliff Bergere	Armacost Miller	Cliff Bergere	Miller*¢	8	90	Miller	red, silver	103.687	32	9	200-80.703
34	Fred Frame	Cooper	Cooper Engineering Co.	Miller*¢	8	90	Cooper	yellow, black	111.328	22	10	193-flagged
28	Frank Brisko	Burbach	Frank Brisko	Miller*	8	89	Miller	white	105.857	29	11	180-flagged
17	Phil Shafer	Miller	Phil Shafer	Miller*¢	8	90	Miller	black, silver	111.628	18	12	150-flagged
3	Lou Moore	Majestic Miller	Charles Haase	Miller*	8	90	Miller	green, white	110.677	13	13	198-con. rod
36	Frank Farmer	Miller	William Albertson	Miller*	8	91	Miller	red, silver	107.9??	26	14	140-supercharger
49	Wes Crawford	Miller	Marian Batten	Miller*	8	90	Fengler	red	108.607	24	15	127-carburetor
4	Peter Kreis	Detroit	Tommy Milton	Miller*¢	8	90	Detroit	black, white	112.528	17	16	91-engine seized
23	Tony Gulotta	Packard Cable	Leon Duray	Miller*	8	90	Miller	violet, yellow	112.146	11	17	91-supercharger
5	Bob McDonough	Miller Front Drive	M. R. Dodds	Miller*¢	8	90	Miller	red	111.614	19	18	74-oil tank
46	Bill Lindau	Pittsburgh Miller	Painter & Hufnagle	Miller*	8	88	Miller	orange	102.509	33	19	70-valve
31	Herman Schurch	Armacost Miller	Fred Schneider	Miller*	8	91	Miller	red, white	107.477	27	20	70-gas tank split
38	Johnny Seymour	Cooper	Cooper Engineering Co.	Miller*¢	8	90	Cooper	yellow, black	114.307	16	21	65-rear axle
21	Leon Duray	Packard Cable	Leon Duray	Miller*	8	90	Miller	violet, yellow	119.087	2	22	65-carburetor
29	Rick Decker	Miller	Rickliffe Decker	Miller*	8	91	Miller	cream	105.288	30	23	61-supercharger
26	Deacon Litz	Rusco Durac	A. B. Litz	Miller*	8	90	Miller	white, black	114.526	9	24	56-con. rod
27	Albert Karnatz	Richards Bros.	Reed & Mulligan	Miller*¢	8	91	Miller	red, white	104.749	31	25	50-gas leak
47	Ernie Triplett	Buckeye Duesenberg	C. H. Cunard	Duesenberg*	8	91	Duesenberg	brown	114.789	20	26	48-con. rod
12	Russ Snowberger	Cooper	Cooper Engineering Co.	Miller*¢	8	90	Cooper	yellow, black	113.622	10	27	45-supercharger
32	Babe Stapp	Spindler Miller	William S. White	Miller*	8	90	Duesenberg	white, blue, red	115.618	4	28	40-universal joint
35	Jules Moriceau	Thompson Products	Thompson Products, Inc.	Amilcar*	6	78	Amilcar	yellow, black	105.609	15	29	30-wrecked NW
37	Peter DePaolo	Boyle Valve	Cliff R. Woodbury	Miller*¢	8	90	Miller	white, red, blue	115.093	5	30	25-steering
18	Ralph Hepburn	Packard Cable	Leon Duray	Miller*¢	8	90	Miller	violet, yellow	116.543	3	31	14-transmission
10	Bill Spence	Duesenberg	A. S. Duesenberg	Duesenberg*	8	91	Duesenberg	lavender, black	111.649	12	32	14-wrecked SE
8	Cliff Woodbury	Boyle Valve	Cliff R. Woodbury	Miller*¢	8	90	Miller	white, red, blue	120.599	1	33	3-wrecked NW

*Supercharged   ¢Front Drive

Lou Meyer

Jimmy Gleason

Carl Marchese

Freddy Winnai

W. H. "Speed" Gardner

Louis Chiron

Billy Arnold

Cliff Bergere

Fred Frame

Frank Brisko

Phil "Red" Shafer

Lou Moore

Frank Farmer

Wes Crawford

Peter Kreis

Tony Gulotta

Bob McDonough

Bill Lindau

Herman Schurch

Johnny Seymour

Leon Duray

Rick Decker

Deacon Litz

Albert Karnatz

Ernie Triplett

Russell Snowberger

Babe Stapp

Jules Moriceau

Peter DePaolo

Ralph Hepburn

Bill Spence

Cliff Woodbury

RALPH HEPBURN   LEON DURAY   ANTHONY GULOTTA.

Above: The Packard Cable Racing Team, owned by Leon Duray.
Left to right are Ralph Hepburn, Duray, and Tony Gulotta.
Middle: The Delage engine, with its Rootes supercharger, in the
car driven to seventh by Louis Chiron. Bottom: Harry Hartz,
recovering from a near-fatal accident on the board track at
Salem, New Hampshire, leans on the tail of Bill White's Miller
which Myron Stevens wrecked a short time later in practice.
Hartz is still an official of the "500", serving on the Technical
Committee.

Below, left: Speedway owner Eddie Rickenbacker takes General Manager T. E. "Pop" Myers for a ride in a LaSalle. Below, right: Lou Meyer not only won the 1928 "500" but he was also crowned National Champion in both 1928 and 1929. Bottom: Lou Meyer's Sampson Miller with the body removed.

1930

Billy Arnold took the lead on the third lap and for all practical purposes the checkered flag might just as well have fallen then. Arnold completely dominated the race, leading 198 laps of the 200, and finished seven-and-a-quarter minutes ahead of Shorty Cantlon. Arnold drove Harry Hartz' Miller in a field of 38 cars, many of which were semi-stock creations. Speedway officials changed the rules so that semi-stock machines would have a reasonably good chance against the specially-built race cars, although it appeared that their performance was still less than adequate. The action started in the first turn when Chet Gardner spun and it took some excellent driving to miss him. On the 23rd lap, DePaolo's relief driver, Red Roberts, Litz, Stapp, Trexler, Seymour, Gleason and Moore, all tangled in the third turn with the Roberts and Moore cars stopping on the wall. There were no serious injuries in this accident but on his 30th lap, Cy Marshall went over the northeast wall and was seriously injured and his brother Paul, serving as riding mechanic, was killed. Charles Moran and Rick Decker, relief for Caccia, also hit the wall but escaped with no serious results. The last half of the race saw few position changes.

Billy Arnold

NO.	DRIVER	CAR	ENTRANT	ENGINE	CYL.	DISP.	CHASSIS	COLOR	QUAL. SPEED	ST.	FIN.	LAPS/SPEED/REASON OUT
4	Billy Arnold	Miller-Hartz	Harry Hartz	Miller¢	8	152	Summers	gray, blue	113.263	1	1	200-100.448
16	Shorty Cantlon	Miller Schofield	William S. White	Miller	4	183	Stevens	white, red, black	109.810	3	2	200- 98.054
23	Louis Schneider	Bowes Seal Fast	Louis F. Schneider	Miller	8	121	Stevens	white, black, red	106.107	4	3	200- 96.752
1	Lou Meyer	Sampson	Alden Sampson, II	Miller	16	201	Stevens	white	111.290	2	4	200- 95.253
6	Bill Cummings	Duesenberg	Peter DePaolo	Duesenberg	8	244	Stevens	banana, black	106.173	22	5	200- 93.579
24	Dave Evans	Jones & Maley	David E. Evans	Miller¢	8	138	Stevens	cream	97.342	33	6	200- 92.571
15	Phil Shafer	Coleman Front Drive	Coleman Motors Corp.	Miller¢	4	183	Coleman	black	102.279	8	7	200- 90.921
22	Russ Snowberger	Russell "8"	Russell Snowberger	Studebaker	8	336	Snowberger	tan	104.577	7	8	200- 89.166
25	Leslie Allen	Allen Miller Products	Leslie Allen	Miller	4	183	Miller	black, red	101.919	9	9	200- 85.749
27	L. L. Corum	Stutz	Milton Jones	Stutz	8	322	Stutz	blue, white	94.130	17	10	200- 85.340
38	Clyde Burton	V8	Ira Vail	Oakland	8	251	Oakland	white, black	95.087	16	11	196-flagged
42	Letterio Cucinotta	Maserati	Letterio Piccolo Cucinotta	Maserati	8	122	Maserati	red	91.584	30	12	185-flagged
41	Chet Miller	Fronty	Thomas J. Mulligan	Fronty-Ford	4	176	Ford T	green, black, white	97.360	15	13	161-flagged
46	Harry Butcher	Butcher Bros.	Harry M. Butcher	Buick	6	332	Buick	orange	87.003	38	14	127-flagged
17	Ernie Triplett	Guiberson	Allen Guiberson	Miller	4	183	Whippet	white	105.618	10	15	125-piston
21	Zeke Meyer	Miller	Zeke Meyer	Miller	8	138	Miller		95.357	34	16	115-con. rod
10	Mel Keneally	MAVV	J. Talbot, Jr.	Miller	4	150	Whippet	black	103.327	23	17	114-valve
35	J. C. McDonald	Romthe	William H. Richards	Studebaker	8	336	Studebaker	blue, white, black	98.953	13	18	112-leaking fuel tank
9	Tony Gulotta	MAVV	J. Talbot, Jr.	Miller	4	150	Whippet	black	100.033	20	19	79-valve
28	Roland Free	Slade	Julius C. Slade	Chrysler	6	268	Chrysler	white, black	89.639	37	20	69-clutch
33	Frank Farmer	Betholine Miller	M. A. Yagle	Miller	8	101	Miller		100.615	11	21	69-wrecked
3	Wilbur Shaw	Empire State	Empire State Motors	Miller	8	152	Smith	black, white, red	106.132	25	22	54-wrist pin
34	Joe Huff	Gauss Front Drive	Herman N. Gauss	Miller¢	8	100	Cooper	yellow, black	101.178	26	23	48-valve
29	Joe Caccia	Alberti	William Alberti	Duesenberg	8	260	Duesenberg	lt. blue	97.606	14	24	43-wrecked (Decker)
44	Bill Denver	Nardi	Gabriel Nardi	Duesenberg	8	260	Duesenberg	black, white	90.650	35	25	41-con. rod
36	Cy Marshall	Duesenberg	George A. Henry	Duesenberg	8	262	Duesenberg	green	100.846	10	26	29-wrecked NE
32	Charles Moran	du Pont	du Pont Motors, Inc.	du Pont	8	322	du Pont	cream	89.733	19	27	22-wrecked NE
7	Jimmy Gleason	Waverly Oil	Thomas J. Mulligan	Miller	8	125	Miller	white	93.709	24	28	22-wrecked NE
14	Lou Moore	Coleman Front Drive	Coleman Motors Corp.	Miller¢	4	183	Coleman	white	99.867	12	29	23-wrecked NE
12	Deacon Litz	Duesenberg	Henry W. Maley	Duesenberg	8	150	Duesenberg	cream, gold	105.755	31	30	22-wrecked NE
8	Babe Stapp	Duesenberg	A. S. Duesenberg	Duesenberg	8	143	Duesenberg	blue, silver	104.950	32	31	18-wrecked NE
39	Johnny Seymour	Gauss Front Drive	Herman N. Gauss	Miller¢	8	100	Cooper	yellow, black	93.376	18	32	21-wrecked NE
5	Peter DePaolo	Duesenberg	Peter DePaolo	Duesenberg	8	244	Stevens	banana, black	99.956	21	33	19-wrecked NE(R.Roberts)
45	Marion Trexler	Trexler	M. M. Lain, Jr.	Lycoming	8	298	Auburn	silver	92.978	29	34	19-wrecked NE
19	Speed Gardner	Miller Front Drive	W. H. Gardner	Miller¢	8	151	Miller	orange, silver	95.585	27	35	14-loose main bearing
48	Rick Decker	Hoosier Pete	Clemons Motors, Inc.	Clemons	4	197	Mercedes	white	92.293	36	36	8-oil tank
26	Baconi Borzachini	Maserati	Alfieri Maserati	Maserati	16	244	Maserati	red	95.213	28	37	7-magneto, plugs
18	Chet Gardner	Buckeye	James H. Booth	Duesenberg	8	150	Duesenberg	gray	105.811	5	38	1-spun SW

¢Front Drive

Shorty Cantlon

Louis Schneider

Lou Meyer

Bill Cummings

Dave Evans

Phil "Red" Shafer

Russell Snowberger

Leslie Allen

L. L. Corum

Clyde Burton

Letterio Cuccinotta

Chet Miller

Harry Butcher

Ernie Triplett

Zeke Meyer

Mel Keneally

J. C. McDonald

Tony Gulotta

Roland Free

Frank Farmer

Wilbur Shaw

Joe Huff

Joe Caccia

Bill Denver

Cy Marshall

Charles Moran

Jimmy Gleason

Lou Moore

Deacon Litz

Babe Stapp

Johnny Seymour

Peter DePaolo

Marion Trexler

W. H. "Speed" Gardner

Rick Decker

Baconi Borzachini

Chet Gardner

Below, left: Billy Arnold and Harry Hartz check one of the Gabriel shock absorbers on the winning Miller-Hartz Special. Below, right: The wrecked Duesenberg driven by "Red" Roberts, which triggered a seven-car crash early in the race, is removed from the crash wall. Pete DePaolo had relinquished the car to Roberts because it was not handling properly. A few laps after returning to the track, Roberts spun in the northeast turn. Also involved were Jimmy Gleason, Lou Moore, Deacon Litz, Babe Stapp, Marion Trexler and Johnny Seymour. There were no serious injuries. Bottom: Shortly before the call to the starting line, cars undergo final preparations on the pit apron. Marion Trexler's car is in the foreground, followed by Rick Decker's "Hoosier Pete".

Top: The winner, Billy Arnold, with riding mechanic Spider Matlock, in Harry Hartz's front-drive Miller. Middle, left: The start. Middle, right: Lou Meyer's Sampson engine, built by gearing two 91-cubic-inch Millers together to make one 16-cylinder, 183-cubic-inch engine. Bottom: Former driver Wade Morton who paced the field in a sleek Cord L-29 roadster.

1931

Lou Schneider survived an accident-filled "500" to win in his Bowes Seal Fast Special. For a while it appeared that Billy Arnold would repeat his 1930 triumph, but a crash on his 167th lap ended this threat. Paul Bost took the lead at the start and led for the first two circuits. Bost's teammate, Bill Cummings, took over for four laps and then Arnold, coming up from the sixth row on the start, went out in front and began pulling away from the pack. The accidents started early when Joe Russo slid and bumped the wall. Harry Butcher, trying to avoid Russo, went over the northwest wall. Wilbur Shaw, relief for Pardee, took the Duesenberg No. 32 over the northeast wall and Freddy Winnai did the same thing a few feet farther down the north chute attempting to miss Shaw. Neither driver nor mechanic was seriously hurt and Shaw came back for another relief assignment in Gleason's Duesey. Arnold, holding a good lead, broke a rear axle on the northwest turn on his 167th lap and was struck by Luther Johnson. Arnold's car crashed in flames and his wheel crossed Georgetown Road and killed 12-year-old Wilbur Brink who was playing in his front yard. Arnold and Spider Matlock were injured. Joe Caccia and his mechanic, Clarence Grove were killed during practice.

Lou Schneider

NO.	DRIVER	CAR	ENTRANT	ENGINE	CYL.	DISP.	CHASSIS	COLOR	QUAL. SPEED	ST.	FIN.	LAPS/SPEED/REASON OUT
23	Lou Schneider	Bowes Seal Fast	B. L. Schneider	Miller	8	151	Stevens	white, black, red	107.210	13	1	200-96.629
34	Fred Frame	Duesenberg	Harry Hartz	Duesenberg	8	150	Duesenberg	dark blue, white	109.273	8	2	200-96.406
19	Ralph Hepburn	Harry Miller	Ralph Hepburn	Miller	8	230	Miller	brown	107.933	10	3	200-94.224
21	Myron Stevens	Jadson	Louis Meyer	Miller	8	230	Stevens	cream	107.463	35	4	200-94.142
4	Russ Snowberger	Russell "8"	Russell Snowberger	Studebaker	8	336	Snowberger	tan	112.796	1	5	200-94.090
33	Jimmy Gleason	Duesenberg	Denny Duesenberg	Duesenberg	8	243	Duesenberg	orange, white	111.400	20	6	200-93.605
25	Ernie Triplett	Buckeye	James H. Booth	Duesenberg	8	151	Duesenberg	black, red	111.034	5	7	200-93.041
36	Stubby Stubblefield	Jones-Miller	Milton Jones	Miller	4	183	Whippet	black, white	108.797	9	8	200-92.424
28	Cliff Bergere	Elco Royale	Elco Grease & Oil Co.	Reo	8	358	Reo	blue, red, white	106.781	14	9	200-91.839
27	Chet Miller	Marr	R. G. "Buddy" Marr	Hudson	8	234	Hudson	blue, silver	106.185	15	10	200-89.580
44	George Howie	G. N. H.	George N. Howie	Chrysler	8	356	Chrysler	beige	102.844	30	11	200-87.651
12	Phil Shafer	Shafer "8"	Phil Shafer	Buick	8	270	Rigling	black, silver	105.103	23	12	200-86.391
8	Dave Evans	Cummins Diesel	Cummins Engine Co.	Cummins	4	361	Duesenberg	white, blue	96.871	17	13	200-86.107
72	Al Aspen	Alberti	William Alberti	Duesenberg	8	266	Duesenberg	black, white	102.509	31	14	200-85.764
59	Sam Ross	Miller	William M. Yahr	Miller	4	158	Smith	white	104.642	37	15	200-85.139
69	Joe Huff	Goldberg Bros.	S. C. Goldberg	Miller¢	8	100	Cooper	light brown	102.386	40	16	180-flagged
5	Deacon Litz	Maley	Henry Maley	Duesenberg	8	151	Duesenberg	rust, black	111.531	4	17	177-wrecked SW(Cummings)
37	Tony Gulotta	Hunt	D. A. "Ab" Jenkins	Studebaker	8	337	Rigling	green, gold	111.725	19	18	167-wrecked NW
1	Billy Arnold	Miller-Hartz	Harry Hartz	Miller¢	8	151	Summers	gray, blue	116.080	18	19	162-wrecked NW
57	Luther Johnson	Bill Richards	William H. Richards	Studebaker	8	336	Studebaker	blue, black	107.652	12	20	156-wrecked NW
55	Billy Winn	Hoosier Pete	F. E. Clemons	Clemons	8	226	Rigling	silver	105.405	36	21	138-flagged
16	Frank Brisko	Brisko-Atkinson	Frank Brisko	Miller	8	151	Stevens	white, red	106.286	27	22	138-steering arm
26	Gene Haustein	Fronty-Ford	Fronty-Ford Sales of Mich.	Fronty-Ford	4	219	Ford T	green, black, white	108.395	34	23	117-lost wheel
41	Joe Russo	Russo	George A. Henry	Duesenberg	8	260	Rigling	white	104.822	16	24	109-oil leak
17	Speed Gardner	Nutmeg State	C. E. Ricketts	Miller¢	8	151	Miller	red	109.820	7	25	107-frame
14	Lou Moore	Boyle Valve	M. J. Boyle	Miller	8	230	Miller	cream, red, blue	103.725	38	26	103-differential
2	Shorty Cantlon	Harry Miller	William S. White	Miller	16	301	Miller	cream, blue	110.372	26	27	88-con. rod
3	Bill Cummings	Empire State	Empire State Gas Motors	Miller	8	215	Cooper	black, red	112.563	2	28	70-oil line
24	Freddy Winnai	Bowes Seal Fast	B. L. Schneider	Miller	8	122	Stevens	white, black, red	105.899	28	29	60-wrecked NS
32	Phil Pardee	Duesenberg	Phil Pardee	Duesenberg	8	243	Duesenberg	orange, white	107.772	11	30	60-wrecked NE (Shaw)
31	Paul Bost	Empire State	Empire State Gas Motors	Miller	8	215	Smith	black, red, silver	112.125	3	31	35-crankshaft
35	Frank Farmer	Jones-Miller	Milton Jones	Miller	4	183	Whippet	maroon	108.303	22	32	32-rod bearing
58	George Wingerter	Wingerter	George Wingerter	Duesenberg	8	266	Duesenberg	dark red	100.139	32	33	29-fuel tank
7	Lou Meyer	Sampson	Alden Sampson, II	Miller	16	200	Stevens	white	113.953	25	34	28-oil leak
39	Babe Stapp	Rigling & Henning	Rigling & Henning	Duesenberg	8	260	Rigling	black	110.125	6	35	9-oil leak/clutch
48	John Boling	Morton & Brett	Grapho Metal Packing Co.	M & B	8	226	M & B	white	102.860	24	36	7-con. rod
54	Leon Duray	Duray	Leon Duray	Duray®£	16	230	Stevens	black, white	103.134	29	37	6-overheating
49	Harry Butcher	Butcher Bros.	Harry H. Butcher	Buick	8	273	Buick	orange	99.343	33	38	6-wrecked NW
10	Herman Schurch	Hoosier Pete	F. E. Clemons	Clemons	8	226	Rigling	gold	102.845	39	39	5-transmission
67	Francis Quinn	Tucker Tappett	James H. Wade	Ford A	4	221	Miller	black, red	111.321	21	40	3-rear axle

®Supercharged   ¢Front Drive   £Two-cycle engine

Fred Frame

Ralph Hepburn

Myron Stevens

Russell Snowberger

Jimmy Gleason

Ernie Triplett

Stubby Stubblefield

Cliff Bergere

Chet Miller

George Howie

Phil "Red" Shafer

Dave Evans

Al Aspen

Sam Ross

Joe Huff

Deacon Litz

Tony Gulotta

Billy Arnold

Luther Johnson

Jimmy Patterson (relief driver)

Frank Brisko

Gene Haustein

Joe Russo

W. H. "Speed" Gardner

Lou Moore

Shorty Cantlon

Bill Cummings

Freddy Winnai

Phil Pardee

Paul Bost

Frank Farmer

George Wingerter

Lou Meyer

Babe Stapp

John Boling

Leon Duray

Harry Butcher

Jimmy Patterson (relief driver)

Francis Quinn

Below, left: Former drivers Cliff Durant and Leon Duray reminisce about past glories. Durant owned large teams of cars and was an enthusiastic driver, as well as being the son of the president of General Motors and head of that company's Oakland, California plant. Duray held the qualifying record at the Speedway from 1928 to 1937. Below, right: L. L. Corum in an almost-stock Stutz "Bearcat". This is a good example of the semi-stock cars that competed in the "500" during the 1930's. This car failed to qualify. Bottom: Forerunner of the Studebaker Team was this entry of D. A. "Ab" Jenkins, famous land speed record holder, and George Hunt, one of Studebaker's top engineers. Left to right are Jenkins, driver Tony Gulotta, mechanic Carl Rescigno and Hunt. In 1932 this car was joined by four duplicates entered by The Studebaker Corporation.

Above: 1930 "500" winner and National Champion Billy Arnold, proudly displays the hard-earned No. 1 on the hood of his Miller-Hartz Special. Owner Harry Hartz stands by in coveralls and cap. Left: The Cummins Diesel engine which powered the car driven by Dave Evans. Evans was the first driver to go non-stop for the 500 miles and finished thirteenth with an average speed of 86.107. It was also the first Diesel-powered car entered in the "500".

1932

For the third straight year, the "500" started out to be a runaway for Billy Arnold but, on the 59th lap, the colorful little driver went over the wall on the third turn and was out of the race, a repetition of 1931 when he also crashed while leading. Ironically, Arnold's broken shoulder and Matlock's broken pelvis were a reverse of their '31 injuries when Arnold broke his pelvis and Matlock his shoulder. With Arnold out, rookie Bob Carey took the lead only to spin three times and bang the wall just before the halfway mark. Carey was able to continue after replacing a bent wheel and finally finished fourth behind Fred Frame, rookie Howdy Wilcox II and Cliff Bergere. Bergere did a fine job in one of the five Studebaker team cars. Al Gordon went through the inside rail coming into the frontstretch on his 4th lap and Gus Schrader hit the wall three laps later. On his 164th, Luther Johnson lost a wheel on the frontstretch and Peter Kreis blew a tire and hit the wall on his 179th. In practice, Milt Jones crashed the southeast wall and was killed while mechanic Harold Gray was injured. Benny Benefield and Harry Cox died over the southwest wall at the same place and in the same car in which Joe Caccia was fatally injured in 1931.

Fred Frame

NO.	DRIVER	CAR	ENTRANT	ENGINE	CYL.	DISP.	CHASSIS	COLOR	QUAL. SPEED	ST.	FIN.	LAPS/SPEED/REASON OUT
34	Fred Frame	Miller-Hartz	Harry Hartz	Miller¢	8	182	Wetteroth	light gray, blue	113.856	27	1	200-104.144
6	Howdy Wilcox, II	Lion Head	William Cantlon	Miller	4	220	Stevens	cream, red, blue	113.468	6	2	200-103.881
22	Cliff Bergere	Studebaker	The Studebaker Corp.	Studebaker	8	337	Rigling	maroon, white	111.503	10	3	200-102.662
61	Bob Carey	Meyer	Louis Meyer	Miller	8	249	Stevens	cream	111.070	14	4	200-101.363
4	Russ Snowberger	Hupp Comet	Russell Snowberger	Hupmobile	8	361	Snowberger	tan	114.326	4	5	200-100.791
37	Zeke Meyer	Studebaker	The Studebaker Corp.	Studebaker	8	337	Rigling	green, white	110.745	38	6	200- 98.476
35	Ira Hall	Duesenberg	G. B. Hall	Duesenberg	8	243	Stevens	blue	114.206	5	7	200- 98.207
65	Freddy Winnai	Foreman Axle Shaft	Henry Maley	Duesenberg	8	151	Duesenberg	dark gray	108.755	35	8	200- 97.437
2	Billy Winn	Duesenberg	Fred Frame	Duesenberg	8	151	Duesenberg	white, blue, black	111.801	9	9	200- 97.421
55	Joe Huff	Highway Parts	S. C. Goldberg	Cooper¢	16	183	Cooper	black, silver	110.402	15	10	200- 87.586
33	Phil Shafer	Shafer "8"	Phil Shafer	Buick	8	272	Rigling	black, silver	110.708	26	11	197-flagged
36	Kelly Petillo	Jones-Miller	Milton Jones	Miller	4	190	Whippet	blue	104.465	40	12	189-flagged
25	Tony Gulotta	Studebaker	The Studebaker Corp.	Studebaker	8	337	Rigling	gray, blue	108.896	20	13	189-flagged
15	Stubby Stubblefield	Gilmore	Sparks & Weirick	Miller	4	220	Adams	cream, red	112.899	25	14	178-flagged
18	Peter Kreis	Studebaker	The Studebaker Corp.	Studebaker	8	337	Rigling	dark blue	110.270	17	15	178-wrecked SW
46	Luther Johnson	Studebaker	The Studebaker Corp.	Studebaker	8	337	Rigling	maroon, silver	111.218	11	16	164-lost wheel FS
3	Wilbur Shaw	Miller	Ralph Hepburn	Miller	8	230	Miller	cream, red	114.326	22	17	157-rear axle
24	Deacon Litz	Bowes Seal Fast	John Rutner	Duesenberg	8	151	Duesenberg	white, black, red	109.546	19	18	152-con. rod
10	Bill Cummings	Bowes Seal Fast	B. L. Schneider	Miller	8	151	Stevens	white, black, red	111.204	12	19	151-crankshaft
57	Malcolm Fox	Richards	William H. Richards	Studebaker	8	336	Studebaker	blue, black	111.149	32	20	132-spring
9	Chet Miller	Hudson	R. G. "Buddy" Marr	Hudson	8	255	Hudson	blue, silver	111.053	29	21	125-engine trouble
7	Ernie Triplett	Floating Power	William S. White	Miller	4	220	Miller	orange, black	114.935	31	22	125-clutch
1	Louis Schneider	Bowes Seal Fast	B. L. Schneider	Miller	8	151	Stevens	white, black, red	110.681	30	23	125-frame
41	Joe Russo	Art Rose	George A. Henry	Duesenberg	8	261	Rigling	white	108.791	21	24	107-con. rod
8	Lou Moore	Boyle Valve	M. J. Boyle	Miller	8	268	Miller	white, blue, red	117.363	1	25	79-timing gear
14	Juan Gaudino	Golden Seal	Juan Gaudino	Chrysler	8	358	Chrysler	green	107.466	36	26	71-clutch
29	Al Miller	Hudson	R. G. "Buddy" Marr	Hudson	8	255	Hudson	blue, silver	110.129	34	27	66-engine trouble
42	Doc MacKenzie	Brady	Ray T. Brady	Studebaker	8	337	Studebaker	lavender, white	108.154	39	28	65-engine trouble
32	Frank Brisko	Brisko-Atkinson	F. Brisko & D. Atkinson	Miller¢	8	151	Stevens	cream, red	111.149	13	29	61-clutch
72	Ray Campbell	Folly Farm	E. D. Stairs, Jr.	Graham	8	245	Graham	blue	108.969	34	30	60-crankshaft
5	Billy Arnold	Miller-Hartz	Harry Hartz	Miller	8	151	Summers	light gray, blue	116.290	2	31	59-wrecked NE
27	Bryan Saulpaugh	Harry Miller	William S. White	Miller	16	303	Miller	cream	114.369	3	32	55-oil line
16	Lou Meyer	Sampson	Alden Sampson, II	Miller	16	220	Stevens	white, black	112.471	7	33	50-crankshaft
21	Al Aspen	Brady & Nardi	G. Nardi & Ray Brady	Studebaker	8	340	Duesenberg	black, red	108.008	23	34	31-con. rod
49	Johnny Kreiger	Consumers Petroleum Oil	Fred P. Duesenberg	Duesenberg	8	138	Duesenberg		109.276	33	35	30-con. rod
48	Wes Crawford	Boyle Valve	M. J. Boyle	Duesenberg¢	8	137	Miller	white, red, blue	110.396	16	36	28-crankshaft
17	Paul Bost	Empire State	Paul B. Bost	Miller¢	8	215	Cooper	red	111.885	8	37	18-crankshaft
58	Bob McDonough	Miller Four Wheel Drive	Four Wheel Drive Auto Co.	Miller 4	8	308	Miller	cream, red	113.276	24	38	17-oil line
45	Gus Schrader	Harry Miller	William Burden	Miller 4	8	308	Miller	red, cream	112.003	28	39	7-wrecked NW
26	Al Gordon	Lion Tamer	G. D. Harrison	Miller	4	220	Miller	blue, white	111.290	37	40	3-wrecked NW

¢Front Drive   4Four wheel drive

Howdy Wilcox, II

Cliff Bergere

Bob Carey

Russell Snowberger

Zeke Meyer

Ira Hall

Freddy Winnai

Billy Winn

Joe Huff

Phil "Red" Shafer

Kelly Petillo

Tony Gulotta

Stubby Stubblefield

Peter Kreis

Luther Johnson

Wilbur Shaw

Deacon Litz

Bill Cummings

Malcolm Fox

Chet Miller

Ernie Triplett

Louis Schneider

Joe Russo

Lou Moore

Juan Gaudino

Al Miller

Doc MacKenzie

Frank Brisko

Ray Campbell

Billy Arnold

Bryan Saulpaugh

Lou Meyer

Al Aspen

Johnny Kreiger

Wes Crawford

Paul Bost

Bob McDonough

Gus Schrader

Al Gordon

Below, left: Cliff Bergere just after he finished third in a Studebaker Special. Below, right: Benny Benifield's wrecked Duesenberg in which mechanic Harry Cox was killed when the car went over the southwest wall and hit a tree. In 1931, Joe Caccia and his mechanic, Clarence Grove, died in the same car and in approximately the same place. Bottom: Fred Frame pulls into Victory Lane and is immediately surrounded by well-wishers, officials and members of the press and radio.

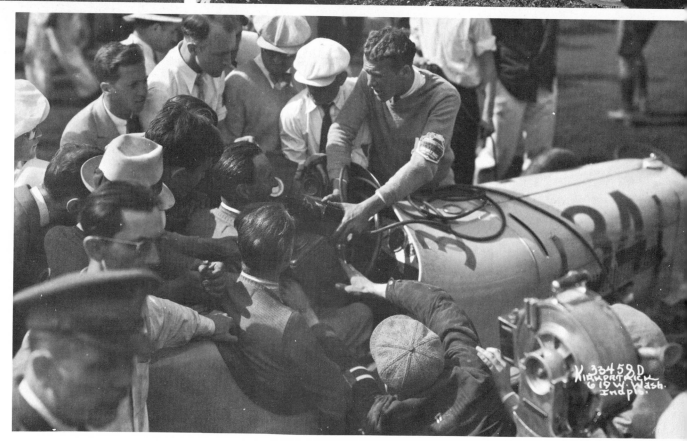

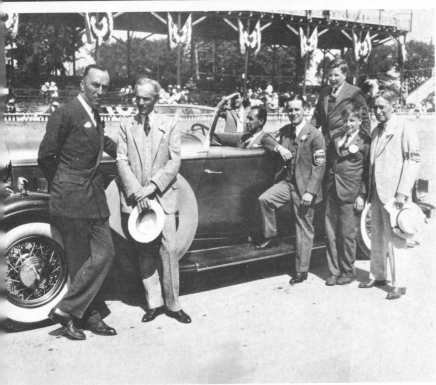

Top: Howdy Wilcox "II", back in the garage area after finishing second driving Shorty Cantlon's Miller. Middle, left: Eddie Rickenbacker, Henry Ford, Harvey Firestone Jr., Henry Ford II, Benson Ford and Harvey Firestone Sr., surround Edsel Ford who is at the wheel of the Lincoln pace car. Middle, right: A front view of the Coleman Four-Wheel-Drive which Fred Merzney failed to qualify. Bottom: Fred Frame and his son Bob prepare to unload Frame's Duesenberg which was driven by Billy Winn. Bob Frame was fatally injured in a sprint car accident during the early 1940's.

1933

1933 was a year of tragedy as five men were killed and one seriously injured. Lou Meyer won his second race in a Miller with Wilbur Shaw and Lou Moore trailing. It was a bad year from the start with the purse reduced and the lap fund unsubscribed due to the Depression. While qualifying, Bill Denver and mechanic Hugh "Bob" Hurst went over the northeast wall and were fatally injured. Before the start of the race a drivers' strike, protesting the medical disqualification of Howdy Wilcox II, held up proceedings until Mauri Rose was named as a replacement driver. Soon after Ira Hall crashed on his 37th lap, Mark Billman hit the wall in the southeast turn and died of injuries. Mechanic Elmer Lombard was badly injured. A short time later a car lost control in the first turn and Malcolm Fox, immediately behind, dodged to avoid contact and swung in front of Lester Spangler. Spangler ran over one of Fox's wheels and flipped from the top of the track to the inside wall. Spangler, along with G. L. "Monk" Jordan, was killed instantly. A little later Wes Crawford lost a wheel and hit the wall, while near the end of the race Kelly Petillo spun and stalled. At the finish Meyer was almost six minutes in front of Wilbur Shaw.

Lou Meyer

NO.	DRIVER	CAR	ENTRANT	ENGINE	CYL.	DISP.	CHASSIS	COLOR	QUAL. SPEED	ST.	FIN.	LAPS/SPEED/REASON OUT
36	Lou Meyer	Tydol	Lou Meyer	Miller	8	258	Miller	cream, red	116.977	6	1	200-104.162
17	Wilbur Shaw	Mallory	Leon Duray	Miller	4	220	Stevens	black, white	115.497	23	2	200-101.795
37	Lou Moore	Foreman Axle	Maley & Scully	Miller	4	255	Duesenberg	gray, red	117.843	4	3	200-101.599
21	Chet Gardner	Sampson Radio	Alden Sampson, II	Miller	16	201	Stevens	white, black	112.319	15	4	200-101.182
8	Stubby Stubblefield	Shafer "8"	Phil Shafer	Buick	8	284	Rigling	black	114.784	10	5	200-100.762
38	Dave Evans	Art Rose	Arthur E. Rose	Studebaker	8	260	Cooper	rose, silver	109.448	36	6	200-100.425
34	Tony Gulotta	Studebaker	Studebaker Corp.	Studebaker	8	336	Rigling	white, blue	113.578	12	7	200- 99.071
4	Russ Snowberger	Russell "8"	Russell Snowberger	Studebaker	8	336	Snowberger	tan, black	110.769	17	8	200- 99.011
9	Zeke Meyer	Studebaker	Studebaker Corp.	Studebaker	8	336	Rigling	green, silver	111.099	16	9	200- 98.122
46	Luther Johnson	Studebaker	Studebaker Corp.	Studebaker	8	336	Rigling	gun metal, silver	110.097	20	10	200- 97.393
6	Cliff Bergere	Studebaker	Studebaker Corp.	Studebaker	8	336	Rigling	maroon, silver	115.643	9	11	200- 97.286
47	L. L. Corum	Studebaker	Studebaker Corp.	Studebaker	8	336	Rigling	gun metal, silver	110.465	18	12	200- 96.458
49	Willard Prentiss	Jack O. Carr	J. W. Kleinschmidt	Duesenberg	8	365	Rigling	black, red	107.776	40	13	200- 93.595
14	Raul Riganti	Golden Seal	Raul Riganti	Chrysler	8	305	Chrysler	green	108.081	27	14	200- 93.244
29	Gene Haustein	Martz	Lawrence J. Martz	Hudson	8	235	Hudson	orange	107.603	28	15	197-flagged
26	Deacon Litz	Bowes Seal Fast	A. B. Litz	Miller	4	220	Miller	white, black, red	113.138	14	16	197-flagged
18	Joe Russo	Wonder Bread	F. P. Duesenberg	Duesenberg	8	275	Duesenberg	white, red, blue	112.531	31	17	192-flagged
51	Doc MacKenzie	Brady	Ray T. Brady	Studebaker	8	340	Duesenberg	black, red	108.073	39	18	192-rear axle
27	Kelly Petillo	Yahr-Miller	William M. Yahr	Miller	4	213	Smith	cream, red	113.037	25	19	168-spun and stalled
28	Chet Miller	Marr	R. G. "Buddy" Marr	Hudson	8	255	Hudson	blue, silver	112.025	32	20	163-con. rod
19	Al Miller	Marr	R. G. "Buddy" Marr	Hudson	8	255	Hudson	blue, silver	109.799	24	21	161-con. rod
68	Bennett Hill	Goldberg Bros.	S. C. Goldberg	Cooper¢	16	190	Cooper	black, red	110.264	19	22	158-con. rod
45	Babe Stapp	Boyle Products	M. J. Boyle	Miller¢	4	221	Miller	white, blue, red	116.626	29	23	156-out of gas
32	Wesley Crawford	Boyle Products	Frank Brisko	Miller¢	8	151	Stevens	cream, red	109.862	26	24	147-wrecked SW (Winn)
5	Bill Cummings	Boyle Products	M. J. Boyle	Miller	8	270	Miller	white, red	118.521	1	25	136-leaking radiator
15	Lester Spangler	Miller	Harry Hartz	Miller	4	255	Miller	light gray, blue	116.903	7	28	132-wrecked SW
65	Freddy Winnai	Kemp	James Kemp	Duesenberg	8	154	Duesenberg	white, red	110.018	35	27	125-engine trouble
57	Malcolm Fox	Universal Service	William Richards	Studebaker	8	337	Studebaker	blue, black	112.922	30	28	121-wrecked SW
12	Fred Frame	Miller-Hartz	Harry Hartz	Miller	8	182	Wetteroth	light gray, blue	117.864	3	29	85-valve
64	Mark Billman	Kemp-Mannix	James Kemp	Duesenberg	8	265	Duesenberg	white, red	112.410	22	30	79-wrecked SE
53	Johnny Sawyer	Lencki-Madis	Lencki & Unger	Miller	4	220	Miller	gun metal blue, red	110.590	34	31	77-clutch
2	Peter Kreis	Frame-Miller	Fred Frame	Miller	8	151	Summers	blue	114.370	11	32	63-universal joint
16	Ernie Triplett	Floating Power	William S. White	Miller	4	220	Weil	red, white	117.685	5	33	61-piston
25	Shorty Cantlon	Sullivan & O'Brien	William Cantlon	Miller	4	220	Stevens	tan, silver	113.384	13	34	50-con. rod
3	Mauri Rose	Gilmore	Joe Marks	Miller	8	248	Stevens	red, silver	117.649	42	35	48-timing gears
58	Frank Brisko	F. W. D.	F. W. D. Auto Co.	Miller 4		308	Miller	cream, red	118.388	2	36	47-oil too hot
10	Ira Hall	Denny Duesenberg	Denny Duesenberg	Duesenberg	8	249	Stevens	dark blue	115.739	8	37	37-piston
23	Ralph Hepburn	Highway Truck Parts	S. C. Goldberg	Cooper¢	16	330	Cooper	blue, white	110.001	41	38	33-con. rod bearing
59	Ray Campbell	G & D	Tulio Gulotta	Hudson	8	244	Hudson	maroon, white	108.650	37	39	24-oil leak
24	Paul Bost	Frame-Miller-Duesenberg	Fred Frame	Miller	4	220	Duesenberg	gray	111.330	33	40	13-oil line
61	Rick Decker	Miller	Bessie Decker	Miller¢	8	167	Miller	white	108.280	38	41	13-manifold
22	Lou Schneider	Edelweiss	W. R. Blackburn	Miller	8	151	Stevens	red	109.850	21	42	1-stalled

¢Front Drive   4Four wheel drive

Wilbur Shaw

Lou Moore

Chet Gardner

Stubby Stubblefield

Dave Evans

Tony Gulotta

Russell Snowberger

Zeke Meyer

Luther Johnson

Cliff Bergere

L. L. Corum

Willard Prentiss

Raul Riganti

Gene Haustein

Deacon Litz

Joe Russo

Doc MacKenzie

Kelly Petillo

Chet Miller

Al Miller

Bennett Hill

Babe Stapp

Wesley Crawford

Bill Cummings

Lester Spangler

Freddy Winnai

Malcolm Fox

Fred Frame

Mark Billman

Johnny Sawyer

Peter Kreis

Ernie Triplett

Shorty Cantlon

Howdy Wilcox (qualifier)

Frank Brisko

Ralph Hepburn

Ray Campbell

Paul Bost

Rick Decker

Lou Schneider

Ira Hall-no picture available

Top: Members of the Studebaker Team stand on the pit wall behind the Studebaker Special, which was driven by Tony Gulotta, and a 1933 Pierce-Arrow. Middle: Though officials would not let him use the number in competition, Lou Schneider kept No. 13 on the tail of his Edelweiss Special long enough to have his picture taken. Bottom: The pace car was a Chrysler.

Below, left: A view with the body removed, of the FWD Special, driven by Frank Brisko. The car is a four-wheel-drive powered by a V8, 303-cubic-inch Miller. Below, right: Winner Lou Meyer and mechanic Lawson Harris in their Tydol Special. Bottom: A stripped view of the Sampson Special, driven by Chet Gardner, showing the spherical fuel tank designed to utilize every drop. The car was also equipped with a short-wave radio for receiving instructions from the pits. Due to the intense vibration, radios have never been especially successful.

1934

"Wild Bill" Cummings, driving Mike Boyle's front-drive Miller, out-dueled Mauri Rose to win the closest race the "500" had seen thus far. At the checkered flag Cummings was a scant 27 seconds ahead of Rose who was driving Leon Duray's squat black Miller. Fuel and oil limitations were in effect in an attempt to slow the cars down and make the race safer, and Cummings averaged a phenomenal 13.9 miles per gallon of gas for the 500 miles, which closely rivaled passenger cars of the day. Wilbur Shaw fell victim to the new rule limiting oil to six gallons. Just as he shot into the lead on the 16th lap, his oil plug came out and the oil was pumped onto the track, causing both George Bailey and Chet Miller to go over the northeast and southwest walls respectively. Gene Haustein later broke an axle and was hit by Doc MacKenzie. After hitting the wall, Haustein climbed out and held his car until help arrived to keep it from rolling down the track. MacKenzie's car, squeezed into the inside wall, finally stopped in the middle of the track. Bailey was the most seriously injured driver with broken ribs and lacerations. During practice, Peter Kreis and mechanic Bob Hahn were killed when their Hartz-Miller went over the southwest wall.

Bill Cummings

NO.	DRIVER	CAR	ENTRANT	ENGINE	CYL.	DISP.	CHASSIS	COLOR	QUAL. SPEED	ST.	FIN.	LAPS/SPEED/REASON OUT
7	Bill Cummings	Boyle Products	H. C. Henning	Miller¢	4	220	Miller	white, red, blue	116.116	10	1	200-104.863
9	Mauri Rose	Leon Duray	Leon Duray	Miller	4	220	Stevens	black, white	116.044	4	2	200-104.697
2	Lou Moore	Foreman Axle	California Racers, Inc.	Miller	4	255	Miller	light gray, red	113.442	20	3	200-103.625
12	Deacon Litz	Stokely Foods	A. B. Litz	Miller	4	220	Miller	white, blue	113.731	19	4	200-100.749
16	Joe Russo	Duesenberg	Joe E. Russo	Duesenberg	8	275	Duesenberg		113.115	24	5	200- 99.893
36	Al Miller	Shafer "8"	Phil Shafer	Buick	8	286	Rigling	black, white	113.307	8	6	200- 98.264
22	Cliff Bergere	Floating Power	William S. White	Miller	4	220	Weil	red, white	115.243	18	7	200- 97.818
10	Russ Snowberger	Russell "8"	Russell Snowberger	Studebaker	8	336	Snowberger	dark blue	111.428	9	8	200- 97.297
32	Frank Brisko	F.W.D.	F.W.D. Auto Co.	Miller	4	255	Miller	cream	116.894	3	9	200- 96.787
24	Herb Ardinger	Lucenti	Angelo Lucenti	Graham	8	265	Graham	blue, gold	111.722	14	10	200- 95.936
17	Kelly Petillo	Red Lion	Joe Marks	Miller	4	255	Adams	cream, red	119.329	1	11	200- 93.432
5	Stubby Stubblefield	Cummins Diesel	Cummins Engin Co.	Cummins £	4	364	Duesenberg	red, white	105.921	29	12	200- 88.566
31	Ralph Hepburn	Miller	Ralph Hepburn	Miller	8	254	Miller	cream, red	114.321	11	13	164-con. rod
18	George Barringer	Boyle Products	H. C. Henning	Miller	8	270	Miller	white, red	113.859	12	14	161-bent front axle
26	Phil Shafer	Shafer "8"	Phil Shafer	Buick	8	292	Rigling	green	113.816	6	15	130-camshaft drive
49	Charles Crawford	Detroit Gasket & Mfg.	Detroit Gasket & Mfg. Co.	Ford V8	8	221	Ford	black	108.784	28	16	110-head gasket
8	Tony Gulotta	Schroeder	Floyd Smith	Studebaker¢	8	250	Cooper	black, silver	113.733	7	17	94-con. rod
1	Lou Meyer	Ring Free	Lou Meyer	Miller	4	255	Stevens	yellow, red	112.332	13	18	92-oil tank
6	Dave Evans	Cummins Diesel	Cummins Engine Co.	Cummins	4	364	Duesenberg	white, red	102.414	22	19	81-transmission
15	Shorty Cantlon	Sullivan & O'Brien	William J. Cantlon	Miller	4	220	Stevens	tan	117.875	15	20	76-crankshaft
4	Chet Gardner	Sampson Radio	Alden Sampson, II	Miller	16	201	Stevens	white, black	114.786	5	21	72-con. rod
51	Al Gordon	Abels & Fink	Paul Weirick	Miller	4	239	Adams	blue, silver	116.273	17	22	66-wrecked SW
35	Rex Mays	Frame Miller-Duesenberg	Fred Frame	Miller	4	220	Duesenberg	gray, blue	113.639	23	23	53-front axle
42	Dusty Fahrnow	Superior Trailer	Irving Goldberg	Cooper¢	16	330	Cooper	black	113.070	25	24	28-con. rod
41	Johnny Sawyer	Burd Piston Ring	Lencki & Unger	Lencki	4	183	Miller	green, black	109.808	21	25	27-con. rod
33	Johnny Seymour	Streamline Miller	Fred Frame	Miller	4	200	Adams	gray, blue	108.591	33	26	22-pinion gear
45	Rick Decker	Carter Carburetor	Rickliffe Decker	Miller¢	8	171	Miller	white	110.895	27	27	17-clutch
3	Wilbur Shaw	Lion Head	Joe Marks	Miller	8	249	Stevens	red, silver	117.647	2	28	15-lost oil
73	Doc MacKenzie	Cresco	Mikan & Carson	Studebaker	8	337	Mikan-Carson	silver, orange	111.933	26	29	15-wrecked NS
29	Gene Haustein	Martz	Lawrence J. Martz	Hudson	8	257	Hudson	orange	109.426	31	30	13-wrecked NW
63	Harry McQuinn	DeBaets	Michel DeBaets	Miller	4	220	Rigling	blue	111.067	30	31	13-con. rod
58	George Bailey	Scott	Roy Scott	Studebaker	8	360	Snowberger	tan, black, white	111.063	16	32	12-wrecked NE
46	Chet Miller	Bohnalite Ford	Bohn Aluminum & Brass Corp.	Ford V8	8	221	Ford	gold, black	109.252	32	33	11-over SW wall

¢Front drive   £ Two-cycle engine

Mauri Rose

Lou Moore

Deacon Litz

Joe Russo

Al Miller

Cliff Bergere

Russell Snowberger

Frank Brisko

Herb Ardinger

Kelly Petillo

Stubby Stubblefield

Ralph Hepburn

George Barringer

Phil ''Red'' Shafer

Charles Crawford

Tony Gulotta

Lou Meyer

Dave Evans

Shorty Cantlon

Chet Gardner

Al Gordon

Rex Mays

Dusty Fahrnow

Johnny Sawyer

Johnny Seymour

Rick Decker

Wilbur Shaw

Doc MacKenzie

Gene Haustein

Harry McQuinn

George Bailey

Chet Miller

Below, left: Winner "Wild Bill" Cummings. Below, right: The cars roar away from their positions on the starting line to circle the track once before taking the green flag. Bottom: Cliff Bergere, in Bill White's Miller, poses with White in front of the Chrysler Airflow that was used as an official car by the chief steward.

CUMMINS-DIESEL MOTOR, 1934

MAURI ROSE'S MOTOR 1934

Top: The pace lap as seen from the pits. Middle, left: The 4-cycle Cummins Diesel engine which powered the car driven by Dave Evans. Middle, right: The Miller engine used in the Duray Special driven to second place by Mauri Rose. This was the popular 4-cylinder, 220-cubic-inch model used for many years in sprint cars. Bottom: The wrecked Miller-Hartz Special in which Peter Kreis and his mechanic, Bob Hahn, crashed to their deaths over the southwest wall. It was broken in half by the impact.

1935

Kelly Petillo, the colorful little driver from Los Angeles, drove a masterful race to beat Wilbur Shaw and set a new track record in the process. The record speed, in excess of 106 miles per hour, might have been higher except for a number of laps under the caution flag, one due to a fatal accident involving Clay Weatherly who crashed coming out of the northwest turn on his 10th lap. Weatherly's mechanic, Eddie Bradburn, received a broken back. A few laps later, Al Gordon's Cocktail Hour Miller hit the northwest wall and flipped upside-down stopping with the hood balanced on the wall and the tail on the track. Near the close of the race, when Shaw was in hot pursuit of Petillo, a light rain brought out the yellow bunting, ending Shaw's chances. The last nine laps were run under the green but there was not enough time for Wilbur to close the gap. Three men died in practice before the race. Johnny Hannon, taking his first lap on the track as a driver at the wheel of Leon Duray's Miller, crashed over the wall on the northeast turn. The car was rebuilt in time for it to be qualified by the ill-fated Weatherly. On their 7th qualifying lap, Stubby Stubblefield and mechanic Leo Whittaker died when their car went over the wall on the south stretch.

Kelly Petillo

NO.	DRIVER	CAR	ENTRANT	ENGINE	CYL.	DISP.	CHASSIS	COLOR	QUAL. SPEED	ST.	FIN.	LAPS/SPEED/REASON OUT
5	Kelly Petillo	Gilmore Speedway	Kelly Petillo	Offy	4	260	Wetteroth	red, cream	115.095	22	1	200-106.240
14	Wilbur Shaw	Pirrung	Gil Pirrung	Offy¢	4	220	Shaw	blue, white	116.854	20	2	200-105.990
1	Bill Cummings	Boyle Products	H. C. Henning	Miller¢	4	221	Miller	white, red, blue	116.901	5	3	200-104.758
22	Floyd Roberts	Abels & Fink	Earl Haskell	Miller	4	255	Miller	dark blue, silver	118.671	3	4	200-103.228
21	Ralph Hepburn	Veedol	Ralph Hepburn	Miller	8	258	Miller	cream, red	115.156	7	5	200-103.177
9	Shorty Cantlon	Sullivan & O'Brien	William J. Cantlon	Miller	4	220	Stevens	tan, silver	118.205	19	6	200-101.140
18	Chet Gardner	Sampson Radio	Alden Sampson, II	Miller	4	220	Stevens	white, black	114.556	9	7	200-101.129
16	Deacon Litz	Sha-litz	A. B. Litz	Miller	4	220	Miller	red, black, white	114.488	13	8	200-100.907
8	Doc MacKenzie	Pirrung	Gil Pirrung	Miller	4	220	Rigling	blue, silver	114.294	15	9	200-100.598
34	Chet Miller	Milac Front Drive	Fred Frame	Miller¢	8	151	Summers	blue	113.552	17	10	200-100.474
19	Fred Frame	Miller-Hartz	Harry Hartz	Miller¢	8	183	Wetteroth	blue, yellow, red	114.701	8	11	200-100.436
36	Lou Meyer	Ring Free	Lou Meyer	Miller	4	255	Stevens	red, white	117.938	4	12	200-100.256
15	Cliff Bergere	Victor Gasket	Phil Shafer	Buick	8	284	Rigling	green, white	114.162	16	13	196-out of gas
62	Harris Insinger	Cresco	Mikan & Carson	Studebaker	8	336	Mikan-Carson	silver, orange, blue	111.729	31	14	185-flagged
4	Al Miller	Boyle Products	H. C. Henning	Miller	4	260	Smith	white, red, blue	115.303	21	15	178-magneto
43	Ted Horn	Ford V8	Harry A. Miller	Ford V8¢	8	220	Miller-Ford	black, white	113.213	26	16	145-steering
33	Rex Mays	Gilmore	Paul Weirick	Miller	4	269	Adams	blue, silver	120.736	1	17	123-spring shackle
7	Lou Moore	Foreman Axle	Lou Moore	Miller	4	255	Miller	red, silver	114.180	23	18	116-con. rod
37	George Connor	Marks-Miller	Joe Marks	Miller	8	248	Stevens	red, white	114.321	14	19	112-transmission
2	Mauri Rose	F. W. D.	Four Wheel Drive Auto Co.	Miller 4	4	255	Miller	buff	116.470	10	20	103-mechanical failure
44	Tony Gulotta	Bowes Seal Fast	Leon Duray	Miller	4	220	Stevens	black, white, red	115.459	6	21	102-magneto
39	Jimmy Snyder	Blue Prelude	Joel Thorne	Studebaker	8	336	Snowberger	blue	112.249	30	22	97-spring
41	Frank Brisko	Art Rose	Kenneth Schroeder	Studebaker¢	8	250	Cooper	black, silver	113.307	24	23	79-universal joint
42	Johnny Seymour	Ford V8	Harry A. Miller	Ford V8¢	8	220	Miller-Ford	blue, silver	112.696	27	24	71-grease leak
17	Babe Stapp	Marks-Miller	Joe Marks	Miller	4	255	Adams	cream, red	116.736	12	25	70-radiator
35	George Bailey	Ford V8	Harry A. Miller	Ford V8¢	8	220	Miller-Ford	silver, red	113.432	29	26	65-steering
3	Russ Snowberger	Boyle Products	H. C. Henning	Miller	8	270	Miller	white, red, blue	114.209	11	27	59-exhaust pipe
26	Louis Tomei	Burd Piston Ring	Joe Lencki	Lencki	8	220	Miller	gun metal blue, red	110.794	32	28	47-valve
46	Bob Sall	Ford V8	Harry A. Miller	Ford V8¢	8	220	Miller-Ford	gold, white	110.519	33	29	47-steering
6	Al Gordon	Cocktail Hour Cigarette	William S. White	Miller	4	220	Weil	cream, blue	119.481	2	30	17-wrecked NW
27	Freddy Winnai	Gyro-Duesenberg	Harry Hartz	Miller	4	234	Duesenberg	gray, blue	115.138	28	31	16-con. rod
45	Clay Weatherly	Bowes Seal Fast	Leon Duray	Miller	4	220	Stevens	black, white, red	115.902	25	32	9-wrecked NW
66	Harry McQuinn	DeBaets	Michel DeBaets	Miller	4	220	Rigling	blue, red	111.111	18	33	4-con. rod

¢Front drive   4Four wheel drive

Wilbur Shaw

Bill Cummings

Floyd Roberts

Ralph Hepburn

Shorty Cantlon

Chet Gardner

Deacon Litz

Doc MacKenzie

Chet Miller

Fred Frame

Lou Meyer

Cliff Bergere

Harris Insinger

Al Miller

Ted Horn

Rex Mays

Lou Moore

George Connor

Mauri Rose

Tony Gulotta

Jimmy Snyder

Frank Brisko

Johnny Seymour

Babe Stapp

George Bailey

Russell Snowberger

Louis Tomei

Bob Sall

Al Gordon

Freddy Winnai

Clay Weatherly

Harry McQuinn

Below, left: Winner Kelly Petillo, who overcame a number of pre-race difficulties to set a track record for the 500 miles despite a drizzle which caused the last part of the race to be run under the caution flag. Below, right: George Bailey in one of the Ford-Millers with designer-builder Harry Miller standing behind the sleek front-drive. Bottom: Part of the Ford-Miller Team lined up on the pit apron. Ten of these identical cars were built by Harry Miller for a group of Ford dealers and, though revolutionary in concept, they had several design defects which prevented any of the four cars that made the race from finishing. The most serious problem was the placement of the steering assembly too near the engine block. The resulting heat caused an expansion of the gears and the eventual freezing of the steering mechanism.

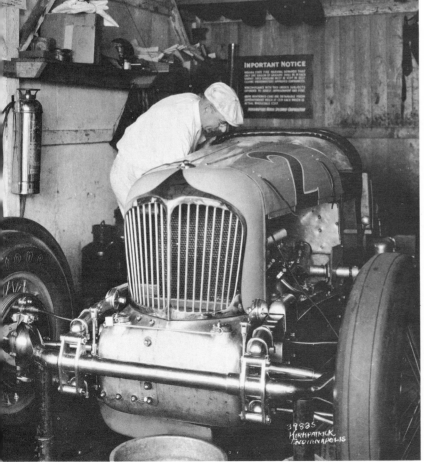

Top, left: The 4-cylinder, 220-cubic-inch engine designed and built by Joe Lencki for his Burd Piston Ring Special which was driven by Louis Tomei. Top, right: The car in which Clay Weatherly was fatally injured on the 9th lap of the race. It is the same car Johnny Hannon drove to his death in practice when he went over the northeast wall on his first lap around the Speedway. Middle, left: Charter members in the Champion 100-Mile-An-Hour Club. Left to right, front row: Howdy Wilcox "II", Wilbur Shaw, Lou Moore, Lou Meyer, Bill Cummings and Dave Evans. Back row, left to right: Cliff Bergere, Fred Frame, Russell Snowberger, Chet Gardner, and Mauri Rose. Middle, right: Stubby Stubblefield and his mechanic, Leo Whittaker, were fatally injured during qualifying when they crashed over the wall on the south straightaway. Bottom: A mechanic works on the FWD Special which was driven by Mauri Rose.

1936

Lou Meyer became the first three-time winner in Speedway history as he tooled his red and white Ring Free Special to victory over Ted Horn and Kelly Petillo, who was driving relief for Doc Mac-Kenzie. Until the 83rd lap it appeared that the race would be a duel between Wilbur Shaw in his new streamlined Gilmore Special and Babe Stapp in the front-drive Pirrung Special that Shaw built the previous year. Loose hood rivets, however, caused Shaw to lose over 17 minutes in the pits and several laps later Stapp withdrew with a broken crankshaft. With Shaw far behind and Stapp out, Meyer found himself in front and he remained there the last half of the race to win in record time. Despite a fuel limit of 37½ gallons, the first five cars broke Petillo's year-old mark, although seven cars ran out of gas before they could finish. Included in this group was pole-driver Rex Mays. The track was entirely revamped for this race with wide safety aprons replacing the infield wall, asphalt paving in the turns and a new outside wall perpendicular to the banked track. Al Miller incurred the only injury during the race when his car broke a crankshaft and hit the wall. He was thrown from the car and fractured his hip. Gulotta, Rose and Hepburn were unhurt in pre-race crashes.

Lou Meyer

NO.	DRIVER	CAR	ENTRANT	ENGINE	CYL.	DISP.	CHASSIS	COLOR	QUAL. SPEED	ST.	FIN.	LAPS/SPEED/REASON OUT
8	Lou Meyer	Ring Free	Lou Meyer	Miller	4	255	Stevens	red, white	114.171	28	1	200-109.069
22	Ted Horn	Miller-Hartz	Harry Hartz	Miller	8	183	Wetteroth	gray, blue	116.564	11	2	200-108.170
10	Doc MacKenzie	Gilmore Speedway	Kelly Petillo	Offy	4	262	Wetteroth	cream, red	116.961	4	3	200-107.460
36	Mauri Rose	F. W. D.	Four Wheel Drive Auto Co.	Miller 4	4	255	Miller	white, red	113.890	30	4	200-107.272
18	Chet Miller	Boyle Products	Boyle Motor Products	Miller¢	4	212	Summers	white, red	117.675	3	5	200-106.919
41	Ray Pixley	Fink Auto	Clarence Felker	Miller	4	203	Miller	dark blue, silver	116.703	25	6	200-105.253
3	Wilbur Shaw	Gilmore	W. Wilbur Shaw	Offy	4	255	Shaw	cream, red	117.503	9	7	200-104.233
17	George Barringer	Kennedy Tank	Phil Shafer	Offy	4	255	Rigling	red	112.700	14	8	200-102.630
53	Zeke Meyer	Boyle Products	Boyle Motor Products	Studebaker¢	8	251	Cooper	white	111.476	32	9	200-101.331
38	George Connor	Marks Miller	Joe Marks	Miller	4	255	Adams	white, red	116.269	5	10	200- 98.931
35	Freddy Winnai	Midwest Red Lion	Midwest Racing Team	Offy	4	255	Stevens	cream, red	116.221	12	11	199-flagged
9	Ralph Hepburn	Art Rose	Ralph Hepburn	Offy	4	255	Miller	white	112.673	24	12	196-flagged
28	Harry McQuinn	Sampson Radio	Alden Sampson, II	Miller	4	247	Stevens	white	114.118	27	13	196-out of gas
7	Shorty Cantlon	Hamilton-Harris	William S. White	Miller	4	247	Weil	cream, red, black	116.912	10	14	194-out of gas
33	Rex Mays	Gilmore	Paul Weirick	Sparks	4	239	Adams	blue, silver	119.644	1	15	192-out of gas
54	Doc Williams	Superior Trailer	Race Car Corp.	Miller¢	4	246	Cooper	blue	112.837	23	16	192-out of gas
32	Lou Moore	Burd Piston Ring	Lou Moore	Offy	4	255	Miller	orange, black	113.996	29	17	185-out of gas
19	Emil Andres	Carew	J. Stewart Carew	Cragar	4	212	Rigling	blue, silver	111.455	33	18	184-flagged
4	Floyd Roberts	Burd Piston Ring	Joe Lencki	Offy	4	255	Stevens	orange, black	112.403	15	19	183-out of gas
14	Frank Brisko	Elgin Piston Pin	Elgin Piston Pin Co.	Brisko	4	255	Miller	orange, blue	114.213	20	20	180-out of gas
12	Al Miller	Boyle Products	Boyle Motor Products	Miller	4	258	Smith	white, red, blue	116.138	17	21	119-wrecked FS
42	Cliff Bergere	Bowes Seal Fast	Bowes Seal Fast Corp.	Miller	4	220	Stevens	black, white, red	113.377	7	22	116-loose engine support
15	Deacon Litz	Deacon Litz	A. B. Litz	Miller	4	220	Miller	white	115.997	26	23	108-crankshaft
21	Babe Stapp	Pirrung	Gil Pirrung	Offy¢	4	255	Shaw	light blue, white	118.945	2	24	89-crankshaft
5	Billy Winn	Harry A. Miller	James M. Winn	Miller	4	255	Miller	white	114.648	19	25	78-crankshaft
52	Frank McGurk	Abels Auto Ford	Charles Worley	Cragar	4	214	Adams	cream, red, black	113.102	22	26	51-crankshaft
27	Louis Tomei	Wheeler's	Babe Stapp	Miller	4	214	Wetteroth	yellow	111.078	8	27	44-engine support arm
44	Herb Ardinger	Bowes Seal Fast	Bowes Seal Fast Corp.	Miller	4	220	Stevens	black, white, red	115.082	6	28	38-transmission
6	Chet Gardner	Gardner	Chester L. Gardner	Offy	4	255	Duesenberg	light blue, red	116.000	18	29	38-clutch
43	Jimmy Snyder	Belanger Miller	Murrell Belanger	Miller	8	249	Stevens	white	111.291	16	30	21-oil leak
47	Johnny Seymour	Sullivan & O'Brien	William L. Cantlon	Miller	4	246	Stevens	cream, red, black	113.169	21	31	13-clutch
46	Fred Frame	Burd Piston Ring	Moore & Fengler	Miller	4	255	Miller	orange, black	112.877	31	32	4-piston
2	Bill Cummings	Boyle Products	Boyle Motor Products	Offy¢	4	255	Miller	white, red, blue	115.939	13	33	0-clutch

¢Front drive   4Four wheel drive

Ted Horn

Doc MacKenzie

Mauri Rose

Chet Miller

Ray Pixley

Wilbur Shaw

George Barringer

Zeke Meyer

George Connor

Freddy Winnai

Ralph Hepburn

Harry McQuinn

Shorty Cantlon

Rex Mays

Doc Williams

Lou Moore

Emil Andres

Floyd Roberts

Frank Brisko

Al Miller

Cliff Bergere

Deacon Litz

Babe Stapp

Billy Winn

Frank McGurk

Louis Tomei

Herb Ardinger

Chet Gardner

Jimmy Snyder

Johnny Seymour

Fred Frame

Bill Cummings

Below, left: The Packard leading the pace lap. Below, right: Lou Meyer and Mrs. Meyer in the Packard pace car which, for the first time, was presented to the winner of the race. Two-time winner, Tommy Milton, is in white suit with field glasses. Bottom: The Firestone crew checks the tires on Harry Hartz's Miller as Hartz talks to Firestone's racing representative, Waldo Stein, wearing vest, outside the Firestone Racing Headquarters in Gasoline Alley. No car is allowed on the track which has not been checked for correct tire pressure.

Above: The Pagoda, which served as the Speedway's nerve center from 1926 until it was razed after the 1956 race to make way for the new Tower. Left: Tony Gulotta's Pirrung Special, which he wrecked in practice in the northwest turn. Gulotta wasn't seriously injured but the car was damaged too badly to be repaired in time for the race.

Tony Gulotta—Wreck
Indianapolis Motor Speedway 1936

1937

Wilbur Shaw, who had previously been denied victory due to assorted mechanical ills, came down the frontstretch just 2.16 seconds in front of Ralph Hepburn to win his first "500". The latter part of the race got a bit hectic for Shaw as his car almost ran out of oil and the rear tires showed a wide breaker strip. Shaw had to reduce his speed to save the tires and engine and hard-charging Hepburn made up a lap and a half disadvantage in the last twenty laps of the race. "Hep" caught Shaw in the last turn but Shaw won with a final burst of speed. Hepburn had received some excellent relief work from Bob Swanson after being temporarily overcome by a broiling sun. Though the race was free from accidents, the practice sessions claimed three lives. Frank McGurk crashed into the infield in the southwest turn. Mechanic Albert Opalko died of injuries and McGurk was seriously hurt. Coming down the frontstretch, Overton "Bunny" Phillips had the crankshaft break on his Duesenberg. The car, in which Mark Billman had died in 1933, spun, narrowly missed Shaw's car and struck a group of people servicing the Ray 8 Special on the pit apron. Otto Rhode, of the Champion Spark Plug Co., and George Warford, a fireman, were killed.

Wilbur Shaw

NO.	DRIVER	CAR	ENTRANT	ENGINE	CYL.	DISP.	CHASSIS	COLOR	QUAL. SPEED	ST.	FIN.	LAPS/SPEED/REASON OUT
6	Wilbur Shaw	Shaw-Gilmore	W. Wilbur Shaw	Offy	4	255	Shaw	cream, red	122.791	2	1	200-113.580
8	Ralph Hepburn	Hamilton-Harris	Louis Meyer	Offy	4	255	Stevens	red, white	118.809	6	2	200-113.565
3	Ted Horn	Miller-Hartz	Harry Hartz	Miller*¢	8	182	Wetteroth	gray, blue	118.608	32	3	200-113.434
2	Lou Meyer	Boyle	H. C. Henning	Miller	8	268	Miller	silver, red	119.619	5	4	200-110.730
45	Cliff Bergere	Midwest Red Lion	George H. Lyons	Offy	4	255	Stevens	cream, red	117.546	16	5	200-108.935
16	Bill Cummings	Boyle	H. C. Henning	Offy¢	4	255	Miller	silver, red	123.455	1	6	200-107.124
28	Billy DeVore	Miller	H. E. Winn	Miller	4	255	Stevens	white, black	120.192	14	7	200-106.995
38	Tony Gulotta	Burd Piston Ring	Joe Lencki	Offy	4	255	Rigling	yellow, red	118.788	7	8	200-105.015
17	George Connor	Marks Miller	Joe Marks	Miller	4	265	Adams	maroon, silver	120.240	12	9	200-103.830
53	Louis Tomei	Sobonite Plastics	S. S. Engineering Co.	Studebaker	8	336	Rigling	maroon	116.437	18	10	200-101.825
31	Chet Gardner	Burd Piston Ring	Chester Gardner	Offy	4	255	Duesenberg	lt. blue, red	117.342	9	11	199-flagged
23	Ronney Householder	Topping	Henry J. Topping, Jr.	Miller	4	234		white, red	116.464	10	12	194-flagged
62	Floyd Roberts	Thorne	Joel Thorne, Inc.	Miller	4	269	Miller	blue, white	116.996	17	13	194-flagged
35	Deacon Litz	Motorola	A. B. Litz	Miller	4	220	Miller	yellow, black	116.372	11	14	191-out of oil
32	Floyd Davis	Thorne	Joel Thorne, Inc.	Miller	4	255	Snowberger	blue, silver	118.942	24	15	190-wrecked NE
34	Shorty Cantlon	Bowes Seal Fast	Bill White Race Cars, Inc.	Miller	4	228	Weil	red, silver	118.555	25	16	182-flagged
42	Al Miller	Thorne	Joel Thorne, Inc.	Miller	4	255	Snowberger	blue, white	118.518	26	17	170-carburetor
1	Mauri Rose	Burd Piston Ring	Lou Moore	Offy	4	270	Miller	red, black, silver	118.540	8	18	127-oil line
41	Ken Fowler	Lucky Teeter	E. M. "Lucky" Teeter	McDowell	4	233	Wetteroth	yellow	117.421	29	19	116-disqualified, pushed
25	Kelly Petillo	Petillo	Kelly Petillo	Offy	4	318	Wetteroth	blue, silver	124.129	20	20	109-out of oil
43	George Bailey	Duray-Sims	Sims & Duray	Miller*	4	220	Stevens	brown	117.497	28	21	107-clutch
54	Herb Ardinger	Chicago Raw Hide Oil Seal	Lewis W. Welch	Offy*	4	255	Welch	copper	121.983	3	22	106-con. rod
24	Frank Brisko	Elgin Piston Pin	Frank Brisko	Brisko¢	6	350	Stevens	maroon silver	118.213	15	23	105-no oil pressure
44	Frank Wearne	Duray	Leon Duray	Miller*	4	220	Stevens	black, white	118.220	33	24	99-carburetor
26	Tony Willman	F.W.D.	Peter DePaolo	Miller 4	4	255	Miller	white, red	118.242	27	25	95-con. rod
10	Billy Winn	Miller	James M. Winn	Miller	4	255	Miller	white	119.922	4	26	85-oil line
12	Russ Snowberger	R.S.	Russ Snowberger	Packard*¢	8	282	Snowberger	brown	117.354	30	27	66-clutch
33	Bob Swanson	Fink	Paul Weirick	Sparks	4	269	Adams	blue, silver	121.920	21	28	52-carburetor
47	Harry McQuinn	Sullivan-O'Brien	Thomas O'Brien	Miller*	4	247	Stevens	white, red	121.822	22	29	47-piston
7	Chet Miller	Boyle	H. C. Henning	Miller¢	8	154	Summers	silver, red	119.213	13	30	36-ignition
15	Babe Stapp	Topping	Henry J. Topping, Jr.	Maserati*	8	305	Maserati	white, red	117.226	31	31	36-clutch
5	Jimmy Snyder	Sparks	Joel Thorne, Inc.	Sparks*	6	337	Adams	blue, white	125.287	19	32	27-transmission
14	Rex Mays	Bowes Seal Fast	Bill White Race Cars, Inc.	Alfa Romeo*	8	232	Alfa Romeo	red, silver	119.968	23	33	24-overheating

*Supercharged   ¢Front drive   4Four wheel drive

Ralph Hepburn

Ted Horn

Lou Meyer

Cliff Bergere

Bill Cummings

Billy DeVore

Tony Gulotta

George Connor

Louis Tomei

Chet Gardner

Ronney Householder

Floyd Roberts

Deacon Litz

Floyd Davis

Shorty Cantlon

Al Miller

Mauri Rose

Ken Fowler

Kelly Petillo

George Bailey

Herb Ardinger

Frank Brisko

Frank Wearne

Tony Willman

Billy Winn

Russell Snowberger

Bob Swanson

Harry McQuinn

Chet Miller

Babe Stapp

Jimmy Snyder

Rex Mays

Top, left: Lee Oldfield with his rear-engined Marmon which was the first rear-engined car to be entered in the "500". It was late arriving at the track and couldn't be prepared in time to qualify. Top, right: Takio "Chickie" Hirashima working on the 6-cylinder Sparks engine which powered the Sparks Special, entered by millionaire sportsman Joel Thorne. When qualifying the car, Jimmy Snyder broke Leon Duray's 10-year-old track record. Middle: The wreckage of the Mannix and Ray 8 Specials. The Mannix, driven by Overton Phillips, broke a crankshaft on the starting line during practice and the car, out of control, spun into the pits, striking the Ray 8 which was being worked on by its crew. Two onlookers were killed and several were seriously injured. Bottom: Wilbur Shaw and Jigger Johnson in Victory Lane.

Below, left: Frank McGurk's Belanger Special after it crashed at the end of the front-stretch during practice, fatally injuring riding mechanic Alex Opalko. Below, right: The starting field of cars on the backstretch during the pace lap. Bottom: The winner Wilbur Shaw in his Shaw-Gilmore Special.

1938

Though Wilbur Shaw was usually quite adept at predicting the speed necessary to win the "500", he miscalculated the potential of Floyd Roberts and his new Burd Piston Ring Special by almost two miles an hour and had to be content with second place. Shaw drove according to his preconceived plan but was never able to catch the flying black and red speedster with the rotund Californ-ian at the wheel. Starting on the pole, Roberts let Rex Mays lead the first few laps but took command by the 200-mile mark. His only pit stop put Jimmy Snyder in the lead but Roberts was back in front at 375 miles when Snyder was forced to stop. Supercharger trouble finally caused Snyder to retire. Chet Miller was running second until five miles from the finish when he made a pit stop, thereby giving second place to Shaw, who was three laps behind Roberts. As fourth place finisher, Ted Horn crossed the line, rain began to fall and the remaining cars finished under the yellow flag. One serious accident resulted in the death of spectator Everett Spence. Emil Andres hit the wall coming out of the southeast turn and rolled over three times into the infield, a wheel from Andres' car strik-ing Spence. Later, Ira Hill hit the wall but was uninjured.

Floyd Roberts

NO.	DRIVER	CAR	ENTRANT	ENGINE	CYL.	DISP.	CHASSIS	COLOR	QUAL. SPEED	ST.	FIN.	LAPS/SPEED/REASON OUT
23	Floyd Roberts	Burd Piston Ring	Lou Moore	Miller	4	270	Wetteroth	red, black, silver	125.681	1	1	200-117.200
1	Wilbur Shaw	Shaw	W. Wilbur Shaw	Offy	4	256	Shaw	cream, red	120.987	7	2	200-115.580
3	Chet Miller	I.B.E.W.	Boyle Racing Headquarters	Offy¢	4	255	Summers	maroon	121.898	5	3	200-114.946
2	Ted Horn	Miller-Hartz	Harry Hartz	Miller*¢	8	182	Wetteroth	gray, blue	121.327	6	4	200-112.203
38	Chet Gardner	Burd Piston Ring	Joe Lencki	Offy	4	257	Rigling	yellow, red, silver	120.435	18	5	200-110.311
54	Herb Ardinger	Offenhauser	Lewis W. Welch	Offy¢	4	255	Miller-Ford	black, white	119.022	14	6	199-109.843
45	Harry McQuinn	Marchese	Carl Marchese	Miller	8	151	Marchese	white	119.492	25	7	197-108.694
58	Billy DeVore	P.R.&W.	Joel Thorne, Inc.	Offy	4	255	Stevens	cream, red	116.339	30	8	185-102.080
22	Joel Thorne	Thorne Engineering	Joel Thorne, Inc.	Offy¢	4	256	Shaw	blue, silver	119.155	13	9	185-102.009
29	Frank Wearne	Indiana Fur	Paul Weirick	Offy	4	270	Adams	blue, silver	121.405	17	10	181- 99.543
43	Duke Nalon	Kohlert-Miller	Henry Kohlert	Miller	8	154	Fengler	red, gold	113.828	33	11	178-flagged
12	George Bailey	Barbasol	Leon Duray	Duray*	4	182	Weil	red, blue, white	116.393	29	12	166-clutch
27	Mauri Rose	I.B.E.W.	Boyle Racing Headquarters	Maserati*	6	91	Maserati	maroon	119.796	9	13	165-supercharger
16	Ronney Householder	Thorne-Sparks	Joel Thorne, Inc.	Sparks*	6	179	Adams	blue, white	125.769	10	14	154-supercharger hose
6	Jimmy Snyder	Sparks-Thorne	Joel Thorne, Inc.	Sparks*	6	179	Adams	blue, white	123.506	15	15	150-supercharger
5	Lou Meyer	Bowes Seal Fast	Bowes Racing, Inc.	Winfield*	8	179	Stevens	ivory, black, red	120.525	12	16	149-oil pump
17	Tony Gulotta	Hamilton-Harris	Tony Gulotta	Offy	4	255	Stevens	red, white	122.499	4	17	130-con. rod
55	Al Miller	Domont's Pepsi-Cola	Jack Holly	Miller	4	255	Miller	bluish gray, red	119.420	22	18	125-clutch
15	George Connor	Marks-Miller	Joseph Marks	Miller	8	272	Adams	maroon	120.326	19	19	119-engine trouble
9	Cliff Bergere	Kraft's Real Rye	George H. Lyons	Miller*	8	151	Stevens	yellow, red	114.464	32	20	111-piston
33	Henry Banks	Kimmel	Louis Kimmel	Voelker	12	273	Miller	blue	116.279	31	21	109-rod bearing
35	Kelly Petillo	Petillo	Kelly Petillo	Offy	4	271	Wetteroth	blue, silver	119.827	21	22	100-camshaft
21	Louis Tomei	P.O.B. Perfect Seal	H. E. Winn	Miller	4	255	Miller	white	121.599	24	23	88-con. rod
7	Bill Cummings	I.B.E.W.	Boyle Racing Headquarters	Miller¢	8	268	Miller	maroon, silver	122.393	16	24	72-radiator tank leak
14	Russ Snowberger	D-X	Russell Snowberger	Miller¢	4	255	Snowberger	tan	124.027	2	25	56-con. rod
34	Babe Stapp	McCoy Auto Service	Bill White Race Cars, Inc.	Miller	4	228	Weil	red	120.595	8	26	54-valve
10	Tony Willman	Belanger	Murrell Belanger	Miller	4	247	Stevens	blue	118.458	26	27	47-valve
8	Rex Mays	Alfa-Romeo	Bill White Race Cars, Inc.	Alfa-Romeo*	8	182	A. R.-Weil	red, silver	122.845	3	28	45-supercharger
42	Emil Andres	Elgin Piston Pin	Elgin Piston Pin Co.	Brisko	6	272	Adams	white, black	117.126	28	29	45-wrecked SE
37	Ira Hall	Greenfield Super Service	Nowiak & Magnee	Studebaker	8	250	Nowiak	white, blue	118.255	27	30	44-eng. seized, hit wall NE
26	Frank Brisko	Shur-Stop Brake Equalizer	Frank Brisko	Brisko¢	6	271	Stevens	red, white	121.921	11	31	39-oil line
36	Al Putnam	Troy Tydol	Arthur M. Sims	Miller	4	220	Stevens	orange, black	116.791	23	32	15-crankshaft
47	Shorty Cantlon	Kamm's	Thomas O'Brien	Miller*	4	247	Stevens	black, white, red	120.906	20	33	13-supercharger loose

*Supercharged   ¢Front Drive

Wilbur Shaw

Chet Miller

Ted Horn

Chet Gardner

Herb Ardinger

Harry McQuinn

Billy DeVore

Joel Thorne

Frank Wearne

Duke Nalon

George Bailey

Mauri Rose

Ronney Householder

Jimmy Snyder

Lou Meyer

Tony Gulotta

Al Miller

George Connor

Cliff Bergere

Henry Banks

Kelly Petillo

Louis Tomei

Bill Cummings

Russell Snowberger

Babe Stapp

Tony Willman

Rex Mays

Emil Andres

Ira Hall

Frank Brisko

Al Putnam

Shorty Cantlon

Right: Winner Floyd Roberts, who first gained prominence on the banks of famed Legion Ascot Speedway in Los Angeles, California. Bottom: Floyd Roberts pulls his Burd Piston Ring Special into Victory Lane.

Left: The Hudson pace car pulls over to the apron as Seth Klein waves the green flag. Winner Floyd Roberts is on the pole. Below, left: A happy Floyd Roberts waves to photographers in Victory Lane. Below, middle: The engine in Lou Meyer's Bowes Seal Fast Special which was designed by Bud Winfield. Below, right: The famous Italian driver Tazio Nuvolari was a popular visitor to the Speedway and here he poses at the wheel of Lou Meyer's car.

Above, left: Winner Floyd Roberts in his Burd Piston Ring Special. Above, right: Jimmy Snyder tries out the seat in the new Joel Thorne car he was to drive, as Rex Mays looks on. Bottom: Harry Miller in one of the radical rear-engined, 6-cylinder cars he designed and built for the Gulf Oil Company. These were the last cars built by Miller and, though revolutionary in many respects, they were not particularly successful.

1939

Wilbur Shaw joined the exclusive ranks of the two-time winners after an action-packed speed duel with Lou Meyer which led to the latter's 197th lap crash and eventual retirement from racing. Held down by a tragic three-car accident that claimed the life of 1938 winner, Floyd Roberts, the speed was far below the 1938 mark set by Roberts. Heavyfooted Jimmy Snyder led the first 100 miles but when he made a pit stop, Shaw took over with Meyer in hot pursuit. Meyer gained the lead, but was passed by Snyder just before the halfway mark. On his 107th lap, Bob Swanson, driving relief for Ralph Hepburn, spun coming into the backstretch. Roberts, directly behind, struck Swanson's car which turned over and burst into flames, throwing Swanson to the track. Roberts' car jumped the outer rail and the impact broke his neck. Chet Miller flipped into the infield to avoid the prostrate Swanson. Swanson wasn't seriously injured but Miller spent many weeks in the hospital. When the green flag finally came out, Meyer was leading Shaw and Snyder. Shaw made his bid and, with 40 miles to go, shot into the lead. Meyer, giving chase, spun and shredded a tire. Although now a lap behind Meyer kept going until he hit the inner rail and was thrown from his car.

Wilbur Shaw

NO.	DRIVER	CAR	ENTRANT	ENGINE	CYL.	DISP.	CHASSIS	COLOR	QUAL. SPEED	ST.	FIN.	LAPS/SPEED/REASON OUT
2	Wilbur Shaw	Boyle	Boyle Racing Headquarters	Maserati*	8	183	Maserati	maroon, cream	128.977	3	1	200-115.035
10	Jimmy Snyder	Thorne Engineering	Joel Thorne, Inc.	Sparks*	6	182	Adams	blue, white	130.138	1	2	200-114.245
54	Cliff Bergere	Offenhauser	Lewis W. Welch	Offy¢	4	270	Miller-Ford	beige, red	123.835	10	3	200-113.698
4	Ted Horn	Boyle	Boyle Racing Headquarters	Miller¢	8	268	Miller	maroon	127.723	4	4	200-111.879
31	Babe Stapp	Alfa Romeo	Bill White Race Cars, Inc.	Alfa Romeo*	8	181	A. R.-Weil	red, silver	125.000	16	5	200-111.230
41	George Barringer	Bill White	Bill White Race Cars, Inc.	Offy	4	228	Weil	red	120.935	15	6	200-111.025
8	Joel Thorne	Thorne Engineering	Joel Thorne, Inc.	Sparks	6	272	Adams	blue, white	122.177	20	7	200-110.416
16	Mauri Rose	Wheeler's	W. Wilbur Shaw	Offy	4	256	Shaw	yellow, red	124.896	8	8	200-109.544
14	Frank Wearne	Burd Piston Ring	Moore & Roberts	Offy	4	270	Wetteroth	black, red	125.074	17	9	200-107.806
26	Billy DeVore	Leon Duray-Barbasol	Leon Duray	Duray*	4	182	Weil	white, red, blue	116.527	33	10	200-104.267
62	Tony Gulotta	Burd Piston Ring	George Lyons	Offy	4	259	Stevens	yellow, red	121.749	27	11	200-103.938
45	Lou Meyer	Bowes Seal Fast	Bowes Racing, Inc.	Winfield*	8	179	Stevens	ivory, black, red	130.067	2	12	197-wrecked BS
18	George Connor	Marks	Joseph Marks	Offy	4	255	Adams	white, red	123.208	12	13	195-stalled
51	Tony Willman	Burd Piston Ring	Joe Lencki	Lencki	6	270	Lencki	yellow, red, silver	122.771	26	14	188-fuel pump
58	Louis Tomei	Alfa-Romeo	Frank T. Griswold	Alfa Romeo*	8	264	Alfa Romeo	red	118.426	30	15	186-flagged
15	Rex Mays	Thorne Engineering	Thorne Engineering Corp.	Sparks*	6	182	Adams	blue, white	126.413	19	16	145-rings
9	Herb Ardinger	Miller-Hartz	Harry Hartz	Miller*¢	8	182	Wetteroth	gray, blue	124.125	9	17	141-clutch
35	Kelly Petillo	Kay Jewelers	Kelly Petillo	Offy	4	270	Wetteroth	brown, silver	123.660	24	18	141-two broken pistons
49	Mel Hansen	Joel Thorne, Inc.	Joel Thorne, Inc.	Offy¢	4	270	Shaw	blue, white	121.683	14	19	113-hit pit wall
38	Harry McQuinn	Elgin Piston Pin	F. Burren	Brisko	6	271	Blume	white	117.287	32	20	110-ignition
3	Chet Miller	Boyle	Boyle Racing Headquarters	Miller¢	4	255	Summers	maroon	126.318	5	21	107-wrecked BS
25	Ralph Hepburn	Hamilton-Harris	Anthony Gulotta	Offy	4	270	Stevens	red, white	122.204	13	22	107-wrecked BS
1	Floyd Roberts	Burd Piston Ring	Lou Moore, Inc.	Offy	4	270	Wetteroth	red, black, silver	128.968	23	23	106-wrecked BS
37	Ira Hall	Greenfield Super Service	Magnee & Nowiak	Studebaker	8	271	Nowiak	white, blue	121.188	18	24	89-head gasket
21	Russ Snowberger	D-X	Russell Snowberger	Miller¢	4	258	Snowberger	brown	123.199	25	25	50-leaking radiator
17	George Bailey	Miller	Harry A. Miller	Miller*R4	4	180	Miller	silver, red	125.821	6	26	47-valve
56	Floyd Davis	W. B. W.	Ed Walsh	Offy	4	255	Miller	blue	119.375	29	27	43-shock absorber
42	Al Miller	Kennedy Tank	Paul Weirick	Offy	4	270	Adams	blue, silver	123.233	28	28	41-accel. pedal bracket
29	Frank Brisko	National Seal	Frank Brisko	Brisko¢	6	272	Stevens	gray, gold	123.351	11	29	38-air pump
44	Emil Andres	Chicago Flash	Jimmy Snyder	Offy	4	255	Stevens	maroon, white	121.212	21	30	22-stripped plug threads
32	Bob Swanson	S.M.I.	Sampson Motors, Inc.	Sampson*	16	183	Stevens	cream, blue	129.431	22	31	19-rear axle
47	Shorty Cantlon	Automotive Service	Associated Enterprises, Ltd.	Offy	4	262	Stevens	silver	125.567	7	32	15-main bearing
53	Deacon Litz	Maserati	Richard T. Wharton	Maserati*	8	182	Maserati	silver, black	117.979	31	33	7-valve

*Supercharged   ¢Front drive   4Four wheel drive   RRear engine

Jimmy Snyder

Cliff Bergere

Ted Horn

Babe Stapp

George Barringer

Joel Thorne

Mauri Rose

Frank Wearne

Billy DeVore

Tony Gulotta

Lou Meyer

George Connor

Tony Willman

Louis Tomei

Rex Mays

Herb Ardinger

Kelly Petillo

Mel Hansen

Harry McQuinn

Chet Miller

Ralph Hepburn

Floyd Roberts

Ira Hall

Russell Snowberger

George Bailey

Floyd Davis

Al Miller

Frank Brisko

Emil Andres

Bob Swanson

Shorty Cantlon

Deacon Litz

Right: In this four-picture sequence, Lou Meyer spins coming out of the southeast turn while trying to overtake Wilbur Shaw on the 198th lap of the race. Meyer was thrown from his car when it collided with the inner rail but he was not seriously injured. After this accident Meyer decided to retire from racing, bringing to a close a very successful career as a driver and paving the way for an equally successful career as an engine manufacturer.

Left: Wilbur Shaw, who scored his second "500" victory. Below, left: 1938 winner, Floyd Roberts, working on the engine of his Burd Piston Ring Special which carried him to his death in a three-car crash on the backstretch. Below, right: The closely packed field of cars takes the green flag from Starter Seth Klein. Middle, left: Herb Ardinger in the Miller-Hartz Special which was one of the most consistent cars during the 1930's. Middle, right: The engine of the 16-cylinder Sampson Special which was basically two 91-cubic-inch Millers with a common crankcase. Originally conceived by 1926 "500" winner Frank Lockhart, the engine powered the Stutz Black Hawk in which Lockhart was fatally injured attempting to break the world's land speed record at Daytona Beach in 1928. Bottom, left: The engine and front end assembly of Wilbur Shaw's Maserati showing the two-stage Rootes supercharger. Bottom, right: The wrecked Barbasol Special after Ronney Householder crashed it into the creek in the southwest turn. The car was repaired and driven in the race by Billy DeVore.

1940

Wilbur Shaw drove perhaps the easiest won race of his illustrious career to take his third "500" and become the first man to win the race twice in succession. Again driving Mike Boyle's maroon Maserati, Shaw was aided considerably by rain which made it necessary to run the last 125 miles under the yellow flag which allowed no passing. Behind Shaw was a formidable array of drivers including Mauri Rose, Rex Mays and Ted Horn. This trio could have given Shaw some serious problems during the last few miles but their bid was thwarted just as Shaw's had been in 1935 when rain stopped him from pressing Kelly Petillo. The race was not devoid of thrills and several happened on the frontstretch in full view of the grandstand spectators who usually see few of the crashes. The most spectacular accident happened, however, in the southeast turn when Raul Riganti, the Argentine champion, spun into the inner rail and rolled twice onto the grass. He was thrown out but not seriously injured. A few laps later Tommy Hinnershitz had his crankshaft break in front of the pits. He smacked the wall several times and spun into the infield just beyond the first turn bridge. Hepburn and Nalon also had front chute trouble with a spin and blown engine respectively.

Wilbur Shaw

NO.	DRIVER	CAR	ENTRANT	ENGINE	CYL.	DISP.	CHASSIS	COLOR	QUAL. SPEED	ST.	FIN.	LAPS/SPEED/REASON OUT
1	Wilbur Shaw	Boyle	Boyle Racing Headquarters	Maserati*	8	179	Maserati	maroon, cream	127.065	2	1	200-114.277
33	Rex Mays	Bowes Seal Fast	Bowes Racing, Inc.	Winfield*	8	180	Stevens	ivory, black, red	127.850	1	2	200-113.742
7	Mauri Rose	Elgin Piston Pin	Lou Moore, Inc.	Offy	4	270	Wetteroth	orange, lt. blue	125.624	3	3	200-113.572
3	Ted Horn	Boyle	Boyle Racing Headquarters	Miller¢	8	268	Miller	maroon, cream	125.545	4	4	199-flagged
8	Joel Thorne	Thorne Donnelly	Joel Thorne, Inc.	Sparks	6	271	Adams	blue, white	122.434	10	5	197-flagged
32	Bob Swanson	Sampson	Sampson Motors, Inc.	Sampson*	16	183	Stevens	yellow, blue	124.882	20	6	196-flagged
9	Frank Wearne	Boyle	Boyle Racing Headquarters	Offy	4	257	Stevens	maroon, cream	123.216	7	7	195-flagged
31	Mel Hansen	Hartz	Harry Hartz	Miller*¢	8	182	Wetteroth	gray, blue	124.753	5	8	194-flagged
16	Frank Brisko	Elgin Piston Pin	Frank Brisko	Brisko¢	6	271	Stevens	red, white	122.716	8	9	193-flagged
49	Rene LeBegue	Lucy O'Reilly Schell	Lucy O'Reilly Schell	Maserati*	8	183	Maserati	blue, silver	118.981	31	10	192-flagged
41	Harry McQuinn	Hollywood Pay Day	Bill White Race Cars, Inc.	Alfa Romeo*	8	181	A. R.-Weil	silver	122.486	15	11	192-flagged
25	Emil Andres	Belanger-Folz	Murrell Belanger	Offy	4	255	Stevens	yellow, blue	122.963	22	12	192-flagged
28	Sam Hanks	Duray	Leon Duray	Duray*	4	182	Weil	black, white	123.064	14	13	192-flagged
6	George Barringer	Hollywood Pay Day	Bill White Race Cars, Inc.	Offy	4	255	Weil	gray, blue	121.889	16	14	191-flagged
42	Joie Chitwood	Kennedy Tank	Paul Weirick	Offy	4	270	Adams	blue, silver	121.757	26	15	190-flagged
26	Louis Tomei	Falstaff	Ed Walsh	Offy	4	270	Miller	blue, silver	119.980	18	16	190-exhaust pipe
34	Chet Miller	Alfa Romeo	Wharton-Dewart Motor Racing	Alfa Romeo*	8	183	Alfa Romeo	red, silver	121.392	27	17	189-flagged
14	Billy DeVore	Bill Holabird	W. Wilbur Shaw	Offy	4	256	Shaw	yellow	122.197	32	18	181-flagged
44	Al Putnam	Refinoil	Anthony Gulotta	Offy	4	255	Adams	green, white	120.818	28	19	179-flagged
61	Floyd Davis	Lencki	Joseph Lencki	Lencki	4	260	Lencki	blue, white	120.797	33	20	157-flagged
35	Kelly Petillo	Indiana Fur	Kelly Petillo	Offy	4	270	Wetteroth	brown, silver	125.331	13	21	128-rear main bearing
21	Duke Nalon	Marks	Joseph Marks	Offy	4	255	Silnes	maroon, silver	121.790	25	22	120-con. rod
17	George Robson	Keller	Marty Keller	Offy¢	4	255	Miller-Ford	black	122.562	23	23	67-shock absorber
24	Babe Stapp	Surber	Frederick K. Surber	Offy	4	262	Stevens	cream, red	123.367	12	24	64-oil line
36	Doc Williams	Quillen Bros. Refrigerator	Doc Williams	Miller¢	4	255	Cooper	blue, white	122.963	19	25	61-oil line
10	George Connor	Lencki	Joseph Lencki	Lencki	6	265	Lencki	red, yellow	124.585	17	26	52-con. rod
5	Cliff Bergere	Noc-Out Hose Clamp	Lou Moore, Inc.	Offy	4	270	Wetteroth	red, black, silver	123.673	6	27	51-oil line
38	Paul Russo	Elgin Piston Pin	Elgin Piston Pin Co.	Brisko	6	271	Blume	white	120.809	29	28	48-oil leak
54	Ralph Hepburn	Bowes Seal Fast	W. C. Winfield	Offy¢	4	270	Miller-Ford	white, black, red	123.860	21	29	47-steering frozen, spun
58	Al Miller	Alfa Romeo	Frank T. Griswold, Jr.	Alfa Romeo*	8	177	Alfa Romeo	maroon	120.288	30	30	41-clutch
19	Russ Snowberger	Snowberger	Russell Snowberger	Miller¢	4	255	Snowberger	dark blue, white	121.564	11	31	38-water pump
27	Tommy Hinnershitz	Marks Offenhauser	Joseph Marks	Offy	4	270	Adams	maroon, silver	122.614	9	32	32-crankshaft, hit wall FS
29	Raul Riganti	Maserati	Raul Riganti	Maserati*	8	183	Maserati	blue, yellow	121.827	24	33	24-wrecked SE

*Supercharged   ¢Front drive

Rex Mays

Mauri Rose

Ted Horn

Joel Thorne

Bob Swanson

Frank Wearne

Mel Hansen

Frank Brisko

Rene LeBegue

Harry McQuinn

Emil Andres

Sam Hanks

George Barringer

Joie Chitwood

Louis Tomei

Chet Miller

Billy DeVore

Al Putnam

Floyd Davis

Kelly Petillo

Duke Nalon

George Robson

Shorty Cantlon (qualifier)

Doc Williams

George Connor

Cliff Bergere

Paul Russo

Ralph Hepburn

Al Miller

Russell Snowberger

Tommy Hinnershitz

Raul Riganti

Above: The pace lap with the Studebaker leading the field through the southwest turn. Right: Three-time winner, Wilbur Shaw, who scored his second straight victory at the wheel of Mike Boyle's Maserati.

Below, left: Chet Miller and his mechanic discuss Chet's Alfa Romeo. Below, right: Rex Mays in the Bowes Seal Fast Special which carried him to second place. Though Mays was always among the leaders and four times sat on the pole with the fastest qualifying time, he was never able to win the race. Bottom: Argentinian Raul Riganti and his new Maserati which was owned by a group of Argentine sportsmen. Riganti was the first driver out of the race when he crashed into the infield on his 24th lap.

1941

An early morning fire, which destroyed several garages as well as one qualified race car, left Wilbur Shaw's Maserati unscathed, although there is a strong possibility that it cost him the race, as well as many painful days in the hospital with a crushed vertebra. A faulty wheel, whose warning chalk marks were washed off by fire hoses, collapsed on Shaw's 152nd lap just as he was nearing his third straight victory. The car spun and struck the wall in the southwest turn. With Shaw out of the running, the race went to little Mauri Rose who did a masterful job of relief driving in a Lou Moore-owned car which had been started by Floyd Davis. When Rose took over the wheel, after his original car withdrew because of spark plug trouble, Davis was running 14th but immediately Rose remedied this situation and was soon battling for first place. When Shaw crashed, Cliff Bergere became the leader although he couldn't keep up the pace and by the 425th mile, Rose was in the lead with Rex Mays second. Bergere, trying to go the distance without a pit stop, was ill from fumes and exhaustion and could do no better than fifth. Shortly after Shaw's accident, Everett Saylor was critically injured when he crashed into the infield in the northwest turn.

Floyd Davis

NO.	DRIVER	CAR	ENTRANT	ENGINE	CYL.	DISP.	CHASSIS	COLOR	QUAL. SPEED	ST.	FIN.	LAPS/SPEED/REASON OUT
16	Floyd Davis-M. Rose	Noc-Out Hose Clamp	Lou Moore, Inc.	Offy	4	270	Wetteroth	red, lt. blue	121.106	17	1	200-115.117
1	Rex Mays	Bowes Seal Fast	Bowes Racing, Inc.	Winfield*	8	180	Stevens	ivory, black, red	128.301	2	2	200-114.459
4	Ted Horn	T. E. C.	Art Sparks	Sparks*	6	181	Adams	blue, white	124.297	28	3	200-113.864
54	Ralph Hepburn	Bowes Seal Fast	Bowes Racing, Inc.	Novi*	8	180	Miller-Ford	ivory, black, red	120.653	10	4	200-113.631
34	Cliff Bergere	Noc-Out Hose Clamp	Cliff Bergere	Offy	4	270	Wetteroth	red, black	123.890	7	5	200-113.528
41	Chet Miller	Boyle	Boyle Racing Headquarters	Miller¢	8	268	Miller	maroon	121.540	9	6	200-111.921
15	Harry McQuinn	Ziffrin	Bill White	Alfa Romeo*	8	181	A. R.-Weil	maroon, gold	125.449	4	7	200-111.795
7	Frank Wearne	Bill Holabird	Arthur M. Sims	Offy	4	255	Shaw	yellow, red	123.890	6	8	200-110.818
45	Paul Russo	Leader Card	Carl Marchese	Miller*	8	137	Marchese	white	125.217	18	9	200-105.628
27	Tommy Hinnershitz	Marks	Joe Marks	Offy	4	270	Adams	maroon, silver	121.021	20	10	200-105.152
53	Louis Tomei	H-3	Hughes Bros.	Offy¢	4	255	Miller-Ford	black	121.074	24	11	200-104.926
55	Al Putnam	Schoof	Val Johnson	Offy	4	255	Wetteroth	orange, black	121.951	31	12	200-101.381
26	Overton Phillips	Phillips	Overton A. Phillips	Miller	8	269	Bugatti	blue, silver	116.298	26	13	187-flagged
25	Joie Chitwood	Blue Crown Spark Plug	Joe Lencki	Lencki	6	265	Lencki	blue, white	120.329	27	14	177-flagged
17	Duke Nalon	Elgin Piston Pin	Elgin Piston Pin Co.	Maserati*	8	183	Maserati	blue, orange	122.951	30	15	173-flagged
14	George Connor	Boyle	Boyle Racing Headquarters	Offy	4	257	Stevens	maroon	123.984	13	16	167-transmission
47	Everett Saylor	Bowles	Mark E. Bowles, M.D.	Offy	4	255	Weil	red, silver	119.860	12	17	155-wrecked NW
2	Wilbur Shaw	Boyle	Boyle Racing Headquarters	Maserati*	8	179	Maserati	maroon	127.836	3	18	151-wrecked SW
23	Billy DeVore	Hollywood PayDay Candy	Frederick K. Surber	Offy	4	272	Stevens	cream, red	121.770	8	19	121-con. rod
62	Tony Willman	Lyons	George Lyons	Offy	4	260	Stevens	yellow, red	123.920	25	20	117-con. rod
42	Russ Snowberger	Hussy's Sportsman Club	Russell Snowberger	Offy	4	255	Snowberger	dark blue	120.104	11	21	107-water pump
32	Deacon Litz	Sampson 16	Sampson Motors, Inc.	Sampson*	16	183	Stevens	yellow, blue	123.440	29	22	89-oil trouble
8	Frank Brisko	Zollner Piston	Frank Brisko	Brisko¢	6	271	Stevens	maroon, silver	123.381	22	23	70-valve spring
36	Doc Williams	Indiana Fur	Aero Marine Finishes Co.	Offy¢	4	255	Cooper	blue, white	124.014	5	24	68-radiator leak
10	George Robson	Gilmore Red Lion	Leon Duray	Duray*	4	182	Weil	black, silver	121.576	16	25	66-oil leak
3	Mauri Rose	Elgin Piston Pin	Lou Moore, Inc.	Maserati*	8	183	Maserati	orange, blue	128.691	1	26	60-spark plug trouble
22	Kelly Petillo	Air Lines Sandwich Shop	Kelly Petillo	Offy	4	270	Wetteroth	white, red, blue	124.417	19	27	48-con. rod
12	Al Miller	Miller	Eddie Offutt	Miller*4	6	180	Miller	blue, white	123.478	14	28	22-transmission
9	Mel Hansen	Fageol	Lou Fageol	Offy¢	4	270	Miller-Ford	white	124.599	21	29	11-con. rod
19	Emil Andres	Kennedy Tank	Joe Lencki	Lencki	6	265	Lencki	yellow, red	122.266	15	30	5-wrecked NE
5	Joel Thorne	Thorne Engineering	Joel Thorne, Inc.	Sparks	6	271	Adams	blue, white	121.163	23	31	5-wrecked NE
35	George Barringer	Miller	Eddie Offutt	Miller*4	6	180	Miller	blue, white	122.299			Destroyed in garage fire
28	Sam Hanks	Tom Joyce 7-Up	Ed Walsh Corp.	Offy	4	270	Kurtis	red	118.211			Wrecked day before race

*Supercharged   ¢Front drive   4Four wheel drive

Rex Mays

Ted Horn

Ralph Hepburn

Cliff Bergere

Chet Miller

Harry McQuinn

Frank Wearne

Paul Russo

Tommy Hinnershitz

Louis Tomei

Al Putnam

Overton Phillips

Joie Chitwood

Duke Nalon

George Connor

Everett Saylor

Wilbur Shaw

Billy DeVore

Tony Willman

Russell Snowberger

Deacon Litz

Frank Brisko

Doc Williams

George Robson

Mauri Rose

Kelly Petillo

Al Miller

Mel Hansen

Emil Andres

Joel Thorne

George Barringer

Sam Hanks

Below, left: Wilbur Shaw was thwarted in his bid for an unprecedented fourth victory when a rear wheel collapsed and he hit the southwest wall. He was leading the race at the time. Below, right: Cliff Bergere in the Noc-Out Hose Clamp Special he drove non-stop to finish fifth. It was the first time that a gas-powered car was able to complete the race without a pit stop. Bergere might have won the race had it not been for cockpit fumes and extreme fatigue which caused him to slow in the latter stages. Bottom: Mauri Rose, co-winner with Floyd Davis, in Victory Lane.

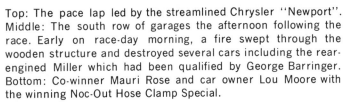

Top: The pace lap led by the streamlined Chrysler ''Newport''.
Middle: The south row of garages the afternoon following the
race. Early on race-day morning, a fire swept through the
wooden structure and destroyed several cars including the rear-
engined Miller which had been qualified by George Barringer.
Bottom: Co-winner Mauri Rose and car owner Lou Moore with
the winning Noc-Out Hose Clamp Special.

1946

The suspension of racing due to World War II seemed to have an adverse effect on much of the racing equipment which had been in storage for over four years. Quite the contrary, it did not have this effect on the throng of race-starved fans that caused a monumental traffic jam trying to gain access to the Speedway grounds. Under the new ownership of Tony Hulman and managed by Wilbur Shaw, the Speedway, in one race, regained its status of "The Greatest Race Course in the World". Although many of the cars fell by the wayside and only nine were running at the finish, the battle for first between George Robson and rookie Jimmy Jackson was excellent and it took all of Robson's skill to push Joel Thorne's car to the wire. Perhaps the most impressive performance was by Ralph Hepburn in the big blue Novi which, although dogged by trouble before dropping out on the 121st lap, captured the hearts of the huge crowd. Also of interest was the Fageol Twin Coach entry driven by Paul Russo which sported two Offy Midget engines: one in the front and one in the rear. Russo was running well until he crashed in the northeast turn and suffered a broken leg. Later, leader Mauri Rose hit the wall in almost the same spot and demolished his car.

George Robson

NO.	DRIVER	CAR	ENTRANT	ENGINE	CYL.	DISP.	CHASSIS	COLOR	QUAL. SPEED	ST.	FIN.	LAPS/SPEED/REASON OUT
16	George Robson	Thorne Engineering	Thorne Engineering Corp.	Sparks*	6	183	Adams	blue, white	125.541	15	1	200-114.820
61	Jimmy Jackson	Jackson	Jimmy Jackson	Offy¢	4	255	Miller	green, gold	120.257	5	2	200-114.498
29	Ted Horn	Boyle Maserati	Boyle Racing Headquarters	Maserati*	8	179	Maserati	red, white	123.980	7	3	200-109.819
18	Emil Andres	Elgin Piston Pin	Frank Brisko	Maserati*	8	183	Maserati	maroon, white, gold	121.139	11	4	200-108.902
24	Joie Chitwood	Noc-Out Hose Clamp	Fred A. Peters	Offy	4	270	Wetteroth	red, lt. blue, silver	119.816	12	5	200-108.399
33	Louis Durant	Alfa Romeo	Milt Marion	Alfa Romeo*	8	182	Alfa Romeo	red, white	118.973	6	6	200-105.073
52	Gigi Villoresi	Maserati	Corvorado Filippini	Maserati*	8	181	Maserati	red, silver	121.249	28	7	200-100.783
7	Frank Wearne	Wolfe Motors Co., Tulsa	Ervin Wolfe	Offy	4	271	Shaw	cream, red	121.233	29	8	197-flagged
39	Bill Sheffler	Jack Maurer	Bill Sheffler	Offy	4	255	Bromme	red, cream	120.611	25	9	139-flagged
17	Billy DeVore	Schoof	William Schoof	Offy	4	255	Wetteroth	orange, black	119.876	31	10	167-spun SW
41	Mel Hansen	Offenhauser	Ross Page	Duray*	4	183	Kurtis	maroon, white, silver	121.431	27	11	143-cranksnaft
25	Russ Snowberger	Jim Hussy's	R. A. Cott	Maserati*	8	183	Maserati	maroon, silver	121.593	10	12	134-differential
14	Harry McQuinn	Mobilgas	Robert J. Flavell	Sparks*	6	183	Adams	white, red	124.499	18	13	124-out of oil
2	Ralph Hepburn	Novi Governor	W. C. Winfield	Novi*¢	8	180	Kurtis	blue, red	133.944	19	14	121-stalled
12	Al Putnam	L.G.S. Spring Clutch	George L. Kuehn	Offy	4	255	Stevens	cream, blue	116.283	13	15	120-magneto, frame
3	Cliff Bergere	Noc-Out Hose Clamp	Shirley Bergere	Offy	4	270	Wetteroth	red, black, silver	126.471	1	16	82-out of oil
45	Duke Dinsmore	Johnston	Fred W. Johnston	Offy	4	255	Adams	maroon	123.279	8	17	82-con. rod
5	Chet Miller	Chet Miller	Chet Miller	Offy¢	4	255	Cooper	blue	124.649	17	18	64-oil line
63	Jimmy Wilburn	Mobiloil	Bill White	Alfa Romeo*	8	181	A. R.-Weil	red, white	125.113	16	19	52-engine trouble
42	Tony Bettenhausen	Bristow-McManus	Robert J. McManus	Miller*¢	8	183	Wetteroth	white	123.094	26	20	47-con. rod
59	Danny Kladis	Grancor V8	Grancor	Ford V8¢	8	274	Miller-Ford	blue, silver	118.890	33	21	46-towed, disqualified
54	Duke Nalon	Maserati	Corvorado Filippini	Maserati*	4	91	Maserati	red, silver	119.682	32	22	45-universal joint
8	Mauri Rose	Blue Crown Spark Plug	Joe Lencki	Lencki	6	265	Lencki	red, blue, silver	124.065	9	23	40-wrecked NE
38	George Connor	Walsh Offenhauser	Ed Walsh	Offy	4	270	Kurtis	red, yellow	120.006	30	24	38-piston
48	Hal Robson	Phillips Miller	Overton A. Phillips	Miller	8	269	Bugatti	blue	121.466	23	25	37-con. rod
15	Louis Tomei	Boxar Tool	Joseph Hosso	Brisko¢	6	271	Stevens	maroon, white	119.193	22	26	34-oil line
31	Henry Banks	Automobile Shippers	Louis Rassey	Offy¢	4	255	Snowberger	orange, black	120.220	21	27	32-stalled
64	Shorty Cantlon	H-3	Charles J. Hughes	Offy¢	4	255	Miller-Ford	black	122.432	20	28	28-clutch
26	George Barringer	Tucker Torpedo	George Barringer	Miller*4R	6	180	Miller	blue, white	120.628	24	29	27-gear trouble
1	Rex Mays	Bowes Seal Fast	Bowes Racing, Inc.	Winfield*	8	180	Stevens	ivory, black	128.861	14	30	26-manifold
32	Sam Hanks	Spike Jones	Gordon Schroeder	Sampson*	16	183	Stevens	cream, blue	124.762	3	31	18-oil line
47	Hal Cole	Don Lee	Don Lee, Inc.	Alfa Romeo*	8	177	Alfa Romeo	maroon	120.728	4	32	16-fuel leak
10	Paul Russo	Fageol Twin Coach	Lou Fageol	2 Offys*★	8	180	Fageol	red, blue, white	126.183	2	33	16-wrecked NE

*Supercharged   ¢Front drive   ★Twin engine; front drove rear wheels, rear drove front

Jimmy Jackson

Ted Horn

Emil Andres

Joie Chitwood

Louis Durant

Gigi Villoresi

Frank Wearne

Bill Sheffler

Billy DeVore

Mel Hansen

Russell Snowberger

Harry McQuinn

Ralph Hepburn

Al Putnam

Cliff Bergere

Duke Dinsmore

Chet Miller

Jimmy Wilburn

Tony Bettenhausen

Danny Kladis

Duke Nalon

Mauri Rose

George Connor

Hal Robson

Louis Tomei

Henry Banks

Shorty Cantlon

George Barringer

Rex Mays

Sam Hanks

Hal Cole

Paul Russo

Top: The first lap. Middle, left: Winner George Robson in his Thorne Engineering Special. Middle, right: Frank McGurk's wrecked Schoof Special after he hit the inside rail during practice. Right: "Gigi" Villoresi has the tires checked on his Maserati before going on the track for practice. This is one of the three Maserati factory entries.

Left: Anton "Tony" Hulman, Jr. who purchased the Speedway from the Rickenbacker interests and began the monumental task of building the rundown track into what is possibly the finest racing plant in the world. Below, left: President and General Manager Wilbur Shaw takes new owner, Tony Hulman, for a ride around the two-and-a-half-mile track in the Firestone tire test car. Below, middle: George Robson, in Victory Lane, is congratulated by Raymond Firestone. Below, right: Ralph Hepburn, in the Novi, breaking the track record during his qualifying run. His speed average was 133.944, five miles an hour faster than his closest competitor, Rex Mays.

Above, left: The start. Above, right: Rex Mays in his Bowes Seal Fast Special. Left: Wilbur Shaw and Cotton Henning let movie actor Donald O'Connor try the Boyle Maserati for size.

1947

A controversial end to an exciting race gave the railbirds some food for discussion for months to come; the Novi Team again showed it is a hard combination to beat; and racing lost one of its most popular veteran drivers. The green flag heralded a brilliant first lap record for Cliff Bergere in the thundering Novi although his lead was to be short-lived due to the terrific tire wear of the big heavy machine. Bill Holland, driving his first "500", shot into the lead when Bergere came into the pits and was running comfortably when the yellow light indicated an accident at the head of the frontstretch involving Paul Russo and Charlie Van Acker. No injuries but both cars were out. In the first turn, while still leading, Holland got sideways on the grass and then whipped back on the track in front of Shorty Cantlon who hit the wall and received fatal injuries. When Holland apparently had the race cinched, car owner Lou Moore gave both of his cars the "E-Z" sign on their pit boards. Holland slowed down considerably but Mauri Rose kept his pace and, as Holland waved, thinking himself a lap ahead, Rose took the lead on the 193rd lap. After Rose received the checker, a surprised and furious Bill Holland pulled in to demand an explanation from Lou Moore.

Mauri Rose

NO.	DRIVER	CAR	ENTRANT	ENGINE	CYL.	DISP.	CHASSIS	COLOR	QUAL. SPEED	ST.	FIN.	LAPS/SPEED/REASON OUT
27	Mauri Rose	Blue Crown Spark Plug	Lou Moore	Offy¢	4	270	Deidt	blue, white	124.040	3	1	200-116.338
16	Bill Holland	Blue Crown Spark Plug	Lou Moore	Offy¢	4	270	Deidt	blue, white	128.756	8	2	200-116.097
1	Ted Horn	Bennett Bros.	H. C. Henning	Maserati*	8	179	Maserati	black, gold	126.564	1	3	200-114.997
54	Herb Ardinger	Novi Governor Mobil	W. C. Winfield	Novi*¢	8	180	Kurtis	red, cream	120.733	4	4	200-113.404
7	Jimmy Jackson	Jim Hussey	H. C. Henning	Offy¢	4	258	Miller	green, gold	122.266	10	5	200-112.834
9	Rex Mays	Bowes Seal Fast	Bowes Racing, Inc.	Winfield*	8	180	Kurtis	black, white, red	124.412	20	6	200-111.056
33	Walt Brown	Permafuse	Milt Marion	Alfa Romeo*	8	182	Alfa Romeo	red, silver	118.355	14	7	200-101.744
34	Cy Marshall	Tattersfield	Bill White	Alfa Romeo*	8	183	A. R.-Weil	red, white	115.644	28	8	197-flagged
41	Fred Agabashian	Ross Page Offenhauser	Ross Page	Duray*	8	183	Kurtis	maroon, white	121.478	23	9	191-flagged
10	Duke Dinsmore	Schoof	Bill Schoof	Offy	4	270	Wetteroth	orange, black	119.840	27	10	167-flagged
58	Les Anderson	Kennedy Tank	Les Anderson	Offy	4	270	Wetteroth	red, white	118.425	7	11	131-flagged
59	Pete Romcevich	Camco Motors Ford	Anthony Granatelli	Ford V8¢	8	256	Miller-Ford	blue, red	117.218	17	12	168-mechanical failure
3	Emil Andres	Preston Tucker Partner	Joe Lencki	Lencki	6	265	Lencki	blue, white	116.781	30	13	150-magneto
31	Frank Wearne	Superior Industries	Louis Rassey	Offy	4	263	Miller	orange, black	117.716	15	14	128-spun NE
47	Ken Fowler	Don Lee Alfa Romeo	Don Lee, Inc.	Alfa Romeo*	8	177	Alfa Romeo	red, silver	123.423	9	15	121-axle
46	Duke Nalon	Don Lee Mercedes	Don Lee, Inc.	Mercedes*	12	183	Mercedes	silver, red	128.082	18	16	119-piston
28	Roland Free	Bristow-McManus	Robert J. McManus	Miller*¢	8	183	Wetteroth	white	119.526	12	17	87-spun SW
29	Tony Bettenhausen	Belanger	Murrell Belanger	Offy	4	255	Stevens	blue, gold	120.980	25	18	79-timing gear
25	Russ Snowberger	Federal Engineering	R. A. Cott	Maserati*	8	183	Maserati	maroon, silver	121.331	6	19	74-oil pump
52	Hal Robson	Palmer	Richard L. Palmer	Offy	4	255	Adams	blue, silver	122.096	16	20	67-transmission
18	Cliff Bergere	Novi Governor Mobil	W. C. Winfield	Novi*¢	8	180	Kurtis	cream, red	124.957	2	21	62-piston
8	Joie Chitwood	Peters	Fred Peters	Offy	4	270	Wetteroth	red, blue	123.157	22	22	51-gears
24	Shorty Cantlon	Automobile Shippers	Louis Rassey	Miller¢	16	272	Snowberger	orange, black	121.462	5	23	40-wrecked SW
43	Henry Banks	Federal Engineering	H. C. Henning	Offy¢	4	255	Miller-Ford	black, red	120.923	26	24	36-oil line
66	Al Miller	Preston Tucker	Clay Ballinger	Miller*4R	6	180	Miller	blue, red	124.848	19	25	33-magneto
14	George Connor	Walsh	Ed Walsh	Offy	4	255	Kurtis	red, yellow	124.874	13	26	32-leaking fuel tank
38	Mel Hansen	Flavell-Duffy	Robert J. Flavell	Sparks*	6	183	Adams	blue, white	117.298	29	27	32-pushed, disqualified
15	Paul Russo	Wolfe Motors, Tulsa	Ervin Wolfe	Offy	4	271	Shaw	red, black	123.967	21	28	24-wrecked FS
44	Charles Van Acker	Preston Tucker Partner	Joe Lencki	Lencki	4	265	Stevens	blue, white	121.049	24	29	24-wrecked FS
53	Milt Fankhouser	Jack Maurer's Club South.	Milt Fankhouser	Offy	4	272	Stevens	maroon, silver	119.932	11	30	16-stalled SE

*Supercharged   ¢Front drive   4Four wheel drive   RRear Engine

Bill Holland

Ted Horn

Herb Ardinger

Jimmy Jackson

Rex Mays

Walt Brown

Cy Marshall

Fred Agabashian

Duke Dinsmore

Les Anderson

Pete Romcevich

Emil Andres

Frank Wearne

Ken Fowler

Duke Nalon

Roland Free

Tony Bettenhausen

Russell Snowberger

Hal Robson

Cliff Bergere

Joie Chitwood

Shorty Cantlon

Henry Banks

Al Miller

George Connor

Mel Hansen

Paul Russo

Charles Van Acker

Milt Fankhouser

Below, left: Rex Mays in action through the southwest turn in his Bowes Seal Fast Special. Below, right: Mauri Rose, right, gives a bit of advice to Tony Hulman and Clark Gable. Bottom: As pit men stand by ready to give assistance, a group of cars roars into the first turn early in the race.

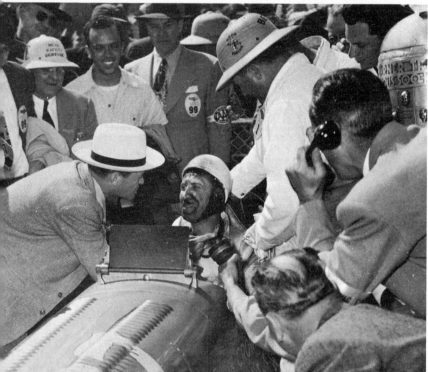

Top: The cars start to pull away from the starting line on the pace lap. Middle, left: General Manager Wilbur Shaw congratulates Mauri Rose in Victory Lane. Before the War, Shaw and Rose were intense competitors. Middle, right: Duke Nalon qualifies the Don Lee Mercedes as Henry Banks gets ready for his run in the No. 43 Federal Engineering Special. Bottom: Johnny Moore and his Firestone crew ready for action on race day.

1948

If Mauri Rose won the 1947 "500" under a cloud of doubt, his 1948 triumph was clear-cut. The daring little pilot drove his usual masterful race and, though Holland again finished second, there was no question that Rose had won on his own merits and without additional help from car owner Lou Moore. Rose's most serious opposition came from Duke Nalon in the powerful Novi, who led a great part of the race and was prevented from winning when an air pocket developed in his fuel tank making an unscheduled stop necessary near the end of the grind. The race was surprisingly free from accidents with Duane Carter being involved in the only one. Going into the second turn on his 60th lap, Carter, who was running sixth, lost his rear wheel and axle and spun. It took a fine job of driving to get the car stopped under these circumstances. Although the race was free from injuries, a pre-race practice session was marked with the death of veteran Ralph Hepburn who crashed one of the two Novis in the northeast turn. Cliff Bergere had earlier resigned his ride in the powerful car after a spin, stating that they were too dangerous to drive. While qualifying, rookie Andy Granatelli lost a wheel and crashed in the southeast turn, receiving a broken wrist.

Mauri Rose

NO.	DRIVER	CAR	ENTRANT	ENGINE	CYL.	DISP.	CHASSIS	COLOR	QUAL. SPEED	ST.	FIN.	LAPS/SPEED/REASON OUT
3	Mauri Rose	Blue Crown Spark Plug	Lou Moore	Offy¢	4	270	Deidt	blue, white	129.129	3	1	200-119.814
2	Bill Holland	Blue Crown Spark Plug	Lou Moore	Offy¢	4	270	Deidt	blue, white	129.515	2	2	200-119.147
54	Duke Nalon	Novi Grooved Piston	W. C. Winfield	Novi*¢	8	180	Kurtis	cream, black, red	131.603	11	3	200-118.034
1	Ted Horn	Bennett Bros.	H. C. Henning	Maserati*	8	179	Maserati	black, gold	126.565	5	4	200-117.844
35	Mack Hellings	Don Lee	Don Lee Division	Offy	4	270	KK2000	red	127.968	21	5	200-113.361
63	Hal Cole	City of Tacoma	Hal Cole	Offy	4	247	KK2000	cream, brown	124.391	14	6	200-111.587
91	Lee Wallard	Iddings	John Iddings	Offy	4	233	Meyer	blue, white	128.420	28	7	200-109.177
33	Johnny Mauro	Mauro Alfa Romeo	Johnny Mauro	Alfa Romeo*	8	182	Alfa Romeo	red	121.790	27	8	198-flagged
7	Tommy Hinnershitz	Kurtis-Kraft	Kurtis-Kraft, Inc.	Offy	4	270	Kurtis	red, silver	125.122	23	9	198-flagged
61	Jimmy Jackson	Howard Keck	Howard Keck Co.	Offy¢	4	270	Deidt	maroon, gold	127.510	4	10	193-spindle, spun
4	Charles Van Acker	South Bend	Walter A. Redmer	Offy	4	270	Stevens	blue, red, silver	125.440	12	11	192-flagged
19	Billy DeVore	Pat Clancy	Pat Clancy	Offy%	4	270	Kurtis	blue	123.967	20	12	190-flagged
98	Johnny Mantz	Agajanian	Smth & Jones Co.	Offy	4	270	KK2000	cream, red	122.791	8	13	185-flagged
6	Tony Bettenhausen	Belanger Motors	Murrell Belanger	Offy	4	270	Stevens	blue, gold	126.396	22	14	167-clutch
64	Hal Robson	Palmer Construction	Palmer Racing, Inc.	Offy	4	247	Adams	blue, white	122.796	18	15	164-valve
36	Bill Cantrell	Fageol Twin Coach	Lou Fageol	Fageol	6	273	Stevens	red, yellow	123.733	7	16	161-steering
55	Joie Chitwood	Nyquist	Ted Nyquist	Offy	4	268	Shaw	white, red	124.619	10	17	138-leaking fuel tank
53	Bill Sheffler	Sheffler Offy	Bayard T. Sheffler	Offy	4	270	Bromme	red, cream	124.529	24	18	132-spark plugs
5	Rex Mays	Bowes Seal Fast	Bowes Racing, Inc.	Winfield*	8	180	Kurtis	black, white, red	130.577	1	19	129-leaking fuel tank
31	Chet Miller	Don Lee Mercedes	Don Lee Division	Mercedes*	12	183	Mercedes	silver, red	127.249	19	20	108-oil trouble
52	Jack McGrath	Sheffler Offy	Bayard T. Sheffler	Offy	4	255	Bromme	red, white	124.580	13	21	70-stalled SE
16	Duane Carter	Belanger Motors	Murrell Belanger	Offy	4	270	Wetteroth	white, gold, red	126.015	29	22	59-lost wheel, spun SE
26	Fred Agabashian	Ross Page Offenhauser	Ross Page	Duray*	4	183	Kurtis	white, maroon, gold	122.737	32	23	58-oil line
34	Les Anderson	Kennedy Tank	Les Anderson	Offy	4	270	Kurtis	cream, red	122.337	9	24	58-gears
17	Mel Hansen	Schafer Gear Works	Paul Weirick	Sparks	4	177	Adams	red, silver	122.117	33	25	42-too slow, disqualified
76	Sam Hanks	Flavell	Robert J. Flavell	Sparks*	6	181	Adams	white, red	124.266	15	26	34-clutch
51	Spider Webb	Fowle Bros.	Louis Bromme	Offy	4	270	Bromme	white, black	125.545	30	27	27-oil line
9	George Connor	Bennett Bros.	H. C. Henning	Miller	8	268	Stevens	black, gold	123.018	17	28	24-drive shaft
74	Doc Williams	Clarke Motors	Ford Moyer	Offy¢	4	255	Cooper	blue, white	124.151	6	29	19-clutch
86	Mike Salay	Terman Marine Supply	John Lorenz	Offy	4	255	Wetteroth	blue, cream, gold	123.393	31	30	13-stalled NE
8	Emil Andres	Tuffy's Offy	C. George Tuffanelli	Offy	4	270	KK2000	maroon, gold	123.550	16	31	11-steering
25	Paul Russo	Federal Engineering	R. A. Cott	Maserati*	8	179	Maserati	maroon, silver	122.595	25	32	7-oil leak
65	Harry McQuinn	Frank Lynch Motors, Inc.	Gerald H. Brisko	Maserati*	8	183	Maserati	maroon, white	122.154	26	33	1-supercharger

*Supercharged   ¢Front drive   %Six-wheeler   KKKurtis-Kraft

Bill Holland

Duke Nalon

Ted Horn

Mack Hellings

Hal Cole

Lee Wallard

Johnny Mauro

Tommy Hinnershitz

Jimmy Jackson

Charles Van Acker

Billy DeVore

Johnny Mantz

Tony Bettenhausen

Hal Robson

Bill Cantrell

Joie Chitwood

Bill Sheffler

Rex Mays

Chet Miller

Jack McGrath

Duane Carter

Fred Agabashian

Les Anderson

Mel Hansen

Sam Hanks

Spider Webb

George Connor

Doc Williams

Mike Salay

Emil Andres

Paul Russo

Harry McQuinn

Below, left: The Novi arrives in Gasoline Alley and its crew begins the unloading operation. Although most cars arrive at the track on trailers, occasionally they are shipped by air or truck. In the days before good highways, most cars, as well as their drivers, traveled from track to track by train. Below, right: The start. Bottom: Winner Mauri Rose lets Mauri, Jr. sit in the Blue Crown in Victory Lane. When asked how he was going to celebrate his third ''500'' victory, Mauri replied, curtly''. . . by going back to work''.

Top, left: Ted Horn, one of the most consistent drivers in "500" history, finished fourth in his last race. On October 10, 1948, Ted was fatally injured when a front spindle broke during the 100-miler at DuQuoin, Illinois. Top, right: The chassis of a Kurtis-Kraft 2000, primarily built for use on dirt tracks but found suitable for "500" competition. Middle, left: The wreckage of Ralph Hepburn's Novi in which the popular veteran driver met his death in practice on May 15th. Middle, right: Ralph Hepburn in the Novi a few minutes before his fatal accident. Left: Rex Mays, right, and his faithful mechanic, Pete Clark, inspect their Bowes Seal Fast Special.

1949

After settling for second the two previous years, Bill Holland finally won the "500" following another battle with teammate Mauri Rose. In this race, Rose was a threat most of the way but Holland remained in command, and when Rose was forced out with eight laps to go, Holland had but to coast the remaining laps to win easily from rookie Johnnie Parsons and George Connor. For owner Lou Moore it was another remarkable triumph. Over the past seven races in which he had starters, Moore's cars finished first five times; second, twice; third, twice; and fifth and ninth, once each. At the end of the first lap, George Lynch spun, bouncing off the wall into the infield. Luckily the field of closely bunched cars was able to miss him. Lynch received a broken ankle. A few laps later, Charlie Van Acker spun, hit the inside rail and overturned in almost the same place on the frontstretch where he and Paul Russo crashed in 1947. Van Acker jumped from the car and signalled that he was O.K. On a qualifying day, a section of old Grandstand B collapsed and a score of fans was injured. In practice, George Metzler, driving Shaw's 1937 winning car, hit the wall in the southwest turn, and died of head injuries several days after the race.

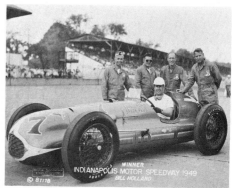

Bill Holland

NO.	DRIVER	CAR	ENTRANT	ENGINE	CYL.	DISP.	CHASSIS	COLOR	QUAL. SPEED	ST.	FIN.	LAPS/SPEED/REASON OUT
7	Bill Holland	Blue Crown Spark Plug	Lou Moore	Offy¢	4	270	Deidt	blue, white, red	128.673	4	1	200-121.327
12	Johnnie Parsons	Kurtis-Kraft	Kurtis-Kraft, Inc.	Offy	4	270	Kurtis	red, silver	132.900	12	2	200-119.785
22	George Connor	Blue Crown Spark Plug	Lou Moore	Offy	4	270	Lesovsky	blue, white	128.228	6	3	200-119.595
2	Myron Fohr	Marchese	Carl Marchese	Offy	4	270	Marchese	white, gold, black	129.776	13	4	200-118.791
77	Joie Chitwood	Wolfe	Ervin Wolfe	Offy	4	270	KK2000	yellow, black, red	126.863	16	5	200-118.757
61	Jimmy Jackson	Howard Keck	Howard Keck Co.	Offy¢	4	268	Deidt	maroon, gold	128.023	7	6	200-117.870
98	Johnny Mantz	Agajanian	J. C. Agajanian	Offy	4	270	KK2000	cream, red	127.786	9	7	200-117.142
19	Paul Russo	Tuffy's Offy	Charles Pritchard	Offy	4	270	KK2000	maroon, gold	129.487	19	8	200-111.862
9	Emil Andres	Tuffy's Offy	Charles Pritchard	Offy	4	243	Langley	maroon, gold	126.042	32	9	197-flagged
71	Norm Houser	Troy Oil Co.	Joe Langley	Offy	4	270	Wetteroth	red, cream	127.756	24	10	181-flagged
68	Jim Rathmann	Pioneer Auto	John Lorenz	Offy	4	270	Wetteroth	red, black	126.516	21	11	175-flagged
64	Troy Ruttman	Carter	Ray W. Carter	Offy	4	270	Deidt	blue, white	125.945	18	12	151-flagged
3	Mauri Rose	Blue Crown Spark Plug	Lou Moore	Offy¢	4	270	Stevens	blue, white, red	127.759	10	13	192-magneto strap
17	Duane Carter	Belanger	Murrell Belanger	Offy	4	270	Olson	blue, gold	128.233	5	14	182-steering, spun NE
29	Duke Dinsmore	Norm Olson	Norm Olson	Offy	4	270	KK2000	black, buff	127.750	15	15	174-radius rod
8	Mack Hellings	Don Lee	Don Lee Motors Corp.	Offy	4	270	Bromme	red, cream	128.260	14	16	172-valve
4	Bill Sheffler	Sheffler Offy	Bill Sheffler	Offy	4	233	Meyer	red, cream	128.521	22	17	160-con. rod
32	Johnny McDowell	Iddings	Henry Meyer	Offy	4	220	KK2000	red, silver	126.139	28	18	142-magneto
14	Hal Cole	Grancor	Grancor Auto Specialists	Sparks*	6	183	Adams	blue, silver	127.168	11	19	117-rod bearing insert
38	George Fonder	Ray Brady	Ray T. Brady	Offy	4	274	Kurtis	blue, silver	127.289	25	20	116-valve
74	Bill Cantrell	Kennedy Tank	Leslie M. Anderson	Offy%	4	270	Kurtis	maroon	127.191	30	21	95-drive shaft
57	Jackie Holmes	Pat Clancy	Pat Clancy	Maserati*	8	181	Maserati	blue, silver	128.087	17	22	65-drive shaft
6	Lee Wallard	Maserati	Indianapolis Race Cars, Inc.	Offy	4	270	KK2000	black, white	128.912	20	23	55-gears
69	Bayliss Levrett	Wynn's Oil	Bayliss Levrett	Novi*¢	8	180	Kurtis	cream, red	129.236	29	24	52-drain plug
5	Rex Mays	Novi Mobil	W. C. Winfield	Offy	4	247	KK2000	maroon, white	129.552	2	25	48-engine trouble
33	Jack McGrath	City of Tacoma	Leo Dobry	Maserati*	8	179	Maserati	black, white	128.884	3	26	39-oil pump
15	Fred Agabashian	Maserati	Indianapolis Race Cars, Inc.	Offy	4	255	Bromme	cream, red	127.007	31	27	38-overheating
52	Manuel Ayulo	Sheffler Offy	Bill Sheffler	Novi*¢	8	180	Kurtis	cream, red	125.799	33	28	24-con. rod
54	Duke Nalon	Novi Mobil	W. C. Winfield	Offy	4	270	KK2000	blue, white	123.939	1	29	23-rear axle, burned NE
18	Sam Hanks	Love Machine & Tool	Milt Marion	Offy	4	270	Stevens	red, white, silver	127.809	23	30	20-oil leak
10	Charley Van Acker	Redmer	Geneva Van Acker	Offy	4	270	Snowberger	orange, black	126.524	27	31	10-wrecked NW
26	George Lynch	Automobile Shippers	Louis Rassey	Offy	4	270	Bromme	black, red	127.823	8	32	1-wrecked SW
37	Spider Webb	Grancor	Lou & Bruce Bromme	Offy	4	270			127.002	26	33	0-transmission

*Supercharged   ¢Front drive   %Six wheel car

Johnnie Parsons

George Connor

Myron Fohr

Joie Chitwood

Jimmy Jackson

Johnny Mantz

Paul Russo

Emil Andres

Norm Houser

Jim Rathmann

Troy Ruttman

Mauri Rose

Duane Carter

Duke Dinsmore

Mack Hellings

Bill Sheffler

Johnny McDowell

Hal Cole

George Fonder

Bill Cantrell

Jackie Holmes

Lee Wallard

Bayliss Levrett

Rex Mays

Jack McGrath

Fred Agabashian

Manuel Ayulo

Duke Nalon

Sam Hanks

Charley Van Acker

George Lynch

Spider Webb

Top: Duke Nalon's flaming crash in the Novi after a rear axle broke and the car hit the northeast wall. The fuel tank ruptured and Nalon was seriously burned before he could jump over the crashwall to safety. Middle, left: Two promising rookies, Jim Rathmann and Pat Flaherty, in their "500" debuts. Although neither driver was able to qualify his original mount, Rathmann made the race in another car. Standing, left to right: unknown, A. J. Watson, Chuck Leighton, Dick Rathmann, sprint car driver Chet Bingham, and Andy Granatelli. Bottom: Stunt driver Joie Chitwood, in the Wolfe Special. Though primarily known by the Thrill Circus that bore his name, Chitwood was one of the top sprint car drivers of the 1930's and a consistent "500" performer.

Left: The start. Below, left: The wrecked Glessner Special in which George Metzler was fatally injured during a practice session when he hit the wall in the southwest turn. Below, middle: The Bowes Seal Fast Team with Mel Hansen in No. 44 and Kenny Eaton in No. 15. Neither car was able to make the starting lineup. Below, right: Firestone's Johnny Moore discusses a tire problem with Bill Cantrell.

Above, left: The contestants pose for the official picture just before the start. Wilbur Shaw is walking toward the camera. Above, right: Rear view of the rear-engined Rounds Rocket built by Emil Deidt, Lujie Lesovsky and Gordon Schroeder. Although it was a well-built, attractive car, it was never able to approach qualifying speeds. Left: Mechanics work on the Thorne Special. The car, which was driven by Joel Thorne, was the Don Lee Mercedes chassis with a 6-cylinder Sparks engine under the hood. It failed to qualify.

1950

The discovery of a small crack in his car's block caused Johnnie Parsons to change his race strategy and because of this change he was leading when the race was stopped by a cloudburst. It was planned for Parsons to go as hard and as long as possible while the engine held together and pick up as much lap money as he could for a sort of consolation prize. When the checkered flag was displayed as he completed his 138th lap, Parsons was still in front, the engine performing faultlessly and his closest competitor, Bill Holland, over a lap behind. Parsons' win heralded a new era which would see a group of drivers up from the ranks of the "Mighty Midgets" almost completely dominate the "500". Just as Legion Ascot Speedway had trained the chargers in the '30s, the United Racing Association and California Racing Association provided the biggest names in the 1950's. Rookie Walt Faulkner had surprised everyone by breaking the track record when qualifying J. C. Agajanian's dirt track car and the days of the heavy front-drives were numbered. Parsons' Kurtis Kraft literally ran away from the Blue Crowns and when the cloudburst struck, causing Jack McGrath and Jackie Holmes to spin, Lou Moore's two cars had been soundly beaten.

WINNER
INDIANAPOLIS MOTOR SPEEDWAY 1950
JOHNNIE PARSONS

Johnnie Parsons

NO.	DRIVER	CAR	ENTRANT	ENGINE	CYL.	DISP.	CHASSIS	COLOR	QUAL. SPEED	ST.	FIN.	LAPS/SPEED/REASON OUT
1	Johnnie Parsons	Wynn's Friction Proofing	Kurtis-Kraft, Inc.	Offy	4	270	Kurtis	yellow, silver	132.044	5	1	138-124.002
3	Bill Holland	Blue Crown Spark Plug	Lou Moore	Offy¢	4	270	Deidt	blue, white, red	130.482	10	2	137-122.638
31	Mauri Rose	Offenhauser	Howard Keck Co.	Offy¢	4	270	Deidt	blue, gold	132.319	3	3	137-121.778
54	Cecil Green	John Zink	M. A. Walker	Offy	4	270	KK3000	blue, white	132.910	12	4	137-121.766
17	Joie Chitwood	Wolfe	Ervin Wolfe	Offy	4	270	KK2000	red, white	130.757	9	5	136-121.755
8	Lee Wallard	Blue Crown Spark Plug	Lou Moore	Offy	4	270	Moore	blue, white, red	132.436	23	6	136-121.009
98	Walt Faulkner	Grant Piston Ring	J. C. Agajanian	Offy	4	270	KK2000	cream, red	134.343	1	7	135-121.094
5	George Connor	Blue Crown Spark Plug	Lou Moore	Offy	4	270	Lesovsky	blue, white, red	132.163	4	8	135-121.086
7	Paul Russo	Russo-Nichels	Paul Russo & Ray Nichels	Offy	4	270	Nichels	black, silver	130.790	19	9	135-119.961
59	Pat Flaherty	Granatelli-Sabourin	Grancor Auto. Specialists	Offy	4	270	KK3000	blue	129.608	11	10	135-119.952
2	Myron Fohr	Bardahl	Carl Marchese	Offy	4	270	Marchese	white, gold, black	131.714	16	11	133-flagged
18	Duane Carter	Belanger	Murrell Belanger	Offy*	4	176	Stevens	blue, gold	131.666	13	12	133-flagged
15	Mack Hellings	Tuffy's Offy	Charles Pritchard	Offy	4	270	KK2000	maroon, gold	130.687	26	13	132-flagged
49	Jack McGrath	Hinkle	Jack B. Hinkle	Offy	4	270	KK3000	maroon, silver	131.868	6	14	131-spun in rain NE
55	Troy Ruttman	Bowes Seal Fast	Bowes Racing, Inc.	Offy	4	270	Lesovsky	black, white, red	131.912	24	15	130-flagged
75	Gene Hartley	Troy Oil	Joe Langley	Offy	4	240	Langley	black, red, silver	129.213	31	16	128-flagged
22	Jim Davies	Pat Clancy	Pat Clancy	Offy	4	270	Ewing	blue, white	130.402	27	17	128-flagged
62	Johnny McDowell	Pete Wales	M. Pete Wales	Offy	4	235	KK2000	blue, silver	129.692	33	18	128-flagged
4	Walt Brown	Tuffy's Offy	Charles Pritchard	Offy	4	270	KK2000	maroon, gold	130.454	20	19	127-flagged
21	Spider Webb	Fadely-Anderson	R. A. Cott	Offy	4	270	Maserati	maroon	129.748	14	20	126-flagged
81	Jerry Hoyt	Morris	Ludson D. Morris, M.D.	Offy	4	270	KK2000	maroon, cream	129.520	15	21	125-flagged
27	Walt Ader	Sampson	Sampson Manufacturing Co.	Offy*	4	177	Rae	white, black	129.940	29	22	123-flagged
77	Jackie Holmes	Norm Olson	Norm Olson	Offy	4	270	Olson	buff, black	129.697	30	23	123-spun in rain NE
76	Jim Rathmann	Pioneer Auto Repair	John Lorenz	Offy	4	270	Wetteroth	black, red	129.959	28	24	122-flagged
12	Henry Banks	I. R. C.	Indianapolis Race Cars, Inc.	Offy*	4	180	Maserati	yellow, black	129.646	21	25	112-flagged
67	Bill Schindler	Automobile Shippers	Louis Rassey	Offy	4	270	Snowberger	orange, black	132.690	22	26	111-universal joint
24	Bayliss Levrett	Palmer	Richard L. Palmer	Offy	4	270	Adams	red, silver	131.181	17	27	108-lost oil pressure
28	Fred Agabashian	Wynn's Friction Proofing	Kurtis-Kraft, Inc.	Offy*	4	177	KK3000	yellow, silver	132.792	2	28	64-oil line
61	Jimmy Jackson	Cummins Diesel	Cummins Engine Co.	Cummins*	6	401	Kurtis	green, gold	129.208	32	29	52-supercharger
23	Sam Hanks	Merz Engineering	Milt Marion	Offy	4	270	KK2000	red	131.593	25	30	42-oil pressure
14	Tony Bettenhausen	Blue Crown Spark Plug	Lou Moore	Offy¢	4	270	Deidt	blue, white, red	130.947	8	31	30-wheel bearing
45	Dick Rathmann	City of Glendale	A. J. Watson	Offy	4	264	Watson	white, blue	130.928	18	32	25-stalled
69	Duke Dinsmore	Brown Motor Co.	Verlin Brown	Offy	4	270	KK2000	brown, white	131.066	7	33	10-oil leak

*Supercharged   ¢Front drive

Bill Holland

Mauri Rose

Cecil Green

Joie Chitwood

Lee Wallard

Walt Faulkner

George Connor

Paul Russo

Pat Flaherty

Myron Fohr

Duane Carter

Mack Hellings

Jack McGrath

Troy Ruttman

Gene Hartley

Jim Davies

Johnny McDowell

Walt Brown

Spider Webb

Jerry Hoyt

Walt Ader

Jackie Holmes

Jim Rathmann

Henry Banks

Bill Schindler

Bayliss Levrett

Fred Agabashian

Jimmy Jackson

Sam Hanks

Tony Bettenhausen

Dick Rathmann

Duke Dinsmore

Below, left: The front gate of the Speedway, at the corner of West 16th Street and Georgetown Road, as it appeared for many years. Below, right: The rickety old Pagoda long a trademark of the "Greatest Race Course in the World". Bottom: Winner Johnnie Parsons in the Wynn's Friction Proofing Special. Ed Walsh sold the car on race day to Jim Robbins, though Robbins received no share in the prize money.

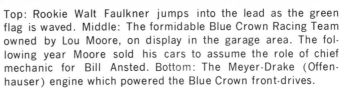

Top: Rookie Walt Faulkner jumps into the lead as the green flag is waved. Middle: The formidable Blue Crown Racing Team owned by Lou Moore, on display in the garage area. The following year Moore sold his cars to assume the role of chief mechanic for Bill Ansted. Bottom: The Meyer-Drake (Offenhauser) engine which powered the Blue Crown front-drives.

1951

After being shut out of the starting lineup in 1950, the Novi crew worked all winter to get their big powerful machines back in racing shape and this effort was rewarded when Duke Nalon set a new qualifying record. Their exuberance was short lived, however, as on the second weekend of time trials, Walt Faulkner beat their average by almost a half-mile an hour in a new Agajanian dirt track car built by Eddie Kuzma. During the race, their defeat was even more humiliating when Nalon was "blown off" on the start by Jack McGrath as well as by Lee Wallard, who was driving a car which appeared to be little more than a stretched midget with the smallest unsupercharged engine in the race. The end of the first lap found the ponderous Novi far back in the pack. After the lead changed hands a number of times in the first 50 miles, Wallard began building up a safe lead over Mike Nazaruk as the blistering pace and blazing sun played havoc with the majority of cars. On lap 126, Mauri Rose broke a wheel, spun, and flipped into the mud in the northeast turn. Although Rose was uninjured, he decided to hang up his goggles. Bettenhausen and Hanks also spun in the northeast turn. The month's only serious injury was sustained by Mike Salay in practice.

Lee Wallard

NO.	DRIVER	CAR	ENTRANT	ENGINE	CYL.	DISP.	CHASSIS	COLOR	QUAL. SPEED	ST.	FIN.	LAPS/SPEED/REASON OUT
99	Lee Wallard	Belanger	Murrell Belanger	Offy	4	241	Kurtis	blue, gold	135.039	2	1	200-126.244
83	Mike Nazaruk	Jim Robbins	J. M. Robbins	Offy	4	270	Kurtis	yellow, silver, red	132.183	7	2	200-125.302
9	Jack McGrath	Hinkle	Jack B. Hinkle	Offy	4	270	KK3000	maroon, silver	134.303	3	3	200-124.745
57	Andy Linden	Leitenberger	George H. Leitenberger	Offy	4	270	Sherman	white, red, black	132.226	31	4	200-123.812
52	Bob Ball	Blakely	John L. McDaniel	Offy	4	270	Schroeder	navy blue, white	134.098	29	5	200-123.709
1	Henry Banks	Blue Crown Spark Plug	Lindsey Hopkins	Offy	4	270	Moore	blue, red, white	133.899	17	6	200-123.304
68	Carl Forberg	Automobile Shippers	Louis Rassey	Offy	4	270	KK3000	orange, black	132.890	24	7	193-flagged
27	Duane Carter	Mobilgas	Rotary Engineering Corp.	Offy¢	4	272	Deidt	blue, white, red	133.749	4	8	180-flagged
5	Tony Bettenhausen	Mobiloil	Rotary Engineering Corp.	Offy¢	4	270	Deidt	blue, white, red	131.950	9	9	178-spun NW
18	Duke Nalon	Novi Purelube	Jean Marcenac	Novi*¢	8	181	Kurtis	white, blue	136.498	1	10	151-stalled BS
69	Gene Force	Brown Motor Co.	Brown Motor Co.	Offy	4	270	KK2000	brown, white, gold	133.102	22	11	142-lost oil pressure
25	Sam Hanks	Schmidt	Peter Schmidt	Offy	4	270	KK3000	red, silver	132.998	12	12	135-spun NE
10	Bill Schindler	Chapman	H. A. Chapman	Offy	4	270	KK2000	yellow, blue	134.033	16	13	129-con. rod
16	Mauri Rose	Pennzoil	Howard Keck Co.	Offy¢	4	270	Deidt	black, yellow, red	133.422	5	14	126-wheel collap., wreck NE
2	Walt Faulkner	Agajanian Grant Piston R.	J. C. Agajanian	Offy	4	270	Kuzma	cream, red	136.872	14	15	123-crankshaft
76	Jim Davies	Parks Offenhauser	L. E. Parks	Offy	4	270	Pawl	cream, red	133.516	27	16	110-rear end gears
59	Fred Agabashian	Granatelli-Bardahl	Grancor Auto. Specialists	Offy	4	270	KK3000	blue, silver	135.029	11	17	109-clutch
73	Carl Scarborough	McNamara	Lee Elkins	Offy	4	270	KK2000	red, cream, gold	135.614	15	18	100-axle
71	Bill Mackey	Karl Hall	Karl Hall	Offy	4	270		maroon, red, white, gold	131.473	33	19	97-clutch shaft
8	Chuck Stevenson	Bardahl	Carl Marchese	Offy	4	270	Marchese	white, black	133.764	19	20	93-caught fire NS
3	Johnnie Parsons	Rya. 's Friction Proofing	Ed Walsh	Offy	4	270	KK3000	yellow, silver, red	132.154	8	21	87-magneto
4	Cecil Green	John Zink	M. A. Walker	Offy	4	270	KK3000	dark yellow, white	131.892	10	22	80-con. rod
98	Troy Ruttman	Agajanian Featherweight	J. C. Agajanian	Offy	4	270	KK2000	cream, red	132.314	6	23	78-bearing
6	Duke Dinsmore	Brown Motors Co.	Brown Motors Co.	Offy	4	270	Schroeder	brown, gold	131.974	32	24	73-overheating
32	Chet Miller	Novi Purelube	Jean Marcenac	Novi*¢	8	181	Kurtis	white, blue	135.798	28	25	56-ignition
44	Walt Brown	Federal Engineering	Federal Engineering Assoc.	Offy	4	270	KK3000	tan, silver	131.907	13	26	55-magneto
48	Rodger Ward	Deck Manufacturing Co.	Louis & Bruce Bromme	Offy	4	270	Bromme	red, black	134.867	25	27	34-oil line
23	Cliff Griffith	Morris	Ludson D. Morris, M.D.	Offy	4	270	KK2000	red, white	133.839	18	28	30-axle
81	Bill Vukovich	Central Excavating	Pete Salemi	Offy	4	270	Trevis	blue, red, white	133.725	20	29	29-oil tank
22	George Connor	Blue Crown Spark Plug	Lou Moore	Offy	4	270	Lesovsky	blue, white, red	133.353	21	30	29-universal joint
19	Mack Hellings	Tuffanelli-Derrico	C. G. Tuffanelli & J. Derrico	Offy¢	4	270	Deidt	maroon, gold	123.925	23	31	18-piston
12	Johnny McDowell	W. J.	Maserati Race Cars	Offy*	4	180	Maserati	mahogony, orange	132.475	26	32	15-gas tank
26	Joe James	Bob Estes Lincoln-Mercury	Bob Estes	Offy	4	270	Watson	blue, white	134.098	30	33	8-drive shaft

*Supercharged ¢Front Drive

Mike Nazaruk

Jack McGrath

Andy Linden

Bob Ball

Henry Banks

Carl Forberg

Duane Carter

Tony Bettenhausen

Duke Nalon

Gene Force

Sam Hanks

Bill Schindler

Mauri Rose

Walt Faulkner

Jim Davies

Fred Agabashian

Carl Scarborough

Bill Mackey

Chuck Stevenson

Johnnie Parsons

Cecil Green

Troy Ruttman

Duke Dinsmore

Chet Miller

Walt Brown

Rodger Ward

Cliff Griffith

Bill Vukovich

George Connor

Mack Hellings

Johnny McDowell

Joe James

Below, left: Lee Wallard is hugged (but not kissed) by actress Loretta Young as Wilbur Shaw and Mrs. Wallard stand by. Sid Collins handles the WIBC microphone. Below, right: Early in the race Lee Wallard noses out Jack McGrath for the lead as Walt Faulkner trails in third place. Middle: The Lutes Special, wrecked in practice by Bill Boyd, is removed from the infield in the southeast turn. Bottom: While attempting to qualify, Bud Sennett spun into the infield in the southwest turn, rolled over and hit a tree. Though his Auto Accessories Special was badly battered, Sennett received only minor injuries.

Left: Lee Wallard makes a pit stop in his Belanger Special. Below, left: Chet Miller charges through the first turn during his qualifying run in the Novi. Below, right: Mechanic Frank "Stoogie" Glidden drives the Brown Motors No. 6 out onto the pit apron.

Above, left: Lee Wallard guides his Belanger Special down the frontstretch toward Victory Lane. When Wallard suffered near-fatal burns driving a sprint car a few days after his "500" victory, Tony Bettenhausen took over the driving chores and proceeded to win the 1951 National Championship in the blue and gold No. 99. Above, middle: When Mike Salay hit the wall in the southwest turn during practice, he was seriously injured. The car was even more seriously injured. Above, left: The time trials on the last weekend before the race were plagued with intermittent rains. Between showers, the unqualified cars flocked back to the track for much-needed practice. Bottom: The Novis await the start of the race as the Purdue Band entertains the spectators on the frontstretch.

1952

After an inauspicious debut in 1951, Bill Vukovich, up from the California midget ranks, showed one and all that he would be the man to beat in future races. The "Mad Russian", actually of Yugoslav parentage, exhibited one of the greatest competitive spirits in history, working his way up from eighth starting position to take command and lead an excellent field of drivers. Included in this group were rookies Art Cross, Jimmy Bryan, Jimmy Reece and Italian champion Alberto Ascari. Early in the race a battle started between Vukovich and big blond Troy Ruttman, the transplanted Oklahoman, who had risen to fame in the California hot rod ranks before he was old enough to drive on the highways. Ascari's Ferrari, while making a creditable showing, broke a wire wheel and spun into the infield in the northwest turn. Pressed by Jim Rathmann, who had charged up from the fourth row to make it a four abreast start, the Vukovich-Ruttman battle continued at fever pitch until it finally appeared that "Vukie" would be the winner. This was not to be, however, as a steering pin broke and the dark gray No. 26 skidded into the northeast wall eight laps from the finish. Ruttman took over and became, at 22, the youngest winner in "500" history.

Troy Ruttman

NO.	DRIVER	CAR	ENTRANT	ENGINE	CYL.	DISP.	CHASSIS	COLOR	QUAL. SPEED	ST.	FIN.	LAPS/SPEED/REASON OUT
98	Troy Ruttman	Agajanian	J. C. Agajanian	Offy	4	263	Kuzma	cream, red	135.364	7	1	200-128.922
59	Jim Rathmann	Grancor-Wynn's Oil	Grancor Auto. Specialists	Offy¢	4	270	KK3000	yellow, silver, red	136.343	10	2	200-126.723
18	Sam Hanks	Bardahl	Ed Walsh	Offy	4	263	KK3000	black, white	135.736	5	3	200-125.580
1	Duane Carter	Belanger Motors	Murrell Belanger	Offy	4	262	Lesovsky	blue, gold	135.522	6	4	200-125.259
33	Art Cross	Bowes Seal Fast	Ray T. Brady	Offy	4	270	KK4000	cream, black, red	134.288	20	5	200-124.292
77	Jimmy Bryan	Schmidt	Peter Schmidt	Offy	4	270	KK3000	red, silver	134.142	21	6	200-123.914
37	Jimmy Reece	John Zink	John Zink	Offy	4	270	KK4000	black, orange	133.993	23	7	200-123.312
54	George Connor	Federal Engineering	Federal Auto. Associates	Offy	4	270	KK3000	tan, cream	135.609	14	8	200-122.595
22	Cliff Griffith	Tom Sarafoff	Tom Sarafoff	Offy	4	263	KK2000	red, white	136.617	9	9	200-122.402
5	Johnnie Parsons	Jim Robbins	J. M. Robbins	Offy	4	270	Kurtis	yellow, red	135.328	31	10	200-121.789
4	Jack McGrath	Hinkle	Jack B. Hinkle	Offy	4	270	KK3000	maroon, silver	136.664	3	11	200-121.428
29	Jim Rigsby	Bob Estes	Bob Estes	Offy	4	270	Watson	blue, white, red	133.904	26	12	200-120.587
14	Joe James	Bardahl	Ed Walsh	Offy	4	263	KK4000	black, white	134.953	16	13	200-120.108
7	Bill Schindler	Chapman	H. A. Chapman	Offy	4	270	Stevens	black, pink	134.988	15	14	200-119.280
65	George Fonder	Leitenberger	George H. Leitenberger	Offy	4	270	Sherman	red, white, blue	135.947	13	15	197-flagged
81	Eddie Johnson	Central Excavating	Pete Salemi	Offy	4	270	Trevis	red, blue, white	133.973	24	16	193-flagged
26	Bill Vukovich	Fuel Injection	Howard Keck Co.	Offy	4	270	KK500A	gray, red, yellow	138.212	8	17	191-steering, hit NE wall
16	Chuck Stevenson	Springfield Welding	Bessie Lee Paoli	Offy	4	263	KK4000	red, white	136.142	11	18	187-flagged
2	Henry Banks	Blue Crown Spark Plug	Lindsey Hopkins	Offy	4	263	Lesovsky	blue, white, orange	135.962	12	19	184-flagged
8	Manuel Ayulo	Coast Grain Co.	Coast Grain Co.	Offy	4	270	Lesovsky	white, blue	135.982	28	20	184-flagged
31	Johnny McDowell	McDowell	Roger G. Wolcott	Offy	4	263	Kurtis	turquoise, gold	133.939	33	21	182-flagged
48	Spider Webb	Granatelli Racing Enter.	Vincent Granatelli	Offy	4	270	Bromme	red, black	135.962	29	22	162-oil leak
34	Rodger Ward	Federal Engineering	Federal Auto. Associates	Offy	4	270	KK4000	tan, cream	134.139	22	23	130-low oil pressure
27	Tony Bettenhausen	Blue Crown Spark Plug	Earl F. Slick	Offy¢	4	270	Deidt	blue, white, red	135.384	30	24	93-starter
36	Duke Nalon	Novi Pure Oil	Lewis W. Welch	Novi*¢	8	181	Kurtis	white, blue	136.188	4	25	84-supercharger shaft
73	Bob Sweikert	McNamara	Lee Elkins	Offy	4	263	KK2000	dark red, gold	134.983	32	26	77-differential
28	Fred Agabashian	Cummins Diesel	Cummins Engine Co.	Cummins*	6	401	Kurtis	red, yellow	138.010	1	27	71-clogged supercharger
67	Gene Hartley	Mel-Rae	Mel B. Wiggers	Offy	4	270	KK4000	white, black	134.343	18	28	65-exhaust pipe
93	Bob Scott	Morris	Ludson D. Morris, M.D.	Offy	4	270	KK2000	red, white	133.953	25	29	49-drive shaft
21	Chet Miller	Novi Pure Oil	Lewis W. Welch	Novi*¢	8	181	Kurtis	blue, white	139.034	27	30	41-supercharger shaft
12	Alberto Ascari	Ferrari	Enzo Ferrari	Ferrari	12	271	Ferrari	red, white	134.308	19	31	40-hub flange, spun NW
55	Bob Ball	Ansted	Rotary Engineering Corp.	Offy	4	270	Stevens	blue, silver, pink	134.725	17	32	34-gear case
9	Andy Linden	Miracle Power	Hart Fullerton	Offy*	4	183	KK4000	yellow, blue, red	137.002	2	33	20-oil leak

*Supercharged   ¢Front Drive

Jim Rathmann

Sam Hanks

Duane Carter

Art Cross

Jimmy Bryan

Jimmy Reece

George Connor

Cliff Griffith

Johnnie Parsons

Jack McGrath

Jim Rigsby

Joe James

Bill Schindler

George Fonder

Eddie Johnson

Bill Vukovich

Chuck Stevenson

Henry Banks

Manuel Ayulo

Johnny McDowell

Spider Webb

Rodger Ward

Tony Bettenhausen

Duke Nalon

Bob Sweikert

Fred Agabashian

Gene Hartley

Bob Scott

Chet Miller

Alberto Ascari

Bob Ball

Andy Linden

Right: Winner Troy Ruttman with his happy crew. Left to right, Chief Mechanic Clay Smith, owner J. C. Agajanian, and Troy's father Ralph Ruttman. Below, left: Alberto Ascari drives his Ferrari back to the garage after some practice laps. Below, middle: Jim Travers checks the fuel, Bill Vukovich checks his watch, and Frank Coon checks Vukovich. Below, right: Wilbur Shaw asks Italian Alberto Ascari how he likes the "Brickyard".

Above, left: Troy Ruttman passes the pits on the way to Victory Lane. Above, right: The Novi Pure Oil Team with Chet Miller in No. 21 and Duke Nalon in No. 36. Right: Bob Ball's wrecked Blakely Oil Special after he crashed on the frontstretch in practice. Fellow driver George Tichenor (wearing crash helmet) surveys the damage.

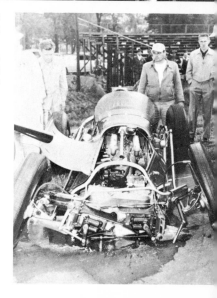

Above: Jack McGrath leads the field through the first turn.
Left: Bill Vukovich returns to the lead after making his first pit stop.

1953

Still smarting from having the 1952 victory snatched from his grasp when almost in sight of the checkered flag, Bill Vukovich set fast time to win the pole position in a driving rainstorm. He then proceeded to lead all but five laps to win the race, during which track temperatures soared above 130 degrees. Freddy Agabashian, Jim Rathmann and Sam Hanks, the only other drivers to win lap money, led those five laps while "Vukie" was in the pits. The "Hottest 500" was one of endurance rather than speed and drivers and cars were tried to their limits. On the third lap, Andy Linden hit the northeast wall and spun into the infield and 50 laps later Gene Hartley did the same thing in the same place. On the 70th lap, veteran Carl Scarborough came in for a routine pit stop and was relieved by Bob Scott. The heat had been too much for Scarborough and he collapsed. Within an hour he was dead in the field hospital. Later, the heat got Pat Flaherty and he hit the north chute wall, receiving serious head injuries. Don Freeland hit the northwest wall on his 76th lap and skidded into the infield. Hartley, driving relief for Bettenhausen, hit the northeast wall and Duke Nalon spun his Novi to miss him. On May 15, Chet Miller died when he hit the southwest wall.

Bill Vukovich

NO.	DRIVER	CAR	ENTRANT	ENGINE	CYL.	DISP.	CHASSIS	COLOR	QUAL. SPEED	ST.	FIN.	LAPS/SPEED/REASON OUT
14	Bill Vukovich	Fuel Injection	Howard Keck Co.	Offy	4	270	KK500A	gray, red, yellow	138.392	1	1	200-128.740
16	Art Cross	Springfield Welding	Bessie Lee Paoli	Offy	4	263	KK4000	red, white	137.310	12	2	200-126.827
3	Sam Hanks	Bardahl	Ed Walsh	Offy	4	270	KK4000	black, white	137.531	9	3	200-126.465
59	Fred Agabashian	Grancor-Elgin Piston Pin	Grancor Auto. Specialists	Offy	4	270	KK500B	blue, red, silver	137.546	2	4	200-126.219
5	Jack McGrath	Hinkle	Jack B. Hinkle	Offy	4	270	KK4000	cream, black	136.602	3	5	200-124.556
48	Jimmy Daywalt	Sumar	Chapman S. Root	Offy	4	270	KK3000	blue, white	135.747	21	6	200-124.379
2	Jim Rathmann	Travelon Trailer	Ernest L. Ruiz	Offy	4	270	KK500B	orange, white	135.666	25	7	200-124.072
12	Ernie McCoy	Chapman	H. A. Chapman	Offy	4	270	Stevens	turquoise, red	135.926	20	8	200-123.404
98	Tony Bettenhausen	Agajanian	J. C. Agajanian	Offy	4	263	Kuzma	cream, red	136.024	6	9	196-axle, wreck. NE(Hartley)
53	Jim Davies	Pat Clancy	Pat Clancy	Offy	4	263	KK500B	gold, red	135.262	32	10	193-flagged
9	Duke Nalon	Novi Governor	Jean Marcenac	Novi*¢	8	181	Kurtis	cream, black	135.461	26	11	191-spun to avoid 98 NE
73	Carl Scarborough	McNamara	Lee Elkins	Offy	4	270	KK2000	mahogony, copper	135.936	19	12	190-flagged
88	Manuel Ayulo	Peter Schmidt	Peter Schmidt	Offy	4	270	Kuzma	red, silver	136.384	4	13	184-con. rod
8	Jimmy Bryan	Blakely Oil	John L. McDaniel	Offy	4	270	Schroeder	red, silver	135.506	31	14	183-flagged
49	Bill Holland	Crawford	Ray Crawford	Offy	4	270	KK500B	red, cream	137.868	28	15	177-cam gear
92	Rodger Ward	M. A. Walker Electric	M. A. Walker	Offy	4	270	Kurtis	blue, cream	137.468	10	16	177-stalled
23	Walt Faulkner	Automobile Shippers	Eugene A. Casaroll	Offy	4	270	KK500A	orange, black	137.117	14	17	176-flagged
22	Marshall Teague	Pure Oil	Hart Fullerton	Offy	4	270	KK4000	blue, white, silver	135.721	22	18	169-oil leak
62	Spider Webb	Lubri-Loy	3-L Racing Team	Offy	4	270	KK3000	white, blue, orange	136.168	18	19	166-oil leak
51	Bob Sweikert	Dean Van Lines	A. E. Dean	Offy	4	270	Kuzma	white, blue	136.872	29	20	151-radius rod
83	Mike Nazaruk	Kalamazoo	Lee Elkins	Offy	4	270	Turner	gold, maroon	135.706	23	21	146-stalled
77	Pat Flaherty	Peter Schmidt	Peter Schmidt	Offy	4	270	KK3000	red, silver	135.668	24	22	115-wrecked NS
55	Jerry Hoyt	John Zink	John Zink	Offy	4	270	KK4000	turquoise, orange	135.731	7	23	107-cockpit too hot
4	Duane Carter	Miracle Power	Murrell Belanger	Offy	4	270	Lesovsky	blue, yellow, red	135.267	27	24	94-ignition
7	Paul Russo	Federal Engineering	Federal Auto. Associates	Offy	4	270	KK3000	yellow, blue	136.219	17	25	89-magneto
21	Johnnie Parsons	Belond Equa-Flow	J. S. Belond	Offy	4	270	KK500B	cream, red	137.667	8	26	86-crankshaft
38	Don Freeland	Bob Estes	Bob Estes	Offy	4	270	Watson	cream, red	136.867	15	27	76-wrecked NW
41	Gene Hartley	Federal Engineering	Federal Auto. Associates	Offy	4	270	KK4000	yellow, blue	137.263	13	28	53-wrecked NE
97	Chuck Stevenson	Agajanian	J. C. Agajanian	Offy	4	270	Kuzma	red, white, black	136.560	16	29	42-fuel leak
99	Cal Niday	Miracle Power	Murrell Belanger	Offy	4	263	Kurtis	yellow, blue, red	136.096	30	30	30-magneto
29	Bob Scott	Belond Equa-Flow	Louis & Bruce Bromme	Offy	4	270	Bromme	cream, red	137.431	11	31	14-oil leak
56	Johnny Thomson	Dr. Sabourin	Dr. R. N. Sabourin, D.C.	Offy	4	270	Del Roy	blue, dark blue	135.262	33	32	6-ignition
32	Andy Linden	Cop-Sil-Loy	Rotary Engineering Corp.	Offy	4	270	Stevens	copper, blue	136.060	5	33	3-wrecked NE

*Supercharged   ¢Front drive

Art Cross

Sam Hanks

Fred Agabashian

Jack McGrath

Jimmy Daywalt

Jim Rathmann

Ernie McCoy

Tony Bettenhausen

Jim Davies

Duke Nalon

Carl Scarborough

Manuel Ayulo

Jimmy Bryan

Bill Holland

Rodger Ward

Walt Faulkner

Marshall Teaque

Spider Webb

Bob Sweikert

Mike Nazaruk

Pat Flaherty

Jerry Hoyt

Duane Carter

Paul Russo

Johnnie Parsons

Don Freeland

Gene Hartley

Chuck Stevenson

Cal Niday

Bob Scott

Johnny Thomson

Andy Linden

Right: Raymond Firestone congratulates Bill Vukovich as Wilbur Shaw arrives with his ''Water from Wilbur and Tony'' bowl. Bill's wife, Esther, prepares to give him a wet towel to wash his oil-covered face. When asked if the broiling heat had bothered him, Bill is reported to have answered ''Think this was hot? Hell, you should drive a tractor in Fresno in July''. Bottom: A pensive, or possibly bored, Bill Vukovich waits for the green light to start a practice session.

Left: The front row with Bill Vukovich on the pole, Freddy Agabashian in the center and Jack McGrath on the outside. Below, left: Johnnie Parsons models one of the new "full coverage" crash helmets, whose basic design was developed by race driver Hal Minyard. Below, middle: A pre-race bull session. Left to right are Jerry Hoyt, Jack McGrath, radio announcer Sid Collins, and Freddy Agabashian. Below, right: Andy Linden's Cop-Sil-Loy Special being pushed to the starting line. It was hardly worth the effort as Linden hit the northeast wall after completing only three laps.

Above, left: Bill Vukovich jumps into the lead as the field is given the green flag. Above, right: Cal Niday makes a pit stop in his Miracle Power Special. Left: Awaiting the words "Gentlemen, start your engines".

1954

Bill Vukovich took things a bit easier than he did in 1953 although the results were the same and he won his second straight "500" a lap ahead of determined Jimmy Bryan. As thoroughbred race cars occasionally do, "Vukie's" Fuel Injection Special became temperamental during pre-race practice and it was the third day of qualifying before he could place it in the lineup. Starting in 19th position, Vukovich took his time and gradually worked toward the front of the pack which was being led at various times by Jimmy Daywalt, Bryan and Jack McGrath, who set a new record when qualifying. Troy Ruttman pressed the leaders so hard that he spun and shredded a tire but returned to the chase after a pit stop. At the halfway point, Vukovich took the lead and stayed a safe distance in front of Bryan. Bill Homeier's was the first car out when his foot slipped off the clutch while pulling out of the pit on his 74th lap. The car lurched into the pit wall and bent the front end. On his 112th lap, Daywalt hit the northwest wall, spun and was struck by Pat Flaherty, who was relieving Jim Rathmann. Both cars were out. Pat O'Connor spun in the southeast turn on his 182nd lap and Rathmann, driving for Hanks, broke a crankshaft and spun down the frontstretch on his 91st.

Bill Vukovich

NO.	DRIVER	CAR	ENTRANT	ENGINE	CYL.	DISP.	CHASSIS	COLOR	QUAL. SPEED	ST.	FIN.	LAPS/SPEED/REASON OUT
14	Bill Vukovich	Fuel Injection	Howard Keck Co.	Offy	4	270	KK500A	gray, red, yellow	138.478	19	1	200-130.840
9	Jimmy Bryan	Dean Van Lines	A. E. Dean	Offy	4	274	Kuzma	white, blue	139.665	3	2	200-130.178
2	Jack McGrath	Hinkle	Jack B. Hinkle	Offy	4	270	KK500C	cream, black	141.033	1	3	200-130.086
34	Troy Ruttman	Automobile Shippers	Eugene A. Casaroll	Offy	4	270	KK500A	orange, black	137.736	11	4	200-129.218
73	Mike Nazaruk	McNamara	Lee Elkins	Offy	4	270	KK500C	gold, red	139.589	14	5	200-128.923
77	Fred Agabashian	Merz Engineering	Miklos Sperling	Offy	4	271	KK500C	maroon, cream	137.746	24	6	200-128.711
7	Don Freeland	Bob Estes	Bob Estes	Offy	4	270	Phillips	cream, red	138.339	6	7	200-128.474
5	Paul Russo	Ansted Rotary	Hoosier Racing Team, Inc.	Offy	4	270	KK500A	dark blue, cream	137.678	32	8	200-128.037
28	Larry Crockett	Federal Engineering	Federal Auto. Associates	Offy	4	270	KK3000	yellow, blue	139.557	25	9	200-126.899
24	Cal Niday	Jim Robbins	Jim Robbins Co.	Offy	4	270	Stevens	maroon, cream, red	139.828	13	10	200-126.895
45	Art Cross	Bardahl	Ed Walsh	Offy	4	270	KK4000	black, white	138.675	27	11	200-126.232
98	Chuck Stevenson	Agajanian	J. C. Agajanian	Offy	4	270	Kuzma	cream, red	138.776	5	12	199-flagged
88	Manuel Ayulo	Schmidt	Peter Schmidt	Offy	4	270	Kuzma	red, silver	138.164	22	13	197-flagged
17	Bob Sweikert	Lutes	Francis Bardazon	Offy	4	270	KK4000	red, yellow	138.206	9	14	197-flagged
16	Duane Carter	Automobile Shippers	Eugene A. Casaroll	Offy	4	270	KK4000	orange, black	138.238	8	15	196-flagged
32	Ernie McCoy	Crawford	Ray Crawford	Offy	4	270	KK500B	cream, red	138.419	20	16	194-flagged
25	Jimmy Reece	Malloy	Emmett J. Malloy	Offy	4	263	Pankratz	black, white, red	138.312	7	17	194-flagged
27	Ed Elisian	Chapman	H. A. Chapman	Offy	4	270	Stevens	turquoise, red	137.794	31	18	193-flagged
71	Frank Armi	Martin Bros.	T. W. & W. T. Martin	Offy	4	270	Curtis	salmon, white	137.673	33	19	193-flagged
1	Sam Hanks	Bardahl	Ed Walsh	Offy	4	270	KK4000	black, white	137.994	10	20	191-spun FS (J. Rathmann)
35	Pat O'Connor	Hopkins	Motor Racers, Inc.	Offy	4	270	KK500C	blue, orange	138.084	12	21	181-spun SE
12	Rodger Ward	Dr. Sabourin	Dr. R. N. Sabourin, D.C.	Offy	4	270	Pawl	white, blue	139.297	16	22	172-stalled BS
31	Gene Hartley	John Zink	John S. Zink	Offy	4	270	KK4000	red, white	139.061	17	23	168-engine trouble
43	Johnny Thomson	Chapman	H. A. Chapman	Offy	4	270	Nichels	red, turquoise	138.787	4	24	165-stalled
74	Andy Linden	Brown Motor Co.	Brown Motor Co.	Offy	4	270	Schroeder	brown, gold	137.820	23	25	165-torsion bar
99	Jerry Hoyt	Belanger	Murrell Belanger	Offy	4	270	Kurtis	blue, gold	137.825	30	26	130-engine trouble
19	Jimmy Daywalt	Sumar	Chapman S. Root	Offy	4	270	KK500C	blue, white	139.789	2	27	111-wrecked NW
38	Jim Rathmann	Bardahl	Ed Walsh	Offy	4	270	KK500C	black, white	138.228	28	28	110-wrecked NW (Flaherty)
10	Tony Bettenhausen	Mel Wiggers	Mel B. Wiggers	Offy	4	270	KK500C	white, red, gold	138.275	21	29	105-con. rod bearing
65	Spider Webb	Advance Muffler	Bruce Bromme	Offy	4	270	Bromme	red, yellow	137.979	29	30	104-oil leak
33	Len Duncan	Brady	Ray T. Brady	Offy	4	270	Schroeder	cream, black, red	139.217	26	31	101-brakes
15	Johnnie Parsons	Belond Equa-Flow Exhaust	So. Calif. Muffler Corp.	Offy	4	270	KK500C	dark yellow, red	139.578	15	32	79-stalled in pits
51	Bill Homeier	Jones & Maley	Cars, Inc.	Offy	4	270	KK500C	red, white	138.948	18	33	74-hit wall leaving pits

Jimmy Bryan

Jack McGrath

Troy Ruttman

Mike Nazaruk

Fred Agabashian

Don Freeland

Paul Russo

Larry Crockett

Cal Niday

Art Cross

Chuck Stevenson

Manuel Ayulo

Bob Sweikert

Duane Carter

Ernie McCoy

Jimmy Reece

Ed Elisian

Frank Armi

Sam Hanks

Pat O'Connor

Rodger Ward

Gene Hartley

Johnny Thomson

Andy Linden

Jerry Hoyt

Jimmy Daywalt

Jim Rathmann

Tony Bettenhausen

Spider Webb

Len Duncan

Johnnie Parsons

Bill Homeier

Top: Jack McGrath leads Johnny Thomson through the first turn. Above, left: The Purdue Band parades before the start of the race. Middle, right, top: The front row. On the pole is Jack McGrath, in the center, Jimmy Daywalt, and on the outside is Jimmy Bryan. Middle, right, bottom: Freddy Agabashian takes the Chinetti Ferrari for a test ride. Right: Bill Homeier is happy after qualifying for his first "500".

Left: Bill Vukovich discusses his Fuel Injection Special with mechanic Frank Coon and Stu Hilborn, the engineer who developed the injection system. Below, left: The J. C. Agajanian crew makes ready for the start. Below, middle: Chapman S. Root's Sumar Racing Team. Left to right: Jimmy Daywalt, Jerry Hoyt, Root and Chief Mechanic John Blouch. Below, right: Frank Coon pumps air pressure into Vukovich's fuel tank while Jim Travers mans the starter.

Above, left: Contestants, pit crews and officials line up for the official picture. Above, right: The first turn during qualifying. Left: Bitter disappointment is seen on the faces of the crews that failed to qualify. Owner Karl Hall (left) and driver Duke Dinsmore push the Commerical Motor Freight Special back to the garages after their last minute qualifying efforts failed.

1955

For many people, the 1955 "500" ended on the 57th lap when the leader, Bill Vukovich, crashed to his death in a four-car accident on the backstretch. The colorful driver, who had completely dominated the '53 and '54 races, was well on his way to an unprecedented third-straight victory when fate stepped in and Rodger Ward's car hit the fence and flipped down the track. Al Keller took to the infield to miss Ward but slid back on the track into Johnny Boyd who, in turn, hit Vukovich. Vukie's car flipped over the outside rail and bounced off several parked cars before coming down on fire. Seeing the accident, Ed Elisian spun into the infield and ran to his friend's aid although Bill had sustained a fatal skull fracture on the first flip. When the green flag was again displayed, it became anybody's race. By the halfway mark, it had narrowed into a three-way duel between Bob Sweikert, Don Freeland and Art Cross. When a pit stop dropped him to third, Sweikert seemingly settled back to let Cross and Freeland fight it out but both had mechanical trouble and Sweikert was flagged the winner. Near the end of the race Cal Niday crashed in the northwest turn, caught fire, and was seriously injured. On May 16th, Manual Ayulo died after hitting the southwest wall in practice.

Bob Sweikert

NO.	DRIVER	CAR	ENTRANT	ENGINE	CYL.	DISP.	CHASSIS	COLOR	QUAL. SPEED	ST.	FIN.	LAPS/SPEED/REASON OUT
6	Bob Sweikert	John Zink	John Zink Co.	Offy	4	270	KK500C	rose, white, black	139.996	14	1	200-128.209
10	Tony Bettenhausen	Chapman	H. A. Chapman	Offy	4	270	KK500C	turquoise, cream, red	139.985	2	2	200-126.733
15	Jim Davies	Bardahl	Pat Clancy	Offy	4	270	KK500B	black, white	140.274	10	3	200-126.299
44	Johnny Thomson	Schmidt	Peter Schmidt	Offy	4	270	Kuzma	red, silver	134.113	33	4	200-126.241
77	Walt Faulkner	Merz Engineering	Merz Engineering, Inc.	Offy	4	270	KK500C	bronze, cream	139.762	7	5	200-125.377
19	Andy Linden	Massaglia	Joseph Massaglia, Jr.	Offy	4	270	KK4000	rose, white	139.098	8	6	200-125.022
71	Al Herman	Martin Bros.	T. W. & W. T. Martin	Offy	4	270	Curtis	salmon, white	139.811	16	7	200-124.794
29	Pat O'Connor	Ansted Rotary	Rotary Engineering Corp.	Offy	4	270	KK500D	cream, black	139.195	19	8	200-124.644
48	Jimmy Daywalt	Sumar	Chapman S. Root	Offy	4	270	Kurtis	blue, white	139.416	17	9	200-124.401
89	Pat Flaherty	Dunn Engineering	Harry Dunn	Offy	4	272	KK500B	white, black	140.149	12	10	200-124.086
98	Duane Carter	Agajanian	J. C. Agajanian	Offy	4	270	Kuzma	cream, red	139.330	18	11	197-flagged
41	Chuck Weyant	Federal Engineering	Federal Auto. Associates	Offy	4	270	KK3000	yellow, blue	138.063	25	12	196-flagged
83	Eddie Johnson	McNamara	Kalamazoo Sports, Inc.	Offy	4	270	Trevis	maroon, gold	134.449	32	13	196-flagged
33	Jim Rathmann	Belond Miracle Power	So. Calif. Muffler Corp.	Offy	4	270	Epperly	yellow, blue	138.707	20	14	191-flagged
12	Don Freeland	Bob Estes	Bob Estes	Offy	4	270	Phillips	cream, red	139.866	21	15	178-transmission
22	Cal Niday	D-A Lubricants	Racing Associates	Offy	4	270	KK500B	yellow, black, white	140.302	9	16	170-wrecked NW
99	Art Cross	Belanger Motors	Murrell Belanger	Offy	4	270	KK500C	blue, gold	138.750	24	17	168-con. rod cap
81	Shorty Templeman	Central Excavating	Pete Salemi	Offy	4	270	Trevis	blue, white	135.014	31	18	142-stalled
8	Sam Hanks	Jones & Maley	Cars, Inc.	Offy	4	270	KK500C	red, white, silver	140.187	6	19	134-transmission
31	Keith Andrews	McDaniel	John L. McDaniel	Offy	4	270	Schroeder	navy blue, white	136.049	28	20	120-ignition
16	Johnnie Parsons	Trio Brass	Carl L. Anderson	Offy	4	270	KK500C	blue, white	136.809	27	21	119-magneto
37	Eddie Russo	Dr. Sabourin	Dr. R. N. Sabourin, D.C.	Offy	4	270	Pawl	white, blue	140.116	13	22	112-ignition
49	Ray Crawford	Crawford	Ray Crawford	Offy	4	270	KK500B	red, cream	139.206	23	23	111-valve
1	Jimmy Bryan	Dean Van Lines	A. E. Dean	Offy	4	270	Kuzma	white, blue	140.160	11	24	90-fuel pump
4	Bill Vukovich	Hopkins	Lindsey Hopkins	Offy	4	269	KK500C	blue, orange, white	141.071	5	25	56-wrecked BS
3	Jack McGrath	Hinkle	Jack B. Hinkle	Offy	4	270	KK500C	cream, black	142.580	3	26	54-magneto
42	Al Keller	Sam Traylor Offy	Samuel W. Traylor, III	Offy	4	270	KK2000	black, gold	139.551	22	27	54-wrecked BS
27	Rodger Ward	Aristo Blue	E. R. Casale	Offy	4	270	Kuzma	white, light blue	135.049	30	28	53-wrecked BS
39	Johnny Boyd	Sumar	Chapman S. Root	Offy	4	270	KK500D	blue, white	136.981	26	29	53-wrecked BS
68	Ed Elisian	Westwood Gauge & Tool	M. Pete Wales	Offy	4	270	KK4000	blue, cream	135.333	29	30	53-stopped at wreck BS
23	Jerry Hoyt	Jim Robbins	Jim Robbins	Offy	4	270	Stevens	maroon, white	140.045	1	31	40-oil leak
14	Fred Agabashian	Federal Engineering	Federal Auto. Associates	Offy	4	270	KK500C	yellow, blue	141.933	4	32	39-spun SE
5	Jimmy Reece	Malloy	Emmett J. Malloy	Offy	4	269	Pankratz	black, white, red	139.991	15	33	10-con. rod, spun SW

Tony Bettenhausen

Jim Davies

Johnny Thomson

Walt Faulkner

Andy Linden

Al Herman

Pat O'Connor

Jimmy Daywalt

Pat Flaherty

Duane Carter

Chuck Weyant

Eddie Johnson

Jim Rathmann

Don Freeland

Cal Niday

Art Cross

Shorty Templeman

Sam Hanks

Keith Andrews

Johnnie Parsons

Eddie Russo

Ray Crawford

Jimmy Bryan

Bill Vukovich

Jack McGrath

Al Keller

Rodger Ward

Johnny Boyd

Ed Elisian

Jerry Hoyt

Fred Agabashian

Jimmy Reece

Top: T. H. Keating, General Manager of the Chevrolet Motor Division of General Motors, leads the Pace Lap with Tony Hulman as his passenger. Middle: Action in the northwest turn. Bottom: Winner Bob Sweikert in the John Zink Special.

Below, left: Bob Sweikert is congratulated by Dinah Shore and Raymond Firestone while Charlie Brockman stands by with the mike and Tony Hulman hands Bob the "Water from Wilbur and Tony" cup. Below, right: Bob Sweikert receives the checkered flag. Bottom: Bill Vukovich, who was fatally injured while on the way to his third straight "500" victory.

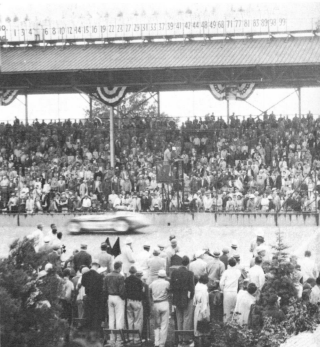

1956

Track Superintendent Clarence Cagle and his crew were the real heroes of the 1956 "500" when a flood inundated the track just three days before the race. Rain washed out all but 57 minutes of the second weekend of qualifying, but this was just time enough to fill the starting field, although some good cars were waiting in line when the track closed. Making one last bid for fame, the Novi, piloted by Paul Russo, was leading the field on lap 22 when it blew a tire and slammed into the southwest wall. As the yellow light flashed, Sam Hanks and Keith Andrews tangled in front of the pits and Ruttman spun to miss them. Johnny Thomson also spun and struck a mechanic working on Johnnie Tolan's car and broke his leg. When action resumed, Pat Flaherty out-battled Pat O'Connor to take the lead and soon the yellow was out again, this time for Ray Crawford who hit the northwest wall. In the next hour, Al Herman hit the pit wall and Andrews spun out. Bob Sweikert spun in the backstretch but kept going. Jimmy Daywalt blew a tire and hit the southeast wall, sustaining serious head injuries. Jim Bryan spun but restarted and Tony Bettenhausen hit the southwest wall, breaking his collar bone. Dick Rathmann crashed after taking the checkered flag.

Pat Flaherty

NO.	DRIVER	CAR	ENTRANT	ENGINE	CYL.	DISP.	CHASSIS	COLOR	QUAL. SPEED	ST.	FIN.	LAPS/SPEED/REASON OUT
8	Pat Flaherty	John Zink	John Zink Co.	Offy	4	270	Watson	rose, white	145.596	1	1	200-128.490
4	Sam Hanks	Jones & Maley	Cars, Inc.	Offy	4	270	KK500C	red, white, silver	142.051	13	2	200-128.303
12	Don Freeland	Bob Estes	Bob Estes	Offy	4	270	Phillips	red, cream	141.699	26	3	200-127.668
98	Johnnie Parsons	Agajanian	J. C. Agajanian	Offy	4	270	Kuzma	cream, red	144.144	6	4	200-126.631
73	Dick Rathmann	McNamara	Kalamazoo Sports, Inc.	Offy	4	270	KK500C	red, gold	144.471	4	5	200-126.133 wrecked SW
1	Bob Sweikert	D-A Lubricant	Racing Associates	Offy	4	270	Kuzma	yellow, white, black	143.033	10	6	200-125.489
14	Bob Veith	Federal Engineering	Federal Auto. Associates	Offy	4	270	KK500C	blue, yellow	142.535	23	7	200-125.048
19	Rodger Ward	Filter Queen	Ed Walsh	Offy	4	270	KK500C	red, maroon, gold	141.171	15	8	200-124.990
26	Jimmy Reece	Massaglia Hotels	Joseph Massaglia, Jr.	Offy	4	270	Lesovsky	white, gold, blue	142.885	21	9	200-124.938
27	Cliff Griffith	Jim Robbins	Jim Robbins	Offy	4	270	Stevens	maroon, white	141.471	30	10	199-flagged
82	Gene Hartley	Central Excavating	Pete Salemi	Offy	4	270	Kuzma	blue, silver	142.846	22	11	196-flagged
42	Fred Agabashian	Federal Engineering	Federal Auto. Associates	Offy	4	270	KK500C	blue, yellow	144.069	7	12	196-flagged
57	Bob Christie	Helse	H. H. Johnson	Offy	4	270	KK500D	maroon, gold	142.236	25	13	196-flagged
55	Al Keller	Sam Traylor	Samuel W. Traylor, III	Offy	4	270	KK4000	blue, gold	141.193	28	14	195-flagged
81	Eddie Johnson	Central Excavating	Pete Salemi	Offy	4	270	Kuzma	blue, silver	139.093	32	15	195-flagged
41	Billy Garrett	Greenman-Casale	E. R. Casale	Offy	4	263	Kuzma	white, lt. blue	140.559	29	16	194-flagged
64	Duke Dinsmore	Shannon's	Shannon Bros.	Offy	4	270	KK500A	blue-green, white	138.530	33	17	191-flagged
7	Pat O'Connor	Ansted Rotary	Ansted Rotary Corp.	Offy	4	270	KK500D	cream, black	144.980	3	18	187-flagged
2	Jimmy Bryan	Dean Van Lines	Dean Van Lines	Offy	4	270	Kuzma	white, blue	143.741	19	19	185-flagged
24	Jim Rathmann	Hopkins	Lindsey Hopkins	Offy	4	270	KK500C	blue, white, orange	145.120	2	20	175-oil trouble
34	Johnnie Tolan	Trio Brass Foundry	Carl L. Anderson	Offy	4	270	KK500C	blue, white	140.061	31	21	173-flagged
99	Tony Bettenhausen	Belanger Motors	Murrell Belanger	Offy	4	270	KK500C	blue, gold	144.602	5	22	160-wrecked SW
10	Ed Elisian	Hoyt Machine	Fred Somers	Offy	4	270	KK500C	metallic rose, white	141.382	14	23	160-stalled
48	Jimmy Daywalt	Sumar	Chapman S. Root	Offy	4	270	KK500D	blue, white	140.977	16	24	134-wrecked SE
54	Jack Turner	Travelon Trailer	Ernest L. Ruiz	Offy	4	270	KK500B	turquoise, white	142.394	24	25	131-engine trouble
89	Keith Andrews	Dunn Engineering	Harry Dunn	Offy	4	270	KK500B	white, black	142.976	20	26	94-spun NW
5	Andy Linden	Chapman	H. A. Chapman	Offy	4	270	KK500C	cream, blue	143.056	9	27	90-oil leak
12	Al Herman	Bardahl	Pat Clancy	Offy	4	270	KK500B	black, white	141.610	27	28	74-wrecked FS
49	Ray Crawford	Crawford	Ray Crawford	Offy	4	270	KK500B	red, cream	140.884	17	29	49-wrecked NW
15	Johnny Boyd	Bowes Seal Fast	George Bignotti	Offy	4	270	KK500E	white, black, red	142.337	12	30	35-engine trouble
53	Troy Ruttman	John Zink	John S. Zink	Offy	4	270	KK500C	rose, white, black	142.484	11	31	22-spun FS
88	Johnny Thomson	Schmidt	Peter Schmidt	Offy	4	270	Kuzma	red, silver	145.549	18	32	22-spun FS
29	Paul Russo	Novi Vespa	Novi Racing Corp., Inc.	Novi*	8	183	Kurtis	red, cream	143.546	8	33	21-blew tire, wrecked SW

*Supercharged

Sam Hanks

Don Freeland

Johnnie Parsons

Dick Rathmann

Bob Sweikert

Bob Veith

Rodger Ward

Jimmy Reece

Cliff Griffith

Gene Hartley

Fred Agabashian

Bob Christie

Al Keller

Eddie Johnson

Billy Garrett

Duke Dinsmore

Pat O'Connor

Jimmy Bryan

Jim Rathmann

Johnnie Tolan

Tony Bettenhausen

Ed Elisian

Jimmy Daywalt

Jack Turner

Keith Andrews

Andy Linden

Al Herman

Ray Crawford

Johnny Boyd

Troy Ruttman

Johnny Thomson

Paul Russo

Below, left: The torrential rains, which played havoc with the final days of qualifying, turned Dry Run Creek into a flood-swollen river. Though many parts of the Speedway grounds were under water two days before the race, Clarence Cagle and his efficient maintenance crew worked around the clock and had the plant ready by race-day morning. Below, right: A perfect start! Middle: Jim Rathmann leads through the south-east turn on the first lap. Bottom: Action down the front stretch. Before the next race, the historic Pagoda and pit area would give way to the ultra-modern Tower Terrace and greatly enlarged pit apron.

Left: Frank Curtis working on the Martin Brothers Special as seen from a garage across "Gasoline Alley". Below, left: Cars wait in the rain for qualifying to resume. The track was too wet for everyone to get an attempt and many fine cars were left waiting in line. Fortunately, the field had been filled in the first three allotted days. Below, right: Jim Rathmann converses with Chief Mechanic Jack Beckley as the Firestone crew checks his tires.

Above, left: former World Road Racing Champion, Giuseppe "Nino" Farina, of Italy, explains his troubles to newsmen. Farina quit the Bardahl-Ferrari Racing Team after disagreements with its American crew, but came back shortly after a rookie driver began turning faster practice laps in his car. Farina was among those waiting in line when rain washed out the final days of qualifying. Above, middle: Bardahl-Ferrari mechanic Jess Beene checks a spark plug while Gary Foley, "Nino" Farina and Farina's personal mechanic watch. Above, right: Billy Garrett is a happy rookie after completing his first "500". Bottom: The front row with Pat Flaherty on the pole, Jim Rathmann in the middle and Pat O'Connor on the outside.

1957

Sam Hanks, the lean, handsome veteran, who had been trying to win the "500" since 1940, finally turned the trick when he teamed up with George Salih's revolutionary "lay-down" speedster. The sleek, low-profiled car performed flawlessly as Hanks beat Jim Rathmann to the wire in a race which saw the first ten cars break the existing record for 500 miles. A new single-file pace lap procedure, designed to utilize the elaborate new pit area, resulted in a crash which eliminated Elmer George and Eddie Russo even before the cars got the green flag. The first few laps found Pat O'Connor, Troy Ruttman and Paul Russo alternating in the lead while Hanks worked up from 13th starting spot to take over from Russo and the Novi on the 37th lap. Jimmy Daywalt hit the northeast wall on his 54th lap, Al Keller did the same thing in the first turn on his 76th and Mike Magill crashed and was hit by Al Herman at the head of the frontstretch near the halfway mark. Late in the race, Don Edmunds, later named "Rookie of the Year", spun in his own oil in the southeast turn. In Victory Lane, a tearful Hanks announced his coming retirement from racing. Early in the month, Keith Andrews was killed when he spun and hit the inside wall coming into the frontstretch.

Sam Hanks

NO.	DRIVER	CAR	ENTRANT	ENGINE	CYL.	DISP.	CHASSIS	COLOR	QUAL. SPEED	ST.	FIN.	LAPS/SPEED/REASON OUT
9	Sam Hanks	Belond Exhaust	George Salih	Offy	4	250	Epperly	cream, maroon	142.812	13	1	200-135.601
26	Jim Rathmann	Chiropractic	Lindsey Hopkins	Offy	4	255	Epperly	blue, pink	139.806	32	2	200-135.382
1	Jimmy Bryan	Dean Van Lines	A. E. Dean	Offy*	4	252	Kuzma	white, blue	141.188	15	3	200-134.246
54	Paul Russo	Novi Auto Air Conditioner	Novi Racing Corp., Inc.	Novi*	8	169	Kurtis	blue, red, white	144.817	10	4	200-133.818
73	Andy Linden	McNamara	Kalamazoo Sports, Inc.	Offy	4	255	KK500G	red, gold	143.244	12	5	200-133.645
6	Johnny Boyd	Bowes Seal Fast	George Bignotti	Offy	4	252	KK500G	white, black, red	142.102	5	6	200-132.846
48	Marshall Teague	Sumar	Chapman S. Root	Offy	4	255	KK500D	blue, white	140.329	28	7	200-132.745
12	Pat O'Connor	Sumar	Chapman S. Root	Offy	4	255	KK500G	blue, white	143.948	1	8	200-132.281
7	Bob Veith	Bob Estes	Bob Estes	Offy	4	255	Phillips	yellow, red	141.016	16	9	200-131.855
22	Gene Hartley	Messaglia Hotels	Joseph Massaglia, Jr.	Offy	4	252	Lesovsky	white, red, blue	141.271	14	10	200-131.345
19	Jack Turner	Bardahl	Pat Clancy	Offy	4	252	KK500G	black, white	140.367	19	11	200-130.906
10	Johnny Thomson	D-A Lubricant	Racing Associates	Offy	4	252	Kuzma	yellow, white, black	143.529	11	12	199-flagged
95	Bob Christie	Jones & Maley	Cars, Inc.	Offy	4	252	KK500C	red, white, black	139.779	33	13	197-flagged
82	Chuck Weyant	Central Excavating	Pete Salemi	Offy	4	252	Kuzma	blue, white	141.105	25	14	196-flagged
27	Tony Bettenhausen	Novi Auto. Air Conditioner	Novi Racing Corp., Inc.	Novi*	8	169	Kurtis	blue, red, white	142.439	22	15	195-flagged
18	Johnnie Parsons	Sumar	Chapman S. Root	Offy	4	255	KK500G	red, white	140.784	17	16	195-flagged
3	Don Freeland	Ansted Rotary	Ansted Rotary Corp.	Offy	4	252	KK500D	cream, black	139.649	21	17	192-flagged
5	Jimmy Reece	Hoyt Machine	Fred & Richard Sommer	Offy	4	255	KK500C	red, yellow, black	142.006	6	18	182-throttle
92	Don Edmunds	McKay	Roy McKay	Offy	4	251	KK500G	lt. lavender, black	140.449	27	19	170-spun SW
28	Johnnie Tolan	Greenman-Casale	Lysle Greenman	Offy	4	252	Kuzma	red, yellow	139.844	31	20	138-clutch
89	Al Herman	Dunn Engineering	Harry Dunn	Offy	4	251	Dunn	white, black	140.007	30	21	111-wrecked FS
14	Fred Agabashian	Bowes Seal Fast	George Bignotti	Offy	4	252	KK500G	white, black, red	142.557	4	22	107-fuel tank
88	Eddie Sachs	Schmidt	Peter Schmidt	Offy	4	251	Kuzma	red, silver	143.872	2	23	105-piston
77	Mike Magill	Dayton Steel Foundry	George Walther, Jr.	Offy	4	252	KK500G	white, blue, red	140.411	18	24	101-wrecked FS
43	Eddie Johnson	Chapman	H. A. Chapman	Offy	4	252	KK500G	cream, blue	140.171	20	25	93-front wheel bearing
31	Bill Cheesbourg	Schildmeier Seal Line	J. S. Donaldson	Offy	4	251	KK500G	red, white	141.565	23	26	81-fuel leak
16	Al Keller	Bardahl	Pat Clancy	Offy	4	252	KK500G	black, white	141.398	8	27	75-wrecked SW
57	Jimmy Daywalt	Helse	H. H. Johnson	Offy	4	252	KK500C	silver, orange, black	140.203	29	28	53-wrecked NE
83	Ed Elisian	McNamara	Kalamazoo Sports, Inc.	Offy	4	255	KK500G	maroon, gold	141.777	7	29	51-timing gear
8	Rodger Ward	Wolcott	Roger Wolcott	Offy*	4	166	Lesovsky	red, white	141.321	24	30	27-supercharger bearing
52	Troy Ruttman	John Zink	John Zink Co.	Offy	4	252	Watson	red, white, black	142.772	3	31	13-overheating
55	Eddie Russo	Sclavi & Amos	Fred Sclavi	Offy	4	252	KK500C	white, light blue	140.862	26	32	0-wrecked on parade lap
23	Elmer George	Travelon Trailer	Ernest L. Ruiz	Offy	4	252	KK500B	blue, white	140.729	9	33	0-wrecked on parade lap

*Supercharged

Jim Rathmann

Jimmy Bryan

Paul Russo

Andy Linden

Johnny Boyd

Marshall Teague

Pat O'Connor

Bob Veith

Gene Hartley

Jack Turner

Johnny Thomson

Bob Christie

Chuck Weyant

Tony Bettenhausen

Dick Rathmann (qualifier)

Don Freeland

Jimmy Reece

Don Edmunds

Johnnie Tolan

Al Herman

Fred Agabashian

Eddie Sachs

Mike Magill

Eddie Johnson

Bill Cheesbourg

Al Keller

Jimmy Daywalt

Ed Elisian

Rodger Ward

Troy Ruttman

Eddie Russo

Elmer George

Right: Sam Hanks receives a kiss from his wife, Alice, in Victory Lane. Below, left: The field lines up behind the Mercury pace car coming out of the southeast turn. The pace lap was marred by an accident involving Elmer George and Eddie Russo. Below, middle: The wreckage of the car in which Keith Andrews was fatally injured. He was testing the car for "Nino" Farina when he spun in the northwest turn, slid across the grass infield and backed into a concrete wall on the inside of the track. Below, right: A tearful Sam Hanks has just announced his imminent retirement from auto racing after a successful 23-year career. Alice Hanks expresses her relief to insurance executive Wes Mahaney.

Above, left: The attractive and functional Tower Terrace replaced the Pagoda and ramshackle bleachers along the inside of the frontstretch. A wide and safe pit apron was a welcome addition for contestants. Above, right: The Novis in action. No. 54 is Paul Russo and No. 27, Tony Bettenhausen. Right: Paul Tea, mechanic for the Frank Kurtis Company puts the finishing touches on a new Bowes Seal Fast Special to be driven by Freddy Agabashian.

Top: The pace lap as seen from the new Tower. Middle left: Tony Bettenhausen compares notes with 1925 winner Peter DePaolo. Middle, right: The "lay down" engine in Sam Hanks' winning Belond Special. Left: The entrance to the new office-museum where famous cars of previous years are on display year-round.

1958

Some masterful driving and a lot of luck got Jimmy Bryan through a first-lap pileup to beat a hard-charging rookie, George Amick, by a narrow margin and win an accident-marred "500". After a parade lap foul-up which found the first three cars a half-lap ahead of the field, necessitating an extra lap, all 33 cars took the flag in a semblance of order but in the third turn, Ed Elisian spun into Dick Rathmann and both cars went into the wall. Jimmy Reece hit the brakes and was spun by Bob Veith. Pat O'Connor flipped over Reece and sustained fatal head injuries before the car burst into flames. Most of the other cars tangled and Jerry Unser drove up on another car and cartwheeled over the outside wall. Miraculously, Unser escaped with a dislocated shoulder. The decimated pack kept going and an excellent battle soon developed between Bryan, Amick and Johnny Boyd. On his 39th lap, Chuck Weyant hit the northwest wall but escaped with minor injuries. Things settled down until the 149th lap when rookie A. J. Foyt spun in the south chute. Near the end of the race Bob Christie spun in the northeast turn and Dempsey Wilson's car caught fire in the pits. Reece, who finished sixth with a wrecked car, had the shortest actual running time on the track.

Jimmy Bryan

NO.	DRIVER	CAR	ENTRANT	ENGINE	CYL.	DISP.	CHASSIS	COLOR	QUAL. SPEED	ST.	FIN.	LAPS/SPEED/REASON OUT
1	Jimmy Bryan	Belond A P	George Salih	Offy	4	252	Epperly	yellow, red	144.185	7	1	200-133.791
99	George Amick	Demler	Norman C. Demler	Offy	4	255	Epperly	yellow, red	142.710	25	2	200-133.517
9	Johnny Boyd	Bowes Seal Fast	Robert M. Bowes, II	Offy	4	252	KK500G	white, black, red	144.023	8	3	200-133.099
33	Tony Bettenhausen	Jones & Maley	Cars, Inc.	Offy	4	252	Epperly	dark red, white	143.919	9	4	200-132.855
2	Jim Rathmann	Leader Card 500 Roadster	Lindsey Hopkins	Offy	4	252	Epperly	blue, pink, white	143.147	20	5	200-132.857
16	Jimmy Reece	John Zink	John Zink	Offy	4	252	Watson	maroon, white	145.513	3	6	200-132.443
26	Don Freeland	Bob Estes	Bob Estes	Offy	4	252	Phillips	yellow, red	143.033	13	7	200-132.403
44	Jud Larson	John Zink	John Zink Co.	Offy	4	252	Watson	red, white	143.512	19	8	200-130.550
61	Eddie Johnson	Bryant Heating & Cooling	J. S. "Duke" Donaldson	Offy	4	251	KK500G	red, white	142.670	26	9	200-130.156
54	Bill Cheesbourg	Novi Auto. Air Conditioner	Novi Racing Corp., Inc.	Novi*	8	169	Kurtis	silver, red	142.546	33	10	200-129.149
52	Al Keller	Bardahl	Pat Clancy	Offy	4	252	KK500G-2	black, white	142.931	21	11	200-128.498
45	Johnnie Parsons	Gerhardt	Fred Gerhardt	Offy	4	252	Kurtis	white, red	144.683	6	12	200-128.254
19	Johnnie Tolan	Greenman-Casale	Lysle Greenman	Offy	4	252	Kuzma	red, yellow	142.309	30	13	200-128.150
65	Bob Christie	Federal Engineering	Federal Auto. Associates	Offy	4	251	KK500C	blue, yellow	142.253	17	14	189-spun NE
59	Dempsey Wilson	Sorenson	Bob Sorenson	Offy	4	252	Kuzma	yellow, black	134.272	32	15	151-clutch pedal, fire
29	A. J. Foyt	Dean Van Lines	Dean Van Lines	Offy	4	252	Kuzma	white, blue	143.130	12	16	148-spun SE
77	Mike Magill	Dayton Steel Foundry	George Walther, Jr.	Offy	4	255	KK500G	white, blue, red	142.276	31	17	136-black flagged
15	Paul Russo	Novi Auto. Air Conditioner	Novi Racing Corp., Inc.	Novi*	8	169	Kurtis	bluish-gray, red	142.959	14	18	122-radiator
83	Shorty Templeman	McNamara	Kalamazoo Sports, Inc.	Offy	4	255	KK500D	maroon, gold	142.817	23	19	116-brakes
8	Rodger Ward	Wolcott Fuel Injection	Roger Wolcott	Offy	4	252	Lesovsky	red, white	143.266	11	20	93-fuel pump
43	Billy Garrett	Chapman	H. A. Chapman	Offy	4	252	KK500G	blue, cream	142.778	15	21	80-cam gear
88	Eddie Sachs	Schmidt	Peter Schmidt	Offy	4	255	Kuzma	red, silver	144.660	18	22	68-universal joint
7	Johnny Thomson	D-A Lubricant	Racing Associates	Offy	4	251	Kurtis	yellow, white, black	142.908	22	23	52-steering damaged
89	Chuck Weyant	Dunn Engineering	Harry Dunn	Offy	4	251	Dunn	white, black	142.608	29	24	38-brakes locked, wrecked
25	Jack Turner	Massaglia Hotels	Joseph Massaglia, Jr.	Offy	4	252	Lesovsky	white, red, blue	143.438	10	25	21-fuel pump
14	Bob Veith	Bowes Seal Fast	Robert M. Bowes, II	Offy	4	252	KK500G	white, black, red	144.881	4	26	1-wrecked NE
97	Dick Rathmann	McNamara	Kalamazoo Sports, Inc.	Offy	4	255	Watson	silver, white, red	145.974	1	27	0-wrecked NE
5	Ed Elisian	John Zink	Ellen McKinney Zink	Offy	4	252	Watson	white, red, black	145.926	2	28	0-wrecked NE
4	Pat O'Connor	Sumar	Chapman S. Root	Offy	4	255	KK500G	blue, white	144.823	5	29	0-wrecked NE
31	Paul Goldsmith	City of Daytona	Henry "Smokey" Yunick	Offy	4	255	KK500G	black, gold	142.744	16	30	0-wrecked NE
92	Jerry Unser	McKay	Roy McKay	Offy	4	251	KK500G	lavender, maroon	142.755	24	31	0-wrecked NE
68	Len Sutton	Jim Robbins	Jim Robbins	Offy	4	255	KK500G	maroon, cream	142.653	27	32	0-wrecked NE
57	Art Bisch	Helse	H. H. Johnson	Offy	4	251	Kuzma	bluish-gray, white	142.631	28	33	0-wrecked NE

*Supercharged

George Amick

Johnny Boyd

Tony Bettenhausen

Jim Rathmann

Jimmy Reece

Don Freeland

Jud Larson

Eddie Johnson

Bill Cheesbourg

Al Keller

Johnnie Parsons

Johnnie Tolan

Bob Christie

Dempsey Wilson

A. J. Foyt

Mike Magill

Paul Russo

Shorty Templeman

Rodger Ward

Billy Garrett

Eddie Sachs

Johnny Thomson

Chuck Weyant

Jack Turner

Bob Veith

Dick Rathmann

Ed Elisian

Pat O'Connor

Paul Goldsmith

Jerry Unser

Len Sutton

Art Bisch

Right: Shirley MacLaine kisses winner Jimmy Bryan. Below, left: Jim Rathmann spins into the pits as he was making a routine stop. Below, right: Johnny Thomson makes a pit stop. Third row, left: Chuck Weyant's car after it hit the northwest wall and spun into the infield. Third row, right: Jimmy Bryan and George Amick neck-and-neck down the front-stretch. Bottom, left: The front row. No. 97, Dick Rathmann, No. 5, Ed Elisian, No. 16, Jimmy Reece. Bottom, right: Dick Rathmann jumps into the lead followed by Ed Elisian.

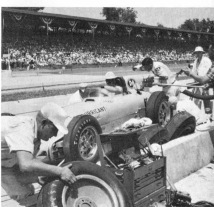

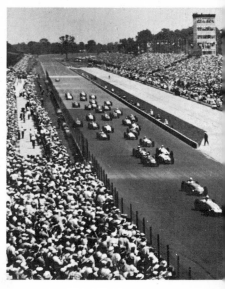

The fifteen-car accident in the northeast turn was triggered when Ed Elisian spun into Dick Rathmann and both cars went into the wall. Pat O'Connor flipped over Jimmy Reece and received fatal head injuries. (top, left). Jerry Unser used Paul Goldsmith for a ramp (top, right) and went end-over-end over the outside wall. He received a dislocated shoulder. The aerial view (above) shows the many cars involved in the accident and the photo at left, some of the wrecked cars which have been removed to the infield. The yellow light is still on as firemen fight the blaze in O'Connor's Sumar Special.

1959

Almost from the start, the 1959 "500" was one of the most competitive races in history. Rodger Ward, Jim Rathmann, Johnny Thomson and Pat Flaherty were evenly matched and the four cars engaged in a see-saw battle for the first three quarters of the race. Only Flaherty's accident and Thomson's mechanical trouble narrowed it down to a two-way fight between Ward and Rathmann. The action started immediately as Ward took the lead in the first turn. Eddie Sachs spun in the first turn on lap 8 with some close calls occuring before he regained control. Len Sutton blew a tire and hit the wall in the southwest turn on his 35th lap and nine laps later Chuck Weyant spun in the northeast. Mike Magill, trying to go by Weyant on the outside, was pinned into the wall and flipped end over end into the infield as Larson and Red Amick tangled to miss him. Magill received a burned neck. Ray Crawford was more seriously injured when he hit the wall in the same place on his 116th lap. On the 163rd lap Flaherty hit the wall and spun to a stop at the pit entrance. Ward finished some 22 seconds in front of Rathmann. In practice, Jerry Unser died of burns in a frontstretch crash and Bob Cortner was fatally injured hitting the northeast wall.

Rodger Ward

NO.	DRIVER	CAR	ENTRANT	ENGINE	CYL.	DISP.	CHASSIS	COLOR	QUAL. SPEED	ST.	FIN.	LAPS/SPEED/REASON OUT
5	Rodger Ward	Leader Card 500 Roadster	Leader Cards, Inc.	Offy	4	252	Watson	white, red, blue	144.035	6	1	200-135.857
16	Jim Rathmann	Simoniz	Lindsey Hopkins	Offy	4	252	Watson	blue, orange, white	144.433	3	2	200-135.619
3	Johnny Thomson	Racing Associates	Racing Associates	Offy	4	252	Lesovsky	pink, black, white	145.908	1	3	200-135.340
1	Tony Bettenhausen	Hoover Motor Express	John R. Wills	Offy	4	252	Epperly	orange, white, black	142.721	15	4	200-134.768
99	Paul Goldsmith	Demler	Norman C. Demler	Offy	4	255	Epperly	yellow, red	142.670	16	5	200-134.573
33	Johnny Boyd	Bowes Seal Fast	Bignotti-Bowes Racing	Offy	4	252	Epperly	white, black, red	142.812	11	6	200-133.867
37	Duane Carter	Smokey's Reverse Torque	Yunick, Glover & Lathrop	Offy	4	252	Kurtis	gold, black	142.795	12	7	200-133.342
19	Eddie Johnson	Bryant Heating & Cooling	J. S. "Duke" Donaldson	Offy	4	251	KK500G	red, gold	144.000	8	8	200-133.336
45	Paul Russo	Bardahl	Fred Gerhardt	Offy	4	252	KK500G	black, white	142.383	27	9	200-133.331
10	A. J. Foyt	Dean Van Lines	A. E. Dean	Offy	4	252	Kuzma	white, blue	142.648	17	10	200-133.297
88	Gene Hartley	Drewry's	R. T. Marley, Sr.	Offy	4	255	Kuzma	red, gold	143.575	9	11	200-132.434
74	Bob Veith	John Zink Heater	John Zink Co.	Offy	4	252	Moore	rose, white, black	144.023	7	12	200-132.169
89	Al Herman	Dunn Engineering	Harry Dunn	Offy	4	251	Dunn	white, black	141.939	23	13	200-131.872
66	Jimmy Daywalt	Federal Engineering	Federal Auto. Associates	Offy	4	251	Kurtis	yellow, blue	144.683	13	14	200-131.861
71	Chuck Arnold	Hall-Mar	Karl Hall	Offy	4	252	Curtis	red, gold	142.118	21	15	200-130.918
58	Jim McWithey	Ray Brady	Ray T. Brady	Offy	4	252	KK500C	red, white	141.215	33	16	200-129.024
44	Eddie Sachs	Peter Schmidt	Peter Schmidt	Offy	4	252	Kuzma	red, silver	145.425	2	17	182-gear tower bolt
57	Al Keller	Helse	H. H. Johnson	Offy	4	251	Kuzma	bluish-gray, white	142.057	28	18	163-piston
64	Pat Flaherty	John Zink Heater	John Zink Co.	Offy	4	252	Watson	rose, white, black	142.399	18	19	162-wrecked FS
73	Dick Rathmann	McNamara Chiropractic	Kalamazoo Sports, Inc.	Offy	4	255	Watson	maroon, gold	144.248	4	20	150-caught fire in pits
53	Bill Cheesbourg	Greenman-Casale	Lysle Greenman	Offy	4	252	Kuzma	white, blue	141.788	30	21	147-magneto
15	Don Freeland	Jim Robbins	Jim Robbins	Offy	4	252	KK500G	maroon, cream	143.056	25	22	136-valve spring
49	Ray Crawford	Meguiar's Mirror Glaze	Ray Crawford	Offy	4	255	Elder	red, cream	141.348	32	23	115-wrecked NE
9	Don Branson	Bob Estes	Bob Estes	Offy	4	253	Phillips	yellow, red	143.312	10	24	112-torsion bar
65	Bob Christie	Federal Engineering	Federal Auto. Associates	Offy	4	251	KK500C	yellow, blue	143.244	24	25	109-rod bolt
48	Bobby Grim	Sumar	Chapman S. Root	Offy	4	255	KK500G	lt. blue, dk. blue	144.225	5	26	85-piston
24	Jack Turner	Travelon Trailer	Ernest L. Ruiz	Offy	4	252	Christensen	green, white, red	143.478	14	27	47-fuel tank
47	Chuck Weyant	McKay	Roy McKay	Offy	4	252	KK500G	yellow, black	141.950	29	28	45-wrecked NE
7	Jud Larson	Bowes Seal Fast	Bignotti-Bowes Racing	Offy	4	252	Kurtis	white, black, red	142.298	19	29	45-wrecked NE
77	Mike Magill	Dayton Steel Foundry	George Walther, Jr.	Offy	4	255	Sutton	bluish-gray, cream	141.482	31	30	45-wrecked NE
87	Red Amick	Wheeler-Foutch	LeRoy E. Foutch, Jr.	Offy	4	255	KK500C	red, bronze	142.925	26	31	45-wrecked NE
8	Len Sutton	Wolcott	Wolcott Memorial Racing Team	Offy*	4	168	Lesovsky	red, white	142.107	22	32	34-wrecked SW
6	Jimmy Bryan	Belond A P Muffler	George Salih	Offy	4	249	Epperly	yellow, red	142.118	20	33	1-clutch, cam gear

*Supercharged

Jim Rathmann

Johnny Thomson

Tony Bettenhausen

Paul Goldsmith

Johnny Boyd

Duane Carter

Eddie Johnson

Paul Russo

A. J. Foyt

Gene Hartley

Bob Veith

Al Herman

Jimmy Daywalt

Chuck Arnold

Jim McWithey

Eddie Sachs

Al Keller

Pat Flaherty

Dick Rathmann

Bill Cheesbourg

Don Freeland

Ray Crawford

Don Branson

Bob Christie

Bobby Grim

Jack Turner

Chuck Weyant

Jud Larson

Mike Magill

Red Amick

Len Sutton

Jimmy Bryan

Below, left: Rodger Ward holding his dog Skippy as his wife Jo (now deceased) and actress Erin O'Brien offer their congratulations. Below, right: Rodger Ward gets the checkered flag from Starter Bill Vandewater. Middle: Rodger and Jo Ward in the Buick pace car which Rodger won. Bottom: Johnny Thomson leading the first lap.

FRONT ROW QUALIFIERS
INDIANAPOLIS MOTOR SPEEDWAY
1959

Left: The front row. Johnny Thomson, No. 3, Eddie Sachs, No. 44, and Jim Rathmann, No. 16. Below, left: Tony Bettenhausen arrives for work. Below, right: The observers' stand at the end of the pit area is the nerve center of the track during practice.

Above, left: Veteran Speedway sign painter, George Gruber paints the number of Jim Packard's Sclavi-Amos Special. Above, middle: Bob Cortner pulls the three "rookie stripes" of tape off the tail of his Cornis Special. The day after passing his driving test, Cortner hit the northeast wall and died that evening. Above, right: Paul Russo utilizes a pneumatic platform to lift his car during a pit stop. Left: Rodger Ward starts his last lap in the Leader Card "500" Roadster.

1960

The red hot battle between Rodger Ward and Jim Rathmann took up right where it left off in 1959, and with Eddie Sachs and Johnny Thomson thrown in for good measure, the competition assumed monumental proportions. Some unplanned action took place during the parade lap when a homemade grandstand collapsed in the northeast turn infield and injured a number of spectators. As Ward, Sachs, Rathmann and Thomson were burning up the track, Don Branson gave pitmen a thrill when he spun coming in for fuel and tires. Eddie Russo ran the tires off his car and hit the wall in the second turn when one finally blew. Eddie was quite seriously injured. A short time later, Chuck Stevenson spun near the scene of Russo's accident and late in the race, Wayne Weiler crashed a little further down the backstretch. Tony Bettenhausen, who had been running with the leaders, broke a connecting rod and the car caught fire as Tony was gingerly guiding it into the pits. Sachs and Thomson also had trouble and the stage was set for a final dogfight between Ward and Rathmann. The two raced almost hub to hub until three laps from the finish when a badly worn tire caused Ward to slow as Rathmann roared to victory.

Jim Rathmann

NO.	DRIVER	CAR	ENTRANT	ENGINE	CYL.	DISP.	CHASSIS	COLOR	QUAL. SPEED	ST.	FIN.	LAPS/SPEED/REASON OUT
4	Jim Rathmann	Ken-Paul	Ken-Paul, Inc.	Offy	4	252	Watson	blue, white, red	146.371	2	1	200-138.767
1	Rodger Ward	Leader Card 500 Roadster	Leader Cards, Inc.	Offy	4	252	Watson	white, red, blue	145.560	3	2	200-138.631
99	Paul Goldsmith	Demler	Norman C. Demler	Offy	4	255	Epperly	yellow, red	142.783	26	3	200-136.792
7	Don Branson	Bob Estes	Bob Estes	Offy	4	252	Phillips	yellow, red	144.753	8	4	200-136.785
3	Johnny Thomson	Adams Quarter Horse	Racing Associates	Offy	4	252	Lesovsky	pink, black, white	146.443	17	5	200-136.750
22	Eddie Johnson	Jim Robbins	Jim Robbins Co.	Offy	4	252	Trevis	maroon, white	145.003	7	6	200-136.137
98	Lloyd Ruby	Agajanian	J. C. Agajanian	Offy	4	252	Watson	maroon, silver	144.208	12	7	200-135.983
44	Bob Veith	Schmidt	Peter Schmidt	Offy	4	252	Meskowski	red, silver	143.363	25	8	200-135.452
18	Bud Tingelstad	Jim Robbins	Jim Robbins Co.	Offy	4	252	Trevis	maroon, white	142.354	28	9	200-133.717
38	Bob Christie	Federal Engineering	Federal Auto. Associates	Offy	4	255	KK500C	yellow, blue	143.638	14	10	200-133.416
27	Red Amick	King O' Lawn	Leonard A. Faas, Sr.	Offy	4	252	Epperly	blue, white, red	143.084	22	11	200-131.946
17	Duane Carter	Thompson Industries	J. Ensley & S. Murphy	Offy	4	252	Kuzma	red, silver, white	142.631	27	12	200-131.882
39	Bill Homeier	Ridgewood Builders	Norman Hall	Offy	4	252	Kuzma	silver, black, orange	141.248	31	13	200-131.367
48	Gene Hartley	Sumar	Chapman S. Root	Offy	4	252	KK500G	lt. blue, dk. blue	143.896	24	14	196-flagged
65	Chuck Stevenson	Leader Card 500 Roadster	Leader Cards, Inc.	Offy	4	252	Watson	white, blue	144.665	9	15	196-flagged
14	Bobby Grim	Bill Forbes	William P. Forbes	Offy	4	252	Meskowski	pearl, red, orange	143.158	21	16	194-flagged
26	Shorty Templeman	Federal Engineering	Federal Auto. Associates	Offy	4	255	KK500C	yellow, blue, black	143.856	19	17	191-flagged
56	Jim Hurtubise	Travelon Trailer	Ernest L. Ruiz	Offy	4	252	Christensen	pink pearl, purple	149.056	23	18	185-con. rod
10	Jimmy Bryan	Metal-Cal	George Salih	Offy	4	252	Epperly	yellow, black	144.532	10	19	152-fuel pump drive
28	Troy Ruttman	John Zink Heater	John Zink Co.	Offy	4	252	Watson	red, white, black	145.366	6	20	134-rear end gear
6	Eddie Sachs	Dean Van Lines	Dean Van Lines Racing Div.	Offy	4	252	Ewing	white, blue	146.592	1	21	132-magneto
73	Don Freeland	Ross-Babcock Traveler	Racing Associates	Offy	4	252	Kurtis	lavender, red, yellow	144.352	11	22	129-magneto
2	Tony Bettenhausen	Dowgard	Lindsey Hopkins	Offy	4	252	Watson	blue, orange, white	145.214	18	23	125-con. rod
32	Wayne Weiler	Ansted Rotary	Ansted Rotary Corp.	Offy	4	252	Epperly	cream, black	143.512	15	24	103-wrecked SE
5	A. J. Foyt	Bowes Seal Fast	Bignotti-Bowes Racing	Offy	4	252	Kurtis	pearl, red, black	143.466	16	25	90-clutch
46	Eddie Russo	Go-Kart	C. O. Prather	Offy	4	255	KK500G	yellow, red, blue	142.203	29	26	84-wrecked SE
8	Johnny Boyd	Bowes Seal Fast	Bignotti-Bowes Racing	Offy	4	252	Epperly	white, black, red	143.770	13	27	77-piston
37	Gene Force	McKay	Roy McKay	Offy	4	255	KK500G	lavender, white, red	143.472	20	28	74-brakes
16	Jim McWithey	Hoover Motor Express	Hoover Motor Express, Inc.	Offy	4	252	Epperly	orange, silver, black	140.378	32	29	60-brakes
9	Len Sutton	S-R Racing Enterprise	Peter Salemi & Nick Rini	Offy	4	252	Watson	tan, yellow, black	145.443	5	30	47-engine trouble
97	Dick Rathmann	Jim Robbins	Jim Robbins Co.	Offy	4	255	Watson	maroon, white	145.543	4	31	42-brake line
76	Al Herman	Joe Hunt Magneto	Joe Hunt	Offy	4	252	Ewing	black, white, red	141.838	30	32	34-clutch
23	Dempsey Wilson	Bryant Heating & Cooling	J. S. "Duke" Donaldson	Offy	4	251	KK500G	red, white	143.215	33	33	11-magneto point spring

Rodger Ward

Paul Goldsmith

Don Branson

Johnny Thomson

Eddie Johnson

Lloyd Ruby

Bob Veith

Bud Tingelstad

Bob Christie

Red Amick

Duane Carter

Bill Homeier

Gene Hartley

Chuck Stevenson

Bobby Grim

Shorty Templeman

Jim Hurtubise

Jimmy Bryan

Troy Ruttman

Eddie Sachs

Don Freeland

Tony Bettenhausen

Wayne Weiler

A. J. Foyt

Eddie Russo

Johnny Boyd

Gene Force

Jim McWithey

Len Sutton

Dick Rathmann

Al Herman

Dempsey Wilson

Right: Jim Rathmann and his wife, Kay, in Victory Lane.
Below: Winner Jim Rathmann in his Ken-Paul Special the
morning after the race.

Left: The wreck of Jack Rounds' Fullerton Special after he hit the inside rail coming out of the northwest turn. Though the car was severely damaged, Rounds was not seriously injured. Below, left: Crews often work late into the night. A mechanic makes some adjustments to Dick Rathmann's Jim Robbins Special in its garage. Below, middle: The Chevrolet engine in the San Diego Steel Products Special. Below, right: Trophies, both modern and historic, are on display in the Speedway Museum.

Above, left: The Oldsmobile pace car, with Sam Hanks at the wheel, leads the thirty-three starters. Eddie Sachs is on the pole. Above right: Fans pour through Gasoline Alley after the race. This is the only time that the area is open to the public during the month of May. Left: A. J. Foyt and Johnny Boyd in the Bowes Seal Fast cars.

1961

The "Golden Anniversary '500'" was one of nostalgia as it brought back many "greats" of racing. The pre-race spectators saw three of them, Harroun, Cooper and Rickenbacker, lap the track in the machines which they drove to fame. The race was every bit as exciting as the 1960 "trophy dash" and it ended in almost the same manner. After Jim Hurtubise led the first segment, Eddie Sachs and Parnelli Jones, driving his first "500", took turns leading. Don Davis spun in his own oil on the starting line and ran to the safety of the pit wall as A. J. Shepherd spun out of control. This triggered an accident involving himself, Jack Turner, Bill Cheesbourg, and Roger McCluskey. Turner went end-over-end down the stretch but was not seriously injured. Jones' car suffered magneto trouble and dropped from the lead, leaving the field clear for a prolonged fight between Sachs and A. J. Foyt. On Foyt's last scheduled pit stop, the fueling equipment malfunctioned and he had to stop on the 184th lap for a refill, apparently giving the race to Sachs. With three laps to go, Sachs had to pit for a tire change and Foyt flashed by to win. On May 12th, Tony Bettenhausen was fatally injured while testing Paul Russo's car. The accident took place in front of the pits.

A. J. Foyt

NO.	DRIVER	CAR	ENTRANT	ENGINE	CYL.	DISP.	CHASSIS	COLOR	QUAL. SPEED	ST.	FIN.	LAPS/SPEED/REASON OUT
1	A. J. Foyt	Bowes Seal Fast	Bignotti-Bowes Racing Assoc.	Offy	4	252	Watson	pearl, black, red	145.903	7	1	200-139.130
12	Eddie Sachs	Dean Van Lines	Dean Van Lines; Racing Div.	Offy	4	252	Ewing	white, blue	147.481	1	2	200-139.041
2	Rodger Ward	Del Webb's Sun City	Leader Cards, Inc.	Offy	4	252	Watson	white, red, blue	146.187	4	3	200-138.539
7	Shorty Templeman	Bill Forbes Racing Team	William P. Forbes	Offy	4	253	Watson	white, maroon	144.341	18	4	200-136.873
19	Al Keller	Konstant Hot	Bruce Homeyer	Offy	4	253	Phillips	black, yellow	146.157	26	5	200-136.034
18	Chuck Stevenson	Metal-Cal	C & H Supply Co.	Offy	4	252	Epperly	yellow, maroon	145.191	28	6	200-135.742
31	Bobby Marshman	Hoover Motor Express	Hoover Motor Express	Offy	4	252	Epperly	orange, silver	144.293	33	7	200-135.534
5	Lloyd Ruby	Autolite	Lindsey Hopkins	Offy	4	254	Epperly	white, rose	146.909	25	8	200-134.860
17	Jack Brabham	Cooper-Climax	Cooper Car Co., Ltd.	Climax R	4	168	Cooper	green, white	145.144	13	9	200-134.116
34	Norm Hall	Federal Engineering	Federal Automotive Assoc.	Offy	4	255	KK500C	blue, yellow	144.555	32	10	200-134.104
28	Gene Hartley	John Chalik	John Chalik	Offy	4	252	Trevis	blue, white	144.817	15	11	198-flagged
98	Parnelli Jones	Agajanian-Willard Battery	J. C. Agajanian	Offy	4	252	Watson	pearl, blue, red	146.080	5	12	192-flagged
97	Dick Rathmann	Jim Robbins	Jim Robbins Co.	Offy	4	252	Trevis	maroon, white, gold	146.033	6	13	164-fuel pump
10	Paul Goldsmith	Racing Associates	Racing Associates	Offy	4	252	Lesovsky	black, gold	144.741	17	14	160-conn. rod
15	Wayne Weiler	Hopkins	Lindsey Hopkins	Offy	4	252	Watson	blue, orange	145.349	12	15	147-wheel bearing
35	Dempsey Wilson	Lysle Greenman	Lysle Greenman	Offy	4	252	Kuzma	blue, white	144.202	31	16	145-fuel pump
32	Bob Christie	North Electric	William Tucker, Inc.	Offy	4	252	Kurtis	white, blue	144.782	16	17	132-burned piston
33	Eddie Johnson	Jim Robbins	Jim Robbins Co.	Offy	4	252	Kuzma	blue, white	145.843	10	18	127-wrecked NW
8	Len Sutton	Bryant Heating & Cooling	Pete Salemi & Nick Rini	Offy	4	252	Watson	blue, white	145.897	8	19	110-clutch
52	Troy Ruttman	John Zink Trackburner	John S. Zink	Offy	4	252	Moore	red, white	144.799	22	20	105-clutch
41	Johnny Boyd	Leader Card 500 Roadster	Leader Cards, Inc.	Offy	4	252	Watson	orange, white	144.092	20	21	105-clutch
99	Jim Hurtubise	Demler	Norm Demler, Inc.	Offy	4	256	Epperly	yellow, red	146.306	3	22	102-piston
86	Ebb Rose	Meyer Speedway	Racing Associates	Offy	4	252	Porter	black, pink	144.338	19	23	93-con. rod
26	Cliff Griffith	McCullough	Edgar R. Elder	Offy	4	252	Elder	yellow, black	145.038	30	24	55-piston
45	Jack Turner	Bardahl	Fred Gerhardt	Offy	4	252	Kurtis	black, white	144.904	21	25	52-wreck FS
73	A. J. Shepherd	Travelon Trailer	Ernest L. Ruiz	Offy	4	252	Watson	silver, gold, blue	144.954	14	26	51-wreck FS
22	Roger McCluskey	Racing Associates	Racing Associates	Offy	4	252	Watson	black, red	145.068	29	27	51-wreck FS
14	Bill Cheesbourg	Dean Van Lines	Dean Van Lines; Racing Div.	Offy	4	252	Kuzma	white, blue	145.873	9	28	50-wreck FS
83	Don Davis	Dart-Kart	Trevis & Morcroft	Offy	4	252	Trevis	blue, white	145.349	27	29	49-wreck FS
4	Jim Rathmann	Simoniz	Ken-Paul, Inc.	Offy	4	252	Watson	black, gold	145.413	11	30	48-magneto
55	Jimmy Daywalt	Schulz Fueling Equipment	C. O. Prather	Offy	4	251	KK500G	red, gold	144.219	23	31	27-brake line
16	Bobby Grim	Thompson Industries	Ansted-Thompson Racing, Inc.	Offy	4	252	Watson	Chinese red, gold	144.029	24	32	26-piston
3	Don Branson	Hoover Motor Express	Hoover Motor Express		4	252	Epperly	orange, silver	146.843	2	33	2-bent valves

RRear Engine

Eddie Sachs

Rodger Ward

Shorty Templeman

Al Keller

Chuck Stevenson

Bobby Marshman

Lloyd Ruby

Jack Brabham

Norm Hall

Gene Hartley

Parnelli Jones

Dick Rathmann

Paul Goldsmith

Wayne Weiler

Dempsey Wilson

Bob Christie

Eddie Johnson

Len Sutton

Troy Ruttman

Johnny Boyd

Jim Hurtubise

Ebb Rose

Cliff Griffith

Jack Turner

A. J. Shepherd

Roger McCluskey

Bill Cheesbourg

Don Davis

Jim Rathmann

Jimmy Daywalt

Bobby Grim

Don Branson

Right: Cars return to "Gasoline Alley" after a practice session. Below, left: As the Purdue Band plays the traditional "On the Banks of the Wabash", the cars are pushed to the starting line. Below, middle: A. J. Shepherd's crew practices a pit stop. Mel Fernandes, on the pit wall, checks their time with a stop watch. Below, right: Eddie Rickenbacker, former driver, official and Speedway owner, takes a lap around the track in a 1915 Duesenberg. His riding mechanic is former racing pilot and aeronautical pioneer, Colonel Roscoe Turner. Rickenbacker, Ray Harroun and Earl Cooper drove their antique cars as a part of the "Golden Anniversary" celebration.

Above, left: On the day before the race, the bricks are vacuumed to remove much of the dust that accumulates in the crevices. This dust could cause poor visibility when thirty-three cars come down for the green flag. Above, right: On the pace lap, the front row lines up as they enter the south chute. Right: Bobby Marshman, who early in May had given up all chances of gaining a ride and returned home, happily removes his "rookie stripes" after being called back to the track to complete his test in the Hoover Motor Express Special. He justified the faith placed in him by earning Co-Rookie of the Year honors with Parnelli Jones.

Top: ''500''Festival Queen Diane Hunt is flanked by 1911 winner Ray Harroun in his Marmon ''Wasp'' and pole driver Eddie Sachs in the Dean Van Lines Special. Above, left: Paul Russo watches his crew weigh the Stearly Motor Freight Special to try to determine what is wrong with its handling characteristics. A few minutes later, Tony Bettenhausen volunteered to test drive the car and crashed to his death on the last lap of the run. Below: The car is removed from the track after the accident which happened directly in front of the pits. Above, right: A. J. Foyt gets the checkered flag from Bill Vandewater after a hectic battle with Eddie Sachs. Left: A. J. Foyt in Victory Lane.

1962

Although Parnelli Jones finally broke the 150-mile-per-hour barrier when he qualified at 150.370, a worn brake line ended his chances of victory as he was holding a commanding lead. Rodger Ward roared to his second "500" triumph in front of teammate Len Sutton and the combination of Ward, Wilke and Watson took home a sizeable piece of the purse. Voluble and popular Eddie Sachs was an impressive third. Jack Turner, for the second straight year, had trouble on the frontstretch and took another nasty flip after becoming involved in a tangle with Allen Crowe, Bob Christie and Chuck Rodee. Turner was more seriously injured, this time with a broken toe and bruises. A. J. Foyt, who was fighting for the lead, lost a wheel shortly after a pit stop and spun out of the race in the southeast turn. A. J. appeared later driving relief for Elmer George. Roger McCluskey, running with the leaders, also spun in the southeast turn when a radiator hose broke on his 170th lap. With Jones and Foyt out of the way, it was comparatively clear sailing for Ward, although Sutton managed to lead a few laps while Rodger was in the pits. Norm Hall crashed into the southwest wall and received severe head injuries while qualifying.

Rodger Ward

NO.	DRIVER	CAR	ENTRANT	ENGINE	CYL.	DISP.	CHASSIS	COLOR	QUAL. SPEED	ST.	FIN.	LAPS/SPEED/REASON OUT
3	Rodger Ward	Leader Card 500 Roadster	Leader Cards, Inc.	Offy	4	252	Watson	white, red, blue	149.371	2	1	200-140.293
7	Len Sutton	Leader Card 500 Roadster	Leader Cards, Inc.	Offy	4	252	Watson	blue, red, white	149.328	4	2	200-140.167
2	Eddie Sachs	Dean-Autolite	Dean Van Lines; Racing Div.	Offy	4	252	Ewing	white, blue	146.431	27	3	200-140.075
27	Don Davis	J. H. Rose Truck Line	Bob Philipp	Offy	4	252	Lesovsky	black, rose	147.209	12	4	200-139.768
54	Bobby Marshma	Bryant Heating & Cooling	Your Bryant Dealer	Offy	4	252	Epperly	black, silver	149.347	3	5	200-138.790
15	Jim McElreath	Schulz Fueling Equipment	C. O. Prather	Offy	4	252	Kurtis	red, white	149.025	7	6	200-138.653
98	Parnelli Jones	Agajanian Willard Battery	J. C. Agajanian	Offy	4	252	Watson	pearl, blue, red	150.370	1	7	200-138.534
12	Lloyd Ruby	Thompson Industries	Ansted-Thompson Racing, Inc.	Offy	4	253	Watson	cream, blue	146.520	24	8	200-138.182
44	Jim Rathmann	Simoniz Vista	Smokey Yunick	Offy	4	252	Watson	black, gold	146.610	23	9	200-136.913
38	Johnny Boyd	Metal-Cal	C & H Supply Co.	Offy	4	252	Epperly	yellow, maroon	147.047	28	10	200-136.600
4	Shorty Templeman	Bill Forbes Racing Team	William P. Forbes	Offy	4	252	Watson	white, maroon	149.050	6	11	200-135.844
14	Don Branson	Mid-Continent Securities	Lindsey Hopkins	Offy	4	252	Epperly	blue, orange	147.312	11	12	200-135.836
91	Jim Hurtubise	Jim Robbins	John Marco Pusilo	Offy	4	252	Trevis	maroon, white	146.963	29	13	200-135.655
86	Ebb Rose	J. H. Rose Truck Line	Herb Porter	Offy	4	252	Porter	black, pink	146.336	32	14	200-134.001
5	Bud Tingelstad	Konstant Hot	Bruce Homeyer	Offy	4	252	Phillips	black, gold	147.753	10	15	200-133.170
17	Roger McCluskey	Bell Lines Trucking	Sclavi, Inc.	Offy	4	252	Watson	yellow, white	147.759	9	16	168-spun SE
21	Elmer George	Sarkes Tarzian	Mari George	Offy	4	252	Lesovsky	blue, maroon	146.092	17	17	146-engine seized
26	Troy Ruttman	Jim Robbins	Jim Robbins Co.	Offy	4	252	Kuzma	ivory, blue	146.765	30	18	140-burned piston
18	Bobby Grim	Morcroft	Gilbert E. Morcroft	Offy	4	252	Trevis	white, red	146.604	15	19	96-oil leak
34	Dan Gurney	Thompson Enterprises	Mickey Thompson	Buick R	8	256	Thompson	white, blue	147.886	8	20	92-rear end gear
19	Chuck Hulse	Federal Engineering	Federal Automotive Assoc.	Offy	4	252	KK500C	blue, yellow	146.377	16	21	91-fuel pump
79	Jimmy Daywalt	Albany, N.Y.	Tassi Vatis	Offy	4	252	Kurtis	blue, orange	146.318	33	22	74-transmission
1	A. J. Foyt	Bowes Seal Fast	Bignotti-Bowes Racing Assoc.	Offy	4	252	Trevis	pearl, red, black	149.074	5	23	69-lost wheel, spun SE
9	Dick Rathmann	Chapman	H. A. Chapman	Offy	4	252	Watson	ivory, gold	147.161	13	24	51-magneto
32	Eddie Johnson	Polyaire Foam	Peter G. Torosian	Offy	4	252	Trevis	blue, red, white	146.592	18	25	38-magneto
53	Paul Goldsmith	Bowes Seal Fast	Bignotti-Bowes Racing Assoc.	Offy	4	252	Epperly	pearl, maroon	146.437	26	26	26-magneto
88	Gene Hartley	Drewry's	M & W Racing Associates	Offy	4	252	Watson	maroon, gold	146.969	20	27	23-steering
62	Paul Russo	Denver-Chicago Trucking	Myron E. Osborn	Offy	4	252	Watson	white, blue, red	146.687	14	28	20-engine trouble
45	Jack Turner	Bardahl	Fred Gerhardt	Offy	4	252	Kurtis	black, white, orange	146.496	25	29	17-wrecked FS
29	Bob Christie	North Electric	William Tucker, Inc.	Offy	4	252	Kurtis	blue, white	146.341	31	30	17-wrecked FS
83	Allen Crowe	S-R Racing Enterprise	Pete Salemi & Nick Rini	Offy	4	252	Watson	blue, white	146.831	22	31	17-wrecked FS
67	Chuck Rodee	Travelon Trailer	Ernest L. Ruiz	Offy	4	252	Watson	pink, purple	146.969	21	32	17-wrecked FS
96	Bob Veith	Meguiar's Mirror Glaze	Ray Crawford	Offy	4	252	Elder	red, yellow	146.157	19	33	12-engine trouble

RRear Engine

Len Sutton

Eddie Sachs

Don Davis

Bobby Marshman

Jim McElreath

Parnelli Jones

Lloyd Ruby

Jim Rathmann

Johnny Boyd

Shorty Templeman

Don Branson

Jim Hurtubise

Ebb Rose

Bud Tingelstad

Roger McCluskey

Elmer George

Troy Ruttman

Bobby Grim

Dan Gurney

Chuck Hulse

Jimmy Daywalt

A. J. Foyt

Dick Rathmann

Eddie Johnson

Paul Goldsmith

Gene Hartley

Paul Russo

Jack Turner

Bob Christie

Allen Crowe

Chuck Rodee

Bob Veith

Below, left: A yard of bricks remains to mark the starting line when the frontstretch is finally paved. Louis Schwitzer, Sr., and Ray Harroun help Tony Hulman lay the gold brick. Schwitzer won the Speedway's first race in 1909. Below, right: The modern version of the famous Novi engine. It has been changed to utilize dual ignition which necessitates sixteen spark plugs. Many other refinements have been made on the engine since it was originally designed by Bud Winfield in 1940. Bottom: Former winners clock their rivals. Left to right, Rodger Ward, Troy Ruttman, Jim Rathmann and A. J. Foyt.

Top, left: Rodger Ward in the cockpit of his Leader Card "500" Roadster. Top, right: Parnelli Jones just after he broke the 150-mile-an-hour barrier. Above, left: Action in the first turn. Left to right, Elmer George, Bob Veith, Eddie Sachs and Lloyd Ruby. Above, right: Cliff Bergere takes a lap around the track before the race in the Studebaker Special he drove to third place in 1932. Left: Bob Veith's crew make some last minute adjustments during practice.

1963

The foreign invasion was on and the days of the "roadsters" were numbered. Colin Chapman brought over a team of rear-engined, Ford-powered Lotuses from England and with Scotsman Jim Clark at the wheel of one and American Dan Gurney in the other, it took exceptional effort by Parnelli Jones to win in an Offy. Clark's car owner, Colin Chapman, claimed that Parnelli had the help of a leaking oil tank but officials decided not to black flag him and he squeaked into Victory Lane by a narrow margin over Clark. The oil situation, by no means all of Jones' making, caused late race spins by Eddie Sachs and Roger McCluskey and a final wheel-loss and crash by Sachs. Hot words were exchanged over the next few days but the finish remained the same. Bobby Unser almost caused a disaster when he spun the Novi on the second lap but everyone missed him. On his 46th lap, Bud Tingelstad hit the southeast wall and a lap later Allen Crowe did the same thing in the southwest. There were a number of pre-race accidents, the worst being Jack Turner's. He spun coming out of the fourth turn and started flipping sideways. Movies showed at least nine rolls and the car stopped on fire. Turner, suffering burns and a crushed vertabra, retired from racing.

Parnelli Jones

NO.	DRIVER	CAR	ENTRANT	ENGINE	CYL.	DISP.	CHASSIS	COLOR	QUAL. SPEED	ST.	FIN.	LAPS/SPEED/REASON OUT
98	Parnelli Jones	Agajanian Willard Battery	J. C. Agajanian	Offy F	4	252	Watson	pearl, blue, red	151.153	1	1	200-143.137
92	Jim Clark	Lotus powered by Ford	Lotus Indianapolis Project	Ford R	8	256	Lotus	green, yellow	149.750	5	2	200-142.752
2	A. J. Foyt	Sheraton-Thompson	Ansted-Thompson Racing	Offy F	4	252	Trevis	pearl, red, blue	150.615	8	3	200-142.210
1	Rodger Ward	Kaiser Aluminum	Leader Cards, Inc.	Offy F	4	252	Watson	white, red, blue	149.800	4	4	200-141.090
4	Don Branson	Leader Card 500 Roadster	Leader Cards, Inc.	Offy F	4	252	Watson	white, blue	150.188	3	5	200-140.866
8	Jim McElreath	Bill Forbes Racing Team	William P. Forbes	Offy F	4	252	Watson	white, maroon	149.744	6	6	200-140.862
93	Dan Gurney	Lotus powered by Ford	Lotus Indianapolis Project	Ford R	8	256	Lotus	white, dk. blue	149.019	12	7	200-140.071
10	Chuck Hulse	Dean Van Lines	Dean Van Lines	Offy R	4	252	Ewing	white, blue	149.340	11	8	200-140.064
84	Al Miller	Thompson Harvey Alum.	Mickey Thompson	Chevy R	8	255	Thompson	orange, cream	149.613	31	9	200-139.524
22	Dick Rathmann	Chapman	Harry Allen Chapman	Offy F	4	252	Watson	red, white	149.130	17	10	200-138.845
29	Dempsey Wilson	Vita Fresh Orange Juice	Gordon Van Liew	Offy F	4	252	Kuzma	white, orange	147.832	30	11	200-138.574
17	Troy Ruttman	Robbins Autocrat S. Belt	Jim Robbins Co.	Offy F	4	252	Kuzma	ivory, blue	148.374	33	12	200-138.244
65	Bob Christie	Travelon Trailer	Ernest L. Ruiz	Offy F	4	252	Watson	pink pearl, purple	149.1238	18	13	200-136.104
32	Ebb Rose	Sheraton-Thompson	Ansted-Thompson Racing	Offy F	4	252	Watson	white, red, blue	148.545	32	14	200-132.347
14	Roger McCluskey	Konstant Hot	Bruce Homeyer	Offy F	4	252	Watson	black, gold	148.680	14	15	198-spun NE
5	Bobby Marshman	Econo-Car Rental	Lindsey Hopkins	Offy F	4	252	Epperly	white, pink	149.458	7	16	196-rear end
9	Eddie Sachs	Bryant Heating & Cooling	D.V.S., Inc.	Offy F	4	252	Watson	yellow, red, silver	149.570	10	17	181-lost wheel NE
99	Paul Goldsmith	Demler	Norm Demler, Inc.	Offy F	4	252	Watson	yellow, red	150.163	9	18	149-crankshaft bearing
52	Lloyd Ruby	John Zink Trackburner	John S. Zink	Offy E	4	252	Moore	red, white	149.1232	19	19	126-hit wall NW
88	Eddie Johnson	Drewry's	M & W Racing Assn.	Offy F	4	252	Watson	maroon, gold	148.509	21	20	112-hit wall BS
45	Chuck Stevenson	Bardahl	Fred Gerhardt	Offy F	4	252	Watson	black, orange, white	148.386	22	21	110-valve
56	Jim Hurtubise	Hotel Tropicana	Novi, Inc.	Novi* F	8	166	Kurtis	rose, white, gold	150.257	2	22	102-oil leak
83	Duane Carter	Thompson Harvey Alum.	Mickey Thompson	Chevy R	8	255	Thompson	red, white	148.002	15	23	100-threw rod
16	Jim Rathmann	Coral Harbour	Lindsey Hopkins	Offy F	4	252	Watson	blue, pink	147.838	29	24	99-magneto
26	Bobby Grim	Morcroft	Gilbert E. Morcroft	Offy F	4	252	Trevis	purple, gold	148.717	20	25	79-oil leak
86	Bob Veith	Racing Associates	Racing Associates	Offy F	4	252	Porter	rose, black	148.289	24	26	74-valve
35	Allen Crowe	Gabriel Shocker	Pete Salemi & Nick Rini	Offy F	4	252	Trevis	white, orange	148.877	13	27	47-lost wheel SW
54	Bud Tingelstad	Hoover, Inc.	Tidewater Associates, Inc.	Offy F	4	252	Epperly	orange, chrome	148.227	25	28	46-hit wall, SE
37	Johnny Rutherford	U. S. Equipment Co.	Ed Kostenuk	Offy F	4	252	Watson	white, red	148.063	26	29	43-transmission
21	Elmer George	Sarkes Tarzian	Mari George	Offy F	4	252	Lesovsky	blue, ivory, maroon	147.893	28	30	21-handling
75	Art Malone	STP	Novi, Inc.	Novi* F	8	166	Kurtis	white, red	148.343	23	31	18-clutch
23	Johnny Boyd	Bowes Seal Fast	Salih-Paddock Corp.	Offy F	4	252	Epperly	pearl, red, black	148.038	27	32	12-oil leak
6	Bobby Unser	Hotel Tropicana	Novi, Inc.	Novi* F	8	166	Kurtis	yellow, black	149.421	16	33	2-hit wall SW

*Supercharged   FFront Engine   RRear Engine

Jim Clark

A. J. Foyt

Rodger Ward

Don Branson

Jim McElreath

Dan Gurney

Chuck Hulse

Al Miller

Dick Rathmann

Dempsey Wilson

Troy Ruttman

Bob Christie

Ebb Rose

Roger McCluskey

Bobby Marshman

Eddie Sachs

Paul Goldsmith

Lloyd Ruby

Eddie Johnson

Chuck Stevenson

Jim Hurtubise

Duane Carter

Jim Rathmann

Bobby Grim

Bob Veith

Allen Crowe

Bud Tingelstad

Johnny Rutherford

Elmer George

Art Malone

Johnny Boyd

Bobby Unser

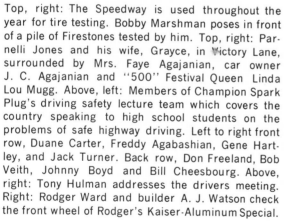

Top, right: The Speedway is used throughout the year for tire testing. Bobby Marshman poses in front of a pile of Firestones tested by him. Top, right: Parnelli Jones and his wife, Grayce, in Victory Lane, surrounded by Mrs. Faye Agajanian, car owner J. C. Agajanian and "500" Festival Queen Linda Lou Mugg. Above, left: Members of Champion Spark Plug's driving safety lecture team which covers the country speaking to high school students on the problems of safe highway driving. Left to right front row, Duane Carter, Freddy Agabashian, Gene Hartley, and Jack Turner. Back row, Don Freeland, Bob Veith, Johnny Boyd and Bill Cheesbourg. Above, right: Tony Hulman addresses the drivers meeting. Right: Rodger Ward and builder A. J. Watson check the front wheel of Rodger's Kaiser-Aluminum Special.

Below, left: The Chrysler pace car pulls off the track and the race is on with a perfect start. Below, right: The Bear Manufacturing Corporation has, for many years, maintained a wheel aligning and balancing service at the Speedway. Technicians utilize the latest equipment to help the contestants with their chassis problems. Bottom: The Purdue University Band plays "Back Home Again in Indiana" just before the start of the "500".

1964

The Speedway was in a state of turmoil for the 1964 "500". Most car owners and drivers, although reluctant to do so, were following the trend to lightweight, rear-engined cars. Safety precautions to cover the new cars lagged behind their mechanical development; a group of drivers unfamiliar with track racing were getting rides and many cars were being run on highly volatile gasoline. This ominous situation produced the Speedway's greatest tragedy when the race was less than two laps old. Rookie Dave MacDonald spun, hit the inside wall coming into the frontstretch and exploded in front of Eddie Sachs, who struck MacDonald's blazing car and likewise exploded. Rutherford's and Duman's cars caught fire and those of Unser, Stevenson and Hall were wrecked too seriously to continue. The race was stopped. Sachs was dead, MacDonald died shortly and Duman was badly burned. The race resumed with Bobby Marshman in front but he soon lost an oil plug, putting Clark in the lead. Clark's tires soon lost their tread and a chunk of rubber mangled his rear end suspension. Parnelli Jones then led but after a refueling stop his car caught fire and burned in front of the pits. A. J. Foyt's reliable "roadster" carried him to his second win.

A. J. Foyt

NO.	DRIVER	CAR	ENTRANT	ENGINE	CYL.	DISP.	CHASSIS	COLOR	QUAL. SPEED	ST.	FIN.	LAPS/SPEED/REASON OUT
1	A. J. Foyt	Sheraton-Thompson	Ansted-Thompson Racing	Offy F	4	252	Watson	pearl, red, blue	154.672	5	1	200-147.350
2	Rodger Ward	Kaiser Aluminum	Leader Cards, Inc.	Offy R	4	252	Watson	white, red, blue	156.406	3	2	200-146.339
18	Lloyd Ruby	Bill Forbes Racing Team	William P. Forbes	Offy F	4	252	Watson	white, maroon	153.932	7	3	200-144.320
99	Johnny White	Demler	Norm Demler, Inc.	Offy F	4	252	Watson	yellow, red	150.893	21	4	200-143.206
88	Johnny Boyd	Vita Fresh Orange Juice	Gordon Van Liew	Offy F	4	252	Kuzma	orange, gold	151.835	13	5	200-142.345
15	Bud Tingelstad	Federal Engineering	Federal Automotive Assoc.	Offy F	4	252	Trevis	cream, blue	151.210	19	6	198-flagged
23	Dick Rathmann	Chapman	Harry Allen Chapman	Offy F	4	252	Watson	maroon, white	151.860	12	7	197-flagged
4	Bob Harkey	Wally Weir Mobilgas	Walter Weir, Jr.	Offy F	4	252	Watson	blue, lt. blue	151.573	27	8	197-flagged
68	Bob Wente	Morcroft-Taylor	G. E. Morcroft-R. Taylor	Offy F	4	252	Trevis	yellow, red	149.869	32	9	197-flagged
16	Bobby Grim	Konstant Hot	Vatis Enterprises, Inc.	Offy F	4	252	Kurtis	yellow, black	151.038	20	10	196-flagged
3	Art Malone	Studebaker-STP	STP Division, Studebaker	Novi* F	8	168	Kurtis	blue, pink	151.222	30	11	194-flagged
5	Don Branson	Wynn's Friction Proofing	Leader Cards, Inc.	Offy R	4	252	Watson	yellow, red	152.672	9	12	187-clutch
53	Walt Hansgen	MG Liquid Suspension	Kjell H. Qvale	Offy F	4	252	Huffaker	blue, white	152.581	10	13	176-flagged
56	Jim Hurtubise	Tombstone Life	D.V.S., Inc.	Offy F	4	252	Hurtubise	red, gold, black	152.542	11	14	141-oil pressure
66	Len Sutton	Bryant Heating & Cooling	Vollstedt Enterprises, Inc.	Offy R	4	252	Vollstedt	silver, red	153.813	8	15	140-fuel pump
62	Bill Cheesbourg	Arizona Apache Airlines	Myron E. Osborn	Offy F	4	252	Epperly	red, silver	148.711	33	16	131-engine trouble
12	Dan Gurney	Lotus Ford	Team Lotus, Ltd.	Ford R	8	255	Lotus	white, blue	154.487	6	17	110-tire wear
14	Troy Ruttman	Dayton Steel Wheel	George Walther, Jr.	Offy F	4	252	Watson	white, blue	151.292	18	18	99-spun NE
54	Bob Veith	MG Liquid Suspension	Kjell H. Qvale	Offy R	4	252	Huffaker	white, blue, red	153.381	23	19	88-burned piston
52	Jack Brabham	Zink-Urschel Trackburner	Zink, Urschel, Slick, Inc.	Offy R	4	252	Brabham	red, white	152.504	25	20	77-split fuel tank
28	Jim McElreath	Studebaker-STP	STP Division, Studebaker	Novi F	8	168	Kurtis	white, red	152.381	26	21	77-engine trouble
77	Bob Mathouser	Dayton Disc Brake	George Walther, Jr.	Offy F	4	252	Walther	blue, white	151.451	28	22	77-brakes
98	Parnelli Jones	Agajanian Bowes Seal Fast	J. C. Agajanian	Offy F	4	252	Watson	pearl, blue, red	155.099	4	23	55-pit fire
6	Jim Clark	Lotus Ford	Team Lotus, Ltd.	Ford R	8	255	Lotus	green, yellow	158.828	1	24	47-rear suspension
51	Bobby Marshman	Pure Oil Firebird	Lindsey Hopkins	Ford R	8	255	Lotus	white, blue	157.857	2	25	39-oil plug
84	Eddie Johnson	Thompson-Sears Allstate	Mickey Thompson	Ford R	8	255	Thompson	white, blue	152.905	24	26	6-fuel pump
86	Johnny Rutherford	Bardahl	Racing Associates	Offy F	4	252	Watson	yellow, black	151.400	15	27	2-wrecked FS
95	Chuck Stevenson	Diet Rite Cola	Leader Cards, Inc.	Offy F	4	252	Watson	white, blue	150.830	29	28	2-wrecked FS
83	Dave MacDonald	Thompson-Sears Allstate	Mickey Thompson	Ford R	8	255	Thompson	red, white	151.464	14	29	1-exploded FS
25	Eddie Sachs	American Red Ball	D.V.S., Inc.	Ford R	8	255	Halibrand	white, gold, red	151.439	17	30	1-hit 83, exploded
64	Ronnie Duman	Clean Wear Service Co.	Nicholas E. Fulbright	Offy F	4	252	Trevis	pink, black	149.744	16	31	1-wrecked FS
9	Bobby Unser	Studebaker-STP	STP Division, Studebaker	Novi* 4 F	8	268	Ferguson	red, chrome	154.865	22	32	1-wrecked FS
26	Norm Hall	Hurst	Pope-Hall Enterprises	Offy F	4	252	Watson	blue, red	150.094	31	33	1-spun, hit wall NW

*Supercharged   R Rear Engine   F Front Engine   4 Four Wheel Drive

Rodger Ward

Lloyd Ruby

Johnny White

Johnny Boyd

Bud Tingelstad

Dick Rathmann

Bob Harkey

Bob Wente

Bobby Grim

Art Malone

Don Branson

Walt Hansgen

Jim Hurtubise

Len Sutton

Bill Cheesbourg

Dan Gurney

Troy Ruttman

Bob Veith

Jack Brabham

Jim McElreath

Bob Mathouser

Parnelli Jones

Jim Clark

Bobby Marshman

Eddie Johnson

Johnny Rutherford

Chuck Stevenson

Dave MacDonald

Eddie Sachs

Ronnie Duman

Bobby Unser

Norm Hall

Right: Tony Hulman prepares to give the traditional command "Gentlemen, start your engines". Below, left: Don Branson in one of the new A. J. Watson rear-engined cars. Below, middle: Rookie of the Year Johnny White, who was critically injured in a sprint car accident shortly after the "500". Below, right: Two of the famous Novis. No. 9 is the four-wheel-drive built in England by Ferguson and No. 28 is one of the rear-drives built in California by Frank Kurtis. Bobby Unser drove No. 9 and Jim McElreath, No. 28.

Above, left: Johnny Rutherford thrilled himself, and several thousand spectators, by driving through the flames of the MacDonald-Sachs crash, over Bobby Unser's Novi and on to safety. Though his car was damaged too badly to continue, Johnny was uninjured. Above, right: The pace lap. Right: Rodger Ward with the old and new tires. The wide profile is greatly responsible for the fantastic speeds of recent years.

Top: The tragic MacDonald-Sachs accident as seen from the Tower. Above, left: Rookie driver Dave MacDonald in action in Mickey Thompson's Sears-Allstate Special. When MacDonald spun and struck the inside wall, the car exploded and careened into the path of Eddie Sachs. Both MacDonald and Sachs were fatally injured and Ronnie Duman was seriously burned. Above, right: Rodger Ward finished second to A. J. Foyt despite several unscheduled pit stops. Middle: Chief Steward Harlan Fengler in the Ford Mustang pace car. Left: Manufacturer Ted Halli-brand discusses his new spot brakes with Sam Hanks.

1965

In sharp contrast with the previous year's race, 1965 was, perhaps, the most injury-free "500" in history. Though there were a number of pre-race accidents, no driver required hospitalization beyond an automatic checkup. Numerous safety regulations were instituted as precautions against a recurrence of the 1964 disaster. The Ford powered "funny cars" were firmly intrenched and were recognized as the only formula for victory. Jim Clark was the favorite, based on his showing in the past two races, but it was A. J. Foyt who took the qualifying honors right after Clark had set a new record. Foyt's average of 161.958 gained him the pole but in the race he was no match for Clark who won with little trouble after the Texan was forced out with gearbox trouble. Parnelli Jones gave chase but was outdistanced and narrowly managed to salvage second from classy rookie Mario Andretti. The race's only accident came when Bud Tingelstad lost a wheel and hit the northeast wall on his 116th lap. In practice, Foyt and Rodger Ward each crashed while Jones wrecked J. C. Agajanian's gold speedster twice. Seconds after Jones received the checkered flag, the engine coughed and died; the fuel tanks were completely empty. Andretti easily won Rookie of the Year honors.

Jim Clark

NO.	DRIVER	CAR	ENTRANT	ENGINE	CYL.	DISP.	CHASSIS	COLOR	QUAL. SPEED	ST.	FIN.	LAPS/SPEED/REASON OUT
82	Jim Clark	Lotus powered by Ford	Team Lotus (Overseas) Ltd.	Ford R	8	255	Lotus	green, yellow	160.729	2	1	200-151.388
98	Parnelli Jones	Agajanian Hurst	J. C. Agajanian	Ford R	8	255	Kuzma-Lotus	gold, ivory	158.625	5	2	200-149.200
12	Mario Andretti	Dean Van Lines	Auto Tecnics, Inc.	Ford R	8	255	Brawner	white, blue	158.849	4	3	200-149.121
74	Al Miller	Jerry Alderman Ford-Lotus	Jerry Alderman Ford Sales	Ford R	8	255	Lotus	white, blue	157.805	7	4	200-146.581
76	Gordon Johncock	Weinberger Homes	Weinberger & Wilseck Ent.	Offy F	4	251	Watson	white, blue	155.012	14	5	200-146.417
81	Mick Rupp	G. C. Murphy	Pete Salemi	Offy R	4	251	Gerhardt	white, blue	154.839	15	6	198-flagged
83	Bobby Johns	Lotus powered by Ford	Team Lotus (Overseas) Ltd.	Ford R	8	255	Lotus	green, yellow	155.481	22	7	197-flagged
4	Don Branson	Wynn	Leader Cards, Inc.	Ford R	8	255	Watson	yellow, red	155.501	18	8	197-flagged
45	Al Unser	Sheraton-Thompson	Ansted-Thompson Racing	Ford R	8	255	Lola	pearl, red, blue	154.440	32	9	196-flagged
23	Eddie Johnson	Chapman	H. Allen Chapman	Offy F	4	251	Watson	maroon, white	153.998	28	10	195-flagged
7	Lloyd Ruby	Dupont Golden 7	David R. McManus	Ford R	8	255	Halibrand	gold, red, white	157.246	9	11	184-blew engine
16	Len Sutton	Bryant Heating & Cooling	Jim Robbins & Vollstedt	Ford R	8	255	Vollstedt	gold, maroon	156.121	12	12	177-flagged
14	Johnny Boyd	Geo. Bryant Racing Project	Geo. Bryant Racing Projects	Ford R	8	255	BRP	lt. blue, white	155.172	29	13	140-gear box
53	Walt Hansgen	MG-Liquid Suspension	Kjell H. Qvale	Offy R	4	251	Huffaker	orange, black	155.662	21	14	117-fuel line
1	A. J. Foyt	Sheraton-Thompson	Ansted-Thompson Racing	Ford R	8	255	Lotus	pearl, red, blue	161.233	1	15	115-rear end gears
5	Bud Tingelstad	American Red Ball	Lindsey Hopkins	Ford R	8	255	Lola	white, gold, red	154.672	24	16	115-hit wall NE
66	Billy Foster	Jim Robbins	Jim Robbins & Vollstedt	Offy R	4	251	Vollstedt	maroon, gold	158.416	6	17	85-water manifold
18	Arnie Knepper	Konstant Hot	Vatis Enterprises, Inc.	Offy F	4	251	Kurtis	black, yellow	154.513	19	18	80-cylinder wall
9	Bobby Unser	STP Gas Treatment	STP Division Studebaker	Novi* 4F	8	167	Ferguson	red, chrome	157.467	8	19	69-oil connection
52	Jim McElreath	Zink-Urschel Trackburner	Zink, Urschel, Slick, Inc.	Offy R	4	251	Brabham	red, white	155.878	13	20	66-rear end gears
94	George Snider	Gerhardt Offy	Fred Gerhardt	Offy R	4	251	Gerhardt	lavender, yellow	154.825	16	21	64-rear end gears
65	Ronnie Duman	Travelon Trailer	Ernest L. Ruiz	Offy R	4	251	Gerhardt	purple, gold	154.533	25	22	62-rear end gears
41	Masten Gregory	George Bryant & Staff	Geo. Bryant Racing Projects	Ford R	8	255	BRP	lt. blue white	154.540	31	23	59-lost oil pressure
54	Bob Veith	MG-Liquid Suspension	Kjell H. Qvale	Offy R	4	251	Huffaker	red, white	156.427	10	24	58-burned piston
88	Chuck Stevenson	Vita Fresh Orange Juice	Gordon Van Liew	Offy F	4	251	Kuzma	pearl, orange, gold	154.725	26	25	50-burned piston
17	Dan Gurney	Yamaha	All American Racers, Inc.	Ford R	8	255	Lotus	white, dk. blue	158.898	3	26	42-timing gears
48	Jerry Grant	Bardahl MG	Kjell H. Qvale	Offy R	4	251	Huffaker	yellow, black	154.606	17	27	30-magneto
19	Chuck Rodee	Wally Weir's Mobilgas	Walter Weir, Jr.	Offy R	4	251	Halibrand	white, orange	154.546	30	28	28-rear end gears
29	Joe Leonard	All American Racers	All American Racers, Inc.	Ford R	8	255	Halibrand	white, blue, red	154.268	27	29	27-oil leak
25	Roger McCluskey	All American Racers	All American Racers, Inc.	Ford R	8	255	Halibrand	white, blue	155.186	23	30	18-clutch
24	Johnny Rutherford	Racing Associates	Racing Associates	Ford R	8	255	Halibrand	white, blue, silver	156.291	11	31	15-transmission
47	Bill Cheesbourg	WIFE Good Guy	Lane-Fulbright Racing Team	Offy R	4	251	Gerhardt	white, black	153.774	33	32	14-magneto
59	Jim Hurtubise	STP-Tombstone Life	Chemical Compounds Division	Novi* F	8	168	Kurtis	red, gold, black	156.863	23	33	1-transmission

*Supercharged   R Rear Engine   F Front Engine   4 Four Wheel Drive

Parnelli Jones

Mario Andretti

Al Miller

Gordon Johncock

Mick Rupp

Bobby Johns

Don Branson

Al Unser

Eddie Johnson

Lloyd Ruby

Len Sutton

Johnny Boyd

Walt Hansgen

A. J. Foyt

Bud Tingelstad

Billy Foster

Arnie Knepper

Bobby Unser

Jim McElreath

George Snider

Ronnie Duman

Masten Gregory

Bob Veith

Chuck Stevenson

Dan Gurney

Jerry Grant

Chuck Rodee

Joe Leonard

Roger McCluskey

Johnny Rutherford

Bill Cheesbourg

Jim Hurtubise

Right: Jim Clark displays a newspaper telling of his triumph. Left of Clark is Chief Mechanic Dave Lazenby and on Clark's right is owner-builder Colin Chapman. Below, left: Just before the start of the "500" thousands of multi-colored balloons are released to soar skyward. Below, middle: Mickey Thompson's front-drive Chevy with Bob Mathouser at the wheel. The unique platform is, in reality, a starter which turns the front wheels. The car failed to qualify. Below, right: The STP mechanics go to work on the Novi while owner Andy Granatelli gives Bobby Unser some advice.

Above: Bobby Johns, Al Unser and A. J. Foyt "stand on it" in the first turn. Right: Dan Gurney contemplates his Lotus.

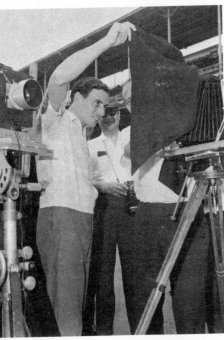

Top: Jim Hurtubise hits the wall in the northeast turn and the car disintegrates. The fuel tanks, though ruptured, did not catch fire due to improved safety precautions. Hurtubise was uninjured and later qualified another car. Above, left: Jim Clark "assists" Speedway Photographer, J. H. "Bud" Jones. Above, right: Closely packed spectators in the first turn picnic, drink, wrestle, sunbathe and occasionally even take time to watch the race. Left: The 8-cylinder Ford engine which has revolutionized the "500".

1966

While Pat Vidan was still waving his green flag, Billy Foster, trying to dodge a lagging car, hit the wall on the starting line and unleashed a chain reaction which caused eleven cars to be wrecked before reaching the first turn. Miraculously, the only injury was to A. J. Foyt's hand which was cut when he vaulted a wire fence to the safety of the grandstand. After an hour and forty minutes delay, Mario Andretti jumped into a short-lived lead as Johnny Boyd crashed into the first turn wall. A few laps later, George Snider spun entering the backstretch and was hit by Chuck Hulse. Jim Clark took the lead when Andretti's car broke a valve, but lost valuable time when he spun, spectacularly, in some oil. Lloyd Ruby led the rapidly depleting field until the three quarter mark when he withdrew with a broken cam stud. The popular Scot, Jackie Stewart, seemingly had the race won with but 10 laps to go when he lost oil pressure and immediately shut off to save John Mecom's $26,000 Ford engine. Graham Hill, in a second Mecom car, became a rather surprised winner and the first rookie to turn the trick since 1927. The death of popular Chuck Rodee, who hit the wall in the southwest turn while qualifying, marred an otherwise injury-free month.

Graham Hill

NO.	DRIVER	CAR	ENTRANT	ENGINE	CYL.	DISP.	CHASSIS	COLOR	QUAL. SPEED	ST.	FIN.	LAPS/SPEED/REASON OUT
24	Graham Hill	American Red Ball	John Mecom, Jr.	Ford R	8	255	Lola	white, red, gold	159.243	15	1	200-144.317
19	Jim Clark	STP Gas Treatment	STP Division Studebaker	Ford R	8	255	Lotus	red, white	164.114	2	2	200-143.843
3	Jim McElreath	Zink-Urschel-Slick	Zink-Urschel-Slick	Ford R	8	255	Brabham	red, white	160.908	7	3	200-143.742
72	Gordon Johncock	Weinberger Homes	W. & W. Enterprises	Ford R	8	255	Gerhardt	blue, white, orange	161.059	6	4	200-143.084
94	Mel Kenyon	Gerhardt Offy	Fred Gerhardt	Offy R	4	251	Gerhardt	lavender, white	158.555	17	5	198-flagged
43	Jackie Stewart	Bowes Seal Fast	John Mecom, Jr.	Ford R	8	255	Lola	white, black, red	159.972	11	6	190-oil pressure
54	Eddie Johnson	Valvoline II	Vatis Enterprises, Inc.	Offy R	4	251	Huffaker	maroon, white, gold	158.898	29	7	175-stalled
11	Bobby Unser	Vita Fresh	Gordon Van Liew	Offy T R	4	168	Huffaker	orange, pearl, gold	159.109	28	8	171-flagged
6	Joe Leonard	Yamaha Eagle	All American Racers	Ford R	8	255	Eagle	dark blue, white	159.560	20	9	170-engine trouble
88	Jerry Grant	Bardahl-Pacesetter Homes	All American Racers	Ford R	8	255	Eagle	blue, silver, green	160.335	10	10	167-flagged
14	Lloyd Ruby	Bardahl Eagle	All American Racers	Ford R	8	255	Eagle	pearl, maroon	162.433	5	11	166-cam stud
18	Al Unser	STP Oil Treatment	STP Division Studebaker	Ford R	8	255	Lotus	red, white	162.372	23	12	161-hit wall NW
8	Roger McCluskey	G. C. Murphy	Lindsey Hopkins	Ford R	8	255	Eagle	blue, white	159.271	21	13	129-oil line
98	Parnelli Jones	Agajanian's Rev 500	J. C. Agajanian	Offy* R	4	168	Shrike	blue, white	162.484	4	14	87-wheel bearing
26	Rodger Ward	Bryant Heating & Cooling	John Mecom, Jr.	Offy* R	4	168	Lola	white, blue	159.468	13	15	74-handling
77	Carl Williams	Dayton Steel Wheel	George Walther, Jr.	Ford R	8	255	Gerhardt	lt. blue, dk. blue	159.645	25	16	38-oil line
56	Jim Hurtubise	Gerhardt Offy	Fred Gerhardt	Offy T R	4	168	Gerhardt	orange, ivory	159.208	22	17	29-oil line
1	Mario Andretti	Dean Van Lines	Dean Racing Enterprises	Ford R	8	255	Brawner	white, blue	165.849	1	18	27-valve
82	George Snider	Sheraton-Thompson	Ansted-Thompson Racing	Ford R	8	255	Coyote	white, red, blue	162.521	3	19	22-wreck SW
12	Chuck Hulse	Wynn's	Leader Cards, Inc.	Ford R	8	255	Watson	yellow, red, white	160.844	8	20	22-hit No. 82
22	Bud Tingelstad	Federal Engineering	Federal Automotive Assoc.	Offy* R	4	168	Gerhardt	blue, white	159.144	27	21	16-radiator
28	Johnny Boyd	Prestone	George R. Bryant	Ford R	8	255	B.R.P.	yellow, red, gold	159.384	14	22	5-hit wall SW
4	Don Branson	Leader Card Racer 4	Leader Cards, Inc.	Ford R	8	255	Gerhardt	dark blue, white	160.385	9	23	0-wreck FS
27	Billy Foster	Jim Robbins	J. M. Robbins	Ford R	8	255	Vollstedt	red, yellow	149.490	12	24	0-wreck FS
53	Gary Congdon	Valvoline	Vatis Enterprises, Inc.	Offy R	4	251	Huffaker	white, blue, gold	158.688	16	25	0-wreck FS
2	A. J. Foyt	Sheraton-Thompson	Ansted-Thompson Racing	Ford R	8	255	Lotus	white, blue, red	161.355	18	26	0-wreck FS
31	Dan Gurney	All American Racers Eagle	All American Racers	Ford R	8	255	Eagle	dark blue, white	160.499	19	27	0-wreck FS
66	Cale Yarborough	Jim Robbins	J. M. Robbins	Ford R	8	255	Vollstedt	red, yellow	159.794	24	28	0-wreck FS
37	Arnie Knepper	Sam Liosi	D. V. S., Inc.	Ford R	8	255	Cecil	blue, white	159.440	26	29	0-wreck FS
75	Al Miller	Jerry Alderman Ford Lotus	Jerry Alderman Ford Sales	Ford R	8	255	Lotus	white, blue	158.681	30	30	0-wreck FS
39	Bobby Grim	Racing Associates	Herb Porter	Offy T F	4	168	Watson	maroon, black	158.367	31	31	0-wreck FS
34	Larry Dickson	Michner Petroleum	Michner Petroleum, Inc.	Ford R	8	255	Lola	black, gold	159.144	32	32	0-wreck FS
96	Ronnie Duman	Harrison	J. Frank Harrison	Ford R	8	255	Eisert	gold, white, black	158.646	33	33	0-wreck FS

*Supercharged   TTurbo Charged   RRear Engine   FFront Engine

Jim Clark

Jim McElreath

Gordon Johncock

Mel Kenyon

Jackie Stewart

Eddie Johnson

Bobby Unser

Joe Leonard

Jerry Grant

Lloyd Ruby

Al Unser

Roger McCluskey

Parnelli Jones

Rodger Ward

Carl Williams

Jim Hurtubise

Mario Andretti

George Snider

Chuck Hulse

Bud Tingelstad

Johnny Boyd

Don Branson

Billy Foster

Gary Congdon

A. J. Foyt

Dan Gurney

Cale Yarborough

Arnie Knepper

Al Miller

Bobby Grim

Larry Dickson

Ronnie Duman

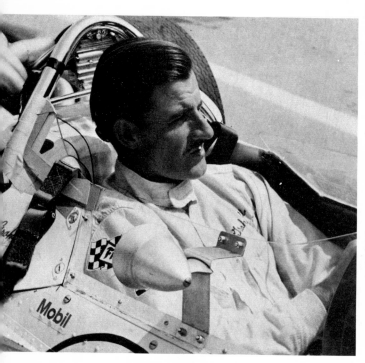

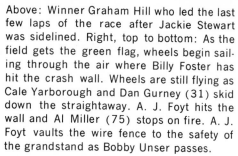

Above: Winner Graham Hill who led the last few laps of the race after Jackie Stewart was sidelined. Right, top to bottom: As the field gets the green flag, wheels begin sailing through the air where Billy Foster has hit the crash wall. Wheels are still flying as Cale Yarborough and Dan Gurney (31) skid down the straightaway. A. J. Foyt hits the wall and Al Miller (75) stops on fire. A. J. Foyt vaults the wire fence to the safety of the grandstand as Bobby Unser passes.

Left: Graham Hill in Victory Lane. Below, left: Johnny Boyd spins in some oil and heads, backwards, for the wall in the southwest turn. Below, right: Boyd climbs out of his car after hitting the wall as one of his wheels narrowly misses Mel Kenyon.

Above, left: Tony Hulman takes 1911 winner Ray Harroun for a ride in a golf cart. Above, middle: Mario Andretti, new track record holder, in the Dean Van Lines Special. Above, right: Lloyd Ruby, who led the race for many laps, with his Chief Mechanic Dave Laycock. Left: Just after the restart, Mario Andretti broke a valve which caused his car to lay a smoke screen and eventually drop from competition.

DRIVER PERFORMANCE RECORDS

Year	No.	Car	Fin.	Remarks
Abell, George				
1927	31	Miller		Relieved Fred Frame
Adams, Bert				
1911	23	McFarlan	25	Flagged
Adams, F. L.				
1913	14	Smada		Did not qualify
Ader, Walt				
1947	6	Olson		Did not qualify
1948	15	Peters		Owner died, withdrawn
	45	Speedway Cocktail		Did not qualify
1950	27	Sampson	22	123—flagged
Agabashian, Freddy				
1947	41	Ross Page	9	191—flagged
1948	26	Ross Page	23	58—oil line
1949	15	Maserati	27	28—overheating
1950	28	Wynn's	28	64—oil line
	12	I. R. C.		Relieved Henry Banks
1951	59	Granatelli	17	109—clutch
1952	28	Cummins Diesel	27	71—clogged superc.
1953	59	Grancor-Elgin	4	200—126.219
1954	77	Merz Engineering	6	200—128.711
1955	14	Federal Eng.	32	39—spun SE
1956	42	Federal Eng.	12	196—flagged
1957	14	Bowes Seal Fast	22	107—fuel tank
1958	56	City of Memphis		142.135, 2nd alt.
	75	D-A Lubricant		141.011, too slow
Aiken, A. C.				
1938	71	Aiken-Howard		Did not qualify
Ainslee, George				
1912	22	Lozier		Relieved Joe Horan
Aitken, Johnny				
1911	4	National	27	125—con. rod
1915	4	Stutz		Relieved Earl Cooper
	5	Stutz		Relieved Gil Anderson
1916	18	Peugeot	15	69—valve
Albertson, Bill				
1929	36	Miller		Relieved Frank Farmer
Allen, Leslie				
1927	36	Burt		Did not qualify
1930	25	Allen Miller	9	200—85.749
Alley, Tom				
1913	25	Tulsa		Relieved George Clark
1915	10	Duesenberg	8	200—79-33
1916	12	Ogren	11	120—73.55
1919	26	Bender	5	200—82.18
1920		T. N. T.		Did not arrive
	15	Revere		Relieved Henderson
1921	27	Frontenac	11	133—con. rod
1922	26	Monroe	9	200—84.20
1924	13	Kess-Line		Did not qualify
1925	13	Kess-Line		Did not qualify
Amick, George				
1957	4	Federal Eng.		139.443, 2nd alt.
1958	99	Demler	2	200—143.517
Amick, Richard "Red"				
1959	87	Wheeler-Foutch	31	45—wrecked NE
1960	27	King O'Lawn	11	200—131.946
Anderson, Les				
1947	58	Kennedy Tank	11	131—flagged
1948	34	Kennedy Tank	24	58—gears
Anderson, Gil				
1911	10	Stutz	11	200—67.73
1912	1	Stutz	16	80—wrecked NE
1913	3	Stutz	12	187—camshaft gears
1914	24	Stutz	26	42—loose cyl. bolts
1914	3	Stutz		Relieved B. Oldfield
1915	5	Stutz	3	200—87.60
1916	28	Premier	13	75—oil line
	29	Premier		Relieved Howdy Wilcox
Andres, Emil				
1935	52	Don Hulbert		Did not qualify
	56	Cresco		109—074, 2nd alt.
1936	56	DeBaets		Didn't complete run
	19	Carew	18	184—flagged
1937	36	Kennedy Tank		Sold, withdrawn
	46	Kennedy Tank		116.243, 1st alt.
	48	Carew		Did not qualify
	42	Thorne		Relieved Al Miller
1938	42	Elgin Piston Pin	29	45—wrecked SE
1939	44	Chicago Flash	30	22—stripped plug threads
1940	25	Belanger-Folz	12	192—flagged
1941	19	Kennedy Tank	30	5—wrecked NE
1946	18	Elgin Piston Pin	4	200—108.902
1947	3	Preston Tucker	13	150—magneto
1948	8	Tuffy's Offy	31	11—steering
1949	9	Tuffy's Offy	9	197—flagged
1950	99	Belanger		Didn't complete run
Andretti, Mario				
1965	12	Dean Van Lines	3	200—149.121
1966	64	Dean Van Lines		Did not qualify
	1	Dean Van Lines	18	27—valve
Andrews, Keith				
1955	31	McDaniel	20	120—ignition
1956	89	Dunn Engineering	26	94—spun NW
1957	62	Farina		Wrecked in practice, died.
Ansterberg, Ernie				
1923	2	Packard		Relieved R. DePalma
	4	Packard		Relieved Dario Resta
1924	10	Duesenberg	22	2—wrecked BS
	9	Duesenberg		Relieved Joe Boyer
Arbuthnot, Robert M. W.				
1946	57	Lagonda		Didn't qualify
Ardinger, Herb				
1934	24	Lucenti	10	200—95.936
1935	24	Welch		Too slow
1936	44	Bowes Seal Fast	28	39—transmission
1937	54	Chicago Raw Hide	22	106—con. rod
1939	9	Miller-Hartz	17	141—clutch
1947	54	Novi Governor	4	200—113.404
Arkus-Duntov, Zora				
1946	49	Talbot		Did not qualify
1947	49	Martin		Did not qualify
Armi, Frank				
1951	64	Bardahl		130.242, too slow
	65	Vulcan Tool		Did not qualify
	58	Scopa		Did not qualify
1953	34	Morris		Didn't complete run
	79	Mel-Rae		Didn't complete run
1954	71	Martin Bros.		Did not qualify
	71	Martin Bros.	19	193—flagged
Arnold, Billy				
1928	43	Boyle Valve	7	200—91.111
1929	9	Boyle Valve	8	200—83.909
1930	4	Miller-Hartz	1	200—100.448
1931	1	Miller-Hartz	19	162—wrecked NW
1932	5	Miller-Hartz	31	59—wrecked NE
Arnold, Charles				
1912	14	White		Relieved John Jenkins
Arnold, Chuck				
1959	72	Speed Enterprise		Did not qualify
	71	Hall-Mar	15	200—130.918
1960	21	Gerhardt		Didn't complete run
1961	62	Denver-Chicago		Didn't complete run
1962	23	Turtle Drilling		145.366, too slow
1962	37	Leader Card		Didn't complete run
	46	Goff Bros.		Didn't complete run
	47	Joe Hunt Magneto		Didn't complete run
	77	Dayton Steel		Did not qualify
1964	71	M. R. C.		Didn't complete run
Ascari, Alberto				
1952	12	Ferrari	31	40—hub flange, spun NW
1953	97	Ferrari		Did not arrive
Aspen, Al				
1931	72	Alberti	14	200—85.764
1932	21	Brady & Nardi	34	31—con. rod
1933	42	Brady & Nardi		Wrecked in practice, SW
Atkins, Dick				
1966	97	Agajanian		158.158, 1st alt.
Ayulo, Manuel				
1948	88	Weidel		Didn't qualify
1949	73	Karl Hall		120.490, too slow
	52	Sheffler Offy	28	24—con. rod
1950	85	Coast Grain		120.000, too slow
1951	31	Coast Grain		131.128, 2nd alt.
	9	Hinkle		Relieved Jack McGrath
1952	8	Coast Grain Co.	20	184—flagged
1953	88	Peter Schmidt	13	184—con. rod
1954	88	Schmidt	13	197—flagged
1955	88	Schmidt		Wrecked in practice, died
Babcock, George C.				
1915	12	Peugeot	17	117—broken cylinder
Bablot, Paul				
1919	33	Ballot	21	63—wrecked
Bailey, George				
1934	58	Scott	32	12—wrecked NE
1935	35	Ford V8	26	65—steering
1936	51	Zauer-Martz		Did not qualify
1937	43	Duray-Sims	21	107—clutch
1938	25	Harry A. Miller		Did not qualify
	12	Barbasol	12	166—clutch
1939	17	Miller	26	47—valve
1940	56	Miller		Wrecked in practice, died
Bailey, Harold				
1946	58	Bee-Gee		Did not qualify
Baker, E. G. "Cannonball"				
1922	3	Frontenac	11	200—79.25
Baker, Joe				
1929	51	Green		Did not qualify
Baldwin, Johnny				
1956	91	Bardahl-Ferrari		Did not qualify
1957	82	Central Ex.		Did not qualify
Ball, Bob				
1951	52	Blakely	5	200—123.709
1952	15	Blakely Oil		Wrecked in practice
	38	Howard Keck		Did not qualify
	55	Ansted	32	34—gear case
Ball, Guy				
1914	37	Great Western		Did not qualify
Banks, Henry				
1935	29	DePalma Miller		110.277, 2nd alt.
1937	49	Kimmell		Did not qualify
1938	33	Kimmell	21	109—rod bearing
1939	39	Cheesman		Did not qualify
	26	Duray-Barbasol		Relieved Billy DeVore
1940	39	Cheesman		Didn't complete run
	34	Alfa Romeo		Relieved Chet Miller
1946	31	Auto Shippers	27	32—stalled
1947	43	Federal Eng.	24	36—oil line
1948	38	Federal Eng.		Did not qualify
1949	21	Federal Eng.		124.939, too slow
	35	Federal Eng.		94.867, too slow
1950	12	I. R. C.	25	112—flagged
1951	1	Blue Crown	6	200—123.304
1952	2	Blue Crown	19	184—flagged
1953	10	Hopkins		Didn't complete run
1954	26	Hopkins		Did not qualify
Barbarino, Salvatore				
1920	3	Monroe		Relieved Louis Chevrolet
Barringer, George				
1933	54	Wonder Bread		Did not qualify
1934	18	Boyle Products	14	161—bent front axle
	23	Ford V8		Didn't complete run
1935	42	Ford V8		Relieved Seymour
1936	17	Kennedy Tank	8	200—102.630
1937	45	Midwest Red Lion		Relieved Cliff Bergere
1939	41	Bill White	6	200—111.025
1940	6	Pay-Day	14	191—flagged
1941	35	Miller		Destroyed in fire
1946	26	Tucker Torpedo	29	27—gear trouble
Barton, Buzz				
1952	58	Wales Trucking		Did not qualify
1953	35	Parks Motor Co.		Did not qualify
Barzda, Joe				
1951	49	Barzda		Spun qualifying
1952	53	Calif. Speed Equipment		121.918, too slow
Basle, Charles				
1911	17	Buick	34	46—Mech. tbl.
Batten, Norman				
1925	12	Duesenberg		Relieved Peter DePaolo
1926	14	Miller	7	151—90.275
1927	8	Miller	30	24—caught fire
1928	22	Miller	5	200—93.228
Bauman, Charles "Dutch"				
1927	26	Miller	20	90—pinion shaft
1928	19	Duesenberg		106.226, Wrecked before race
	8	Stutz Blackhawk		Relieved Tony Gulotta
Beardsley, Ralph				
1911	38	Simplex	20	flagged
Beeder, Frank				
1938	12	Duray Barbasol		Wrecked in practice
Belcher, Fred				
1911	15	Knox	9	200—68.63
Belt, C. W.				
1925	32	Super Ford		Did not qualify
1928	41	Green	27	32—valve
Benifield, Benny				
1932	73	Jones & Maley		Wrecked in practice, mechanic Cox died.
Bergdoll, Erwin R.				
1915	18	Bergdoll		Did not qualify
Bergdoll, Grover C.				
1915	19	Bergdoll		Did not qualify
Bergere, Cliff				
1927	25	Miller	9	200—79.929
1928	21	Miller	28	7—supercharger
	4	Miller		Relieved Leon Duray
1929	25	Armacost Miller	9	200—80.703
1931	25	Elco Royale	9	200—91.839
1932	22	Studebaker	3	200—102.662
1933	6	Studebaker	11	200—97.286
1934	22	Floating Power	7	200—97.818
1935	15	Victor Gasket	13	196—out of gas
1936	42	Bowes Seal Fast	22	116—loose engine support
	32	Burd Piston Ring		Relieved Lou Moore
1937	45	Midwest Red Lion	5	200—108.935
1938	9	Kraft's Real Rye	20	111—piston
1939	54	Offenhauser	3	200—113.698

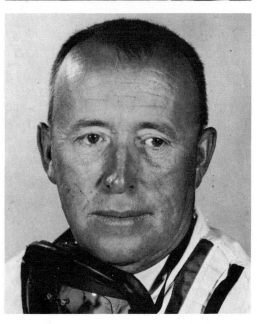

Left to right—Top: Mario Andretti, Henry Banks, Billy Arnold. Middle: Tony Bettenhausen, Cliff Bergere, Jack Brabham. Bottom: Joe Boyer, Don Branson.

Left to right—Top: Duane Carter, Shorty Cantlon. Middle: Earl Cooper, Bill Cheesbourg, Jimmy Bryan. Bottom: Jimmy Clark, Gaston Chevrolet.

Year	No.	Car	Fin.	Remarks
1940	5	Noc-Out	27	51—oil line
1941	34	Noc-Out	5	200—113.528
1946	3	Noc-Out	16	82—out of gas
1947	18	Novi Governor	21	62—piston
	54	Novi Governor		Relieved Ardinger
1948	85	Grancor-Werner		Did not qualify
Bettenhausen, Tony				
1946	27	Marchese		Qualified, withdrawn
	42	Bristow-McManus	20	47—con. rod
1947		Thorne Eng.		Did not qualify
	29	Belanger	18	79—timing gear
1948	6	Belanger Motors	14	167—clutch
1949	16	Alfa Romeo		125.156, too slow
	46	Flavell		125.764, 1nd alt.
1950	14	Blue Crown	31	30—wheel bearing
	17	Wolfe		Relieved Joie Chitwood
1951	5	Mobiloil	9	178—spun NW
1952	99	Belanger Motors		Wrecked qualifying SS
	27	Blue Crown Spark Plug	24	93—starter
1953	98	Agajanian	9	196—axle, wrecked NE (Hartley)
1954	10	Mel Wiggers	29	105—con. rod bearing
1955	10	Chapman	2	200—126.733
1956	99	Belanger Motors	22	160—wrecked SW
1957	27	Novi Air Con.	15	195—flagged
1958	33	Jones & Maley	4	200—134.768
1960	2	Dowgard	23	126—con. rod
1961	24	Stearly		Wrecked in practice, died
Bienke, Randall				
1949	42	Worline		Did not qualify
Bigelow, Charles				
1911	37	Mercer	15	Flagged
Billman, Mark				
1933	64	Kemp-Mannix	30	79—wrecked SE, died
Bisch, Art				
1958	17	Ansted Rotary		141.376, too slow
	57	Helse	33	0—wrecked NE
Boillot, Andre				
1919	37	Baby Peugeot	15	195—wrecked BS
1920	17	Peugeot	23	16—engine trouble
1921	14	Talbot-Darracq	20	41—con. rod
Boillot, Georges				
1914	7	Peugeot	14	141—broken frame
Boling, John				
1920	32	Richards	11	199—flagged
1931	48	Morton & Brett	36	7—conn. rod
Bonadies, Tony				
1955	36	Donaldson		Did not qualify
1956	25	Duke Donaldson		Did not qualify
1957	15	Ray Brady		Did not qualify
	81	Central Ex.		Didn't complete run
Bonedeo, Joseph				
1932	14	Golden Seal		Relieved Juan Gaudino
Bordino, Pietro				
1925	22	Fiat	10	200—94.75
Borzachini, Baconi				
1930	26	Maserati	37	7—magneto, plugs
Bost, Paul				
1930	41	Fronty Ford		Relieved Chet Miller
1931	31	Empire State	31	35—crankshaft
1932	17	Empire State	37	18—crankshaft
1933	24	Frame	40	13—oil line
1935	2	F. W. D.		Relieved Mauri Rose
Bothwell, Lindley				
1949	66	Peugeot		Did not qualify
Boyer, Joe				
1919	39	Frontenac	31	30—rear axle
1920	6	Frontenac	12	192—wrecked NE
1921	7	Duesenberg	17	74—rear axle
	9	Duesenberg		Relieved Albert Guyot
1923	3	Packard	18	59—Differential
1924	9	Duesenberg	18	177—hit wall SW
	15	Duesenberg		Relieved L. L. Corum
Boyd, Bill				
1951	42	Lutes Truck Parts		Wrecked in practice
1952	48	Granatelli		Didn't complete run
1953	86	Merz Engineering		Did not qualify
Boyd, Johnny				
1955	25	Lutes Truck Parts		Did not qualify
	39	Sumar	29	53—wrecked BS
1956	15	Bowes Seal Fast	30	35—engine trouble
1957	6	Bowes Seal Fast	6	200—132.846
1958	9	Bowes Seal Fast	3	200—133.099
1959	33	Bowes Seal Fast	6	200—133.867
1960	8	Bowes Seal Fast	27	77—piston
1961	41	Leader Card	21	105—clutch
1962	38	Metal-Cal	10	200—136.600
1963	23	Bowes Seal Fast	32	12—oil leak
1964	88	Vita Fresh	5	200—142.345
1965	14	Geo. Bryant	13	140—gear box
1966	28	Prestone	22	5—Hit wall SW
Brabham, Jack				
1961	17	Cooper-Climax	9	200—134.116
1964	52	Zink-Urschel	20	77—split fuel tank
Bragg, Caleb				
1911	39	Fiat	37	24—wrecked in pits
1912	3	Fiat		Relieved Tetzlaff
1913	19	Mercer	15	128—pump shaft
1914	21	Mercer	19	117—camshaft
Brandfon, Benny				
1931	66	Duesenberg		Did not qualify
Branson, Don				
1959	9	Bob Estes	24	112—torsion bar
1960	7	Bob Estes	4	200—136.785
1961	3	Hoover	33	2—bent valves
1962	14	Mid-Continent	12	200—135.836
1963	4	Leader Card	5	200—140.866
1964	4	Wynn's	12	187—clutch
1965	5	Wynn's	8	197—flagged
1966	91	Leader Card		Did not qualify
	4	Leader Card	23	0—wrecked FS
Brett, Riley J.				
1921	17	Junior	15	91—hit wall, damaged
Brisko, Frank				
1929	28	Burbach	11	180—flagged
1931	16	Brisko-Atkinson	22	138—steering arm
1932	32	Brisko-Atkinson	29	61—clutch
	10	Bowes Seal Fast		Relieved Cummings
1933	58	F. W. D.	36	47—oil too hot
	5	Boyle Products		Relieved Cummings
	68	Goldberg Bros.		Relieved Bennett Hill
1934	32	F. W. D.	9	200—96.787
1935	41	Art Rose	23	79—universal joint
	19	Miller-Hartz		Relieved Fred Frame
1936	14	Elgin Piston Pin	20	180—out of gas
1937	24	Elgin Piston Pin	23	105—no oil pressure
1938	26	Shur-Stop Brake	31	39—oil line
1939	29	National Seal	29	38—air pump
	9	Miller-Hartz		Relieved Herb Ardinger
1940	16	Elgin Piston Pin	9	193—flagged
1941	8	Zollner Piston	23	70—valve spring
1949	48	Frank J. Lynch		Did not qualify
Brock, S. F.				
1914	48	Ray	30	5—camshaft
Brooke, Henry				
1947	35	E. R. A.		Did not qualify
Brooks, Bert				
1961	79	Hall-Mar		143.415, too slow
Brown, W. W. "Cockeyed"				
1915	7	DuChesneau		Did not qualify
1919	5	Richards	32	14—con. rod
Brown, Walt				
1947	33	Permafuse	7	200—101.744
1948	69	Werner-Grancor		Did not qualify
1949	9	Tuffy's Offy		Relieved Emil Andres
1950	4	Tuffy's Offy	19	127—flagged
1951	44	Federal Eng.	26	55—magneto
Brubaker, Jim				
1946	68	Maserati		Did not qualify
1947	86	Jack Mauer		Did not qualify
1948	14	Maserati		Did not qualify
1949	79	Brubaker		Did not qualify
Bruce-Brown, David				
1911	28	Fiat	3	200—72.73
1912	29	National	22	25—valve trouble
Brunmeier, Arvol				
1939	62	Guiberson		Did not qualify
1946	67	Offenhauser		Did not qualify
Bryan, Jimmy				
1951	72	Viking Trailer		124.176, too slow
1952	77	Schmidt	6	200—123.914
1953	8	Blakely Oil	14	183—flagged
1954	9	Dean Van Lines	2	200—130.178
1955	1	Dean Van Lines	24	90—fuel pump
1956	2	Dean Van Lines	19	185—flagged
1957	1	Dean Van Lines	3	200—134.246
1958	1	Belond AP	1	200—133.791
1959	6	Belond AP Muffler	33	1—clutch, cam gear
1960	10	Metal-Cal	19	152—fuel pump drive
Bucknum, Ronnie				
1966	69	Arciero		Did not qualify
Burany, Frank				
1949	24	Schoof		Wrecked in practice
Burbach, Eddie				
1927	35	Elcar		Relieved Al Cotey
1931	61	B & C		Did not qualify
Burch, Mike				
1950	84	George Hoster		Did not qualify
Burke, Marvin				
1950	65	Offenhauser		Did not qualify
Burman, Bob				
1911	45	Benz	19	flagged
1912	15	Cutting	12	157—wrecked SE
1913	4	Keeton	11	200—flagged
1914	17	Burman	24	47—con. rod
	31	Keeton		Relieved Billy Kniper
1915	33	Burman		Did not qualify
	8	Peugeot	6	200—80.36
Burton, Clyde				
1930	38	V8	11	196—flagged
Butcher, Harry				
1930	46	Butcher Bros.	14	127—flagged
1931	49	Butcher Bros.	38	6—wrecked NW
Butler, Paul				
1933	56	Sacks Bros.		Did not qualify
Butler, Wally				
1924	34	Roof		Did not qualify
Buxton, Jack				
1929	31	Armacost-Miller		Relieved Schurch
Buzane, George				
1919	16	Premier		Did not qualify
Byron, "Red"				
1947	22	Pauley Ford		Did not qualify
1948	43	Parks-Vogt		Did not qualify
Caccia, Joe				
1930	29	Alberti	24	43—wrecked (Decker)
1931	38	Jones & Maley		Wrecked in practice, died, SW
Cain, A. Dan				
1926	37	K. & M.		Did not qualify
1927	37	K. & M.		Did not qualify
Callahan, Jesse				
1914	28	Stafford		Did not qualify
Callaway, "Buddy"				
1932	64	Callaway		Did not qualify
Campbell, Ray				
1932	72	Folly Farm	30	60—crankshaft
1933	59	G & D	39	24—oil leak
Canthacuzino, M. Ghica				
1928	42	Cozette M. G. C.		Did not arrive
Cantlon, William "Shorty"				
1928	36	Bugatti		Did not arrive
	29	Elgin Piston Pin		Relieved Henry Kohlert
1930	16	Miller Schofield	2	200—98.054
1931	2	Harry Miller	27	88—con. rod
1933	25	Sullivan & O'Brien	34	50—con. rod
	28	Marr		Relieved Chet Miller
1934	15	Sullivan & O'Brien	20	76—crankshaft
1935	9	Sullivan & O'Brien	6	200—101.140
1336	7	Hamilton-Harris	14	194—out of gas
1937	34	Bowes Seal Fast	16	182—flagged
1938	47	Kamm's	33	13—supercharger
1939	47	Automotive Serv.	32	15—main bearing
1940	24	Surber		Qualified, driven by Stapp
1946	64	H-3	28	28—clutch
1947	24	Automobile Shippers	23	40—wrecked SW, died.
Cantrell, Bill				
1948	36	Fageol	16	161—steering
1949	36	Fageol		125.022, too slow
	74	Kennedy Tank	21	95—drive shaft
1950	44	Bowes Seal Fast		Didn't complete run
	24	Palmer		Relieved Levrett
1951	62	Motor Trend		Did not qualify
	72	Fullerton		Didn't complete run
1952	52	Pat Clancy		Did not qualify
Cantrell, Willard				
1953	42	Malloy		Did not qualify
Caracciola, Rudolph				
1946	44	Thorne Eng.		Wrecked in practice
	72	Mercedes		Did not arrive
Carey, Bob				
1932	61	Meyer	4	200—101.363
Cariens, Ray				
1925	3	Miller		Qualified, driven by B. Hill
Carlson, Billy				
1914	25	Maxwell	9	200—70.97
1915	19	Maxwell	9	200—78.96
Carter, Duane				
1947	32	Kuehl-Osborne		Did not qualify
1948	16	Belanger Motors	22	59—lost wheel, spun
1949	17	Belanger	14	182—steering, spun
1950	18	Belanger	12	133—flagged
1951	27	Mobilgas	8	180—flagged
1952	1	Belanger Motors	4	200—125.259
1953	4	Miracle Power	24	94—ignition
	3	Bardahl		Relieved Sam Hanks
1954	16	Auto. Shippers	15	196—flagged
	34	Auto. Shippers		Relieved Troy Ruttman
1955	98	Agajanian	11	197—flagged
1959	17	Reverse Torque	7	200—133.342
1960	17	Thompson	12	200—131.882
1961	61	Roy		Did not qualify
	94	McCullough		Didn't complete run
1962	72	John Zink		145.867, too slow
1963	83	Thompson Harvey	23	100—threw rod
	17	Hopkins		Did not qualify
1964	75	D. V. S.		Did not qualify
Carter, Neal				
1952	25	Auto. Shippers		Didn't complete run
Carter, Ray				
1933	63	Billings		Did not qualify
Chamberlain, Ted				
1930	34	Gauss		Relieved Joe Huff
1931	68	Miller S. L.		99.182, 1st alt.
Chandler, William				
1914	38	Braender Bulldog	21	69—con. rod
1915	22	Duesenberg		Relieved Ralph Mulford
1916	24	Crawford	9	120—74.20
Chassagne, Jean				
1914	12	Sunbeam	29	20—wrecked NW
1919	33	Ballot		Relieved Paul Bablot
1920	26	Ballot	7	200—79.94
1921	19	Peugoet	18	65—lost hood
Cheesbourg, Bill				
1956	84	H. B. T.		Did not qualify
1957	45	Las Vegas Club		138.878, too slow
	31	Schildmeier Seal Line	26	81—fuel leak
1958	54	Novi Air Con.	10	200—129.149
1959	25	Hardwood Door		Did not qualify
	53	Greenman-Casale	21	147—magneto
1960	45	Braund Plywood		Did not qualify
1961	14	Dean Van Lines	28	50—wrecked FS
1962	35	Harvey Aluminum		Didn't complete run
	59	Tropicana		Did not qualify
	88	Drewry's		Relieved Gene Hartley
1963	27	U. S. Equipment		Didn't complete run
	85	Thompson		Did not qualify
1964	62	Arizona Apache Airlines	16	131—engine trouble
1965	62	Wilbur Clark		Did not qualify
	47	WIFE Good Guy	32	14—magneto
1966	79	Stein Porsche		Did not qualify
	99	Jack Adams		Did not qualify
Chevrolet, Arthur				
1911	16	Buick	36	30—mechanical trouble
1916	7	Frontenac	18	35—magneto

Year	No.	Car	Fin.	Remarks
Chevrolet, Gaston				
1919	41	Frontenac	10	200—79.50
1920	4	Monroe	1	200—88.16
Chevrolet, Louis				
1915	27	Cornelian	20	76—valve
1916	6	Frontenac		87.69, cracked cylinder
	8	Frontenac	12	82—con. rod
1919	7	Frontenau	7	200—81.03
1920	3	Monroe	18	94—steering
Chiron, Louis				
1929	6	Delage	7	200—87.728
Chittum, Bill				
1934	59	G. & D.		Did not qualify
Chitwood, Joie				
1940	42	Kennedy Tank	15	190—flagged
1941	25	Blue Crown	14	17—flagged
1946	24	Noc-Out	5	200—108.399
1947	8	Peters	22	51—gears
1948	55	Nyquist	17	138—leaking fuel tank
1949	77	Wolfe	5	200—118.757
1950	17	Wolfe	5	136—121.755
Christiaens, Josef				
1914	9	Excelsior	6	200—77.44
1916	14	Sunbeam	4	120—79.96
Christie, Bob				
1954	66	Christie		Didn't complete run
1955	7	Dean Van Lines		Wrecked, warm-up lap
1956	57	Helse	13	196—flagged
1957	95	Jones & Maley	13	197—flagged
1958	65	Federal Eng.	14	189—spun NE
1959	65	Federal Eng.	25	109—rod bolt
1960	38	Federal Eng.	10	200—133.416
1961	32	North Electric	17	132—burned piston
1962	29	North Electric	30	17—wrecked FS
1963	28	Stearly		Did not qualify
	65	Travelon Trailer	13	200—136.104
1964	33	Robbins Auto-Crat		147.583, too slow
1965	21	Kemerly		153.472, too slow
1966	55	Barnett Bros.		Didn't complete run
Clark, George				
1913	25	Tulsa	10	200—62.99
1914	33	Texas		Did not qualify
Clark, Jim				
1963	92	Lotus Ford	2	200—142.752
1964	6	Lotus Ford	24	47—rear suspension
1965	82	Lotus Ford	1	200—151.388
1966	10	STP Oil Treatment		Did not arrive
	19	STP Gas Treatment	2	200—143.843
Clark, Maynard				
1934	56	Smith		Did not qualify
1935	39	Blue Prelude		Did not qualify
Cleberg, Bob				
1960	61	Detroiter		Wrecked in practice
1961	6	Bell Lines		143.672, 2nd alt.
Clemons, "Bud"				
1957	59	Chiropractic		Did not qualify
1958	59	Sorenson		Did not qualify
Clemons, Fred "Jap"				
1911	22	McFarlan		Did not qualify
	6	Pope-Hartford		Relieved Frank Fox
1932	39	Hoosier Pete		Did not qualify
Clum, Leon				
1961	77	Dayton Steel		Didn't complete run
1962	6	Sclavi		Didn't complete run
	23	Turtle Drilling		Didn't complete run
Cobe, Harry				
1911	25	Jackson	10	200—67.90
Coffey, Jim				
1911	15	Knox		Relieved Frank Belcher
Cole, Hal				
1946	47	Don Lee	32	16—fuel leak
1948	63	City of Tacoma	6	200—111.587
1949	14	Grancor	19	117—rod bearing
1950	16	Pritchard		Wrecked qualifying
Comer, Fred				
1924	14	Durant	7	200—93.43
1925	5	Miller	11	200—93.67
	28	Miller		Relieved Leon Duray
1926	8	Miller	4	155—92.323
1928	25	Boyle Valve	9	200—88.889
Comotti, Gianfranco				
1929	57	Talbot		Withdrawn
Congdon, Gary				
1966	53	Valvoline	25	0—wrecked FS
Congdon, Russ				
1960	79	Hall-Mar		Didn't complete run
1961	69	Eelco		Didn't complete run
Conley, Jack				
1962	89	Chapman		Did not qualify
1963	89	J. E. Engineering		Did not qualify
1966	89	Conley & McManus		Did not qualify
Connor, George				
1934	39	Ward		Did not qualify
1935	37	Marks-Miller	19	112—transmission
1936	38	Marks-Miller	10	200—98.931
1937	17	Marks	9	200—103.830
1938	15	Marks-Miller	19	119—engine trouble
1939	18	Marks	13	195—stalled
1940	10	Lencki	26	52—con. rod
	14	Bill Holabird		Relieved Billy DeVore
	61	Lencki		Relieved Floyd Davis
1941	14	Boyle	16	167—transmission
1946	38	Walsh Offy	24	38—piston
	12	L. G. S.		Relieved Al Putnam
1947	14	Walsh	26	32—leaking fuel tank
	3	Tucker Partner		Relieved Emil Andres
1948	9	Bennett Bros.	28	24—drive shaft
1949	22	Blue Crown	3	200—119.595
1950	5	Blue Crown	8	135—121.086
1951	22	Blue Crown	30	29—universal joint
1952	54	Federal Eng.	8	200—122.595
1953	25	Chrysler		135.237, 1st alt.
Cooper, Earl				
1913	2	Stutz		Relieved Charles Merz
	3	Stutz		Relieved Charles Merz
1914	2	Stutz	18	118—broken wheel
1915	4	Stutz	4	200—87.11
1919	8	Stutz	12	200—78.60
1923	29	Durant	21	21—wrecked BS
	6	Durant		Relieved Eddie Hearne
1924	8	Studebaker	2	200—97.79
1925	2	Miller	17	127—wrecked SW
1926	5	Front Drive Miller	16	73—transmission
	1	Front Drive Miller		Relieved Dave Lewis
Cooper, Joe				
1915	18	Sebring	15	154—wrecked SS
Copp, Tommy				
1962	58	Sorenson		Did not qualify
Cortner, Bob				
1958	93	McKay Bulldog		Did not qualify
1959	51	Cornis Eng.		Wrecked in practice, NE; died
Corum, Lora L. "Slim"				
1922	27	Monroe	17	169—engine trouble
1923	23	Barber-Warnock	5	200—82.58
1924	15	Duesenberg	1	200—98.23
1925	16	Miller		Did not qualify
	8	Miller		Relieved R. DePalma
1926	23	Schmidt	20	44—shock absorbers
1927	28	Duesenberg		94.694, 1st alt.
	43	Miller		Relieved Schneider
1928	17	Duesenberg		96.172, wrecked before race
				Relieved Winnai
1929	42	Duesenberg		
1930	27	Stutz	10	200—85.340
1931	29	Stutz Bearcat		97.389, too slow
	44	G. N. H.		Relieved George Howie
1932	47	Studebaker	12	200—96.458
1935	49	Ford V8		Did not qualify
Cosman, Tommy				
1937	63	Wehr Rotary		Did not qualify
Cotey, Al				
1919	35	Ogren		82.9, 2nd alt.
1927	35	Elcar	21	87—universal joint
Cox, G. C.				
1915	25	Cino-Purcell	24	12—timing gears
Coy, Johnny				
1962	68	White Spot		Didn't complete run
	92	WRD		Did not qualify
Crawford, Charles				
1934	49	Detroit Gasket & Mfg.	16	110—head gasket
1938	31	Shafer 8		112.762, 1st alt.
	51	Stewart		Didn't complete run
1947	67	Murphy		Did not qualify
Crawford, Ray				
1955	49	Crawford	23	111—valve
1956	49	Crawford	29	49—wrecked NW
1957	49	Meguiar		139.093, too slow
1958	49	Meguiar		141.688, too slow
1959	49	Meguiar	23	115—wrecked NE
1961	94	McCullough		Did not qualify
1963	47	Crawford		Didn't complete run
Crawford, Wesley				
1927	25	Miller		Relieved Cliff Bergere
1928	23	Miller		Relieved Deacon Litz
1929	49	Miller	15	127—carburetor
1931	17	Nutmeg State		Relieved "Speed" Gardner
1932	48	Boyle Valve	36	28—crankshaft
1933	32	Boyle Products	24	147—wrecked SW (Winn)
1934	44	Garcia Grande		Didn't complete run
1935	48	Ford V8		Did not qualify
1940	62	Corley Miller		Did not qualify
Crockett, Larry				
1954	28	Federal Eng. Detroit	9	200—126.899
Cross, Art				
1952	44	Bowes Seal Fast		Did not qualify
	33	Bowes Seal Fast	5	200—124.292
1953	33	Ray Brady		Didn't complete run
	16	Springfield	2	200—126.827
1954	6	Springfield		137.362, too slow
	45	Bardahl	11	200—126.232
1955	99	Belanger Motors	17	168—con. rod cap
Crowe, Allen				
1962	83	S-R Racing	31	17—wrecked FS
1963	35	Gabriel Shocker	27	47—lost wheel, SW
Cucinotta, Letterio				
1930	42	Maserati	12	185—flagged
Cummings, Bill				
1930	6	Duesenberg	5	200—93.579
1931	3	Empire State	28	70—oil line
	5	Maley		Relieved Deacon Litz
1932	10	Bowes Seal Fast	19	151—crankshaft
	1	Bowes Seal Fast		Relieved Schneider
1933	5	Boyle Products	25	136—leaking radiator
1934	7	Boyle Products	1	200—104.863
1935	1	Boyle Products	3	200—104.758
1936	2	Boyle Products	33	0—clutch
1937	16	Boyle Products	6	200—107.124
1938	7	I. B. E. W.	24	72—radiator tank leak
Curley, Terry				
1933	66	C. O. Warnock		Did not qualify
	65	Kemp		Relieved Winnai
Curtner, Jack				
1922	18	Fronty Ford	14	160—flagged
Daigh, Chuck				
1959	98	Agajanian		Did not qualify
1961	35	Harvey Aluminum		Did not qualify
D'Alene, Wilbur				
1916	3	Duesenberg		Did not arrive
	1	Duesenberg	2	120—83.15
1919	22	Duesenberg	2	120—83.15
1922	25	Monroe	15	160—flagged
Daponte, Jorge				
1953	95	Wayne		Did not qualify
Davidson, Frank				
1933	76	Davidson		Did not qualify
Davies, Jim				
1950	22	Pat Clancey	17	128—flagged
1951	76	Parks Offy	16	110—rear end gears
1953	99	Miracle Power		Didn't complete run
	53	Pat Clancy	10	193—flagged
1954	53	Pat Clancy		137.583, 2nd alt.
	1	Bardahl		Relieved Sam Hanks
1955	15	Bardahl	3	200—126.299
1956	31	Novi		Did not qualify
1957	32	Trio Brass		138.462, too slow
1959	41	Sumar		Didn't complete run
1960	34	Turner		Did not qualify
1963	63	Kimberly		Did not qualify
Davis, Don				
1961	85	Federal Eng.		Didn't complete run
	83	Dart-Kart	29	49—wreck FS
1962	27	J. H. Rose	4	200—139.768
Davis, Floyd				
1937	32	Thorne	15	190—wrecked NE
1938	59	Woestman		Did not qualify
1939	56	W. B. W.	27	43—shock absorber
1940	61	Lencki	20	157—flagged
1941	16	Noc-Out	1	200—115.117
Dawson, Joe				
1911	31	Marmon	5	200—72.34
1912	8	National	1	200—78.72
1913	7	Deltal		Did not qualify
1914	26	Marmon	25	45—wrecked BS
Day, Dany				
1932	81	Silver Marshall		Did not qualify
1934	62	Miller		Did not qualify
	24	Lucenti		Relieved Ardinger
Daywalt, Jimmy				
1949	56	Bill & Bud		Did not qualify
1951	33	Iddings		Wrecked in practice
	47	Merkler Machine		Did not qualify
1952	64	Merkler Machine		Did not qualify
1953	48	Sumar	6	200—124.379
1954	19	Sumar	27	111—wrecked NW
1955	48	Sumar	9	200—124.401
1956	48	Sumar	24	134—wrecked SE
1957	57	Helse	28	53—wrecked NE
1958	69	Federal Eng.		Did not qualify
	92	Central Excavat.		Didn't complete run
1959	66	Federal Eng.	14	200—131.861
1960	23	Bryant Heating		Qualified, driven by D. Wilson
	79	Albany, N. Y.	31	27—brake line
1961	55	Schulz Fueling		Wrecked in practice
1962	46	Goff Bros.	22	74—transmission
1963	25	Wynn's		Didn't complete run
de Alsaga, Martin				
1923	21	Bugatti	24	6—con. rod
	35	Miller		Relieved Bennett Hill
Decker, Rick				
1929	29	Miller	23	61—supercharger
1930	31	Decker		Did not qualify
	48	Hoosier Pete	36	8—oil tank
	29	Alberti		Relieved Joe Caccia
1931	46	Miller		98.061, 2nd alt.
1933	61	Miller	41	13—manifold
1934	45	Carter Carb.	27	17—clutch
1938	44	Miller		Did not qualify
de Cystria, Prince				
1923	19	Bugatti	9	200—77.64
DeFraties, Port				
1940	51	W. & A.		Did not qualify
DeHart, Leon				
1932	44	Veedol		Did not qualify
1933	55	Morton & Brett		Did not qualify
Delaney, Ernest				
1911	27	Cutting	23	Flagged
Delling, E. H.				
1913	7	Deltal		Did not qualify
Dempsey, Elmer				
1924	22	Dempsey		Did not qualify
	31	Schmidt		Relieved Ora Haibe
Denslow, Bruce				
1946	56	Green-Holland		Did not qualify
Denver, Bill (William Oram)				
1930	44	Nardi	25	41—con. rod
1931	42	B & N		96.085, too slow
	72	Alberti		Relieved Al Aspen
1933	42	Brady & Nardi		Over wall NE, died
DePalma, John				
1915	17	Delage	21	41—loose flywheel
DePalma, Ralph				
1911	2	Simplex	6	200—71.13
1912	4	Mercedes	11	198—con. rod
1913	21	Mercer	23	15—burned bearing

Left to right—Top: George Connor, Bill Cummings. Middle: Peter DePaolo, Joe Dawson, Ronnie Duman. Bottom: Ralph DePalma, Floyd Davis.

Left to right—Top: Dave Evans, Pat Flaherty, Billy Foster. Middle: Cliff Durant, A. J. Foyt, Fred Frame. Bottom: Don Freeland, Jules Goux.

Year	No.	Car	Fin.	Remarks
	19	Mercer		Relieved Caleb Bragg
	22	Mercer		Relieved Wishart
1914	18	Mercedes		Qualified, withdrawn
1915	2	Mercedes	1	200—89.84
1919	4	Packard	6	200—81.04
1920	2	Ballot	5	200—82.12
1921	4	Ballot	12	112—con. rod
1922	17	Duesenberg	4	200—90.61
1923	2	Packard	15	69—head gasket
1925	8	Miller	7	200—96.85
1929	44	Miller		Did not qualify
1931	18	Miller-Wehr		Did not qualify
DePaolo, Peter				
1922	7	Frontenac	20	110—wrecked NE
1924	12	Duesenberg	6	200—94.30
1925	12	Duesenberg	1	200—101.13
1926	12	Duesenberg	5	153—91.544
1927	3	Perfect Circle	26	31—supercharger
	9	Miller		Relieved Tony Gulotta
	14	Cooper		Relieved McDonough
	27	Miller		Relieved Tony Gulotta
1928	1	Flying Cloud		Wrecked qualifying NE
1929	37	Boyle Valve	30	25—steering
1930	5	Duesenberg	33	19—wrecked NE (R. Roberts)
1934	27	Miller		Withdrawn
1935	42	Ford V8		Did not qualify
DeVigne, Jules				
1916	21	Delage	16	61—wrecked NS
de Viscaya, Pierre				
1923	18	Bugatti	12	166—con. rod
DeVore, Billy				
1937	28	Miller	7	200—106.995
1938	58	P. R. & W.	8	185—102.080
1939	26	Duray-Barbasol	10	200—104.267
1940	14	Bill Holabird	18	181—flagged
1941	23	Pay-Day	19	121—con. rod
1946	17	Schoof	10	167—spun SW
1947	10	Schoof		Relieved Dinsmore
1948	19	Pat Clancy	12	190—flagged
1950	58	Scopa		Did not qualify
1954	93	White Truck		Did not qualify
DeVore, Earl				
1925	24	Miller	13	198—flagged
1927	10	Miller	2	200—93.868
1928	6	Chromolite	18	161—wrecked SW
Dickson, Larry				
1966		Michner	32	0—wrecked FS
Dingley, Bert				
1912	12	Simplex	13	116—con. rod
Dinsmore, Duke				
1946	45	Johnston	17	82—con. rod
1947	10	Schoof	10	167—flagged
1949	29	Norm Olson	15	174—radius rod
1950	69	Brown Motor Co.	33	10—oil leak
1951	6	Brown Motor Co.	24	73—overheating
1952	68	Vulcan Tool		Didn't complete run
1953	52	Tom Sarafoff		Did not qualify
1954	62	Comm'l Motor Freight		137.096, too slow
	67	D-A Lubricant		Didn't complete run
1956	64	Shannon's	17	191—flagged
1960	36	McKay		Did not qualify
	95	Safety Auto Glass		Did not qualify
Disbrow, Louis				
1911	5	Pope-Hartford	35	45—wrecked FS
1912	5	Case	18	67—differential pin
1913	31	Case	8	200—66.80
1914	1	Burman	16	128—con. rod
Dreyfus, Rene				
1940	22	Lucy Schell		118.831, 2nd alt.
	49	Lucy Schell		Relieved LeBegue
Droeger, Bob				
1948	44	Baldwin		Did not qualify
Drollinger, Lee				
1960	58	Brady		Wrecked in practice
Duff, John				
1926	18	Elcar	9	147—87.551
Duman, Ronnie				
1961	43	Ray Brady		Didn't complete run
1962	29	Stearly		145.908, 2nd alt.
1963	15	Federal Eng.		Wrecked in practice
1964	64	Clean Wear	31	1—wrecked FS
1965	65	Travelon Trailer	22	62—rear end gears
1966	17	Jim Robbins		Didn't complete run
	96	Harrison	33	0—wrecked FS
Duncan, Len				
1953	31	Caccia Motors		133.487, too slow
	81	Central Excavat.		Did not qualify
1954	33	Brady	31	101—brakes
1955	24	Ray Brady		133.245, 1st alt.
	73	McNamara		Wrecked in practice
1956	51	Ray Brady		Did not qualify
Duncan, Ted				
1949	72	Lutes		Did not qualify
1950	16	Pritchard		Did not qualify
Durant, Cliff				
1919	1	Chevrolet	24	54—steering
1920	1	Chevrolet		Did not qualify
1922	34	Durant	12	200—77.75
1923	8	Durant	7	200—82.17
1924	16	Durant	13	199—out of gas
1926	9	Locomobile Jr. 8	17	60—gas tank leak
1928	5	Detroit	16	175—supercharger
Durant, Louis				
1940	12	Schoof		117.218, too slow
1941	44	B. & S.		116.152, 1st alt.
	45	Leader Card		Relieved Paul Russo
	55	Schoof		Relieved Al Putnam

Year	No.	Car	Fin.	Remarks
1946	33	Alfa Romeo	6	200—105.073
1947	23	Boggs		Did not qualify
1948	29	Auto. Shippers		117.666
	33	Mauro Alfa Romeo		Relieved Johnny Mauro
Duray, Arthur				
1914	14	Peugeot	2	200—80.99
Duray, Leon (James Stewart)				
1922	4	Frontenac	22	94—broken axle
1923	28	Durant	13	136—con. rod
1925	28	Miller	6	200—96.91
1926	10	Locomobile Jr. 8	23	33—broken axle
	6	Miller		Relieved Frank Elliott
1927	12	Miller Front Drive	27	26—leaking fuel tank
1928	4	Miller	19	133—overheating
1929	21	Packard Cable	22	65—carburetor
1931	79	Leon Duray		Withdrawn
	54	Duray	37	6—overheating
1932	54	Mallory		Did not qualify
1934	54	Leon Duray		Did not qualify
Easton, Rex				
1958	10	Hoover		140.972, too slow
	72	Wyandotte Tool		Did not qualify
1959	39	Massaglia Hotels		139.438, 1st alt.
Eaton, Kenny				
1949	55	Bowes Seal Fast		Did not qualify
1959	19	Lutes		Didn't complete run
	99	Belanger		Did not qualify
1951	66	Jeanie-Lee		Didn't complete run
Eckerle, Nick				
1925	34	Rotary		Did not qualify
Edmonds, Louis				
1911	43	Cole		Did not qualify
Edmunds, Don				
1957	67	Braund Birch		136.400, too slow
	92	McKay	19	170—spun SW
1959	54	Bill Forbes		Did not qualify
Eldridge, E. A. D.				
1926	26	Eldridge	19	45—tie rod
	27	Eldridge		Relieved W. Douglas Hawkes
Elisian, Ed				
1954	68	Wales Trucking		136.581, too slow
	27	Chapman	18	193—flagged
1955	68	Westwood Gauge	30	53—stopped, BS
1956	10	Hoyt Machine	23	160—stalled
1957	83	McNamara	29	51—timing gear
1958	5	John Zink	28	0—wrecked NE
Ellingboe, Jules				
1920	23	Ellingboe		Did not arrive
1921	22	Frontenac	19	49—steering
	23	Frontenac		Relieved Percy Ford
1922	23	Duesenberg	26	25—wrecked
	24	Duesenberg		Relieved Wonderlich
	31	Duesenberg		Relieved Ora Haibe
1924	18	Miller	11	200—90.47
1925	10	Miller	22	24—steering key
	3	Miller		Relieved Bennett Hill
1926	7	Miller	22	39—supercharger
	16	Miller		Relieved Bennett Hill
1927	18	Cooper	29	25—wrecked
Elliott, Frank				
1916	24	Crawford		Relieved Chandler
1920	35	T. N. T.		Did not arrive
1922	9	Leach	16	195—axle
1923	31	Durant	6	200—82.22
1924	18	Elliott		Withdrawn
	21	Miller	20	149—gas tank
1925	27	Miller	12	200—92.23
1926	6	Miller	6	152—90.917
1927	5	Junior 8	10	200—78.244
Ellis, Fred				
1911	24	Jackson	38	22—withdrawn
Endicott, Harry				
1911	3	Inter-state	16	Flagged
1912	18	Schacht		Relieved Bill Endicott
1913	1	Nyberg	21	23—transmission
Endicott, William				
1911	42	Cole	26	Flagged
1912	18	Schacht	5	200—74.25
1913	33	Case	27	1—drive shaft
Engle, Chuck				
1963	77	Dayton All Star		Wrecked in practice
Ensley, Jack				
1958	17	Ansted Rotary		Did not qualify
1959	92	McKay		Did not qualify
1961	84	Ansted-Thompson		Did not qualify
1962	95	Safety Auto Glass		Did not qualify
Evans, Dave				
1927	21	Duesenberg	5	200—90.782
1928	12	Boyle Valve	12	200—87.401
1930	24	Jones & Maley	6	200—92.571
1931	8	Cummins Diesel	13	200—86.107
1933	38	Art Rose	6	200—100.425
1934	6	Cummins Diesel	19	81—transmission
	5	Cummins Diesel		Relieved Stubblefield
1935	32	Ford V8		109.937, 1st alt.
1936	25	D. & G.		Did not qualify
1937	21	Elgin Piston Pin		Didn't complete run
Evans, Robert				
1911	26	Jackson		Relieved Jack Tower
1913	5	Mason	13	158—clutch
Fahrnow, "Dusty"				
1931	74	United Cab		Did not qualify
1932	95	Highway Parts		Did not qualify
	55	Highway Parts		Relieved Joe Huff

Year	No.	Car	Fin.	Remarks
1934	42	Superior Trailer	24	28—con. rod
1935	53	Superior Trailer		109.138, too much fuel
1936	55	Superior Trailer		Didn't complete run
Fairman, Jack				
1963	78	DeVilliers		Did not qualify
Falt, Harry				
1933	71	H. A. F.		Did not qualify
Fankhouser, Milt				
1947	53	Jack Maurer's	30	16—stalled, SE
1948	23	Milt Frankhouser		Did not qualify
1949	73	Karl Hall		Did not qualify
1950	41	Karl Hall		Did not qualify
Fansin, Fred				
1930	53	Fansin		Did not qualify
Farino, Giuseppe "Nino"				
1950	46	Maserati		Did not arrive
1956	9	Bardahl-Ferrari		Did not qualify
Farmer, Al "Cotton"				
1960	31	Bardahl		Did not qualify
1961	23	Bardahl		Didn't complete run
Farmer, Frank				
1929	36	Miller	14	140—supercharger
1930	33	Betholine Miller	21	69—wrecked
1931	9	Pedrick Piston R.		Did not qualify
	35	Jones-Miller	32	32—rod bearing
Farr, W. H.				
1912	17	Marquette-Buick		Relieved Billy Liesaw
Faulkner, Walt				
1950	98	Grant Piston Ring	7	135—121.094
1951	2	Agajanian Grant	15	123—crankshaft
1952	3	Sid Street Motors		Did not qualify
	25	Auto. Shippers		Didn't complete run
1953	23	Auto. Shippers	17	176—flagged
1954	44	Schmidt		137.065, too slow
	97	Belanger		Did not qualify
	98	Agajanian		Relieved Stevenson
1955	77	Merz Engineering	5	200—125.377
Fedricks, Johnny				
1950	34	Kupiec		Did not qualify
1952	82	Cal Connell		Did not arrive
1953	46	Dunn		Did not qualify
1957	71	Gdula		Did not qualify
Fengler, Harlan				
1923	26	Durant	16	69—gas tank
1924	6	Wade		Wrecked in practice
Fernic, George				
1927	46	Bugatti		Did not qualify
Fetterman, I. P.				
1922	21	Duesenberg	7	200—87.99
Fitch, John				
1953	74	Brown Motor Co.		Did not qualify
	32	Crawford		Didn't complete run
Flaherty, Pat				
1949	43	Grancor V8		120.846, too slow
1950	59	Granatelli	10	135—119.952
1953	77	Peter Schmidt	22	115—wrecked NS
1954	39	Shouse Motors		Did not qualify
	89	Dunn Engineering		Didn't complete run
	38	Bardahl		Relieved Jim Rathmann
1955	89	Dunn Engineering	10	200—124.086
1956	8	John Zink	1	200—128.490
1959	64	John Zink Heater	19	162—wrecked FS
Fohr, Myron				
1948	32	Marchese		121.531, 2nd alt.
1949	2	Marchese	4	200—118.791
1950	2	Bardahl	11	133—flagged
1951	56	Shaheen		Didn't complete run
Foley, Jack				
1926	32	Duesenberg		Did not qualify
Fonder, George				
1949	38	Ray Brady	20	116—valve
1950	26	Ray Brady		127.918, 2nd alt.
1951	26	Ray Brady		Did not qualify
	53	Hancock Dome		128.892, too slow
	63	Ray Brady		Did not qualify
1952	65	Leitenberger	15	197—flagged
1953	52	Tom Sarafoff		Didn't complete run
	76	Leitenberger		133.547, too slow
1954	36	Ed Stone		Didn't complete run
	33	Brady		Relieved Len Duncan
	71	Martin Bros.		Relieved Frank Armi
Fontaine, Louis				
1921	18	Junior	21	33—wrecked FS
Forberg, Carl				
1950	74	Jewell		Did not qualify
1951	68	Auto. Shippers	7	193—flagged
1952	23	Fadely Anderson		Did not qualify
Force, Gene				
1951	69	Brown Motor Co.	11	142—lost oil pressure
1952	96	Brown Motor Co.		133.789, too slow
1957	64	Shannon Bros.		Didn't complete run
1959	55	Sclavi & Amos		Didn't complete run
	78	Midwest Mfg.		Didn't complete run
1960	37	McKay	28	74—brakes
Ford, Percy				
1921	23	Chicago Frontenac	3	200—85.02
Foster, Billy				
1965	66	Jim Robbins	17	85—water manifold
1966	27	Jim Robbins	24	0—wrecked FS
Fowler, Ken				
1937	41	Lucky Teter	19	116—disqualified, pushed
1947	47	Don Lee Alfa	15	121—axle
1948	41	Don Lee Alfa		120.446, too slow
	31	Don Lee Mercedes		Relieved Chet Miller
Fox, Frank				
1911	6	Pope-Hartford	22	Flagged
1913	12	Gray Fox		Relieved Howdy Wilcox

Year	No.	Car	Fin.	Remarks
Fox, Malcolm				
1931	63	Duesenberg		Did not qualify
1932	57	Richards	20	132—spring
1933	57	Universal Service	28	121—wrecked SW
Foyt, A. J.				
1958	29	Dean Van Lines	16	148—spun SE
1959	10	Dean Van Lines	10	200—133.297
1960	5	Bowes Seal Fast	25	90—clutch
1961	1	Bowes Seal Fast	1	200—139.130
1962	1	Bowes Seal Fast	23	69—lost wheel, spun SE
1963	2	Sheraton-Thompson	3	200—142.210
1964	1	Sheraton-Thompson	1	200—147.350
1965	1	Sheraton-Thompson	15	115—rear end gears
1966	45	Sheraton-Thompson		Wrecked in practice
	2	Sheraton-Thompson	26	0—wrecked FS
Frame, Fred				
1927	31	Miller	11	199—flagged
	5	Junior 8		Relieved Frank Elliott
1928	27	State Auto Ins.	8	200—90.079
1929	34	Cooper	10	193—flagged
1931	34	Duesenberg	2	200—96.406
1932	34	Miller-Hartz	1	200—104.144
1933	12	Miller-Hartz	29	85—valve
1934	34	Frame Front-Drive		Wrecked in practice
1935	19	Miller-Hartz	11	200—100.436
1936	46	Burd Piston Ring	32	4-piston
1937	28	Miller		Relieved Billy DeVore
1938	32	Hulbert		Did not qualify
Franchi, Aldo				
1916	23	Peusun	21	9—engine trouble
Frayer, Lee				
1911	30	Firestone-Columbus	13	Flagged
1912	16	Firestone-Columbus	21	43—intake valve
Frazier, Dick				
1949	59	Grancor		Did not qualify
1950	52	Iddings		Did not qualify
1952	63	Jeannie-Lee		Did not qualify
Free, Roland				
1930	28	Slade	20	69—clutch
1947	28	Bristow-McManus	17	87—spun SW
1948	73	Gustafson K. F.		Did not qualify
Freeland, Don				
1953	38	Bob Estes	27	76—wrecked NW
1954	7	Bob Estes	7	200—128.474
1955	12	Bob Estes	15	178—transmission
1956	12	Bob Estes	3	200—127.668
1957	3	Ansted Rotary	17	192—flagged
1958	26	Bob Estes	7	200—132.403
1959	15	Jim Robbins	22	136—valve spring
1960	73	Ross-Babcock	22	129—magneto
1961	27	Chapman		Didn't complete run
	47	Joe Hunt Magneto		141.476, too slow
1962	36	Fullerton		145.366, too slow
1963	62	White Spot		Didn't complete run
Frey, Howard				
1911	37	Mercer		Relieved Bigelow
Friedrich, Ernst				
1914	34	Bugatti	15	134—drive pinion
Fuller, George				
1912	27	Continental		Did not qualify
Furci, Andy				
1957	58	Ray Brady		Didn't complete run
Gardner, Chester "Chet"				
1929	19	Boyle Valve		Burned rod qualifying
	48	Chromolite		Relieved W. H. Gardner
1930	18	Buckeye	38	1—spun SW
1933	21	Sampson Radio	4	200—101.182
1934	4	Sampson Radio	21	72—con. rod
	18	Boyle Products		Relieved Barringer
1935	6	Gardner	29	38—clutch
1937	31	Burd Piston Ring	11	199—flagged
1938	38	Burd Piston Ring	5	200—110.311
Gardner, W. H. "Speed"				
1929	48	Chromolite	6	200—88.390
1930	19	Miller Front Drive	35	14—loose main bearing
1931	17	Nutmeg State	25	107—frame
	69	Goldberg Bros.		Relieved Joe Huff
1932	31	Allegheny Metal		Did not qualify
1933	31	Allegheny Metal		Wrecked in practice
Garrett, Billy				
1956	41	Greenman-Casale	16	194—flagged
1957	33	Federal Eng.		139.546, 1st alt.
1958	43	Chapman	21	80—cam gear
Gaudino, Juan				
1930	52	Chrysler		Did not qualify
1932	14	Golden Seal	26	71—clutch
1933	14	Golden Seal		Relieved Raul Riganti
Gelnaw, J. Franklin				
1911	14	Fal		Did not qualify
George, Elmer				
1955	74	Walmotor		Wrecked in practice
1957	23	Travelon Trailer	33	0—wrecked on parade lap
1958	28	Ansted Rotary		Did not qualify
1962	21	Sarkes Tarzian	17	146—engine seized
1963	21	Sarkes Tarzian	30	21—handling
1964	21	Sarkes Tarzian		Didn't complete run
Gerard, Louis				
1946	35	Alfa Romeo		Did not qualify
	36	Maserati-Schell		Did not qualify
Giba, Joe				
1958	62	Carl Anderson		Did not qualify
Gibbons, Arthur				
1911	40	Velie		Withdrawn
Gilhooley, Ray				
1914	49	Isotta	27	41—wrecked BS
Gleason, Jimmy				
1928	39	Duesenberg	15	195—magneto
1929	53	Duesenberg	3	200—93.699
1930	7	Waverly Oil	28	22—wrecked NE,
1931	76	Mercedes		Withdrawn
	33	Duesenberg	6	200—93.605
Goacher, Potsy				
1953	36	Sid Street		134.620, too slow
1954	67	D-A Lubricant		Wrecked in practice
Goldsmith, Paul				
1958	31	City of Daytona	30	0—wrecked NE
1959	99	Demler	5	200—134.53
1960	99	Demler	3	200—136.792
1961	10	Racing Associates	14	160—con. rod
1962	53	Bowes Seal Fast	26	26—magneto
1963	99	Demler	18	149—crankshaft bearing
1964	36	Jack Adams		Withdrawn
Goode, Frank				
1911	38	Simplex		Relieved Beardsley
Gordon, Al				
1932	26	Lion Tamer	40	3—wrecked NW
1934	51	Abels & Fink	22	66—wrecked SW
1935	6	Cocktail Hour	30	17—wrecked NW
Goux, Jules				
1913	16	Peugeot	1	200—75.93
1914	6	Peugeot	4	200—79.49
1919	6	Peugeot	3	200—85.93
1920	16	Peugeot	15	148—engine trouble
1922	14	Ballot	25	25—boken axle
1923	16	Schmidt		Withdrawn
Graham, Roy				
1962	55	Metzloff Jetfire		Did not qualify
Granatelli, Andy				
1948	39	Grancor V8		Did not qualify
	59	Grancor-Werner		Wrecked in practice
Grant, Harry				
1911	19	Alco	33	51—bearings
1913	26	Isotta	24	14—gas tank
	10	Henderson		Relieved Billy Knipper
1914	27	Sunbeam	7	200—77.44
1915	14	Sunbeam	12	184—loose mud apron
Grant, Jerry				
1964	45	Bardahl		Did not qualify
1965	48	Bardahl MG	27	30—magneto
1966	88	Bardahl	10	167—flagged
Greco, Sam				
1929	45	Miller		88.849, too slow
1930	49	Scranton		Did not qualify
1932	76	Samcliff		Did not qualify
Green, Cecil				
1950	54	John Zink	4	137—121.766
1951	4	John Zink	22	80—con. rod
Green, Carl R.				
1925	32	Super Ford		Did not qualify
Gregg, Bob				
1950	63	Esmeralda		Did not qualify
Gregory, Masten				
1963	81	Harvey Aluminum		147.517, too slow
	82	Harvey Titanium		Didn't complete run
1964	82	Thompson-Sears		148.038, 2nd alt.
1965	41	George Bryant	23	59—lost oil pressure
1966	78	G. C. Murphy		Didn't complete run
Greiner, Arthur				
1911	44	Amplex	40	12—wrecked BS, mech. Dickson died
Griffith, Cliff				
1950	66	Sarafoff		129.014, 1st alt.
1951	23	Morris	28	30—axle
1952	22	Tom Sarafoff	9	200—122.402
1953	24	Bardahl		Wrecked in practice
1954	22	Tom Sarafoff		Did not qualify
1956	27	Jim Robbins	10	199—flagged
1960	29	North Electric		Did not qualify
1961	26	McCullough	24	55—piston
1962	84	Thompson Rocket		Did not qualify
1963	72	Lencki		Didn't complete run
1964	35	Central Excavat.		Did not qualify
Grim, Bobby				
1959	48	Sumor	26	85—piston
1960	14	Bill Forbes	16	194—flagged
1961	16	Thompson	32	26—piston
1962	18	Morcroft	19	96—oil leak
1963	26	Morcroft	25	79—oil leak
1964	16	Konstant Hot	10	196—flagged
1965	86	Racing Associates		153.309, too slow
	95	Leader Card		Did not qualify
1966	39	Racing Associates	31	0—wrecked FS
Gulotta, Anthony "Tony"				
1926	31	Miller	11	142—flagged
1927	27	Miller	3	200—93.139
1928	8	Stutz	10	200—88.888
1929	23	Packard Cable	17	91—supercharger
1930	9	Mavv	19	79—valve
1931	37	Hunt	18	167—wrecked NW
1932	25	Studebaker	13	184—flagged
1933	34	Studebaker	7	200—99.071
1934	8	Schroeder	17	94—con. rod
1935	44	Bowes Seal Fast	21	102—magneto
	7	Foreman Axle		Relieved Lou Moore
1936	31	Pirrung		Wrecked in practice
	56	Pirrung		Didn't complete run
	42	Bowes Seal Fast		Relieved Cliff Bergere
1937	38	Burd Piston Ring	8	200—105.015
1938	17	Hamilton-Harris	17	130—con. rod
1939	62	Burd Piston Ring	11	200—103.938
Gurney, Dan				
1962	52	John Zink		Did not qualify
	34	Thompson	20	92—rear end gear
1963	91	Lotus Ford		Wrecked qualifying
	93	Lotus Ford	7	200—140.071
1964	12	Lotus Ford	17	110—tire wear
1965	17	Yamaha	26	42—timing gears
1966	31	All American	27	0—wrecked FS
Guyot, Albert				
1913	9	Sunbeam	4	200—70.92
1914	10	Delage	3	200—80.20
1919	32	Ballot	4	200—84.44
1921	9	Duesenberg	6	200—83.03
1923	24	Roland-Pilain		Withdrawn
1925	10	Guyot		Did not arrive
1926	39	Guyot	28	8—steering knuckle
Haddad, Ed				
1949	47	Page		Did not qualify
Hahn, Peter J.				
1952	74	Helin Flyer		Did not qualify
Haibe, Ora				
1916	9	Osteweg	10	120—74.00
1919	17	Hudson	14	200—
1921	16	Sunbeam	5	200—84.28
1922	31	Duesenberg	5	200—90.58
1924	31	Schmidt	15	182—flagged
1925	27	Miller		Relieved Frank Elliot
Hall, Howard				
1911	41	Velie	17	Flagged
Hall, Ira				
1928	26	Duesenberg	21	115—wrecked SW
1932	35	Duesenberg	7	200—98.207
1933	10	D. Duesenberg	37	37—piston
1937	37	Precise Tool		Didn't complete run
	56	Lafayette, Ind.		Disqualified
1938	17	Greenfield Super Service	30	44—engine seized, hit wall, NE
1939	17	Greenfield S.S.	24	89—Head gasket
1940	47	Magnee & Nowiak		Did not qualify
1941	38	Kimmell		Wrecked in practice
Hall, Norman				
1960	92	Thompson		Did not qualify
1961	88	Drewry's		Didn't complete run
	92	Concannon		141.861, too slow
	34	Federal Eng.	10	200—134.104
1962	25	Dean-Autolite		Wrecked in practice
	41	Bill Forbes Racing		Wrecked qualifying SW
1963	55	Demler		Did not qualify
	61	Federal Eng.		Didn't complete run
1964	26	Hurst	33	1—spun, hit wall NW
1965	8	Pope-Hall		153.407, too slow
Hamilton, "Red"				
1953	91	Dillon		Did not qualify
Hanks, Sam				
1940	28	Duray	13	192—flagged
1941	28	Tom Joyce 7-Up		Wrecked before race
1946	32	Spike Jones	31	18—oil line
	24	Noc-Out		Relieved Chitwood
1948	76	Flavell	26	34—clutch
1949	35	Federal Eng.		Did not qualify
	18	Love Machine	30	20—oil leak
1950	23	Merz Engineering	30	42—oil pressure
1951	25	Schmidt	12	135—spun NE
1952	18	Bardahl	3	200—125.580
1953	3	Bardahl	3	200—126.465
1954	1	Bardahl	20	191—spun (J. Rathmann) FS
1955	8	Jones & Maley	19	134—transmission
1956	4	Jones & Maley	2	200—128.303
1957	9	Belond Exhaust	1	200—135.601
Hannon, Johnny				
1935	45	Bowes Seal Fast		Wrecked in practice NE, died
Hansen, Mel				
1939	49	Joel Thorne, Inc.	19	113—hit pit wall
	58	Alfa Romeo		Relieved Louis Tomei
1940	31	Hartz	8	194—flagged
1941	9	Fageol	29	11—con. rod
	26	Phillips		Relieved Phillips
1946	41	Offenhauser	11	143—crankshaft
1947	38	Flavell-Duffy	27	32—pushed, disqualified
1948	28	Brady		Did not qualify
	17	Schafer Gear Works	25	42—too slow, disqualified
1949	44	Bowes Seal Fast		Did not qualify
	38	Ray Brady		Relieved George Fonder
Hansgen, Walt				
1964	53	MG Liquid Sus.	13	176—flagged
1965	53	MG Liquid Sus.	14	117—fuel line
Harder, Fred				
1924	27	Barber-Warnock	17	176—flagged
1925	7	Skelly		Relieved M. C. Jones
Harkey, Bob				
1963	31	American Rubber		Wrecked in practice
1964	4	Wally Weir	8	197—flagged
1965	10	Federal Eng.		Did not qualify
1966	48	Prather		Did not qualify
	81	Central Excavat.		Did not qualify

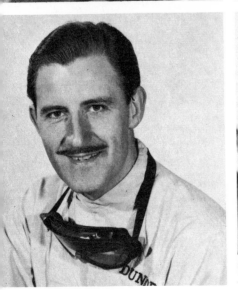

Left to right—Top: Bobby Grim, Sam Hanks, Middle: Gene Hartley, Ray Harroun, Ralph Hepburn. Bottom: Graham Hill, Bill Holland.

Left to right—Top: Ted Horn, Ronney Householder. Middle: Eddie Johnson, Jim Hurtubise, Parnelli Jones. Bottom: Ray Keech, Gordon Johncock.

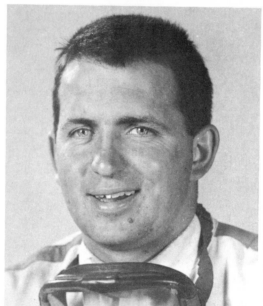

Year	No.	Car	Fin.	Remarks
	85	Caves Buick Offy		Didn't complete run
Harriman, Vern				
1961	91	Honeymoon Exp.		Did not arrive
Harroun, Ray				
1911	32	Marmon "Wasp"	1	200—74.59
Hartley, C. G.				
1924	29	Hartley		Did not qualify
Hartley, Gene				
1950	75	Troy Oil	16	128—flagged
1952	67	Mel-Rae	28	65—exhaust pipe
1953	41	Federal Eng.	28	53—wrecked NE
1954	31	John Zink	23	168—engine trouble
1955	28	Commercial Motor Freight		Didn't complete run
1956	82	Central Excavat.	11	196—flagged
1957	22	Messaglia Hotels	11	200—131.345
1958	24	Hoyt Machine		142.231, 1st alt.
1959	88	Drewry's	11	200—132.434
1960	48	Sumar	14	196—flagged
1961	28	John Chalik	11	198—flagged
1962	88	Drewry's	27	23—steering
Hartsfield, Art				
1948	27	Corley		Did not qualify
Hartz, Harry				
1922	12	Duesenberg	2	200—93.53
1923	7	Durant	2	200—90.06
1924	4	Durant	4	200—96.55
1925	6	Miller	4	200—98.89
1926	3	Miller	2	158—94.481
1927	1	Erskine Miller	25	38—crankshaft
Haupt, Willie				
1913	35	Mason	9	200—63.48
1914	43	Duesenberg	12	200—66.66
1915	24	Bergdoll		Did not qualify
	28	Emden	11	200—70.75
1920	34	Meteor	16	146—con. rod
Haustein, Gene				
1931	26	Fronty Ford	23	117—lost wheel
1932	23	Fronty Ford		Did not qualify
1933	29	Martz	15	197—flagged
1934	29	Martz	30	13—wrecked NW
1935	28	Yahr Bros.		Did not qualify
	21	Veedol		Relieved Ralph Hepburn
Hawkes, W. Douglas				
1922	22	Bentley	13	200—74.95
1926	27	Eldridge	14	91—frozen camshaft
Headley, Mervin E.				
1921	26	Frontenac		Did not qualify
Hearne, Eddie				
1911	18	Fiat	21	flagged
1912	6	Case	20	55—burned bearing
1913	32	Case		Relieved Joe Nikrent
1919	14	Durant	2	200—87.09
1920	31	Duesenberg	6	200—80.15
1921	1	Revere	13	111—oil line
1922	15	Ballot	3	200—93.04
1923	6	Durant	4	200—86.65
	8	Durant		Relieved Cliff Durant
1924	1	Durant	19	151—fuel line
1926	9	Locomobile Jr. 8		Relieved Cliff Durant
1927	16	Miller	7	200—90.064
Heath, Allen				
1925	32	Engle-Stanko		Wrecked qualifying
	97	Agajanian		Did not qualify
1953	65	Commercial Motor Freight		Did not qualify
	51	Dean Van Lines		Didn't complete run
Hellings, Mack				
1948	58	Blue Crown		Did not qualify
	35	Don Lee	5	200—113.361
1949	8	Don Lee	16	172—valve
1950	15	Tuffy's Offy	13	132—flagged
1951	19	Tuffanelli-Derrico	31	18—piston
Hemmings, Jim				
1962	65	Kurtis-Kraft		Didn't complete run
	94	Speed Enterprise		Did not qualify
Henderson, Pete				
1916	2	Duesenberg		Did not arrive
	4	Maxwell	6	120—78.30
1920	15	Revere	10	200—67.93
Hepburn, Ralph				
1925	17	Miller	16	144—gas tank
1926	19	Miller	8	151—89.882
1927	19	Boyle Valve	24	39—leaking fuel line
1928	16	Miller	24	48—timing gears
	7	Miller		Relieved Babe Stapp
1929	18	Packard Cable	31	14—transmission
	21	Packard Cable		Relieved Leon Duray
1931	19	Harry Miller	3	200—94.224
1933	23	Highway Parts	38	33—con. rod bearing
1934	31	Miller	13	164—con. rod
1935	21	Veedol	5	200—103.177
1936	9	Art Rose	12	196—flagged
1937	8	Hamilton-Harris	2	200—113.565
1938	4	Harry A. Miller		Left at line
1939	25	Hamilton-Harris	22	107—wrecked BS
1940	54	Bowes Seal Fast	29	47—steering frozen, spun
1941	54	Bowes Seal Fast	4	200—113.631
1946	2	Novi Governor	14	121—stalled
1948	12	Novi Grooved Piston		Wrecked in practice, NE, died
Herman, Al				
1953	93	Traylor Eng.		Did not qualify
1954	36	Ed Stone		Did not qualify
1955	71	Martin Bros.	7	200—124.794
1956	12	Bardahl	28	74—wrecked FS
1957	89	Dunn Engineering	21	111—wrecked FS
1958	75	D-A Lubricant		Did not qualify
1959	89	Dunn Engineering	13	200—131.872
1960	76	Joe Hunt Magneto	32	34—clutch
Herr, Don				
1912	8	National		Relieved Joe Dawson
1913	8	Stutz	26	7—clutch shaft
Hickey, Denny				
1919	21	Stickle	9	200—80.22
Hill, Bennett "Benny"				
1920	7	Frontenac	17	115—wrecked
1921	21	Duesenberg Straight 8	8	200—79.13
1923	35	Miller	19	44—crankshaft
1924	3	Miller	5	200—96.46
1925	21	Miller Front Drive		105.708, poor handling
	3	Miller	18	69—rear spring
	1	Junior 8		Relieved Dave Lewis
	14	Miller		Relieved McDonough
1926	16	Miller	12	136—flagged
1927	4	Cooper	28	26—rear spring shackle bolt
1933	68	Goldberg Bros.		Did not qualify
	68	Goldberg Bros.	22	158—con. rod
Hill, George				
1915	26	Bugatti	23	20—water pump gear
Hill, Graham				
1963	83	Harvey Aluminum		Wrecked in practice
1966	25	Red Ball	1	200—144.317
Hill, Herb				
1962	69	Grizzly Brake		Did not qualify
Hill, Jim				
1927	42	Nickel Plate	12	197—flagged
1928	31	Marion Chevrolet		Did not qualify
Hill, J. R.				
1915	41	Bals		Did not qualify
Hinnershitz, Tommy				
1939	33	Kimmell		Did not qualify
1940	27	Marks-Offenhauser	32	32—crankshaft, hit wall FS
1941	27	Marks	10	200—105.152
1946	34	Maserati		Did not qualify
1947	5	T. H. E.		Did not qualify
1948	7	Kurtis-Kraft	9	198—flagged
Hitke, Kurt				
1919	12	Roamer	23	56—rod bearing
1920	27	Kenworthy		Did not arrive
Hoffman, Sam				
1933	27	Yahr-Miller		Relieved Kelly Petillo
1934	47	Mannix		Did not qualify
Holland, Bill				
1947	16	Blue Crown	2	200—116.097
1948	2	Blue Crown	2	200—119.147
1949	7	Blue Crown	1	200—121.327
1950	3	Blue Crown	2	137—122.638
1953	61	Slick Racers, Inc.		134.439, too slow
	49	Crawford	15	177—cam gear
Holmes, Jackie				
1948	24	Indiana Plywood		Did not qualify
	93	Jimmy Chai		Did not qualify
1949	57	Pat Clancy	22	65—drive shaft
1950	77	Norm Olson	23	123—spun in rain NE
1951	24	Palmer		129.259, too slow
	45	C. R. C.		Didn't complete run
1952	41	Speed		Did not qualify
1953	71	Merkler Machine		Did not qualify
Holmes, Ralph				
1927	41	Thompson Valve		Relieved Wade Morton
Homeier, Bill				
1953	84	Coast Grain		Did not qualify
	87	Cal Connell		Did not qualify
1954	51	Jones & Maley	33	74—hit wall leaving pits
1955	72	Travelon Trailer		Did not qualify
	77	Merz Engineering		Relieved Walt Faulkner
1958	74	Kurtis-Kraft		Did not qualify
	95	Safety Auto Glass		Didn't complete run
1959	42	Go-Kart		Threw rod qualifying
	62	Rusco		130.928, too slow
1960	39	Ridgewood	13	200—131.367
Horan, Joe				
1912	22	Lozier	8	200—71.50
1914	29	Metropol		Did not qualify
Horn, Eylard T. "Ted"				
1934	53	Mick		Did not qualify
1935	43	Ford V8	16	145—steering
1936	22	Miller-Hartz	2	200—108.170
1937	3	Miller-Hartz	3	200—112.203
1939	4	Boyle	4	200—111.879
1940	3	Boyle	4	199—flagged
1941	4	T. E. C.	3	200—113.864
1946	29	Boyle Maserati	3	200—109.819
1947	1	Bennett Bros.	3	200—114.997
1948	1	Bennett Bros.	4	200—117.844
Horne, Byron				
1949	39	Grancor V8		Did not qualify
Horvath, Don				
1964	37	Dean Van Lines		Did not qualify
Householder, Ronney				
1937	23	Topping	12	194—flagged
1938	16	Thorne-Sparks	14	154—supercharger hose
1939	26	Duray-Barbasol		Wrecked in practice SW
1948	68	Speedway Cocktail		Did not qualify
Houser, Norm				
1947	69	Robert Allison		Did not qualify
1949	71	Troy Oil Co.	10	181—flagged
1950	65	Offenhauser		Didn't complete run
1951	61	Tom Sarafoff		Didn't complete run
Houser, Thane				
1926	33	Abell	13	102—flagged
1929	41	Duesenberg		Broken supercharger
	53	Duesenberg		Relieved Gleason
Howard, C. Glenn				
1920	24	Ellingboe		Did not arrive
1922	19	Fronty Ford	18	165—engine trouble
Howard, Ray				
1919	48	Peugeot	16	130—lost oil pressure
1920	9	Peugeot	13	150—camshaft
Howie, George				
1931	44	G. N. H.	11	200—87.651
1932	47	Howie		103.490, 1st alt.
1933	48	Howie		Withdrawn
	4	Russell 8		Relieved Snowberger
Hoyt, Jerry				
1950	81	Morris	21	125—flagged
1951	14	Pat Clancy		127.700, too slow
1953	55	John Zink	23	107—cockpit too hot
1954	23	Sumar		Didn't complete run
	99	Belanger	26	130—engine trouble
	4	Anstead Rotary		Relieved Paul Russo
1955	23	Jim Robbins	31	40—oil leak
Hudson, "Skip"				
1965	93	Harrison		Did not qualify
Huff, Joe				
1930	34	Gauss Front-Drive	23	48—valve
1931	69	Goldberg Bros.	16	180—flagged
1932	55	Highway Parts	10	200—87.586
Hughes, Hughie				
1911	36	Mercer	12	200—67.73
1912	21	Mercer	3	200—76.13
1913	4	Keeton		Relieved Bob Burman
1915	26	F. R. P.		Did not qualify
	19	Maxwell		Relieved Billy Carlson
Hulse, Chuck				
1960	43	Chapman		Wrecked in practice
	69	Sorenson		137.174, too slow
1961	37	Vatis Enterprises		Wrecked in practice
1962	19	Federal Eng.	21	91—fuel pump
1963	10	Dean Van Lines	8	200—140.064
1966	86	Leader Card		Did not qualify
	12	Wynn's	20	22—hit 82 SW
Hunt, Bill				
1924	26	Barber-Warnock	14	191—flagged
Hunt, Harry				
1932	78	Brooks Romo		Did not qualify
1934	43	Duesenberg		Did not qualify
1935	25	Duesenberg		Didn't complete run
1936	58	Duesenberg		Did not qualify
Hurt, Bob				
1965	43	Jim Robbins		Did not qualify
1966	36	Viking Racing		Didn't complete run
Hurtubise, Jim				
1960	56	Travelon Trailer	18	185—con. rod
1961	99	Demler	22	102—piston
1962	99	Demler		Wrecked qualifying
	91	Jim Robbins	13	200—135.655
1963	56	Hotel Tropicana	22	102—oil leak
1964	56	Tombstone Life	14	141—oil pressure
1965	56	Tombstone Life		Wrecked in practice
	59	STP-Tombstone	33	1—transmission
1966	56	Gerhardt Offy	17	29—oil line
Insinger, Harris				
1935	62	Cresco	14	185—flagged
Jackson, Jimmy				
1946	61	Jackson	2	200—114.498
1947	7	Jim Hussey	5	200—112.834
1948	61	Howard Keck	10	193—spindle, spun
1949	61	Howard Keck	6	200—117.870
1950	61	Cummins Diesel	29	52—supercharger
1952	61	Auto. Shippers		133.824, 2nd alt.
Jacobi, Bruce				
1962	22	Frohde		144.939, too slow
1966	68	Western Racing		Did not qualify
Jagersberger, Joe				
1911	8	Case	31	87—wrecked FS
James, Joe				
1950	63	Esmeralda		127.438, too slow
	82	Bob Estes		124.176, too slow
1951	26	Bob Estes	33	8—drive shaft
1952	14	Bardahl	13	200—120.108
Jeffkins, Rupert				
1911	40	Velie		Did not qualify
		Cole		Did not qualify
	41	Velie		Relieved Howard Hall
Jenkins, D. A. "Ab"				
1929	49	Miller		Did not qualify
Jenkins, John				
1911	42	Cole		Relieved Bill Endicott
1912	14	White	7	200—73.25
1913	18	Schacht	25	13—crankshaft
1914	35	Great Western		Did not qualify
Johncock, Gordon				
1965	76	Weinberger	5	200—146.417
1966	5	Weinberger		Did not qualify
	72	Weinberger	4	200—143.084
Johns, Bobby				
1964	47	Hurst Floor Shift		Wrecked qualifying
1965	83	Lotus Ford	7	197—flagged
1966	41	Prestone		Didn't complete run
Johnson, Art				
1916	26	Crawford	8	120—74.40

Year	No.	Car	Fin.	Remarks
Johnson, Eddie				
1952	81	Central Excavat.	16	193—flagged
1953	26	City of Detroit		Did not qualify
	2	Travelon Trailer		Relieved J. Rathmann
1954	83	McNamara		137.599, 1st alt.
	12	Dr. Sabourin		Relieved Rodger Ward
1955	83	McNamara	13	196—flagged
1956	81	Central Excavat.	15	195—flagged
1957	43	Chapman	25	93—front wheel bearing
1958	61	Bryant Heating	9	200—130.156
1959	19	Bryant Heating	8	200—133.336
1960	22	Jim Robbins	6	200—136.137
1961	33	Jim Robbins	18	127—wrecked NW
1962	32	Polyaire Foam	25	38—magneto
1963	88	Drewry's	20	112—hit wall BS
1964	84	Thompson-Sears	26	6—fuel pump
1965	23	Chapman	10	195—flagged
1966	54	Valvoline II	7	175—engine trouble
Johnson, "Junior"				
1963	73	American Rubber		Did not qualify
Johnson, Luther				
1931	57	Bill Richards	20	156—wrecked NW
1932	46	Studebaker	16	164—lost wheel FS
1933	46	Studebaker	10	200—97.393
1936	49	Bugatti		Did not qualify
1937	66	Mannix		Did not qualify
Johnson, Van				
1958	59	Ray Brady		Wrecked in practice
Jones, Ben				
1926	29	Duesenberg	18	54—wrecked
Jones, Dan				
1961	47	Joe Hunt Magneto		Wrecked in practice
Jones, Dee				
1964	65	Travelon Trainer		Didn't complete run
Jones, Herbert				
1925	29	Jones	19	69—wrecked SS
1926	18	Elcar		Wrecked NW, died
Jones, M. C.				
1925	7	Skelly	21	33—transmission
Jones, Milt				
1932	19	Jones		Wrecked in practice, died, SE
Jones, Rufus P. "Parnelli"				
1961	98	Agajanian-Willard	12	192—flagged
1962	98	Agajanian-Willard	7	200—138.534
1963	98	Agajanian-Willard	1	200—143.137
1964	97	Agajanian-Bowes		Did not qualify
	98	Agajanian-Bowes	23	55—pit fire
1965	98	Agajanian-Hurst	2	200—149.200
1966	98	Agajanian Rev 500	14	87—wheel bearing
Jones, Walter				
1911	12	Amplex		Relieved W. Turner
Jones, Will				
1911	9	Case	28	122—steering
Kalen, George				
1932	83	McPherson-Kalen		Did not qualify
Karnatz, Albert "Bert"				
1929	27	Richards Bros.	25	50—gas leak
1931	15	All Oil		Did not qualify
Kay, Johnny (John Kapustinski)				
1953	67	Jeanie-Lee		Did not qualify
1955	76	Leitenberger		132.193, too slow
1956	35	Pete Wales		Did not qualify
1959	17	Safety Auto Glass		Did not qualify
Keech, Ray				
1928	15	Simplex Piston R.	4	200—93.320
1929	2	Simplex Piston R.	1	200—97.585
Keene, Charles				
1914	5	Beaver Bullet	8	200—74.82
1915	27	F. R. P.		Did not qualify
Keller, Al				
1955	42	Sam Traylor Offy	27	54—wrecked BS
1956	55	Sam Traylor	14	195—flagged
1957	16	Bardahl	27	75—wrecked SW
1958	52	Bardahl	11	200—128.498
1959	57	Helse	18	163—piston
1960	35	McKay		138.264, too slow
	57	Helse		Did not qualify
1961	19	Konstant Hot	5	200—136.034
Keneally, Mel				
1930	21	Miller	17	114—valve
Kenyon, Mel				
1965	27	Federal Eng.		153.597, 2nd alt.
1966	94	Gerhardt Offy	5	200—139.456
Kilpatrick, I. J.				
1913	31	Case		Relieved Disbrow
Kirkpatrick, Charles				
1919	19	Detroit	20	69—con. rod
Kladis, Danny				
1946	59	Grancor V8	21	46—towed, disqualified
1949	58	Speedway Cocktail		Did not qualify
1950	39	Federal Eng.		Didn't complete run
1951	89	Trainor Chicago		Bkn. rod qualifying
1952	19	Tuffanelli-Derrico		Did not qualify
1954	65	Advance Muffler		Relieved Spider Webb
1955	93	Roy McKay		Didn't complete run
1957	72	Morgan Eng.		124.412, too slow
	84	Safety Auto Glass		Did not qualify
Klar, Russ				
1955	61	Brady		131.301, too slow
Klein, Art				
1914	15	King	20	87—valve
1915	9	Kleinart	18	111—disqualified, smoking
1919	29	Peugeot	19	70—oil line
1920	8	Frontenac	21	40—wrecked
	28	Monroe		Relieved Joe Thomas
1922	6	Frontenac	21	105—con. rod
	9	Leach		Relieved Frank Elliott
Klemos, James				
1930	37	Morton & Brett		Did not qualify
Kloepfer, Barney				
1929	3	Majestic Miller		Relieved Lou Moore
Knight, Harry				
1911	7	Westcott	30	90—wrecked FS
1912	10	Lexington	23	6—engine trouble
Knepper, Arnie				
1965	18	Konstant Hot	18	80—cylinder wall
1966	37	Sam Liosi	29	0—wrecked FS
Knepper, Ray				
1951	78	Bardahl		Did not qualify
Knipper, Billy				
1911	46	Benz	18	flagged
1912	2	Stutz		Relieved Len Zengel
	28	Stutz		Relieved Charles Merz
1913	10	Henderson	16	125—clutch
1914	31	Keeton	13	200—65.79
Koetzla, Dave				
1922	1	Disteel Dues.		Relieved Ira Vail
Kohlert, Henry				
1927	23	Elgin Piston Pin		Relieved Lecklider
1928	29	Elgin Piston Pin	13	180—flagged
Kostenuk, Ed				
1962	37	Leader Card		Did not qualify
1964	37	Dean Van Lines		Did not qualify
Kreiger, Johnny				
1930	35	Romthe		Relieved McDonald
1932	49	Consumers Oil	35	30—con. rod
Kreis, Peter				
1925	35	Duesenberg	8	200—96.32
1927	9	Cooper	17	123—bent front axle
1928	32	Marmon	22	73—rod bearings
1929	4	Detroit	16	91—engine seized
	25	Armacost-Miller		Relieved Cliff Bergere
1931	22	Coleman Motors		Qualified, withdrawn
	19	Harry Miller		Relieved Hepburn
1932	18	Studebaker	15	178—wrecked SW
1933	2	Frame-Miller	32	63—universal joint
1934	14	Miller-Hartz		Wrecked in practice SW, died
Krause, Bill				
1963	82	Harvey Titanium		Wrecked in practice
Langley, Joe				
1946	55	Clemons		Did not qualify
Larson, Jud				
1952	39	Iddings		Did not qualify
1953	96	Helin		Did not qualify
1957	25	John Zink		139.061, too slow
1958	44	John Zink	8	200—130.550
1959	52	Leader Card Duo		Did not qualify
	7	Bowes Seal Fast	29	45—wrecked NE
1964	85	Kaiser Aluminum		147.432, too slow
1965	15	Wynn		Wrecked in practice
1966	9	Michner		Did not qualify
Larson, Norske				
1931	64	Buehrig		Did not qualify
Lariviere, L. A.				
1933	75	L. & L.		Did not qualify
Lautenschlager, Christian				
1923	14	Mercedes	23	14—wrecked SW
LeBegue, Rene				
1940	49	Lucy O'Reilly Schell	10	192—flagged
1941	21	Talbot		116.000, 2nd alt.
LeCain, Jack				
1914	25	Maxwell		Relieved Billy Carlson
1916	22	Delage		82.48 crankshaft
	21	Delage		Relieved DeVigne
Lecklider, Fred				
1926	17	Nickel Plate	24	24—con. rod
	4	Miller		Relieved Phil Shafer
1927	23	Elgin Piston Pin	23	49—wrecked SW (Kohlert)
	44	Miller		Relieved Al Melcher
1930	25	Allen-Miller		Relieved Leslie Allen
LeCocq, Louis				
1919	15	Roamer	18	96—wrecked NE, died
Leighton, Chuck				
1950	79	Cantarano		121.065, too slow
Leipert, Edward				
1932	74	Leipert Miller		Did not qualify
Leonard, Joe				
1965	29	All American	29	27—oil leak
1966	6	Yamaha Eagle	9	170—magneto
Levrett, Bayliss				
1949	69	Wynn't Oil	24	52—drain plug
1950	24	Palmer	27	108—lost oil pressure
1951	46	Hunt Magneto		128.329, too slow
1952	69	Brown Motor Co.		Did not qualify
Lewis, Dave				
1916	25	Crawford	14	71—loose gas tank
1919	38	Duesenberg		Did not qualify
1922	34	Durant		Relieved Cliff Durant
1923	10	Scheel Frontenac		Did not qualify
	31	Durant		Relieved Frank Elliott
1925	1	Junior 8	2	200—100.82
1926	1	Front Drive Miller	15	91—broken valve
1927	7	Miller Front Drive	33	21—front spring pad
Lewis, Harry M.				
1933	44	Bud's Auto Parts		Did not qualify
1934	52	Don Hulbert		2nd alt.
Liesaw, Billy				
1912	17	Marquette-Buick	17	72—caught fire
1913	17	Anel	14	148—loose rods
Light, Mark				
1950	51	Glessner		Did not qualify
	52	Iddings		Didn't complete run
Limberg, Carl				
1915	31	Sunbeam		Did not qualify
Lindau, Bill				
1929	46	Pittsburgh Miller	19	70—valve
Linden, Andy				
1950	9	Bromme		Did not qualify
1951	57	Leitenberger	4	200—123.812
1952	9	Miracle Power	33	20—oil leak
1953	32	Cop-Sil-Loy	33	3—wrecked NE
	55	John Zink		Relieved Jerry Hoyt
	92	M. A. Walker		Relieved Rodger Ward
1954	74	Brown Motor Co.	25	165—torsion bar
	43	Chapman		Relieved Thomson
1955	19	Massaglia	6	200—125.022
1956	5	Chapman	27	90—oil leak
1957	73	McNamara	5	200—133.645
Lipscomb, Bill				
1940	5	Watson		Did not qualify
1941	57	Greene		Did not qualify
Liguori, Ralph				
1959	12	El Dorado Italia		136.395, too slow
	41	Sumar		Did not qualify
1962	68	White Spot		Did not qualify
1963	3	Schulz Refueling		147.620, 2nd alt.
1964	38	Ollie Prather		Did not qualify
1965	99	Demler		Wrecked in practice
1966	35	Flynn		Did not qualify
Litz, A. B. "Deacon"				
1928	23	Miller	14	161—flagged
1929	26	Deacon Litz	24	56—con. rod
1930	12	Duesenberg	30	22—wrecked NE
1931	5	Maley	17	177—wrecked SW (Cummings)
1932	24	Bowes Seal Fast	18	152—con. rod
1933	26	Bowes Seal Fast	16	197—flagged
1934	12	Stokley Foods	4	200—100.749
1935	16	Sha-litz	8	200—100.907
1936	15	Deacon Litz	23	108—crankshaft
1937	35	Motorola	14	191—out of oil
1938	52	Sampson-Litz		Did not qualify
1939	53	Maserati	33	7—valve
1941	32	Sampson 16	22	89—oil trouble
Livingood, Virgil				
1933	69	Duesenberg		Wrecked qualifying
Lockhart, Frank				
1926	15	Miller	1	160—95.885
1927	2	Perfect Circle	18	120—con. rod
Luptow, Frank				
1952	56	Bardahl		Did not qualify
Lux, Ron				
1966	55	Barnett Bros.		Did not qualify
Lynch, George				
1948	56	Lisher & Lynch		Did not qualify
1949	36	Auto. Shippers	32	1—wrecked SW
1950	36	Auto. Shippers		Did not qualify
1951	36	Rassey		Did not qualify
Lytle, Herbert				
1911	35	Apperson		82—wrecked in pits
MacDonald, Dave				
1964	83	Thompson-Sears	29	1—exploded FS, died
MacKenzie, George "Doc"				
1930	43	Ambler		Did not qualify
1932	42	Brady	28	65—engine trouble
1933	51	Brady	18	192—rear axle
1934	73	Cresco	29	15—wrecked NS
1935	8	Pirrung	9	200—100.598
1936	10	Gilmore	3	200—107.460
Mackey, Bill (William C. Gretsinger, Jr.)				
1951	71	Karl Hall	19	97—clutch shaft
Madden, Ed				
1913	1	Nyberg		Relieved H. Endicott
Magill, Mike				
1956	74	Chesty Foods		Did not qualify
1957	77	Dayton Steel	24	101—wrecked FS
1958	77	Dayton Steel	17	136—black flagged
1959	77	Dayton Steel	30	45—wrecked NE
1960	77	Dayton Steel		Did not qualify
1961	82	San Diego Steel Pdts.		Didn't complete run
Mais, John A.				
1915	24	Mais	22	23—left course
Malone, Art				
1963	75	STP	31	18—clutch
1964	3	Studebaker-STP	11	194—flagged
1965	67	G. C. Murphy		Didn't complete run
1966	32	Wally Weir		Wrecked in practice
Mantz, Johnny				
1948	98	Agajanian	13	185—flagged
1949	98	Agajanian	7	200—117.142
1963	23	Auto. Shippers		Relieved Faulkner
Marchese, Carl				
1929	43	Marchese	4	200—93.541
Marion, Milt				
1931	43	Duesenberg		Did not qualify
1932	53	Duesenberg		Did not qualify
1934	57	Miller		Did not qualify
1937	65	Crystal Flash		Did not qualify
Marquette, Mel				
1911	23	McFarlan		Relieved Bert Adams
1912	23	McFarlan	19	63—broken wheels
Marr, R. G. "Buddy"				
1928	35	B. W. Cooke		109.685
Marshall, Cyrus "Cy"				
1928	6	Chromolite		Relieved Earl DeVore

Left to right—Top: Joe Leonard,
Andy Linden, Frank Lockhart.
Middle: Bobby Marshman, Rex Mays,
Al Keller. Bottom: Roger McCluskey,
Jack McGrath.

Left to right—Top: Alfred Moss, Tommy
Milton. Middle: Lou Meyer, Chet
Miller, Jimmy Murphy. Bottom: Duke
Nalon, Johnnie Parsons.

Year	No.	Car	Fin.	Remarks
1930	36	Duesenberg	26	29—wrecked NE
1947	34	Tattersfield	8	197—flagged
1950	78	Vulcan Tool		Did not qualify
Marshman, Bobby				
1961	31	Hoover	7	200—135.534
1962	54	Bryant Heating	5	200—138.790
1963	5	Econo-Car Rental	16	196—rear end
1964	51	Pure Oil Firebird	25	39—oil plug
Mason, George				
1914	13	Mason	23	66—piston
Mathouser, Bob				
1962	43	Ray Brady		Wrecked in practice
1963	3	Schulz Refueling		Did not qualify
	15	Federal Eng.		Didn't complete run
1964	77	Dayton Disc Brake	22	77—brakes
1965	77	Dayton Disc Brake		Did not qualify
	87	M/T Challenger		Threw rod qualifying
1966	17	Jim Robbins		Didn't complete run
Matson, Joe				
1912	25	Lozier	14	110—crankshaft
Mauro, Johnny				
1947	64	Phil Kraft		Did not qualify
1948	37	Miller		Did not qualify
	33	Mauro Alfa Romeo	8	198—flagged
1949	16	Alfa Romeo		Did not qualify
1950	25	Alfa Romeo		Did not qualify
1952	35	Kennedy Tank		Did not qualify
1953	47	Ferrari		Did not arrive
May, Rollin				
1930	51	J. M.		Did not qualify
1933	27	Yahr-Miller		Did not qualify
May, Walt				
1931	65	Tucker Tappett		Did not qualify
Mays, Rex				
1934	35	Frame Miller-Duesenberg	23	53—front axle
	32	F. W. D.		Relieved Frank Brisko
1935	33	Gilmore	17	123—spring shackle
1936	33	Gilmore	15	192—out of gas
1937	14	Bowes Seal Fast	33	24—overheating
	34	Bowes Seal Fast		Relieved Cantlon
	38	Burd Piston Ring		Relieved Tony Gulotta
1938	8	Alfa Romeo	28	45—supercharger
1939	15	Thorne Eng.	16	145—rings
1940	33	Bowes Seal Fast	2	200—113.742
1941	1	Bowes Seal Fast	2	200—114.459
1946	1	Bowes Seal Fast	30	26—manifold
	3	Noc-Out		Relieved Cliff Bergere
1947	9	Bowes Seal Fast	6	200—111.056
1948	5	Bowes Seal Fast	19	129—leaking fuel tank
1949	5	Novi Mobil	25	48—engine trouble
Mazzucco, Joe				
1914	45	Tatters		Did not qualify
McCarver, Jack				
1926	28	Hamlin	25	23—con. rod
McCluskey, Roger				
1961	22	Racing Associates	27	51—wreck FS
1962	17	Bell Lines	16	168—spun SE
1963	14	Konstant Hot	15	198—spun NE
1965	25	All American	30	18—clutch
1966	8	G. C. Murphy	13	129—oil leak
McCoy, Ernie				
1953	12	Chapman	8	200—123.404
1954	32	Crawford	16	194—flagged
1955	69	LaVilla		133.038, 2nd alt.
McCoy, J. J.				
1919	36	McCoy	30	36—oil line
McDonald, J. C.				
1930	35	Romthe	18	112—leaking fuel
McDonough, Bob				
1924	19	Miller	10	200—90.51
1925	14	Miller	14	188—truss rod
1926	2	Duesenberg		Did not qualify
	19	Miller		Relieved Hepburn
1927	14	Cooper	6	200—90.410
1928	5	Detroit		Relieved Cliff Durant
1929	5	Miller Front Drive	18	74—oil tank
1932	58	Miller F.W.D.	38	17—oil line
McDougall, R. G. "Bon"				
1926	34	Miller	26	19—valve
McDowell, Johnny				
1949	32	Iddings	18	142—magneto
1950	62	Pete Wales	18	128—flagged
1951	12	W. J.	32	15—gas tank
1952	31	McDowell	21	182—flagged
McElreath, Jim				
1962	15	Schultz Fueling	6	200—138.653
1963	8	Bill Forbes	6	200—140.862
1964	28	Studebaker-STP	21	77—engine trouble
1965	52	Zink-Urschel	20	66—rear end gears
1966	52	Zink-Urschel		Did not qualify
	3	Zink-Urschel	3	200—143.742
McGrath, Jack				
1948	52	Sheffler Offy	21	70—stalled SE
1949	33	City of Tacoma	26	39—oil pump
1950	49	Hinkle	14	131—spun in rain NE
1951	9	Hinkle	3	200—124.745
1952	4	Hinkle	11	200—121.428
1953	5	Hinkle	5	200—124.556
1954	2	Hinkle	3	200—130.086
1955	3	Hinkle	26	54—magneto
McGreevy, Mike				
1962	46	Goff Bros.		Did not qualify
1966	65	Travelon Trailer		Did not qualify
McGurk, Frank				
1936	52	Abels Auto Ford	26	51—crankshaft
1937	39	Belanger Miller		Wrecked qualifying, mech. Opalko died
McKee, Herschell				

Year	No.	Car	Fin.	Remarks
1926	26	Eldridge		Relieved Eldridge
1935	51	Frigenor		106.638, too slow
McKenna, Barney				
1932	69	Finneran		Did not qualify
McNay, Edward				
1915	36	Cino		Did not qualify
McQuinn, Harry				
1934	63	DeBaets	31	13—con. rod
1935	66	DeBaets	33	4—con. rod
1936	28	Sampson Radio	13	196—out of gas
1937	47	Sullivan-O'Brien	29	47—piston
	35	Motorola		Relieved Deacon Litz
1938	45	Marchese	7	197—108.694
1939	38	Elgin Piston Pin	20	110—ignition
	62	Burd Piston Ring		Relieved Tony Gulotta
1940	45	Leader Card		Did not qualify
	41	Pay-Day	11	192—flagged
1941	15	Ziffrin	7	200—111.795
1946	14	Mobilgas	13	124—out of oil
1948	65	Frank Lynch	33	1—supercharger
McVey, Max				
1919	25	Hudson		Did not qualify
McWithey, Jim				
1956	77	Dayton Steel		Did not qualify
1957	34	Federal Eng.		Wrecked, warm up lap NE
1958	66	Federal Eng.		Did not qualify
1959	58	Ray Brady	16	200—129.024
1960	16	Hoover	29	60—brakes
1961	29	Fullerton		Didn't complete run
Melaun, Fred				
1914	47	Titzie Flyer		Did not qualify
Melcher, Al				
1927	44	Miller	15	144—supercharger
Mertz, Jack				
1932	79	Mertz		Did not qualify
Merz, Charles				
1911	20	National	7	200—70.37
1912	28	Stutz	4	200—76.00
1913	28	Stutz	3	200—73.38
1916	19	Peugeot	19	25—lubrication
Merzney, Fred				
1932	63	Coleman F.W.D.		Did not qualify
Metzler, George				
1947	55	Dixon		Did not qualify
1948	47	Glessner Motors		Did not qualify
1949	67	Glessner		Wrecked in practice, SW, died
Meyer, Lou				
1927	29	Jynx		Relieved Wilbur Shaw
1928	14	Miller	1	200—99.482
1929	1	Miller	2	200—95.596
1930	1	Sampson	34	28—oil leak
	21	Jadson		Relieved Stevens
1932	16	Sampson	33	50—crankshaft
1933	36	Tydol	1	200—104.162
1934	1	Ring Free	18	92—oil tank
	31	Miller		Relieved Hepburn
1935	36	Ring Free	12	200—100.256
1936	8	Ring Free	1	200—109.069
1937	2	Boyle	4	200—110.730
1938	5	Bowes Seal Fast	16	149—oil pump
1939	45	Bowes Seal Fast	12	197—wrecked BS
Meyer, Zeke				
1927	10	Miller		Relieved Earl DeVore
1928	22	Miller		Relieved Batten
1929	16	Miller		Too dark to qualify
	49	Miller		Relieved W. Crawford
1930	21	Miller	16	115—con. rod
1931	78	Woods		Withdrawn
1932	37	Studebaker	6	200—98.476
1933	9	Studebaker	9	200—98.122
1934	45	Carter Carburetor		Did not qualify
	26	Shafer 8		Relieved Phil Shafer
	36	Shafer 8		Relieved Al Miller
1935	31	Victor Gasket		Didn't complete run
1936	53	Boyle Products	9	200—101.331
1937	52	Joel Thorne		Did not qualify
1939	27	Miller		Did not qualify
Meyers, Ned				
1932	35	Duesenberg		Relieved Ira Hall
Miller, Al				
1932	29	Hudson	27	66—engine trouble
	9	Hudson		Relieved Chet Miller
1933	19	Marr	21	161—con. rod
1934	36	Shafer 8	6	200—98.264
1935	4	Boyle Products	15	178—magneto
1936	12	Boyle Products	21	119—wrecked FS
1937	42	Thorne	17	170—carburetor
1938	55	Domont's	18	125—clutch
1939	42	Kennedy Tank	28	41—accelerator pedal bracket
1940	58	Alfa Romeo	30	41—clutch
1941	12	Miller	28	22—transmission
1946	9	Blue Crown		Did not qualify
1947	66	Preston Tucker	25	33—magneto
1948	66	Preston Tucker		Did not qualify
1950	83	Trainor		Did not qualify
Miller, Al				
1962	64	Federal Eng.		Didn't complete run
1963	84	Harvey Aluminum	9	200—139.524
1964	93	Gerhardt-DeOrian		147.227, too slow
1965	74	Jerry Alderman	4	200—146,581
1966	75	Jerry Alderman	30	0—wrecked FS
Miller, Bruce				
1927	33	Jones-Whitaker		Did not qualify
Miller, Chet				
1928	35	B. W. Cooke		Wrecked in practice
1930	41	Fronty	13	161—flagged

Year	No.	Car	Fin.	Remarks
1931	27	Marr	10	200—89.580
1932	9	Hudson	21	125—engine trouble
1933	28	Marr	20	163—con. rod
1934	46	Bohnalite Ford	33	11—over SW wall
1935	34	Milac Front Drive	10	200—100.474
1936	18	Boyle Products	5	200—106.919
1937	7	Boyle	30	36—ignition
	16	Boyle Products		Relieved Cummings
1938	3	I. B. E. W.	3	200—114.946
1939	3	Boyle	21	107—wrecked BS
1940	34	Alfa Romeo	17	189—flagged
1941	41	Boyle	6	200—111.921
1946	5	Chet Miller	18	64—oil line
1948	31	Don Lee	20	108—oil trouble
1950	43	Novi Mobil		Did not qualify
1951	32	Novi Purelube	25	56—ignition
1952	21	Novi Pure Oil	30	41—supercharger shaft
1953	15	Novi Governor		Wrecked in practice, SW, died
Miller, Eddie				
1921	5	Duesenberg	4	200—84.65
Miller, Ralph				
1929	55	Hoefle		Did not qualify
Milton, Tommy				
1919	9	Duesenberg	25	50—con. rod
1920	10	Duesenberg	3	200—86.52
1921		Duhrn Dues.		Withdrawn
	2	Frontenac	1	200—89.62
1922	8	Leach	24	44—loose gas tank
1923	1	H. C. S.	1	200—90.95
1924	5	Miller	21	110—gas tank
1925	4	Miller	5	200—97.26
1927	6	Detroit	8	200—85.081
Minyard, Hal				
1966	49	Ring Free-Ansen		Did not qualify
Mitchell, Walter "Wally"				
1946	43	Mitchell Corp.		Did not qualify
Moore, Lou				
1928	28	Miller	2	200—99.241
1929	3	Majestic Miller	13	198—con. rod
1930	14	Coleman	29	23—wrecked NE
1931	22	Coleman Motors		Did not qualify
	14	Boyle Valve	26	103—differential
1932	8	Boyle Valve	25	79—timing gear
1933	37	Foreman Axle	3	200—101.599
1934	2	Foreman Axle	3	200—103.625
1935	7	Foreman Axle	18	116—con. rod
1936	32	Burd Piston Ring	17	185—out of gas
Moorhouse, Johnny				
1959	91	Binter		Wrecked in practice
Moran, Charles				
1930	32	duPont	27	22—wrecked NE
1931	51	Model A Ford		Did not qualify
Moriceau, Jules				
1929	35	Thompson	29	30—wrecked NW
Morton, Wade				
1920	34	Meteor		Relieved Willie Haupt
1922	10	Duesenberg		Relieved Joe Thomas
1923	33	Duesenberg		Did not qualify
	34	Duesenberg		Relieved Phil Shafer
1924	7	Durant		Relieved Wonderlich
	14	Miller		Relieved Fred Comer
1925	23	Duesenberg	15	156—wrecked NW
	5	Miller		Relieved Fred Comer
	9	Duesenberg		Relieved Phil Shafer
1926	8	Miller		Relieved Fred Comer
1927	41	Thompson Valve	14	152—wrecked Winnai
Moss, Alfred E.				
1924	28	Barber-Warnock	16	177—flagged
1925	29	Jones-Whitaker		Relieved Herb Jones
Motter, Earl				
1959	21	Dean Van Lines		Wrecked in practice
Mourre, Antoine				
1924	32	Mourre		Wrecked in practice
1925	23	Duesenberg	9	200—91.76 Qualified, driven by W. Morton
	22	Fiat		Relieved Bordino
	23	Duesenberg		Relieved Wade Morton
Mulford, Ralph				
1911	33	Lozier	2	200—74.29
1912	19	Knox	10	200—56.29
1913	29	Mercedes	7	200—66.95
1914	23	Mercedes	11	200—69.55
1915	35	Mulford		Did not qualify
	22	Duesenberg	16	124—con. rod
1916	10	Peugeot	3	120—82.60
1919	2	Frontenac	29	37—driveshaft
1920	33	Mulford	9	200—68.33
1921	8	Frontenac	9	177—flagged
1922	5	Frontenac	19	161—con. rod
1926	38	Duesenberg		Did not qualify
Mundy, Frank (Frank Menendez)				
1954	41	McDaniel		Did not qualify
Murphy, Dave				
1911	11	Mercedes		Relieved Wishart
Murphy, Jimmy				
1920	12	Duesenberg	4	200—85.10
1921	24	Duesenberg	14	107—wrecked FS
	5	Duesenberg		Relieved Eddie Miller
1922	35	Murphy	1	200—94.48
1923	5	Durant	3	200—88.08
1924	2	Miller	3	200—97.27
Nalon, Dennis C. "Duke"				
1935		Jeeter-Morris		Withdrawn
1937	21	Elgin Piston Pin		Did not qualify
1938	43	Kohlert-Miller	11	178—flagged

Year	No.	Car	Fin.	Remarks
1939	7	Belanger		Did not qualify
1940	21	Marks	22	120—con. rod
1941	17	Elgin Piston Pin	15	173—flagged
1946	54	Maserati	22	45—universal joint
	25	Jim Hussy		Relieved Snowberger
1947	46	Don Lee	16	119—Piston
1948	54	Novi	3	200—118.034
1949	54	Novi Mobil	29	23—rear axle, hit wall, burned NE
1950	38	Novi Mobil		Did not qualify
1951	18	Novi Purelube	10	151—stalled BS
1952	36	Novi Pure Oil	25	84—supercharger shaft
1953	9	Novi Governor	11	191—spun to avoid 98 NE
1954	8	Novi		136.395, too slow
Nazaruk, Mike				
1951	83	Jim Robbins	2	200—125.302
1952	66	John Zink		133.844, 1st alt.
1953	83	Kalamazoo	21	146—stalled
1954	73	McNamara	5	200—128.923
Nemish, Steve				
1926	24	Schmidt	21	41—transmission
1927	21	Duesenberg		Relieved Dave Evans
Neuman, Roy				
1953	43	Maserati		Did not qualify
Nichols, Harry				
1928	41	Green		Relieved C. W. Belt
Niday, Cal				
1953	78	Storey-Ricketts		134.927, too slow
	99	Miracle Power	30	30—magneto
1954	24	Jim Robbins	10	200—126.895
1955	22	D-A Lubricants	16	170—wrecked NW
Nikrent, Joe				
1913	32	Case	18	67—burned bearing
1915	21	Mercer		Did not qualify
Nuvolari, Tazio				
1938	48	Alfa Romeo		Withdrawn
Oakes, Danny				
1952	6	Grant Piston Ring		Didn't complete run
1953	63	Hopkins		Didn't complete run
1954	47	Ferrari		Did not qualify
	49	Micro-Nut		137.237, too slow
O'Connor, Pat				
1953	28	Slick Racers, Inc.		Did not qualify
	64	Engle-Stanko		133.571, too slow
	74	Brown Motor Co.		134.363, too slow
1954	35	Hopkins	21	181—spun SE
1955	29	Ansted Rotary	8	200—124.644
1956	7	Ansted Rotary	18	187—flagged
1957	12	Sumar	8	200—132.281
1958	4	Sumar	29	0—wrecked NE
O'Donnell, Eddie				
1915	15	Duesenberg	5	200—81.47
1919	10	Duesenberg	22	60—piston
1920	29	Duesenberg	14	149—oil line
Oldfield, Barney				
1914	3	Stutz	5	200—78.15
1915	22	Mercer		Did not qualify
1916	15	Delage	5	120—79.20
Oldfield, Lee				
1912	31	Mason		Did not qualify
1913	5	Mason		Relieved Bob Evans
	17	Anel		Relieved Billy Liesaw
	35	Mason		Relieved Willie Haupt
1914	13	Mason		Relieved Mason
1937	72	Oldfield		Did not qualify
O'Neal, Floyd				
1935	57	Preston		Did not qualify
Ormsby, Homer				
1922	18	Fronty Ford		Relieved Jack Curtner
Ormsby, Len				
1912	24	Opel	24	5—con. rod
O'Rourke, Cletus "Cowboy"				
1948	45	Spdwy Cocktail		Did not qualify
Ornduff, Vern				
1934	62	Miller		Did not qualify
1937	67	Ray 8		Hit by 66 in pits, burned
Orr, Tom				
1915	34	Harroun		Did not qualify
	21	Maxwell	13	168—axle bearing
Orstrander, Don				
1927	42	Nickel Plate		Relieved Jim Hill
Packard, Jim				
1959	55	Sclavi & Amos		Wrecked in practice
1960	71	Sclavi & Amos		Didn't complete run
Painter, Roy				
1931	52	Painter		Did not qualify
1932	51	Lupasa		Did not qualify
1933	72	Crow Eight		Did not qualify
1935	51	Frigenor		Did not qualify
1936	34	Amer. Twist Drill		109.867 too slow
Palmer, Sam				
1933	41	R. & W. Cam Co.		105.998, 2nd alt.
	6	Studebaker		Relieved Cliff Bergere
	46	Studebaker		Relieved L. Johnson
Pardee, Phil				
1929	44	Miller		111.211 Wrecked before race
1931	32	Duesenberg	30	60—wrecked NE (Shaw)
Parker, E. H.				
1911	18	Fiat		Relieved Eddie Hearne
Parsons, Johnnie				
1949	12	Kurtis-Kraft	2	200—119.785
1950	1	Wynn's	1	138—124.002
1951	3	Wynn's	21	87—magneto
1952	6	Grant's Piston R.		Did not qualify
	5	Jim Robbins	10	200—121.780
1953	21	Belond Equa-Flow	26	86—crankshaft
1954	15	Belond Equa-Flow	32	79—stalled in pits
	45	Bardahl		Relieved Art Cross
1955	16	Trio Brass	21	119—magneto
1956	98	Agajanian	4	200—126.631
1957	98	Agajanian		138.975, too slow
	18	Sumar	16	195—flagged
1948	45	Gerhardt	12	200—128.254
Patschke, Cyrus				
1911	31	Marmon		Relieved Joe Dawson
	32	Marmon "Wasp"		Relieved Ray Harroun
Patterson, James				
1931	56	Cacace		Did not qualify
	55	Hoosier Pete		Relieved Billy Winn
1932	75	Duesenberg		101.246 2nd alt.
	2	Duesenberg		Relieved Billy Winn
Paul, Dave				
1966	23	Paul Enterprise		Did not qualify
Pearce, Billy				
1911	13	Fal		Did not qualify
Pennebaker, Robert				
1913	24	Pennebaker		Did not qualify
Perkins, Joe				
1948	62	Kurtis-Kraft		Did not qualify
Peters, Fred "Jiggs"				
1955	32	Glessner		Did not qualify
Petillo, Kelly				
1928	29	Elgin Piston Pin		Wrecked in practice
1932	36	Jones-Miller	12	189—flagged
1933	43	Ward		Withdrawn
	27	Yahr-Miller	19	168—spun and stalled
1934	17	Red Lion	11	200—93.432
1935	5	Gilmore Speedway	1	200—106.240
1936	10	Gilmore Speedway		Relieved MacKenzie
1937	25	Petillo	20	109—out of oil
1938	35	Petillo	22	100—camshaft
1939	35	Kay Jewelers	18	141—two broken pistons
1940	35	Indiana Fur	21	128—rear main bearing
1941	22	Air Lines S.S.	27	48—con. rod
	15	Ziffrin		Relieved McQuinn
Petticord, Jack				
1927	22	Boyle Valve	32	22—supercharger
1928	26	Duesenberg		Did not qualify
	26	Duesenberg		Relieved Ira Hall
1934	52	Don Hulbert		Did not qualify
1938	57	Miller-Dues.		Did not qualify
Phillips, Overton "Bunny"				
1937	66	Mannix-Dues.		Wrecked in practice
1940	46	Phillips		Didn't complete run
1941	26	Phillips	13	187—flagged
Pickard, T. W.				
1926	57	Sievers Jr.		Did not qualify
Pifer, Marvin				
1956	75	Commercial Motor Freight		Wrecked in practice
Pilette, Theodore				
1913	23	Mercedes-Knight	5	200—68.15
Pixley, Ray				
1936	41	Fink Auto	6	200—105.253
Pollard, Art				
1966	44	Hegar & Compton		157.985, 2nd alt.
Porporato, Jean				
1915	6	Sunbeam	14	164—piston
1920	19	Gregoire	22	23—car fell apart
Pratt, Ralph				
1948	87	Lutes-Gdula-Pratt		Did not qualify
1949	34	Belanger Motors		125.764, 1st alt.
1950	19	Lutes		Did not qualify
	47	Gdula		Did not qualify
Prentiss, Willard				
1933	49	Jack C. Carr	13	200—93.595
1934	59	G. & D.		1st alt.
	64	Wehr Rotary		Did not qualify
Price, Ray				
1914	36	Great Western		Did not qualify
Pullen, Eddie				
1914	22	Mercer		Did not qualify
	21	Mercer		Relieved Caleb Bragg
1915	22	Mercer		Did not qualify
1921	25	Duesenberg		Qualified, driven by J. Thomas
	24	Duesenberg		Relieved Murphy
Putnam, Al				
1936	26	Shafer		110.485, 1st alt.
	48	Mikan		Withdrawn
1937	46	Kennedy Tank		Did not qualify
	23	Topping		Relieved Householder
1938	36	Troy Tydol	32	15—crankshaft
1939	38	Elgin Piston Pin		Relieved McQuinn
1940	44	Refinoil	19	179—flagged
1941	55	Schoof	12	200—101.381
1946	12	L. G. S.	15	120—magneto, frame
Quinn, Francis				
1931	67	Tucker Tappett	40	3—rear axle
Rachwitz, Keith "Porky"				
1962	33	Kimberly		Did not qualify
1963	61	Federal Eng.		Did not qualify
	64	Kimberly		Did not qualify
Rader, Bill				
1912	9	National		Relieved Wilcox
1914	2	Stutz		Relieved Earl Cooper
Rae, Johnny				
1935	47	Ford V8		Did not qualify
Randall, Bill				
1961	95	Safety Auto Glass		Wrecked in practice
Rathmann, Dick				
1950	45	City of Glendale	32	25—stalled
1956	73	McNamara	5	200—126.133 wrecked SW 202nd lap
1957	18	Sumar		Qualified, driven by Parsons
1958	97	McNamara	27	0—wrecked NE
1959	73	McNamara	20	150—caught fire in pits
1960	97	Jim Robbins	31	42—brake line
1961	75	Paxton Products		Did not qualify
	97	Jim Robbins	13	164—fuel pump
1962	9	Chapman	24	51—magneto
1963	22	Chapman	10	200—138.845
1964	23	Chapman	7	197—flagged
Rathmann, Jim				
1949	63	Grancor		Did not qualify
	68	Pioneer Auto	11	175—flagged
1950	76	Pioneer Auto	24	122—flagged
1952	59	Grancor-Wynn's	2	200—126.723
1953	6	Wynn's		Did not qualify
	2	Travelon Trailer	7	200—124.072
	49	Crawford		Relieved Bill Holland
1954	59	Elgin Piston Pin		137.132, too slow
	38	Bardahl	28	110—wrecked NW (Flaherty)
1955	33	Belond	14	191—flagged
1956	24	Hopkins	20	175—oil trouble
1957	26	Chiropractic	2	200—135.382
1958	2	Leader Card	5	200—132.857
1959	16	Simoniz	2	200—135.619
1960	4	Ken-Paul	1	200—138.767
1961	4	Simoniz	30	48—magneto
1962	10	Simoniz		Did not qualify
	44	Simoniz Vista	9	200—136.913
1963	16	Coral Harbour	24	99—magneto
Rawlings, E.				
1919	23	Shannon		Relieved Shannon
Ray, Elmer				
1911	1	Case		Relieved Lewis Strang
Reece, Jimmy				
1952	37	John Zink	7	200—123.312
1953	16	Springfield		Didn't complete run
1954	25	Malloy	17	194—flagged
1955	5	Malloy	33	10—con. rod, spun SW
1956	26	Massaglia Hotels	9	200—124.938
1957	5	Hoyt Machine	18	182—throttle
1958	16	John Zink	6	200—132.443
Reeder, C. C.				
1931	45	Copper		95.613, too slow
Reese, Dickie				
1956	87	McDonald		Did not qualify
Reid, Gordon				
1951	67	Johnson-Herbert		118.234, too slow
Reid, Wallace				
1922	13	Duesenberg		Withdrawn
Resta, Dario				
1915	3	Peugeot	2	200—88.91
1916	17	Peugeot	1	120—83.26
1923	4	Packard	14	88—head gasket
Reynolds, J. M.				
1919	24	Hudson		83.5, 1st alt.
Rice, Paul				
1932	52	All American		Did not qualify
Rickenbacker, Eddie				
1911	30	Firestone-Columbus		Relieved Lee Frayer
1912	16	Firestone-Columbus		Relieved Lee Frayer
1914	42	Duesenberg	10	200—70.83
1915	23	Maxwell	19	103—con. rod
1916	5	Maxwell	20	9—steering
	4	Maxwell		Relieved Henderson
Riegel, William "Red"				
1966	87	California S. & S.		Wrecked in practice
Rienke, Al				
1931	67	Tucker Tappett		Did not qualify
Riganti, Raul				
1923	22	Bugatti	22	19—gas leak
1933	14	Golden Seal	14	200—93.244
1940	29	Maserati	33	24—wrecked SE
Rigsby, Jim				
1950	85	Coast Grain		Did not qualify
1952	29	Bob Estes	12	200—120.587
Roberts, Floyd				
1935	22	Abels & Fink	4	200—103.228
1936	4	Burd Piston Ring	19	183—out of gas
1937	62	Thorne	13	194—flagged
1938	23	Burd Piston Ring	1	200—117.200
1939	1	Burd Piston Ring	23	106—wrecked BS
Roberts, Johnny				
1953	82	Burns		Did not qualify
Roberts, Mortimer				
1914	39	Pope-Bullet		Did not qualify
Roberts, "Red"				
1930	5	Duesenberg		Relieved DePaolo
Robinson, Bill				
1929	24	Duesenberg		Not ready to qualify
Robson, George				
1939	23	W.-A. Rotary		Did not qualify
	28	Deacon Litz		116.305, alternate
1940	17	Keller	23	67—shock absorber
1941	37	Greenfield S.S.		Did not qualify

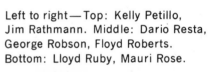

Left to right—Top: Kelly Petillo,
Jim Rathmann. Middle: Dario Resta,
George Robson, Floyd Roberts.
Bottom: Lloyd Ruby, Mauri Rose.

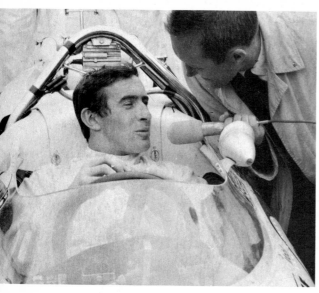

Left to right—Top: Paul Russo,
Eddie Sachs, Troy Ruttman. Middle:
Jackie Stewart, Lou Schneider,
Wilbur Shaw. Bottom: Russell
Snowberger, George Souders.

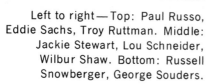

Year	No.	Car	Fin.	Remarks
	10	Gilmore Red Lion	25	66—oil leak
	27	Marks		Relieved Tommy Hinnershitz
1946	16	Thorne Eng.	1	200—114.820
Robson, Hal				
1946	48	Phillips Miller	25	37—con. rod
1947	52	Palmer	20	67—transmission
1948	64	Palmer	15	164—valve
1949	23	Miller		Did not qualify
1953	57	Voelker		Did not qualify
Rodee, Chuck (Charles Rodeghier)				
1959	82	Central Excavat.		Did not qualify
1960	89	Dunn Engineering		140.100, 1st alt.
1961	89	Dunn Engineering		Didn't complete run
1962	67	Travelon Trailer	32	17—wrecked FS
1963	25	Wynn's		Didn't complete run
	38	Konstant Hot		147.197, too slow
	7	Dean Van Lines		Did not qualify
1964	81	Joe Hunt Magneto		146.466, too slow
	87	American Rubber		Did not qualify
1965	19	Wally Weir's	28	28—rear end gears
1966	92	Leader Card		Wrecked qualifying, SW, died
Rodriquez, Pedro				
1963	48	B. M. C.		146.689, too slow
1964	48	MG Liquid Sus.		Wrecked in practice
Rogers, C. L.				
1914	5	Beaver Bullet		Relieved Keene
Rogers, Charles				
1948	89	Jewell		Did not qualify
Roll, Franco				
1950	48	Maserati		Did not arrive
Romcevich, Pete				
1947	59	Camco Motors	12	168—mechanical failure
1948	49	Norm Olson		Did not qualify
Rooney, Tom				
1916	27	Premier	17	48—wrecked SS
1920	36	Revere		Did not arrive
Rose, Bud (Harry Eisele)				
1946	69	Purdy Offy		Did not qualify
1950	10	I. R. C.		Didn't complete run
Rose, Jesse "Ebb"				
1960	41	Ellen Zink		138.153, too slow
1961	86	Meyer Speedway	23	93—con. rod
1963	46	Racing Associates	14	200—134.001
1962	86	J. H. Rose		147.293, too slow
	32	Sheraton-Thompson	14	200—132.347
1965	79	Racing Associates		Wrecked in practice
	86	Racing Associates		Did not qualify
Rose, Mauri				
1932	36	Jones		Did not qualify
1933	39	Iroquois		Broken radius rod
	3	Gilmore	35	48—timing gears
1934	9	Leon Duray	2	200—104,697
1935	2	F. W. D.	20	103—mechanical failure
1936	36	F. W. D.	4	200—107.272
1937	1	Burd Piston Ring	18	127—oil line
1938	27	I. B. E. W.	13	165—supercharger
1939	16	Wheeler's	8	200—109.544
1940	7	Elgin Piston Pin	3	200—113.572
1941	3	Elgin Piston Pin	26	60—spark plug
	16	Noc-Out		Relieved Floyd Davis
1946	8	Blue Crown	23	40—wrecked NE
1947	27	Blue Crown	1	200—116.338
1948	3	Blue Crown	1	200—119.814
1949	3	Blue Crown	13	192—magneto strap
1950	31	Offenhauser	3	137—121.778
1951	16	Pennzoil	14	126—wheel collapsed, wrecked NE
Ross, Sam B.				
1926	35	Green Super Ford		Did not qualify
1928	38	Aranem	20	132—timing gears
1931	59	Miller	15	200—85.139
1932	12	Yahr Miller		Did not qualify
Rossi, Jimmy				
1929	29	Miller		Relieved Rick Decker
1930	26	Maserati		Relieved Borzachini
Rounds, Jack				
1960	52	Fullerton		Wrecked in practice
1961	19	Konstant Hot		Did not qualify
	44	Schmidt		Threw rod, spun
	87	M. P. C.		Did not qualify
Ruby, Lloyd				
1960	98	Agajanian	7	200—135.983
1961	9	Kelso		Didn't complete run
	5	Autolite	8	200—134.860
1962	12	Thompson	8	200—138.182
1963	52	John Zink	19	126—hit wall NW
1964	18	Bill Forbes	3	200—144.320
1965	7	Dupont Golden 7	11	184—blew engine
1966	14	Bardahl Eagle	11	166—cam stud
Ruckstell, Grover				
1915	20	Mercer		Did not qualify
Rupp, Mick				
1965	81	G. C. Murphy	6	198—flagged
Rush, "Buddy"				
1946	37	Enlist in Army		116.268, 1st alt.
Russing, Roy				
1940	35	Indiana Fur		Wrecked in practice
Russo, Eddie				
1954	37	Federal Eng.		Didn't complete run
1955	37	Dr. Sabourin	22	112—ignition
1956	33	Belond		Did not qualify
	10	Merz Engineering		Relieved Ed Elisian
1957	55	Scalavi & Amos	32	0—wrecked on parade lap
1958	55	Scalavi & Amos		Did not qualify
1959		Turner		Did not qualify

Year	No.	Car	Fin.	Remarks
	78	Midwest Mfg.		Didn't complete run
	93	McKay		Did not qualify
	98	Agajanian		Didn't complete run
1960	62	Bob Jones		Did not qualify
	46	Go-Kart	26	84—wrecked SE
Russo, Joe				
1931	41	Russo	24	109—oil leak
1932	41	Art Rose	24	107—con. rod
1933	18	Wonder Bread	17	192—flagged
1934	16	Duesenberg	5	200—99.893
Russo, Paul				
1940	38	Elgin Piston Pin	28	48—oil leak
1941	45	Leader Card	9	200—105.628
1946	10	Fageol Twin Coach	33	16—wrecked NE
1947	15	Wolfe Motors	28	24—wrecked FS
1948	25	Federal Eng.	32	7—oil leak
	55	Nyquist		Relieved Chitwood
1949	19	Tuffy's Offy	8	200—111.862
1950	7	Russo-Nichels	9	135—119.961
1951	7	Kennedy Tank		121.914, too slow
1952	10	Lutes Offy		Did not qualify
1953	7	Federal Eng.	25	89—magneto
	59	Grancor-Elgin		Relieved Agabashian
1954	5	Ansted Rotary		Did not qualify
	5	Ansted Rotary	8	200—128.037
1955	21	Wolcott		Wrecked in practice
	10	Chapman		Relieved Bettenhausen
1956	29	Novi Vespa	33	21—blew tire, wrecked SW
1957	54	Novi	4	200—133.818
1958	15	Novi	18	122—radiator
1959	38	Novi Diesel		Did not qualify
	45	Bardahl	9	200—133.331
1960	49	Novi		Did not qualify
1961	21	Bryant Heating		143.983, 1st alt.
1962	62	Denver-Chicago		Did not qualify
	62	Denver-Chicago	28	20—engine trouble
	21	Sarkes Tarzian		Relieved Elmer George
1963	53	Spirit of St. Louis		Did not qualify
1964	21	Kemerly		148.644, 1st alt.
1965	21	Kemerly		Did not qualify
Rutherford, Johnny				
1963	27	U.S. Equipment		Did not qualify
	37	U.S. Equipment	29	43—transmission
1964	10	Racing Associates		Did not qualify
	86	Bardahl	27	2—wrecked FS
1965	24	Racing Associates	31	15—transmission
Ruttman, Troy				
1949	64	Carter	12	151—flagged
1950	55	Bowes Seal Test	15	130—flagged
1951	98	Agajanian	23	78—bearing
1952	98	Agajanian	1	200—128,922
1954	34	Auto. Shippers	4	200—129.218
1955	18	Novi		Didn't complete run
1956	53	John Zink	31	22—spun FS
1957	52	John Zink	31	13—overheating
1958	98	Agajanian		Did not qualify
1960	28	John Zink Heater	20	134—rear end gear
1961	52	John Zink	20	105—clutch
1962	26	Jim Robbins	18	14—burned piston
1963	17	Robbins Autocrat	12	200—138.244
1964	14	Dayton Steel	18	99—spun NE
Sachs, Eddie				
1953	34	Morris		Spun on driver's test
1954	54	Marion Eng.		Did not qualify
1956	58	Ray Brady		137.373, 1st alt.
1957	88	Schmidt	23	105—piston
1958	88	Schmidt	22	68—universal joint
1959	44	Peter Schmidt	17	182—gear tower bolt
1960	6	Dean Van Lines	21	132—magneto
1961	12	Dean Van Lines	2	200—139.041
1962	2	Dean-Autolite	3	200—140.075
1963	9	Bryant Heating	17	181—lost wheel NE
1964	25	American Red Ball	30	1—hit 83, exploded, died
Sailer, Karl				
1923	15	Mercedes		Relieved Max Sailer
Sailer, Max				
1923	15	Mercedes	8	200—80.68
	16	Mercedes		Relieved Werner
Salay, Mike (Szalai)				
1948	95	Kuehl-Osborne		Did not qualify
	86	Terman Marine	30	13—stalled NE
1949	49	Szalai		Did not qualify
1951	41	Szalai Offy		Wrecked in practice
Sall, Bob				
1935	46	Ford V8	29	47—steering
Sarles, Roscoe				
1919	28	Oldfield	33	8—rocker arm
1920	5	Monroe	20	58—wrecked NW
1921	6	Duesenberg	2	200—88.61
1922	2	Frontenac	23	88—con. rod
Saulpaugh, Bryan				
1931	27	Marr		Relieved Chet Miller
1932	37	Harry Miller	32	55—oil line
Sawyer, Johnny				
1933	53	Lencki-Madis	31	77—clutch
1934	41	Burd Piston Ring	25	27—con. rod
1935	63	Miller		Did not qualify
	16	Shaler-Rislone		Relieved Litz
1938	53	Uhl		Did not qualify
Saylor, Everett				
1941	47	Bowles	17	155—wrecked NW
Scales, Jack				
1920	21	Gregoire		Did not qualify
Scarborough, Carl				
1951	73	McNamara	18	100—axle
1952	73	McNamara		Didn't complete run

Year	No.	Car	Fin.	Remarks
1953	73	McNamara	12	190—flagged. Died of heat exhaustion
Scheel, Herbert				
1923	13	Scheel Frontenac		Did not qualify
1924	35	Sinclair		Did not qualify
Schell, Harry				
1946	46	Maserati		Did not qualify
Schindler, Bill				
1950	67	Auto. Shippers	22	111—universal joint
1951	10	Chapman	13	129—con. rod
1952	7	Chapman	14	200—119.280
Schisler, Donald				
1961	36	Jerry Alderman		Did not arrive
Schneider, Louis				
1927	43	Miller	16	137—timing gears
1928	24	Armacost-Miller	11	200—87.964
	28	Miller		Relieved Lou Moore
1930	23	Bowes Seal Fast	3	200—96.752
1931	23	Bowes Seal Fast	1	200—96.629
1932	1	Bowes Seal Fast	23	125—frame
1933	22	Edelweiss	42	1—stalled
Schrader, Gus				
1932	45	Harry Miller	39	7—wrecked NW
Schroeder, Bob				
1959	78	Midwest Mfg.		Did not qualify
Schultz, Glenn				
1925	24	Miller		Relieved Earl DeVore
Schurch, Herman				
1928	37	Sievers Jr.		Did not qualify
1929	31	Armacost Miller	20	70—gas tank split
1930	16	Miller-Schofield		Relieved Cantlon
1931	10	Hoosier Pete	39	5—transmission
Schwitzer, Louis				
1911	25	Jackson		Relieved Harry Cobe
Scott, Bob				
1951	82	Bob Estes		Did not qualify
1952	93	Morris	29	49—drive shaft
1953	29	Belond Equa-Flow	31	14—oil leak
	73	McNamara		Relieved Scarborough
1954	18	Brady		Didn't complete run
	21	Travelon Trailer		137.504, too slow
	74	Brown Motor Co.		Relieved Andy Linden
Scroggin, Colby				
1963	24	American Rubber		Did not qualify
Selser, Wayne				
1953	75	Christy		Did not qualify
Sennett, Bud				
1951	51	Auto Accessories		Wrecked qualifying
Sessions, Sam				
1966	38	Federal Eng.		Didn't complete run
Seymour, Johnny				
1928	33	Marmon	17	170—supercharger
1929	38	Cooper	21	65—rear axle
	34	Cooper		Relieved Fred Frame
1930	39	Gauss Front-Drive	32	21—wrecked NE
1931	71	Highway Parts		Did not qualify
1934	33	Streamline Miller	26	22—pinion gear
1935	42	Ford V8	24	71—grease leak
1936	47	Sullivan & O'Brien	31	13—clutch
1937	51	Stewart		Didn't complete run
	12	Snowberger		Relieved Snowberger
1938	61	Clemons		Did not qualify
1939	61	Miller		Wrecked in practice
Shafer, Phil "Red"				
1922	21	Duesenberg		Relieved Fetterman
1923	34	Duesenberg	10	200—74.98
1924	16	Durant		Relieved Cliff Durant
1925	9	Duesenberg	3	200—100.18
1926	4	Miller	10	146—87.096
1929	17	Miller	12	150—flagged
1930	15	Coleman	7	200—90.921
1931	12	Shafer "8"	12	200—86.391
1932	33	Shafer "8"	11	197—flagged
1933	7	Ables-Fink Auto		107.972, 1st alt.
1934	26	Shafer "8"	15	130—camshaft drive
1935	31	Victor Gasket		Did not qualify
1936	26	Shafer		Did not qualify
Shackelford, Johnny				
1948	48	Johnston Offy		121.745, 1st alt.
Shambaugh, Charles				
1912	26	Shambaugh		Did not qualify
1915	40	Shambaugh		Did not qualify
1923	38	Shambaugh		Withdrawn
1924	36	Hoosier		Did not qualify
1925	33	Hoosier		Did not qualify
1926		Shambaugh		Did not qualify
Shanebrook, "Doc"				
1951	77	Elgin Piston Pin		Did not qualify
1952	76	Parks Offy		Did not qualify
Shannon, Elmer T.				
1919	23	Shannon	13	200—76.75
Shattuc, Dr. W. E. "Doc"				
1925	15	Miller	9	200—95.74
1926	22	Miller	27	15—valve
1927	17	Miller	22	83—valve
Shaw, Harold				
1933	49	Jack C. Carr		Relieved Prentiss
1934	65	Kleinschmidt		Did not qualify
Shaw, W. Wilbur				
1927	29	Jynx	4	200—93.110
1928	1	Flying Cloud	25	42—timing gears
	15	Simplex Piston R.		Relieved Ray Keech
1930	3	Empire State	22	54—wrist pin
1931	6	Duesenberg		Broken crankshaft
	32	Duesenberg		Relieved Phil Pardee
	33	Duesenberg		Relieved Gleascn
1932	3	Miller	17	157—rear axle
1933	17	Mallory	2	200—101.795
1934	3	Lion Head	28	15—lost oil

Year	No.	Car	Fin.	Remarks
	2	Foreman Axle		Relieved Lou Moore
1935	14	Pirrung	2	200—105.990
1936	3	Gilmore	7	200—104.233
1937	6	Shaw-Gilmore	1	200—113.580
1938	1	Shaw	2	200—115.580
1939	2	Boyle	1	200—115.035
1940	1	Boyle	1	200—114.277
1941	2	Boyle	18	151—wrecked SW
Sheffler, Bayard T. "Bill"				
1946	39	Jack Maurer	9	139—flagged
1948	53	Sheffler, Offy	18	132—spark plugs
1949	4	Sheffler Offy	17	160—con. rod
Shepherd A. J.				
1961	73	Travelon Trailer	26	51—wreck FS
Shoaff, Benny				
1927	24	Perfect Circle	13	198—rear end gears
1928	18	Duesenberg	26	35—wrecked SW
	27	State Auto Ins.		Relieved Fred Frame
Simpson, Ted				
1929	49	Miller		Did not qualify
Skelly, H. J.				
1925	7	Skelly		Qualified, driven by M. Jones
Smith, Carl				
1931	73	C. C. Smith		Did not qualify
Smith, Orville				
1934	61	Anglemeyer		Did not qualify
Smith, Steven				
1925	18	Cough Drop		Did not qualify
1927	45	Rausie		Did not qualify
1928	52	Rausie		Did not qualify
Snell, Overton				
1933	52	Snell		Did not qualify
1935	58	Snell Bros.		99.699, too slow
1936	24	Snell Bros.		109.561, too slow
Snider, George				
1965	94	Gerhardt Offy	21	64—rear end gears
1966	82	Sheraton-Thompson	19	22—wrecked SE
Snowberger, Russell				
1928	34	Cooper	29	4—supercharger
	39	Duesenberg		Relieved Gleason
1929	12	Cooper	27	45—supercharger
1930	22	Russell "8"	8	200—89.166
1931	4	Russell "8"	5	200—94.090
1932	4	Hupp Comet	5	200—100.791
1933	4	Russell "8"	8	200—99.011
1934	10	Russell "8"	8	200—97.297
1935	3	Boyle Products	27	59—exhaust pipe
1936	23	D & G		Wrecked in practice.
1937	12	R. S.	27	66—clutch
1938	14	D-X	25	56—con. rod
	54	Offenhauser		Relieved Ardinger
1939	21	D-X	25	50—leaking radiator
1940	19	Snowberger	31	38—water pump
1941	42	Jim Hussy's	21	107—water pump
1946	25	Jim Hussy's	12	134—differential
1947	25	Federal Eng.	19	74—oil pump
Snyder, Jimmy				
1935	53	Superior Trailer		Did not qualify
	39	Blue Prelude	22	97—spring
1936	43	Belanger Miller	30	21—oil leak
	19	Carew		Relieved Emil Andres
1937	5	Sparks	32	27—transmission
	54	Chicago Raw Hide		Relieved Ardinger
1938	6	Sparks-Thorne	15	150—supercharger
1939	10	Thorne Eng.	2	200—114.245
Sockwell, Bill				
1933	74	Sockwell 8		Did not qualify
Souders, George				
1927	32	Duesenberg	1	200—97.545
1928	3	State Auto Ins.	3	200—98.034
Sostillio, Joe				
1953	17	Belanger Motors		Did not qualify
Spangler, Lester				
1933	15	Miller	26	132—wrecked SW, died
Sparks, Floyd "Sparky"				
1931	47	DeBiase		Burned in pits
Spence, Bill				
1928	43	Boyle Valve		Relieved Billy Arnold
1929	10	Duesenberg	32	14—wrecked SE, died
Stapp, Egbert "Babe"				
1927	38	Duesenberg	31	24—universal joint
	24	Perfect Circle		Relieved Benny Shoaff
1928	7	Miller	6	200—92.638
1929	32	Spindler Miller	28	40—universal joint
1930	8	Duesenberg	31	18—wrecked NE
1931	39	Rigling & Henning	35	9—oil leak/clutch
1933	45	Boyle Products	23	156—out of gas
1934	44	Garcia Grande		Wrecked in practice
	54	Leon Duray		Used too much gas
	12	Stokely Foods		Relieved Deacon Litz
1935	12	Toledo Valve		Did not qualify
	17	Marks-Miller	25	70—radiator
1936	21	Pirrung	24	89—crankshaft
1937	15	Topping	31	36—clutch
1938	34	McCoy Auto	26	54—valve
1939	31	Alfa-Romeo	5	200—111.230
1940	4	Wheeler		Didn't complete run
	24	Surber	24	64—oil line
Stein, Waldo				
1920	14	Oldfield		Did not qualify
Stephens, Laurence "Gig"				
1956	85	Slick Airway		Did not qualify
1962	61	Automatic Radio		Did not qualify
1963	43	Hook Lobster Co.		Did not qualify
1964	63	Hall-Fran		Did not qualify
1965	69	New Boston		Did not qualify
1966	71	Fairchild Hiller		Did not qualify
Stevens, Myron				
1929	33	White		Wrecked in practice
1931	21	Jadson	4	200—94.142
Stevenson, Chuck				
1951	8	Bardahl	20	93—caught fire NS
1952	16	Springfield	18	187—flagged
1953	97	Agajanian	29	42—fuel leak
	98	Agajanian		Relieved Bettenhausen
1954	98	Agajanian	12	199—flagged
1960	65	Leader Card	15	196—flagged
1961	18	Metal-Cal	6	200—135.742
1962	16	Tropicana		Did not qualify
1963	45	Bardahl	21	110—valve
1964	95	Diet Rite Cola	28	2—wrecked FS
1965	88	Vita Fresh	25	50—burned piston
1966	7	Vita Fresh		Did not qualify
Stewart, Jackie				
1966	43	Bowes Seal Fast	6	190—lost oil pressure
Stine, Otis				
1952	84	B. & M.		Did not qualify
Stokes, Wally				
1949	75	Kupiec		Did not qualify
Strang, Lewis				
1911	1	Case	29	109—steering
Stringer, Mel				
1914	41	Washington		Did not qualify
Stubblefield, W. H. "Stubby"				
1930	25	Allen-Miller		Did not qualify
1931	36	Jones-Miller	8	200—92.424
1932	15	Gilmore	14	178—flagged
1933	8	Shafer "8"	5	200—100.762
1934	5	Cummins Diesel	12	200—88.566
1935	29	Victor Gasket		Wrecked qualifying, SW, died
Sutton, Len				
1956	62	Wolcott		Did not qualify
1958	82	Central Excavat.		Did not qualify
	68	Jim Robbins	32	0—wrecked NE
1959	8	Wolcott	32	34—wrecked SW
1960	9	S-R Racing	30	47—engine trouble
1961	8	Bryant Heating	19	110—clutch
1962	7	Leader Card	2	200—140.167
1963	7	Leader Card		147.372, too slow
	47	Crawford		147.620, 1st alt.
1964	66	Bryant Heating	15	140—fuel pump
1965	16	Bryant Heating	12	177—flagged
Swank, Sam				
1927	34	Green		Did not qualify
Swanson, Bob				
1937	33	Fink	28	52—carburetor
	8	Hamilton-Harris		Relieved Hepburn
1939	32	S. M. I.	31	19—rear axle
	25	Hamilton-Harris		Relieved Hepburn
1940	32	Sampson	6	196—flagged
Sweigert, Frank				
1929	54	Duesenberg		99.585, 1st alt.
Sweikert, Bob				
1950	64	Carter		Did not qualify
1951	37	Marion Eng.		131.224, 1st alt.
1952	52	Pat Clancy		132.553, too slow
	71	Marion Eng.		Did not qualify
	73	McNamara	26	77—differential
1953	64	Engle-Stanko		Didn't complete run
	51	Dean Van Lines	20	151—radius rod
1954	17	Lutes	14	197—flagged
1955	6	John Zink	1	200—128.209
1956	1	D-A Lubricant	6	200—125.489
Tansy, Loral				
1948	71	Tansy		Did not qualify
Tattersall, Bob				
1966	61	McManus		Did not qualify
Taylor, Bill				
1949	51	Rounds Rocket		Did not qualify
1951	47	Blue Crown		Didn't complete run
1953	39	Blue Crown		Did not qualify
Teague, Marshall				
1953	22	Pure Oil	18	169—oil leak
1954	3	Fullerton		137.552, too slow
	16	Auto. Shippers		Relieved Duane Carter
1954	31	John Zink		Relieved Gene Hartley
1956	3	Dean Van Lines		Did not qualify
	47	Sumar		Did not qualify
1957	48	Sumar	7	200—132.745
1958	18	Sumar		Didn't complete run
Templeman, Clark "Shorty"				
1955	81	Central Excavat.	18	142—stalled
1956	46	Glessner		Did not qualify
1958	83	McNamara	19	116—brakes
1959	69	Frank Arciero		Didn't complete run
	76	Braund Plywood		139.023, 2nd alt.
1960	26	Federal Eng.	17	191—flagged
1961	7	Bill Forbes	4	200—136.873
1962	4	Bill Forbes	11	200—135.844
Tetzlaff, Teddy				
1911	34	Lozier	39	20—wrecked FS
1912	3	Fiat	2	200—76.75
1913	27	Isotta	17	118—drive chain
1914	8	Maxwell	28	33—rocker arm
Theisen, Al				
1932	59	Marr		Did not qualify
Thicksten, Harry				
1921	17	Junior 8		Relieved Riley Brett
1923	37	Clements		Did not qualify
1924	34	Roof		Qualified too late
1925	18	Cough Drop		Did not qualify
	36	Schmidt		Did not arrive
Thomas, Joe				
1920	28	Monroe	8	200—78.60
1921	18	Junior		Qualified, driven by Fontaine
	25	Duesenberg	22	25—steering
1922	10	Duesenberg	10	200—82.50
1931	53	Finneran		91.403
Thomas, Rene				
1914	16	Delage	1	200—82.47
1919	31	Ballot	11	200—78.75
1920	25	Ballot	2	200—87.47
1921	15	Sunbeam	10	144—water connection
Thomson, Johnny				
1953	56	Dr. Sabourin	32	6—ignition
	62	Lubri-Loy		Relieved Spider Webb
7954	43	Chapman	24	165—stalled
1955	44	Schmidt	4	200—126.241
1956	88	Schmidt	32	22—spun FS
1957	10	D-A Lubricant	12	199—flagged
1958	7	D-A Lubricant	12	199—flagged
1959	3	Racing Associates	3	200—135.340
1960	3	Adams	5	200—136.750
Thorne, Joel				
1937	22	Thorne		115.607, 1st alt.
1938	22	Thorne Eng.	9	185—102.009
1939	8	Thorne Eng.	7	200—110.416
1940	8	Thorne Donnelly	5	197—flagged
1941	5	Thorne Eng.	31	5—wrecked NE
1948	57	Thorne Eng.		Did not qualify
1949	81	Thorne Eng.		Did not qualify
1950	33	Thorne Eng.		Did not qualify
1951	88	Thorne		Didn't complete run
Thurman, Arthur				
1919	18	Thurman	27	44—wrecked NE, died
Tichenor, George				
1952	88	Schmidt		133.427, too slow
1953	65	Commercial Motor Freight		Didn't complete run
1954	22	Tom Sarafoff		Didn't complete run
1955	78	Hopkins		Did not qualify
Tingelstad, Bud				
1960	18	Jim Robbins	9	200—133.717
1961	54	Dean Van Lines		Didn't complete run
1962	5	Konstant Hot	15	200—133.170
1963	18	Auto-Power		Did not qualify
	54	Hoover, Inc.	28	46—hit wall, SE
1964	15	Federal Eng.	6	198—flagged
1965	5	American Red Ball	16	115—hit wall NE
1966	22	Federal Eng.	21	16—radiator
Toft, Omar				
1919	43	Toft	28	44—con. rod
Tolan, Johnny				
1951	34	Wales Trucking		Didn't complete run
1953	66	Chrysler		Did not qualify
	85	Blakely Oil		134.852, too slow
1954	69	W. P. T.		Did not qualify
1956	34	Trio Brass	21	173—flagged
1957	28	Greenman-Casale	20	138—clutch
1958	19	Greenman-Casale	13	200—128.150
1959	43	Chapman		Didn't complete run
1960	24	Greenman-Casale		Did not qualify
Tomei, Louis				
1935	63	Miller		Did not qualify
	26	Burd Piston Ring	28	47—valve
1936	27	Wheeler's	27	44—engine support arm
	15	Litz		Relieved Deacon Litz
1937	53	Sobonite Plastics	10	88—con. rod
1939	55	Indiana Fur		Did not qualify
	58	Alfa-Romeo	15	186—flagged
1940	26	Falstaff	16	190—exhaust pipe
1941	53	H-3	11	200—104.926
1946	15	Boxar Tool	26	34—oil line
	5	Miller		Relieved Chet Miller
1947	44	Miller		Did not qualify
	57	Camco Motors		Did not qualify
	31	Superior Ind.		Relieved Wearne
1948	10	Tom Sarafoff		Did not qualify
1949	42	Worline		Did not qualify
Tower, Jack				
1911	26	Jackson	24	flagged
1913	6	Mason	19	51—wrecked SW
Tramison, Charles				
1934	72	Economy Gas		Used too much gas
Trexler, Marion M.				
1930	45	Trexler	34	19—wrecked NE
1931	45	Cooper		Did not qualify
1932	56	Jack C. Carr		Did not qualify
Triplett, Ernie				
1929	47	Buckeye Dues.	26	48—con. rod
1930	25	Allen-Miller		Did not qualify
	17	Guiberson	15	125—piston
1931	67	Tucker-Tappett		Did not qualify
	25	Buckeye	7	200—93.041
1932	7	Floating Power	22	125—clutch
1933	16	Floating Power	33	61—piston
Trucco, Vincenzo				
1913	28	Isotta	20	39—loose gas tank
Truchan, Steve				
1946	28	Offenhauser		Did not qualify
Turgeon, Henry				
1929	56	Miller		Did not qualify
Turner, Curtis				
1963	12	Fiberglas		Wrecked in practice
Turner, Jack				
1956	54	Travelon Trailer	25	131—engine trouble
1957	19	Bardahl	11	200—130.906
1958	25	Massaglia Hotels	25	21—fuel pump
1959	24	Travelon Trailer	27	47—fuel tank
1960	25	Kelso		Didn't complete run

Left to right — Top: Rene Thomas, Bob Sweikert. Middle: Len Sutton, Babe Stapp, Mel Hansen. Bottom: Shorty Templeman, Johnny Thomson.

Left to right—Top: Bob Veith,
Bobby Unser, Al Unser. Middle:
Jack Turner, Bill Vukovich, Lee Wallard.
Bottom: Howdy Wilcox, Rodger Ward.

Year	No.	Car	Fin.	Remarks
1961	45	Bardahl	25	52—wreck FS
1962	45	Bardahl	29	18—wreck FS
1963	44	Precision P.R.		Wrecked in practice
Turner, W. H. "Jack"				
1911	12	Amplex	8	200—68.82
Unser, Al				
1965	63	Arciero Bros.		Did not qualify
	96	Harrison		Didn't complete run
	45	Sheraton-Thompson	9	196—flagged
1966	84	STP		Did not arrive
	18	STP	12	161—hit wall, NW
Unser, Bobby				
1963	6	Hotel Tropicana	33	2—hit wall SW
1964	9	Studebaker-STP	32	1—wrecked FS
1965	6	STP		Wrecked in practice
	9	STP	19	69—oil connection
1966	11	Vita Fresh	8	171—flagged
Unser, Jerry				
1958	48	Sumar		Did not qualify
	52	Duncan		Did not qualify
	92	McKay	31	0—wrecked NE
1959	57	Helse		Wrecked in practice, died
Vail, Ira				
1919	27	Hudson	8	200—80.49
1920	22	Philbrin		Did not arrive
	6	Frontenac		Relieved Joe Boyer
1921	3	Leach	7	200—86.15
1922	1	Disteel Dues.	8	200—86.15
1923	9	Scheel Frontenac		Did not qualify
1924	6	Ira Vail	8	200—92.45
1925	19	R. J.	20	63—con. rod
1927	16	Miller		Relieved Eddie Hearne
Van Acker, Charles				
1946	62	Singer		115.666, 2nd alt.
1947	44	Preston Tucker	29	24—wrecked FS
1948	4	South Bend	11	192—flagged
1949	10	Redmer	31	10—wrecked NW
1950	29	Redmer		Did not qualify
Vance, John				
1929	51	Green		Did not qualify
Van Gorder, Harold				
1911	29	Lozier		Did not qualify
Van Raalte, Noel (Norman Graham)				
1915	7	Sunbeam	10	200—75.87
Van Ranst, Cornelius W.				
1921	28	Frontenac	16	87—water connection
1923	12	Scheel Frontenac		Did not qualify
1924	6	Ira Vail		Relieved Ira Vail
1927	6	Detroit		Relieved Milton
Varzi, Achille				
1946	53	Maserati		Did not qualify
Veith, Bob				
1956	14	Federal Eng.	7	200—125.048
1957	7	Bob Estes	9	200—131.855
1958	14	Bowes Seal Fast	26	1—wrecked NE
1959	74	John Zink Heater	12	200—132.169
1960	44	Schmidt	8	200—135.452
1961	23	Bardahl		143.581, too slow
	25	Shaler Rislone		143.062, too slow
	44	Schmidt		Didn't complete run
	85	Federal Eng.		Didn't complete run
1962	85	Federal Eng.		Didn't complete run
1962	96	Meguiar's	33	12—engine trouble
1963	86	Racing Associates	26	74—valve
1964	54	MG Liquid Susp.	19	88—burned piston
1965	54	MG Liquid Susp.	24	58—burned piston
1966	63	MG Liquid Susp.		Did not qualify
	67	MG Liquid Susp.		Didn't complete run
Villoresi, Luigi "Gigi"				
1946	52	Maserati	7	200—100.783
Vukovich, Bill				
1950	10	I. R. C.		Did not qualify
	87	R. E. C.		Did not qualify
1951	81	Central Excavat.	29	29—oil tank
1952	26	Fuel Injection	17	191—steering, hit NE wall
1953	14	Fuel Injection	1	200—128.740
1954	14	Fuel Injection	1	200—130.840
1955	4	Hopkins	25	56—wrecked BS, died
Wagner, Louis				
1919	34	Ballot	26	44—broken wheel
Wall, Larry				
1932	73	Jones & Maley		Did not qualify
Wallace, Bob				
1934	53	Mick		Did not qualify
Wallard, Lee				
1948	67	G. & M.		Did not qualify
	91	Iddings	7	200—109.177
1949	6	Maserati	23	55—gears
1950	8	Blue Crown	6	136—121.009
1951	99	Belanger	1	200—126.244
Ward, Rodger				
1951	48	Deck Mfg.	27	34—oil line
1952	34	Federal Eng.	23	130—low oil pressure
1953	92	M. A. Walker	16	177—stalled
1954	12	Dr. Sabourin	22	172—stalled BS
1955	27	Aristo Blue	28	53—wrecked BS
1956	19	Filter Queen	8	200—124.990
1957	8	Wolcott	30	27—supercharger bearing
1958	8	Wolcott	20	93—fuel pump
1959	5	Leader Card	1	200—135.857
1960	1	Leader Card	2	200—138.631
1961	2	Sun City	3	200—138.539
1962	3	Leader Card	1	200—140.293
1963	1	Kaiser Aluminum	4	200—141.090
1964	2	Kaiser Aluminum	2	200—146.339
1965	2	Moog-St. Louis		153.623, 1st alt.
1966	26	Bryant Heating	15	87—handling trouble
Warriner, Leroy				
1951	75	Heller		Did not qualify
1953	44	Jim Robbins		Did not qualify
1955	64	Ansted Rotary		Did not qualify
1956	93	McKay's Bulldog		Did not qualify
1958	95	Safety Auto Glass		Did not qualify
Wearne, Frank				
1937	44	Duray	24	99—carburetor
1938	29	Indiana Fur	10	181—99.543
1939	14	Burd Piston Ring	9	200—107.806
1940	9	Boyle	7	195—flagged
1941	7	Bill Holabird	8	200—110.818
1946	7	Wolfe Motors	8	197—flagged
1947	31	Suprior Ind.	14	128—spun NE
Weatherly, Clay				
1935	56	Cresco		Did not qualify
	45	Bowes Seal Fast	32	9—wrecked NW, died
Weaver, George				
1947	44	Miller		Did not qualify
Webb, Louie				
1937	58	Superior Trailer		Didn't complete run
1939	59	Woestman		Did not qualify
1940	37	Kimmell		Did not qualify
Webb, Travis "Spider"				
1948	72	Anderson Offy		121.421, too slow
	51	Fowle Bros.	27	27—oil line
1949	37	Grancor	33	0—transmission
1950	21	Fadely-Anderson	20	126—flagged
1952	51	Blue Crown		132.660, too slow
	48	Granatelli	22	162—oil leak
1953	89	Fadely-Anderson		Did not qualify
	62	Lubri-Loy	19	166—oil leak
1954	65	Advance Muffler	30	104—oil leak
1955	9	Walsh		Didn't complete run
Wehr, Rudolph				
1922	28	D'Wehr		Did not qualify
Weiler, Wayne				
1960	32	Ansted Rotary	24	103—wrecked SE
1961	15	Hopkins	15	147—wheel bearing
Weld, Greg				
1966	15	STP		Wrecked qualifying warm-up lap
	76	Pure Firebird 76		Wrecked in practice
Wells, F. H.				
1923	32	F. H. W.		Did not qualify
1924	17	Wells Hornet		Wrecked cualifying
1925	17	Wells Hornet		Killed racing in N.Y.
Wente, Bob				
1964	68	Morcroft-Taylor	9	197—flagged
1965	67	G. C. Murphy		Did not qualify
1966	65	Travelon Trailer		Didn't complete run
	85	Caves Buick Offy		Did not qualify
Werner, Christian				
1923	16	Mercedes	11	200—74.65
Weyant, Chuck				
1952	92	Pipe Fitters		Did not qualify
1954	52	Parks Motor Co.		Did not qualify
1955	41	Federal Eng.	12	196—flagged
1957	35	Jim Robbins		wrecked NW
1958	89	Dunn Engineering		139.104, too slow
			24	38—brakes locked,
1959	47	McKay	28	45—wrecked NE
1960	87	Wheeler-Foutch		Did not qualify
	88	Hardwood Door		Did not qualify
1961	88	Drewry's		Did not qualify
Whalen, Neil				
1912	5	Case		Relieved Disbrow
1912	6	Case		Relieved Hearne
1915	28	F. R. P.		Did not qualify
White, Johnny				
1964	99	Demler	4	200—143.206
Wilburn, Jimmy				
1946	63	Mobiloil	19	52—engine trouble
	14	Mobilgas		Relieved Harry McQuinn
Wilcox, Howard "Howdy"				
1911	21	National	14	flagged
1912	9	National	9	200—69.30
1913	12	Gray Fox	6	200—67.65
1914	4	Gray Fox	22	67—valve
1915	1	Stutz	7	200—80.11
1916	29	Premier	7	120—76.80
1919	3	Premier	7	120—76.80
1920	18	Peugeot	1	200—88.05
1921	10	Peugeot	23	22—con. rod
1922	16	Peugeot	27	7—valve spring
1923	25	H. C. S.	17	60—clutch
	1	H. C. S.		Relieved Milton
Wilcox, Howdy "II"				
1932	6	Lion Head	2	200—103.881
1933	3	Gilmore		Qualified, driven by Rose
Williams, Carl				
1965	33	Dayton Steel		Didn't complete run
1966	77	Dayton Steel	16	38—oil leak
Williams, Merril "Doc"				
1933	66	C. O. Warnock		104.538, too slow
1934	38	Highway Parts		Did not qualify
1935	64	Harry Henderson		Wrecked in practice
1936	54	Superior Trailer	16	192—out of gas
1937	57	Superior Trailer		Did not qualify
1938	46	Ben Been		Didn't complete run
1939	36	Quillen Bros.		Did not qualify
1940	36	Quillen Bros.	25	61—oil line
1941	36	Indiana Fur	24	68—radiator leak
1948	74	Clarke Motors	29	19—clutch
1949	65	Sarafoff		125.161, too slow
Willman, Tony				
1937	26	F. W. D.	25	95—con. rod
1938	10	Belanger	27	95—con. rod
	46	Marchese		Relieved McQuinn
1939	51	Burd Piston Ring	14	188—fuel pump
1940	45	Leader Card		118.914, 1st alt.
	24	Surber		Relieved Babe Stapp
1941	62	Lyons	20	117—con. rod
Wilson, Bob				
1935	59	Phillips 66		Did not qualify
Wilson, Dempsey				
1956	22	Martin Bros.		Didn't complete run
	79	Parks		Did not qualify
1957	42	Martin Bros.		139.109, too slow
1958	71	Hall-Mar		142.029, too slow
	59	Sorenson	15	151—clutch pedal, fire in pits
1959	34	Novi Diesel		Didn't complete run
	82	Central Excavat.		Didn't complete run
1960	47	Novi		Did not qualify
	23	Bryant Heating	33	11—magneto point spring
1961	35	Lysle Greenman	16	145—fuel pump
1962	31	Lysle Greenman		146.086, 1st alt.
1963	41	Lysle Greenman		Did not qualify
	29	Vita Fresh	11	138.574
1964	8	Vita Fresh		Wrecked qualifying
	24	New England Speed Equipment		Did not qualify
1965	44	Vita Fresh		Wrecked in practice
1966	51	Greenman-Wilson		Did not qualify
Wilson, Lou				
1923	26	Durant		Relieved Fengler
1928	24	Armacost-Miller		Relieved Schneider
Wingerter, George				
1931	58	Wingerter	33	29—fuel tank
1932	68	Duesenberg		Did not qualify
1936	57	G. W.		Did not qualify
Winn, Billy				
1931	55	Hoosier Pete	21	138—flagged
1932	39	Hoosier Pete		Did not qualify
	2	Duesenberg	9	200—97.421
1933	32	Boyle Products		Relieved Crawford
1934	15	Sullivan & O'Brien		Relieved Cantlon
	22	Floating Power		Relieved Cliff Bergere
1935	10	Ford V8		Didn't complete run
	9	Sullivan & O'Brien		Relieved Cantlon
1936	5	Harry A. Miller	25	78—crankshaft
1937	10	Miller	26	85—oil line
	31	Burd Piston Ring		Relieved Chet Gardner
1938	18	Harry A. Miller		Didn't complete run
	24	Harry A. Miller		Didn't complete run
	16	Sparks-Thorne		Relieved Householder
Winnai, Freddy				
1929	42	Duesenberg	5	200—88.792
1930	6	Duesenberg		Relieved Cummings
1931	24	Bowes Seal Fast	29	60—wrecked NS
1932	43	C. B.		Did not qualify
	65	Foreman Axle	8	200—9.437
1933	65	Kemp	27	125—engine trouble
1935	27	Gyro-Duesenberg	31	16—con. rod
1936	35	Midwest Red Lion	11	199—flagged
1940	59	Walt Woestman		Did not qualify
1946	71	Jewell		Didn't complete run
Wishart, Spencer				
1911	11	Mercedes	4	200—72.65
1912	7	Mercedes	15	82—water connection
1913	12	Mercer	2	200—73.49
1914	19	Mercer	17	122—camshaft
Wonderlich, Jerry				
1920	7	Frontenac		Relieved Bennett Hill
1921	21	Duesenberg		Relieved Bennett Hill
1922	24	Duesenberg	6	200—88.79
1923	34	Duesenberg		Did not qualify
1924	7	Durant	12	200—85.48
Woodbury, Cliff				
1926	36	Boyle	3	158—94.131
1927	15	Boyle Valve	19	108—supercharger
1928	10	Boyle Valve	23	55—timing gears
	25	Boyle Valve		Relieved Fred Comer
1929	8	Boyle Valve	33	3—wrecked NW
	5	Miller Front-Drive		Relieved McDonough
	9	Boyle Valve		Relieved Billy Arnold
	17	Miller		Relieved Phil Shafer
Woodford, Woody				
1937	61	Yeager		Did not qualify
Yarborough, Cale				
1966	66	Jim Robbins	28	0—wrecked FS
Yarbrough, Lee Roy				
1965	96	Harrison		Did not qualify
1966	76	Pure Firebird 76		Spun in practice
Yeager, Ray				
1937	61	Yeager		Did not qualify
Zale, Wally				
1931	62	Midway Motors		Did not qualify
Zalucki, Eddie				
1948	21	Auto. Shippers		Did not qualify
Zbrowski, Count L.				
1923	27	Bugatti	20	41—con. rod
Zengel, Len				
1912	2	Stutz	6	200—73.83
Zuccarelli, Paul				
1913	15	Peugeot	22	18—main bearing

RELIEF DRIVERS

NO.	CAR	STARTING DRIVER	RELIEF DRIVER
		1911	
1	Case	Lewis Strang	Elmer Ray
6	Pope-Hartford	Frank Fox	Fred "Jap" Clemons
11	Mercedes	Spencer Wishart	Dave Murphy
12	Amplex	W. H. "Jack Turner	Walter Jones
15	Knox	Fred Belcher	Jim Coffey
18	Fiat	Eddie Hearne	E. H. Parker
23	McFarlan	Bert Adams	Mel Marquette
25	Jackson	Harry Cobe	Louis Schwitzer
26	Jackson	Jack Tower	doD Evans
30	Firestone-Columbus	Lee Frayer	Eddie Rickenbacker
31	Marmon	Joe Dawson	Cyrus Patschke
32	Marmon "Wasp"	Ray Harroun	Cyrus Patschke
37	Mercer	Charles Bigelow	Howard Frey / E. H. Sherwood
38	Simplex	Ralph Beardsley	Frank Goode
41	Velie	Howard Hall	Rupert Jeffkins
42	Cole	Bill Endicott	John Jenkins
		1912	
2	Stutz	Len Zengel	Billy Knipper
3	Fiat	Teddy Tetzlaff	Caleb Bragg
5	Case	Louis Disbrow	Neil Whalen
6	Case	Eddie Hearne	Neil Whalen
8	National	Joe Dawson	Don Herr
9	National	Howdy Wilcox	Bill Rader
14	White	John Jenkins	Charles Arnold
16	Firestone-Columbus	Lee Frayer	Eddie Rickenbacker
17	Marquette-Buick	Billy Liesaw	W. H. Farr
18	Schacht	Bill Endicott	Harry Endicott
22	Lozier	Joe Horan	George Ainslee
28	Stutz	Charles Merz	Billy Knipper
		1913	
1	Nyberg	Harry Endicott	Ed Madden
2	Stutz	Charles Merz	Earl Cooper
3	Stutz	Gil Anderson	Earl Cooper
4	Keeton	Bob Burman	Hughie Hughes
5	Mason	Bob Evans	Lee Oldfield
10	Henderson	Billy Knipper	Harry Grant
12	Gray Fox	Howdy Wilcox	Frank Fox
17	Anel	Billy Liesaw	Lee Oldfield
19	Mercer	Caleb Bragg	Ralph DePalma
22	Mercer	Spencer Wishart	Ralph DePalma
25	Tulsa	George Clark	Tom Alley
31	Case	Louis Disbrow	I. J. Kilpatrick
32	Case	Joe Nikrent	Eddie Hearne
35	Mason	Willie Haupt	Lee Oldfield
		1914	
2	Stutz	Earl Cooper	Bill Rader
3	Stutz	Barney Oldfield	Gil Anderson
5	Beaver Bullett	Charles Keene	C. L. Rogers
13	Mason	George Mason	Lee Oldfield
21	Mercer	Caleb Bragg	Eddie Pullen
25	Maxwell	Billy Carlson	Jack LeCain / Harry Goetz
31	Keeton	Billy Knipper	Bob Burman
		1915	
4	Stutz	Earl Cooper	Johnny Aitken
5	Stutz	Gil Anderson	Johnny Aitken
19	Maxwell	Billy Carlson	Hughie Hughes
22	Duesenberg	Ralph Mulford	William Chandler
		1916	
4	Maxwell	Pete Henderson	Eddie Rickenbacker
21	Delage	Jules DeVigne	Jack LeCain
24	Crawford	William Chandler	Frank Elliott

NO.	CAR	STARTING DRIVER	RELIEF DRIVER
29	Premier	Howdy Wilcox	Gil Anderson
		1919	
23	Shannon	Elmer Shannon	E. Rawlings
33	Ballot	Paul Bablot	Jean Chassagne
		1920	
3	Monroe	Louis Chevrolet	Salvatore Barbarino
6	Frontenac	Joe Boyer	Ira Vail
7	Frontenac	Bennett Hill	Jerry Wonderlich
15	Revere	Pete Henderson	Tom Alley
28	Monroe	Joe Thomas	Art Klein
34	Meteor	Willie Haupt	Wade Morton
		1921	
5	Duesenberg	Eddie Miller	Jimmy Murphy
9	Duesenberg	Albert Guyot	Joe Boyer / Eddie Miller
17	Junior 8	Riley Brett	Harry Thicksten
21	Duesenberg	Bennett Hill	Jerry Wonderlich
23	Frontenac	Percy Ford	Jules Ellingboe
24	Duesenberg	Jimmy Murphy	Eddie Pullen
		1922	
1	Disteel Duesenberg	Ira Vail	Dave Koetzla
9	Leach	Frank Elliott	Art Klein
10	Duesenberg	Joe Thomas	Wade Morton / Pete DePaolo
18	Fronty-Ford	Jack Curtner	Homer Ormsby
21	Duesenberg	I. P. Fetterman	Phil Shafer
24	Duesenberg	Jerry Wonderlich	Jules Ellingboe
31	Duesenberg	Ora Haibe	Jules Ellingboe
34	Durant	Cliff Durant	Dave Lewis
		1923	
1	H.C.S.	Tommy Milton	Howdy Wilcox
2	Packard	Ralph DePalma	Ernie Ansterberg
4	Packard	Dario Resta	Ernie Ansterberg / Joe Boyer
6	Durant	Eddie Hearne	Earl Cooper
8	Durant	Cliff Durant	Eddie Hearne
15	Mercedes	Max Sailer	Karl Sailer
16	Mercedes	Christian Werner	Max Sailer / C. Lautenschlager
26	Durant	Harlan Fengler	Lou Wilson
31	Durant	Frank Elliott	Dave Lewis
34	Duesenberg	Phil Shafer	Wade Morton / Jerry Wonderlich / Ora Haibe / Thane Houser
35	Miller	Bennett Hill	Martin De Alsaga
		1924	
6	Ira Vail	Ira Vail	C. W. Van Ranst
7	Durant	Jerry Wonderlich	Wade Morton
9	Duesenberg	Joe Boyer	Ernie Ansterberg / L. L. Corum / Thane Houser
14	Miller	Fred Comer	Wade Morton
15	Duesenberg	L. L. Corum	Joe Boyer
16	Durant	Cliff Durant	Phil Shafer / Eddie Hearne
31	Schmidt	Ora Haibe	Elmer Dempsey
		1925	
1	Junior 8	Dave Lewis	Bennet Hill
3	Miller	Bennett Hill	Jules Ellingboe / Jerry Wonderlich / Ray Cariens
5	Miller	Fred Comer	Wade Morton
7	Skelly	M. C. Jones	Fred Harder
8	Miller	Ralph DePalma	L. L. Corum
9	Duesenberg	Phil Shafer	Wade Morton
12	Duesenberg	Peter DePaolo	Norman Batten
14	Miller	Bob McDonough	Bennett Hill
22	Fiat	Pietro Bordino	Antoine Mourre
23	Duesenberg	Wade Morton	Antoine Mourre / Jimmy Gleason
24	Miller	Earl DeVore	Glenn Schultz
27	Miller	Frank Elliott	Ora Haibe

NO.	CAR	STARTING DRIVER	RELIEF DRIVER
28	Miller	Leon Duray	Fred Comer
29	Jones-Whitaker	Herbert Jones	Alfred Moss
		1926	
1	Front Drive Miller	Dave Lewis	Earl Cooper
4	Miller	Phil Shafer	Fred Lecklider
6	Miller	Frank Elliott	Leon Duray
8	Miller	Fred Comer	Wade Morton
9	Locomobile Jr. 8	Cliff Durant	Eddie Hearne
16	Miller	Bennett Hill	Jules Ellingboe
19	Miller	Ralph Hepburn	Bob McDonough
26	Eldridge	E. A. D. Eldridge	Herschell McKee
27	Eldridge	W. Douglas Hawkes	E. A. D. Eldridge
		1927	
5	Junior 8	Frank Elliott	Fred Frame
6	Detroit	Tommy Milton	C. W. Van Ranst / Leon Duray / Ralph Hepburn
9	Miller	Tony Gulotta	Peter DePaolo
10	Miller	Earl DeVore	Zeke Meyer
14	Cooper	Bob McDonough	Peter DePaolo
16	Miller	Eddie Hearne	Ira Vail / Leon Duray / Harry Hartz
21	Duesenberg	Dave Evans	Steve Nemish
23	Elgin Piston Pin	Fred Lecklider	Henry Kohlert
24	P. C. Duesenberg	Benny Shoaff	Babe Stapp
25	Miller	Cliff Bergere	Wesley Crawford
27	Miller	Tony Gulotta	Peter DePaolo
29	Jynx	Wilbur Shaw	Lou Meyer
31	Miller	Fred Frame	George Abell / George Fernic
35	Elcar	Al Cotey	Eddie Burbach
41	Thompson Valve	Wade Morton	Ralph Holmes / Freddy Winnai
42	Nickel Plate	Jim Hill	Don Orstrander
43	Miller	Louis Schneider	L. L. Corum / Dutch Bauman
44	Miller	Al Melcher	Fred Lecklider / Jack Petticord
		1928	
4	Miller	Leon Duray	Cliff Bergere
5	Detroit	Cliff Durant	Bob McDonough
6	Chromolite	Earl DeVore	Cy Marshall
7	Miller	Babe Stapp	Ralph Hepburn
8	Stutz Blackhawk	Tony Gulotta	Dutch Bauman
15	Simplex Piston Ring	Ray Keech	Wilbur Shaw
22	Miller	Norman Batten	Zeke Meyer
23	Miller	Deacon Litz	Wesley Crawford
24	Armacost Miller	Lou Schneider	Lou Wilson
25	Boyle Valve	Fred Comer	Cliff Woodbury
26	Duesenberg	Ira Hall	Jack Petticord
27	State Auto Ins.	Fred Frame	Benny Shoaff / Ralph Hepburn
28	Miller	Lou Moore	Lou Schneider
29	Elgin Piston Pin	Henry Kohlert	Shorty Cantlon / "Doc" Shattuc
39	Duesenberg	Jimmy Gleason	Russ Snowberger
41	Green	C. W. Belt	Harry Nichols
43	Boyle Valve	Billy Arnold	Bill Spence
		1929	
3	Majestic Miller	Lou Moore	Barney Kloepfer
5	Miller Front Drive	Bob McDonough	Cliff Woodbury
9	Boyle Valve	Billy Arnold	Cliff Woodbury / Red Roberts
17	Miller	Phil Shafer	Cliff Woodbury / Russ Snowberger
21	Packard Cable	Leon Duray	Ralph Hepburn
25	Armacost-Miller	Cliff Bergere	Peter Kreis
29	Miller	Rick Decker	Jimmy Rossi
31	Armacost-Miller	Herman Schurch	Jack Buxton / Bert Karnatz
34	Cooper	Fred Frame	Johnny Seymour
36	Miller	Frank Farmer	Bill Albertson
42	Duesenberg	Freddy Winnai	L. L. Corum / Roscoe Ford

NO.	CAR	STARTING DRIVER	RELIEF DRIVER
48	Chromolite	Speed Gardner	Chet Gardner
49	Miller	Wesley Crawford	Zeke Meyer / Ted Simpson / Dave Evans
53	Duesenberg	Jimmy Gleason	Thane Houser / Ernie Triplett

1930

NO.	CAR	STARTING DRIVER	RELIEF DRIVER
5	Duesenberg	Peter DePaolo	Red Roberts
6	Duesenberg	Bill Cummings	Freddy Winnai
16	Miller-Schofield	Shorty Cantlon	Herman Schurch
25	Allen-Miller	Leslie Allen	Fred Lecklider / Stubby Stubblefield
26	Maserati	Baconi Borzachini	Jimmy Rossi
29	Alberti	Joe Caccia	Rick Decker
34	Gauss	Joe Huff	Ted Chamberlain / Speed Gardner
35	Romthe	J. C. McDonald	Johnny Kreiger
41	Fronty Ford	Chet Miller	Paul Bost

1931

NO.	CAR	STARTING DRIVER	RELIEF DRIVER
5	Maley	Deacon Litz	Bill Cummings
17	Nutmeg State	Speed Gardner	Wesley Crawford
19	Harry Miller	Ralph Hepburn	Peter Kreis
21	Jadson	Myron Stevens	Lou Meyer
27	Marr	Chet Miller	Bryan Saulpaugh
32	Duesenberg	Phil Pardee	Wilbur Shaw
33	Duesenberg	Jimmy Gleason	Wilbur Shaw
44	G. N. H.	George Howie	L. L. Corum / Herman Schurch
55	Hoosier Pete	Billy Winn	Jimmy Patterson
69	Goldberg Bros.	Joe Huff	Speed Gardner
72	Alberti	Al Aspen	Bill Denver

1932

NO.	CAR	STARTING DRIVER	RELIEF DRIVER
1	Bowes Seal Fast	Lou Schneider	Bill Cummings
2	Duesenberg	Billy Winn	Jimmy Patterson
9	Hudson	Chet Miller	Al Miller
10	Bowes Seal Fast	Bill Cummings	Frank Brisko
14	Golden Seal	Juan Gaudino	Joseph Bonedeo
35	Duesenberg	Ira Hall	Ned Meyers
55	Highway Parts	Joe Huff	Dusty Fahrnow

1933

NO.	CAR	STARTING DRIVER	RELIEF DRIVER
4	Russell 8	Russ Snowberger	George Howie / Mauri Rose
5	Boyle Products	Bill Cummings	Frank Brisko
6	Studebaker	Cliff Bergere	Sam Palmer
14	Golden Seal	Raul Riganti	Juan Gaudino
27	Yahr-Miller	Kelly Petillo	Sam Hoffman
28	Marr	Chet Miller	Shorty Cantlon
32	Boyle Products	Wesley Crawford	Billy Winn
46	Studebaker	Luther Johnson	Sam Palmer / Ralph Hepburn
49	Jack C. Carr	Willard Prentiss	Harold Shaw
65	Kemp	Freddy Winnai	Terry Curley
68	Goldberg Bros.	Bennett Hill	Frank Brisko

1934

NO.	CAR	STARTING DRIVER	RELIEF DRIVER
2	Foreman Axle	Lou Moore	Wilbur Shaw
5	Cummins Diesel	Stubby Stubblefield	Dave Evans
12	Stokely Foods	Deacon Litz	Babe Stapp
15	Sullivan & O'Brien	Shorty Cantlon	Billy Winn
18	Boyle Products	George Barringer	Chet Gardner
22	Floating Power	Cliff Bergere	Billy Winn / Tony Gulotta
24	Lucenti	Herb Ardinger	Dany Day
26	Shafer 8	Phil Shafer	Zeke Meyer
31	Miller	Ralph Hepburn	Lou Meyer
32	F. W. D.	Frank Brisko	Rex Mays
36	Shafer 8	Al Miller	Zeke Meyer

1935

NO.	CAR	STARTING DRIVER	RELIEF DRIVER
2	F. W. D.	Mauri Rose	Paul Bost
7	Foreman Axle	Lou Moore	Tony Gulotta
9	Sullivan & O'Brien	Shorty Cantlon	Billy Winn
16	Shaler-Rislone	Deacon Litz	Johnny Sawyer / Babe Stapp

NO.	CAR	STARTING DRIVER	RELIEF DRIVER
19	Miller-Hartz	Fred Frame	Frank Brisko
21	Veedol	Ralph Hepburn	Gene Haustein
42	Ford V8	Johnny Seymour	George Barringer

1936

NO.	CAR	STARTING DRIVER	RELIEF DRIVER
10	Gilmore Speedway	Doc MacKenzie	Kelly Petillo
15	Litz	Deacon Litz	Louis Tomei
19	Carew	Emil Andres	Jimmy Snyder
32	Burd Piston Ring	Lou Moore	Cliff Bergere
42	Bowes Seal Fast	Cliff Bergere	Tony Gulotta / Herb Ardinger

1937

NO.	CAR	STARTING DRIVER	RELIEF DRIVER
8	Hamilton-Harris	Ralph Hepburn	Bob Swanson
12	Snowberger	Russ Snowberger	Johnny Seymour
16	Boyle Products	Bill Cummings	Chet Miller
23	Topping	Ronney Householder	Al Putnam / Henry Banks / Ken Fowler
28	Miller	Billy DeVore	Fred Frame
31	Burd Piston Ring	Chet Gardner	Billy Winn
34	Bowes Seal Fast	Shorty Cantlon	Rex Mays
35	Motorola	Deacon Litz	Harry McQuinn
38	Burd Piston Ring	Tony Gulotta	Rex Mays / Jimmy Snyder
42	Thorne	Al Miller	Emil Andres / Mauri Rose
45	Midwest Red Lion	Cliff Bergere	George Barringer
54	Chicago Raw Hide	Herb Ardinger	Jimmy Snyder

1938

NO.	CAR	STARTING DRIVER	RELIEF DRIVER
16	Sparks-Thorne	Ronney Householder	Billy Winn
45	Marchese	Harry McQuinn	Tony Willman
54	Offenhauser	Herb Ardinger	Russ Snowberger / Cliff Bergere

1939

NO.	CAR	STARTING DRIVER	RELIEF DRIVER
9	Miller-Hartz	Herb Ardinger	Frank Brisko / Mel Hansen
25	Hamilton-Harris	Ralph Hepburn	Bob Swanson
26	Duray-Barbasol	Billy DeVore	Henry Banks
38	Elgin Piston Pin	Harry McQuinn	Al Putnam / Frank Brisko / George Robson
58	Alfa Romeo	Louis Tomei	Mel Hansen
62	Burd Piston Ring	Tony Gulotta	Harry McQuinn

1940

NO.	CAR	STARTING DRIVER	RELIEF DRIVER
14	Bill Holabird	Billy DeVore	George Connor
24	Surber	Babe Stapp	Tony Willman
34	Alfa Romeo	Chet Miller	Henry Banks
49	Lucy O'R. Schell	Rene LeBegue	Rene Dreyfus
61	Lencki	Floyd Davis	George Connor / Louie Webb

1941

NO.	CAR	STARTING DRIVER	RELIEF DRIVER
15	Ziffrin	Harry McQuinn	Kelly Petillo
16	Noc-Out Hose Clamp	Floyd Davis	Mauri Rose
26	Phillips	Overton Phillips	Mel Hansen
27	Marks	Tommy Hinnershitz	George Robson
45	Leader Card	Paul Russo	Louis Durant
55	Schoof	Al Putnam	Louis Durant

1946

NO.	CAR	STARTING DRIVER	RELIEF DRIVER
3	Noc-Out Hose Clamp	Cliff Bergere	Rex Mays
5	Miller	Chet Miller	Louis Tomei
12	L. G. S. Spring Clutch	Al Putnam	George Connor
14	Mobilgas	Harry McQuinn	Jimmy Wilburn
24	Noc-Out Hose Clamp	Joie Chitwood	Sam Hanks
25	Jim Hussy	Russ Snowberger	Duke Nalon

1947

NO.	CAR	STARTING DRIVER	RELIEF DRIVER
3	Tucker Partner	Emil Andres	George Connor
10	Schoof	Duke Dinsmore	Billy DeVore
31	Superior Industries	Frank Wearne	Louis Tomei
54	Novi Governor Mobil	Herb Ardinger	Cliff Bergere

1948

NO.	CAR	STARTING DRIVER	RELIEF DRIVER
31	Don Lee Mercedes	Chet Miller	Ken Fowler / Louis Tomei

NO.	CAR	STARTING DRIVER	RELIEF DRIVER
33	Mauro Alfa Romeo	Johnny Mauro	Louis Durant
55	Nyquist	Joie Chitwood	Paul Russo / Johnny Shackelford

1950

NO.	CAR	STARTING DRIVER	RELIEF DRIVER
12	I. R. C.	Henry Banks	Fred Agabashian
17	Wolfe	Joie Chitwood	Tony Bettenhausen
24	Palmer	Bayliss Levrett	Bill Cantrell

1949

NO.	CAR	STARTING DRIVER	RELIEF DRIVER
9	Tuffy's Offy	Emil Andres	Walt Brown
38	Ray Brady	George Fonder	Mel Hansen

1951

NO.	CAR	STARTING DRIVER	RELIEF DRIVER
9	Hinkle	Jack McGrath	Manual Ayulo

1952

NONE

1953

NO.	CAR	STARTING DRIVER	RELIEF DRIVER
2	Travelon Trailer	Jim Rathmann	Eddie Johnson
3	Bardahl	Sam Hanks	Duane Carter
23	Automobile Shippers	Walt Faulkner	Johnny Mantz
49	Crawford	Bill Holland	Jim Rathmann
55	John Zink	Jerry Hoyt	Andy Linden / Chuck Stevenson
59	Grancor-Elgin	Fred Agabashian	Paul Russo
62	Lubri-Loy	Spider Webb	Johnny Thomson / Jackie Holmes
73	McNamara	Carl Scarborough	Bob Scott
92	M. A. Walker Electric	Rodger Ward	Andy Linden / Duke Dinsmore
98	Agajanian	Tony Bettenhausen	Chuck Stevenson / Gene Hartley

1954

NO.	CAR	STARTING DRIVER	RELIEF DRIVER
1	Bardahl	Sam Hanks	Jim Davies / Jim Rathmann
5	Ansted Rotary	Raul Russo	Jerry Hoyt
12	Dr. Sabourin	Rodger Ward	Eddie Johnson
16	Automobile Shippers	Duane Carter	Marshall Teague / Jimmy Jackson / Tony Bettenhausen
27	Chapman	Ed Elisian	Bob Scott
31	John Zink	Gene Hartley	Marshall Teague
33	Brady	Len Duncan	George Fonder
34	Automobile Shippers	Troy Ruttman	Duane Carter
38	Bardahl	Jim Rathmann	Pat Flaherty
43	Chapman	Johnny Thomson	Andy Linden / Bill Homeier
45	Bardahl	Art Cross	Johnnie Parsons / Sam Hanks / Andy Linden / Jim Davies
65	Advance Muffler	Spider Webb	Danny Kladis
71	Martin Bros.	Frank Armi	George Fonder
74	Brown Motor Co.	Andy Linden	Bob Scott
98	Agajanian	Chuck Stevenson	Walt Faulkner

1955

NO.	CAR	STARTING DRIVER	RELIEF DRIVER
10	Chapman	Tony Bettenhausen	Paul Russo
77	Merz Engineering	Walt Faulkner	Bill Homeier

1956

NO.	CAR	STARTING DRIVER	RELIEF DRIVER
10	Merz Engineering	Ed Elisian	Eddie Russo

1957 1958 1959 1960 1961

NONE

1962

NO.	CAR	STARTING DRIVER	RELIEF DRIVER
21	Sarkes Tarzian	Elmer George	Paul Russo / A. J. Foyt
88	Drewry's	Gene Hartley	Bill Cheesbourg

1963 1964 1965 1966

NONE

CARS AND DRIVERS WHICH FAILED TO QUALIFY

NO.	DRIVER	CAR	ENTRANT	ENGINE	REMARKS
		1911			
13	Billy Pearce	Fal	Fal Motor Car	Fal	
14	J. Franklin Gelhaw	Fal	Fal Motor Car	Fal	
22	Fred "Jap" Clemons	McFarlan	McFarlan Motor Car Co.	McFarlan	
29	Harold Van Gorder	Lozier	W. H. Chambers	Lozier	
40	Rupert Jeffkins / Arthur Gibbons	Velie	Velie Motors Co.	Velie	Withdrawn
43	Louis Edmonds	Cole	Cole Motor Car Co.	Cole	
	Rupert Jeffkins	Cole	Cole Motor Car Co.	Cole	
		Lozier	Lozier Motor Co.	Lozier	
		1912			
26	Chas. Shambaugh	Shambaugh	Charles Shambaugh		
27	George Fuller	Continental	F. N. Martindale	Continental	
31	Lee Oldfield	Mason	F. S. Duesenberg	Mason	
		1913			
7	E. H. Delling / Joe Dawson	Deltal	E. H. Delling	Mercer	
14	F. L. Adams	Smada	F. L. Adams		
24	R. Pennebaker	Pennebaker	Robert Pennebaker	Knight	
		1914			
18	Ralph DePalma	Mercedes	E. C. Patterson	Mercedes	Qualified, withdrawn
22	Eddie Pullen	Mercer	Mercer Motors Co.	Mercer	
28	Jess Callahan	Stafford	Terry Stafford	Stafford	
29	Joe Horan	Metropol	Metropol Motor Works	Metropol	
32		Maxwell	A. S. Bennett	Maxwell	
33	George Clark	Texas	Clark & Trammell		
35	John Jenkins	Great Western	John Jenkins	Great Western	
36	Ray Price	Great Western	John Jenkins	Great Western	
37	Guy Ball	Great Western	Edward A. Myers	Great Western	
39	Mortimer Roberts	Pope-Bullet	Pope Manufacturing Co.	Pope	
41	Mel Stringer	Washington	Carter Motor Car Corp.	Washington	
45	Joe Mazzucco	Tatters	Louis & John Tatter		
47	Fred Melaun	Titze Flyer	A. Titze		
		1915			
7	W. W. Brown	DuChesneau	F. A. DuChesneau	Brown	
18	Erwin Bergdoll	Bergdoll	Bergdoll Bros.		
19	Grover Bergdoll	Bergdoll	Bergdoll Bros.		
20	Grover Ruckstell	Mercer	Mercer Motor Co.	Mercer	
21	Joe Nikrent	Mercer	Mercer Motor Co.	Mercer	
22	Barney Oldfield / Eddie Pullen	Mercer	Mercer Motor Co.	Mercer	
24	Willie Haupt	Bergdoll	Bergdoll Bros.		
26	Hughie Hughes	F. R. P.	Finlay R. Porter	Porter	
27	Charles Keene	F. R. P.	Finlay R. Porter	Porter	
28	Neil Whalen	F. R. P.	Finlay R. Porter	Porter	
31	Carl Limberg	Sunbeam	Fortuna Racing Team Inc.	Sunbeam	
33	Bob Burman	Burman	Bob Burman	Peugeot	
34	Tom Orr	Harroun	Ray Harroun	Mercer	
35	Ralph Mulford	Mulford	Lutcher Brown		
36	Edward McNay	Cino	Edward D. McNay	Mercer	
40	Chas. Shambaugh	Shambaugh	Charles Shambaugh	Buick	
41	James R. Hill	Bals	Wilson T. Bals		

NO.	DRIVER	CAR	ENTRANT	ENGINE	REMARKS
		1916			
2	Pete Henderson	Duesenberg	F. S. Duesenberg	Duesenberg	Did not arrive
3	Wilbur D'Alene	Duesenberg	F. S. Duesenberg	Duesenberg	Did not arrive
6	Louis Chevrolet	Frontenac	Louis Chevrolet	Frontenac	87.69, cracked cyl.
22	Jack Le Cain	Delage	Harry Harkness	Delage	82.48, bkn. crank
23		Delage	Harry Harkness	Delage	Did not arrive
		1919			
16	George Buzane	Premier	Indapls. Speedway Team	Premier	
24	J. M. Reynolds	Hudson	J. M. Reynolds	Hudson	83.5, 1st. alt.
25	Max McVey	Hudson	J. M. Reynolds	Hudson	
35	Al Cotey	Ogren	Ogren Motor Car Co.	Duesenberg	82.9, 2nd. alt.
38	Dave Lewis	Duesenberg	Meteor Motor Co.	Duesenberg	
47		Premier	Indapls. Speedway Team	Premier	
		1920			
1	Cliff Durant	Chevrolet	R. Cliff Durant	Miller	
14	Waldo Stein	Oldfield	Barney Oldfield	Miller	
21	Jack Scales	Gregoire	Jean Porporato	Gregoire	
22	Ira Vail	Philbrin	Ira Vail	Duesenberg	Did not arrive
23	Jules Ellingboe	Ellingboe	Ellingboe Motor Corp.		Did not arrive
24	C. Glenn Howard	Ellingboe	Ellingboe Motor Corp.		Did not arrive
27	Kurt Hitke	Kenworthy	Kenworthy Motors	Duesenberg	Did not arrive
35	Frank Elliott	T. N. T.		Miller	Did not arrive
36	Tom Rooney	Revere	Revere Motor Car Corp.	Duesenberg	Did not arrive
	Tom Alley	T. N. T.		Miller	Did not arrive
		1921			
26	M. E. Headley	Frontenac	Mervin E. Headley	Frontenac	
	Tommy Milton	Duhrn Duesenberg		Duesenberg	Withdrawn
		1922			
13	Wallace Reid	Duesenberg	Wallace Reid	Duesenberg	Withdrawn
28	Rudolph Wehr	D'Wehr	Rudolph Wehr		
29		Frontenac	Louis Chevrolet	Frontenac	
33		Mystery			Did not arrive
		1923			
9	Ira Vail	Scheel Frontenac	Herbert Scheel	Frontenac	
10	Dave Lewis	Scheel Frontenac	Herbert Scheel	Frontenac	
12	C. W. Van Ranst	Scheel Frontenac	Herbert Scheel	Frontenac	
13	Herbert Scheel	Scheel Frontenac	Herbert Scheel	Frontenac	
16	Jules Goux	Schmidt	Albert Schmidt		Withdrawn
24	Albert Guyot	Roland-Pilain	Albert Guyot	Roland-Pilain	Withdrawn
32	F. H. Wells	F. H. W.	F. H. Wells		
33	Wade Morton	Duesenberg	Duesenberg Bros.	Duesenberg	
34	Jerry Wonderlich	Duesenberg	Duesenberg Bros.	Duesenberg	
37	Harry Thicksten	Clements	L. C. Milner	Fronty-Ford	
38	Chas. Shambaugh	Shambaugh	Charles Shambaugh		Withdrawn

1911   Rupert Jeffkins

1914   Ralph DePalma

1914   Hughie Hughes

1915   Eddie Pullen

1924   Harlan Fengler

1924   Harry Thicksten

1924   Herbert Scheel

1925   Tom Alley

1925   Steve Smith

1925   Ora Haibe

1925   Charles Shambaugh

1926   Jack Foley

1926   T. W. Pickard

1927   L. L. Corum

1927   Sam Swank

1928   L. L. Corum

1928   "Dutch" Bauman

1928   R. G. "Buddy" Marr

1928   Herman Schurch

1929   Zeke Meyer

1929   Chet Gardner

1929   Bill Robinson

1929   Thane Houser

1929   Ralph DePalma

1924

NO.	DRIVER	CAR	ENTRANT	ENGINE	REMARKS
6	Harlan Fengler	Wade	George L. Wade	Miller	Wrecked in practice
13	Tom Alley	Kess-Line	Kess-Line Motors	Frontenac	
17	F. H. Wells	Wells Hornet	F. H. Wells		Wrecked qualifying
18	Frank Elliott	Elliott	Frank R. Elliott		Withdrawn
22	Elmer Dempsey	Dempsey	Elmer Dempsey	Frontenac	
25		Kess-Line	M. C. Kessler		Withdrawn
29	C. G. Hartley	Hartley	C. G. Hartley	Fronty-Ford	
34	Harry Thicksten / Wally Butler	Roof	Laurel Motors Corp.	Fronty-Ford	Qualified too late
35	Herbert Scheel	Sinclair	Herbert Scheel	Frontenac	
36	Chas. Shambaugh	Hoosier	Charles Shambaugh		
24	Bill Robinson	Duesenberg	Ray Keech	Duesenberg*	
33	Myron Stevens	White	William S. White	Miller*	Wrecked in practice
41	Thane Houser	Duesenberg	Tommy Milton	Duesenberg*	Bkn. supercharger
44	Phil Pardee / Ralph DePalma	Miller	Alden Sampson, II	Miller*	111.211, wrecked
45	Sam Greco	Miller	Ralph Malamud	Miller*	88.849, too slow
51	Joe Baker / John Vance	Green	Green Engineering Works	Green*	
52	Steven Smith	Rausie	Steven S. Smith		
54	Frank Sweigert	Duesenberg	W. M. Yahr	Duesenberg*	99.585, 1st. alt.
55	Ralph Miller	Hoefle	Ralph S. Miller		
56	Henry Turgeon	Miller	C. E. Ricketts	Miller*¢	
57	G. Comotti	Talbot	Gionfranco Comotti	Talbot*	Withdrawn

1925

NO.	DRIVER	CAR	ENTRANT	ENGINE	REMARKS
10	Albert Guyot	Guyot	Albert Guyot		Did not arrive
12		Guyot	Albert Guyot		Did not arrive
13	Tom Alley	Kess-Line	M. C. Kessler	Frontenac	
14		Guyot	Albert Guyot		Did not arrive
16	L. L. Corum	Miller	Ralph DePalma	Miller	
17	F. H. Wells	Wells Hornet	F. H. Wells		Killed racing in N.Y.
18	Harry Thicksten	Cough Drop	Steven S. Smith		
21	Bennett Hill	Miller Front Drive	Harry A. Miller	Miller*¢	105.708, poor handl.
32	C. W. Belt / Carl R. Green	Super Ford	Green Engineering Co.	Ford	
33	Chas. Shambaugh	Hoosier	Charles Shambaugh		
34	Nick Eckerle	Rotary	J. Hulesman		
36	Harry Thicksten	Schmidt	Albert Schmidt	Mercedes	Did not arrive

1926

NO.	DRIVER	CAR	ENTRANT	ENGINE	REMARKS
2	Bob McDonough	Duesenberg	Duesenberg Bros.	Duesenberg*	
21		Miller	Ralph DePalma	Miller*	
25		Schmidt	Albert Schmidt	Continental*	
32	Jack Foley	Duesenberg	Duesenberg Bros.	Duesenberg*	
35	Sam Ross	Green Super Ford	Carl R. Green	Ford	
37	A. Dan Cain	K.&M.	K.&M. Machine Co.	K.&M.*	
38	Ralph Mulford	Duesenberg	Duesenberg Bros.	Duesenberg*	
57	T. W. Pickard	Sievers Jr.	M. R. Dodds	Sievers	
	Chas. Shambaugh	Shambaugh	Charles Shambaugh		

1927

NO.	DRIVER	CAR	ENTRANT	ENGINE	REMARKS
28	L. L. Corum	Duesenberg	Jack LeCain	Duesenberg*	94.694, 1st. alt.
33	Bruce Miller	Jones-Whittaker	Stanley L. Reed	Miller*¢	
34	Sam Swank	Green	Green Engineering Works	Green*	
36	Leslie Allen	Burt	Andy Burt	Miller*	
37	A. Dan Cain	K.&M.	K.&M. Machine Co.	K.&M.*	
39		Duesenberg	Duesenberg Bros.	Duesenberg*	
45	Steven Smith	Ransie	Steven S. Smith		
46	George Fernic	Bugatti	George Fernic	Bugatti*	

1928

NO.	DRIVER	CAR	ENTRANT	ENGINE	REMARKS
17	L. L. Corum	Duesenberg	Duesenberg Bros.	Duesenberg*	96.172, wrecked
19	Dutch Bauman	Duesenberg	A. S. Kirkby	Duesenberg*	106.226, wrecked
31	Jim Hill	Marion Chevrolet	Marion Chevrolet Co.	Miller*	
35	Buddy Marr / Chet Miller	B. W. Cooke	William Horn	Miller*	109.685 Wrecked
36	Shorty Cantlon	Bugatti	William Horn	Bugatti*	Did not arrive
37	Herman Schurch	Sievers Jr.	M. R. Dodds	Sievers	
42	M. Canthacuzino	Cozette M.G.C.	M. Ghica Canthacuzino		Did not arrive

1929

NO.	DRIVER	CAR	ENTRANT	ENGINE	REMARKS
16	Zeke Meyer	Miller	Zeke Meyer	Miller*	Too dark to qualify
19	Chet Gardner	Boyle Valve	Chester Gardner	Miller*	Burned rod

1930

NO.	DRIVER	CAR	ENTRANT	ENGINE	REMARKS
31	Rick Decker	Decker	Bessie Decker	Duesenberg	
37	James Klemos	Morton & Brett	Morton & Brett	M & B	
43	Doc MacKenzie	Ambler	Auto Engineering Co.	Buick	
47		Duesenberg	A. S. Duesenberg	Duesenberg	
49	Sam Greco	Scranton	Sam Greco		
51	Rollin May	J. M.	Rollin W. May	Chevrolet	
52	Juan Gaudino	Chrysler	Juan Gaudino	Chrysler	
53	Fred Fansin	Fansin	Fred M. Fansin		

1931

NO.	DRIVER	CAR	ENTRANT	ENGINE	REMARKS
6	Wilbur Shaw	Duesenberg	A. S. Duesenberg	Duesenberg	Bkn. crankshaft
9	Frank Farmer	Pedrick Piston Ring	M. A. Yagle	Miller	
15	Bert Karnatz	All Oil	William S. White	Miller	
18	Ralph DePalma	Miller-Wehr	William Van B. Claussen	Miller	
22	Peter Kreis / Lou Moore	Coleman Motors	Coleman Motors Corp.	Miller¢	97.389, too slow / Qualified, withdrawn
29	L. L. Corum	Stutz Bearcat	Stutz Motor Car Co.	Stutz	
38	Joe Caccia	Jones & Maley	Alvin R. Jones	Duesenberg	Wrecked in practice
42	Bill Denver	B & N	Brady & Nardi	Duesenberg	96.085, too slow
43	Milt Marion	Duesenberg	Milt Marion	Duesenberg	
45	M. M. Trexler / C. C. Reeder	Copper	C. C. Reeder	Lycoming	95.613, too slow / 98.061, 2nd. alt.
46	Rick Decker	Miller	Bessie Decker	Miller¢	
47	Floyd Sparks	De Biase	Anna De Biase	Curtiss	Burned in pits
51	Charles Moran	Model A Ford	Charles Moran, Jr.	Ford A	
52	Roy Painter	Painter	Roy W. Painter	Miller	
53	Joe Thomas	Finneran	Andrew E. Finneran	Miller	91.403
56	James Patterson	Cacace	John T. Cacace	Miller	
61	Eddie Burbach	B & C	Burbach & Classon	Duesenberg	
62	Wally Zale	Midway Motors	Charles H. Burk	Lycoming¢	
63	Malcolm Fox	Duesenberg	Charles Burgert	Duesenberg	
64	Norske Larson	Buehrig	James H. Wade	Duesenberg	
65	Walt May	Schofield-Curlett	Schofield Auto. Eng. Ltd.	Ford A	
66	Ben Brandfon	Duesenberg	Benny Brandfon	Duesenberg	
68	Ted Chamberlain	Miller S. L.	Paul C. Searles, Jr.	Miller	99.182, 1st. alt.
71	Johnny Seymour	Highway Truck Parts	S. C. Goldberg	Cooper¢	
73	Carl Smith	C. C. Smith	Carl C. Smith	Mercer	
74	Dusty Fahrnow	United Cab	Leon Duray	Duesenberg	
75		Duesenberg	Dick Woods	Duesenberg	Withdrawn
76	Jimmy Gleason	Mercedes Grand Prix	Dick Woods	Mercedes	Withdrawn
77		Duesenberg	Dick Woods	Duesenberg	Withdrawn
78	Zeke Meyer	Woods	Dick Woods	Lycoming	Withdrawn
79	Leon Duray	Leon Duray	Leon Duray	Miller	Withdrawn

1932

NO.	DRIVER	CAR	ENTRANT	ENGINE	REMARKS
12	Sam Ross	Yahr Miller	William Yahr	Miller	
19	Milt Jones	Jones	Milt Jones	Miller	Wrecked in practice
23	Gene Haustein	Fronty Ford	Fronty Sales Corp.	Ford A	
31	Speed Gardner	Allegheny Metal	Mikan, Carson & Gardner	Studebaker	
38	L. L. Corum	Duesenberg	Kleinschmidt & Rigling	Duesenberg	

*Supercharged   ¢Front Drive

1929 Sam Greco

1929 Steve Smith

1929 Henry Turgeon

1930 James Klemos

1931 Wilbur Shaw

1931 Frank Farmer

1931 Albert Karnatz

1931 Joe Caccia

1931 Bill Denver

1931 Milt Marion

1931 Floyd Sparks

1931 Joe Thomas

1931 Norske Larson

1932 Sam Ross

1932 Gene Haustein

1932 W. H. "Speed" Gardner

1932 George Howie

1932 Roy Painter

1932 Paul Rice

1932 Milt Marion

1932 Leon Duray

1932 Marion Trexler

1932 Fred Merzney

1932 Buddy Callaway

NO.	DRIVER	CAR	ENTRANT	ENGINE	REMARKS
			1932 (Cont.)		
39	Fred Clemons / Billy Winn	Hoosier Pete	F. E. Clemons	Clemons	
43	Freddy Winnai	C. B.	Charles Burgert	Duesenberg	
44	Leon DeHart	Veedol	E. M. Morton	Morton-Brett	
47	George Howie	Howie	George N. Howie	Chrysler	103.490, 1st. alt.
51	Roy Painter	Lupasa	Lupasa Co.	Graham	
52	Paul Rice	All American	George S. Gerrard	Oakland	
53	Milt Marion	Duesenberg	Virgil O. Williams	Duesenberg	
54	Leon Duray	Mallory	Leon Duray	Duray	
56	M. M. Trexler	Jack C. Carr	Albert H. Walker	Lycoming	
59	Al Theisen	Marr	Tulio Gulotta	Hudson	
62	Arvol Brunmeier	Guiberson	Allen Guiberson	Ford A¢	
63	Fred Merzney	Coleman Four Wheel Dr.	Coleman Motors Corp.	Miller	
64	Buddy Callaway	Callaway	Buddy Callaway	Hisso	
68	Geo. Wingerter	Duesenberg	George Wingerter	Duesenberg	
69	Barney McKenna	Finneran	Andrew E. Finneran	Miller	
71	A. C. Aiken	Aiken-Howard	Aiken & Howard	Stutz	
73	Larry Wall / Ben Benifield	Jones & Maley	Alvin R. Jones	Duesenberg	Wrecked in practice
74	Edward Leipert	Leipert Miller	Edward Leipert	Miller	
75	Jim Patterson	Duesenberg	Louis Katz	Duesenberg	101.246, 2nd. alt.
76	Sam Greco	Samcliff	Sam Greco		
78	Harry Hunt	Brooks Romo	Harold Brooks	Lycoming	
79	Jack Mertz	Mertz	Jack Mertz	Hudson	
81	Dany Day	Silver Marshall Radio	Steve Gregory	Duesenberg	
83	Geo. Kalen	McPherson-Kalen	J. B. McPherson, IV	Duesenberg	
95	Dusty Fahrnow	Highway Truck Parts	S. C. Goldberg	Cooper¢	
			1933		
7	Phil Shafer	Ables-Fink Auto	Phil Shafer	Buick	107.972, 1st. alt.
31	Speed Gardner	Allegheny Metal	Mikan, Carson & Gardner	Studebaker	Wrecked in practice
35		Fronty Ford	Fronty Sales Co.	Ford A	
39	Mauri Rose	Iroquois	Moyer & Dunning	DeSoto¢	Bkn. radius rod
41	Sam Palmer	R. & W. Cam Co.	George A. Henry	Duesenberg	105.998, 2nd. alt.
42	Al Aspen / Bill Denver	Brady & Nardi	Ray T. Brady	Studebaker	Wrecked in pract. Over wall, NE, died
43	Kelly Petillo	Ward	Harvey Ward	Miller	Withdrawn
44	Harry Lewis	Bud's Auto Parts	Edward M. Cauble	Miller¢	
48	George Howie	Howie	George N. Howie	Chrysler	Withdrawn
52	Overton Snell	Snell	Overton H. Snell	Studebaker	
54	Geo. Barringer	Wonder Bread	F. E. Clemons	Clemons	
55	Leon DeHart	Morton & Brett	Morton & Brett, Inc.	Morton & Brett	
56	Paul Butler	Sacks Bros.	Paul Butler	Lincoln	
63	Ray Carter	Billings	R. M. Carter		
66	Terry Curley / Doc Williams	C. O. Warnock	C. O. Warnock Co.	Ford V8	104.538, too slow
68	Bennett Hill	Goldberg Bros.	S. C. Goldberg	Cooper¢	
69	Virgil Livingood	Duesenberg	Curt Gosma	Duesenberg	Wrecked qualifying
71	Harry Falt	H. A. F.	Harry A. Falt	Lycoming¢	
72	Roy Painter	Crow Eight	Wilbur Crow	Graham	
74	Bill Sockwell	Sockwell 8	Bill Sockwell		
75	L. A. Lariviere	L. & L.	L. A. Lariviere	Duesenberg	
76	Frank Davidson	Davidson	Frank Davidson		
			1934		
14	Peter Kreis	Miller-Hartz	Harry Hartz	Miller¢	Wrecked in practice
27	Peter DePaolo	Miller	California Racers, Inc.	Miller 4	Withdrawn
34	Fred Frame	Frame Front Drive	Fred Frame	Miller¢	Wrecked in practice
38	Doc Williams	Highway Truck Parts	Irving Goldberg	Cooper¢	
39	George Connor	Ward	Harvey Ward	Miller	
43	Harry Hunt	Duesenberg	Harry P. Hunt	Duesenberg	
44	Babe Stapp / Wes. Crawford	Garcia Grande	Roscoe L. Dunning	DeSoto¢	Wrecked in practice Didn't complete run
47	Sam Hoffman	Mannix	J. L. Mannix	Duesenberg	
52	Jack Petticord / Harry Lewis	Don Hulbert	Don Hulbert, Inc.	Ford V8	Did not qualify, 2nd. alt.
53	Ted Horn / Bob Wallace	Mick	J. J. Mick	Duesenberg	

NO.	DRIVER	CAR	ENTRANT	ENGINE	REMARKS
54	Leon Duray / Babe Stapp	Leon Duray	Leon Duray	Duray	Used too much gas
55		York	M. York	Miller	Withdrawn
56	Maynard Clark	Smith	E. H. Smith	Clemons	
57	Milt Marion	Miller	Milt Marion	Miller	
59	Bill Chittum / Will. Prentiss	G. & D.	Tulio Gulotta	Hudson	1st. alternate
61	Orville Smith	Anglemyer Miller	Alfred A. Anglemyer	Miller	
62	Vern Ornduff / Dany Day	Miller	John L. Buckley	Miller	
64	Will. Prentiss	Wehr Rotary Valve	Frank J. Fabian	Wehr	
65	Harold Shaw	Kleinschmidt	J. W. Kleinschmidt	Duesenberg	
72	Chas. Tramison	Economy Gas	Wilbur J. Crow	Graham	Used too much gas
			1935		
10	Billy Winn	Ford V8	Harry A. Miller	Ford V8¢	Didn't complete run
12	Babe Stapp	Toledo Valve	Lou Matheson	Miller	
23	Geo. Barringer	Ford V8	Harry A. Miller	Ford V8¢	Didn't complete run
24	Herb Ardinger	Welch	Lewis Welch	Ford V8	Too slow
25	Harry Hunt	Duesenberg	Harry P. Hunt	Duesenberg	Engine tbl., 4th lap
28	Gene Haustein	Yahr Bros.	William Yahr	Miller	
29	S. Stubblefield	Victor Gasket	Phil Shafer	Buick	Wrecked qualifying
31	Phil Shafer / Zeke Meyer	Victor Gasket	Phil Shafer	Buick	Didn't complete run
32	Dave Evans	Ford V8	Harry A. Miller	Ford V8¢	109.937, 1st. alt.
38		Elgin Piston Pin	Elgin Piston Pin Co.	Brisko	
47	Johnny Rae	Ford V8	Harry A. Miller	Ford V8¢	
48	Wes Crawford	Ford V8	Harry A. Miller	Ford V8¢	
49	L. L. Corum	Ford V8	Harry A. Miller	Ford V8¢	
51	Roy Painter / Hershell McKee	Frigenor	Roy W. Painter	Graham	106.638, too slow
52	Emil Andres	Don Hulbert	Don Hulbert, Inc.	Ford V8¢	
53	Dusty Fahrnow / Jimmy Snyder	Superior Trailer	Race Car Corp.	Cooper¢	109.138, used too much fuel
54		Welch	Lewis Welch	Ford V8	
56	Clay Weatherly / Emil Andres	Cresco	J. C. Schmidlapp	Miller	109.074, 2nd. alt.
57	Floyd O'Neal	Preston	A. J. Preston	Morton-Brett	
58	Overton Snell	Snell Bros.	Overton H. Snell	Ford V8	99.669, too slow
59	Bob Wilson	Phillips 66	Tulio Gulotta	Hudson	
61		Wehr Rotary Valve	Frank J. Fabian	Wehr Rotary	Withdrawn
63	Johnny Sawyer / Louis Tomei	Miller	Lem'nd, Magnee, Nowiak	Miller	
64	Doc Williams	Harry Henderson	Harry Henderson	Ford V8	Wrecked in practice
65		Farmcrest	Lawrence J. Martz	Hudson	
	Duke Nalon	Jeeter-Morris	Jeeter & Morris	Ford V8	Withdrawn
			1936		
23	R. Snowberger	D & G	Joel Thorne, Inc.	Dodge	Wrecked in pract.
24	Overton Snell	Snell Bros.	Overton H. Snell	Miller	109.561, too slow
25	Dave Evans	D & G	Joel Thorne, Inc.	Dodge	
26	Phil Shafer / Al Putnam	Shafer	Phil Shafer	Buick	110.485, 1st. alt.
29	Henry Banks	DePalma Miller	Louis Kimmell	Miller	110.277, 2nd. alt.
31	Tony Gulotta	Pirrung	Gil Pirrung	Miller	Wrecked in practice
34	Roy Painter	American Twist Drill	T. Nowiak & C. Magnee	Studebaker	109.867, too slow
37		Miller-Hibbard	Ira Vail	Miller	
39		Lucky Teter	E. M. "Lucky" Teter	Ford V8	Withdrawn
48	Al Putnam	Mikan	Ivan Mikan	Studebaker	Withdrawn
49	Luther Johnson	Bugatti	Overton A. Phillips	Bugatti*	
51	George Bailey	Zauer-Martz	Lawrence J. Martz	Hudson	
55	Dusty Fahrnow	Superior Trailer	Race Car Corp.	Miller¢	Didn't complete run
56	Emil Andres / Tony Gulotta	DeBaets	Michel DeBaets sold to.... Gil Pirrung	Miller	Didn't complete run Didn't complete run
57	Geo. Wingerter	G. W.	George Wingerter	Duesenberg	
58	Harry Hunt	Duesenberg	Harry Hunt	Duesenberg	
59		Dunning	Roscoe Dunning		Withdrawn

*Supercharged   ¢Front drive   4Four wheel drive

1932   A. C. Aiken

1932   Jimmy Patterson

1932   Dany Day

1933   W. H. "Speed" Gardner

1933   Al Aspen

1933   Harry Lewis

1933   George Barringer

1933   Leon DeHart

1933   Ray Carter

1933   Virgil Livingood

1933   Harry A. Falt

1934   George Connor

1934   Babe Stapp

1934   Jack Petticord

1934   Willard Prentiss

1934   Charles Tramison

1935   Babe Stapp

1935   Stubby Stubblefield

1935   Phil "Red" Shafer

1935   Dave Evans

1935   Floyd O'Neal

1935   Overton Snell

1935   Louis Tomei

1936   Russell Snowberger

1937

NO.	DRIVER	CAR	ENTRANT	ENGINE	REMARKS
21	Duke Nalon / Dave Evans	Elgin Piston Pin	Elgin Piston Pin Co.	Brisko	Didn't complete run
22	Joel Thorne	Thorne	Joel Thorne, Inc.	Offy	115.607, 1st. alt.
36	Emil Andres	Kennedy Tank & Mfg.	Phil Shafer sold to... Joel Thorne	Buick	116.243, sold... withdrawn
37	Ira Hall	Precise Tool	Magnee & Nowiak	Studebaker	Didn't complete run
39	Frank McGurk	Belanger Miller	Murrell Belanger	Miller	Wrecked qualifying
46	Al Putnam / Emil Andres	Kennedy Tank	Phil Shafer	Buick	116.243, 1st. alt.
48	Emil Andres	Carew	J. Stewart Carew	Cragar	
49	Henry Banks	Kimmell	Louis Kimmell	Voelker	
51	Johnny Seymour	Stewart	William Stewart	Morton-Brett	Didn't complete run
52	Zeke Meyer	Joel Thorne	Joel Thorne, Inc.	Studebaker¢	
56	Ira Hall	Lafayette, Indiana	Souders & Galaval	Duesenberg	Disqualified
57	Doc Williams	Superior Trailer	Race Car Corp.	Cooper¢	
58	Louie Webb	Superior Trailer	Race Car Corp.	Miller	Didn't complete run
61	Ray Yeager / Woody Woodford	Yeager	Ray Yeager	Studebaker	
63	Tom Cosman	Wehr Rotary Valve	Rudolph Wehr	Wehr*	
64		Wehr Rotary Valve	Rudolph Wehr	Wehr*	
65	Milt Marion	Crystal Flash	Milt Marion	Miller	
66	Luther Johnson / Overton Phillips	Mannix-Duesenberg	J. L. Mannix	Duesenberg	Wrecked in practice
67	Vern Ornduff	Ray 8	Ray T. Brady	Studebaker	Hit by 66 in pits
72	Lee Oldfield	Oldfield	Lee Oldfield	Marmon* R	

1938

NO.	DRIVER	CAR	ENTRANT	ENGINE	REMARKS
4	Ralph Hepburn	Harry A. Miller	Harry A. Miller	Miller 4 R	Left at line
18	Billy Winn	Harry A. Miller	Harry A. Miller	Miller	Didn't complete run
24	Billy Winn	Harry A. Miller	Harry A. Miller	Miller	Didn't complete run
25	George Bailey	Harry A. Miller	Harry A. Miller	Miller 4 R	
31	Chas. Crawford	Shafer 8	Phil Shafer	Buick	112.762, 1st. alt.
32	Fred Frame	Hulbert Duesenberg	Frame & McDaniel	Duesenberg	
44	Rick Decker	Miller	Robert V. Dunn	Miller¢	
46	Doc Williams	Ben Been	Ben Been	Miller¢	Didn't complete run
48	Tazio Nuvolari	Alfa Romeo	Alfia San Felippo	Alfa Romeo*	Withdrawn
49		Kirkham Maserati	Hollis A. Cheesman	Maserati*	
51	Chas. Crawford	Stewart	William Stewart	Morton-Brett	Didn't complete run
52	Deacon Litz	Sampson-Litz	J. C. Calvert	Offy	
53	Johnny Sawyer	Uhl	Edwin J. Uhl	Duesenberg	
56	Johnny Seymour	Clemons Indep. Susp.	F. E. Clemons	Clemons	
57	Jack Petticord	Miller-Duesenberg	H. Jack Petticord	Duesenberg	
59	Floyd Davis	Woestman	Walt Woestman	McDowell	

1939

NO.	DRIVER	CAR	ENTRANT	ENGINE	REMARKS
7	Duke Nalon	Belanger	Murrell Belanger	Miller	
12		Marchese	Carl Marchese	Miller*	
23	George Robson	W. A. Rotary Valve	Wehr & Anderson	Wehr*	
27	Zeke Meyer	Miller	Harry A. Miller	Miller* 4 R	
28	George Robson	Deacon Litz	J. L. Litz	Maserati	116.305, alt.
33	Tom Hinnershitz	Kimmell	Louis Kimmell	Voelker	
36	Doc Williams	Quillen Bros. Refrig.	Merrell Williams	Miller¢	
39	Henry Banks	Cheesman Maserati	Hollis A. Cheesman	Maserati*	
43		Kohlert's Miller	Henry Kohlert	Miller*	
46		Lucky Teter	"Lucky" Teter	Offy	
48		Miller-Purdy	Richard H. Purdy	Miller	
52		Miller-Gardner	W. H. Gardner	Miller¢	
55	Louis Tomei	Indiana Fur	Phil Shafer	Buick	
57		Gordner	F. M. Gordner	Offy	
59	Louie Webb	Woestman-McDowell	Walt Woestman	McDowell	
61	John Seymour	Miller	Harry A. Miller	Miller* 4 R	Wrecked in practice

1940

NO.	DRIVER	CAR	ENTRANT	ENGINE	REMARKS
4	Babe Stapp	Wheeler	Wheeler's Lunch	Miller*	Didn't complete run
12	Louis Durant	Schoof	William A. Schoof	Offy	117.218, too slow
22	Rene Dreyfus	Lucy O'Reilly Schell	Lucy O'Reilly Schell	Maserati*	118.831, 2nd. alt.
37	Louie Webb	Kimmell	Louis Kimmell	Voelker	
39	Henry Banks	Cheesman Maserati	Hollis A. Cheesman	Maserati*	Didn't complete run
45	Tony Willman / Harry McQuinn	Leader Card	Leader Card Works	Miller*	Didn't complete run 118.914, 1st. alt.
46	Overton Phillips	Phillips	V. H. Phillips	Miller	
47	Ira Hall	Magnee & Nowiak	Magnee & Nowiak		
51	Port DeFraties	W. & A.	Rudolph Wehr	Wehr*	
55		Shafer 8	Phil Shafer	Buick	
56	George Bailey	Miller	Eddie Offutt	Miller* 4 R	Wrecked in practice
57	Bill Lipscomb	Watson	Donald J. Greene	Miller	
59	Freddy Winnai	Walt Woestman	Walt Woestman	McDowell	
62	Wes Crawford	Corley Miller	William A. Corley	Miller	
63		Miller	Eddie Offutt	Miller* 4 R	
64		Thorne Donnelly	Joel Thorne, Inc.	Offy¢	

1941

NO.	DRIVER	CAR	ENTRANT	ENGINE	REMARKS
21	Rene LeBegue	Talbot	Rene LeBegue	Talbot	116.000, 2nd. alt.
37	George Robson	Greenfield Super Serv.	C. Magnee & T. Nowiak	Studebaker	
38	Ira Hall	Kimmell	Louis Kimmell	Voelker	Wrecked in practice
44	Louis Durant	G. & S.	Glane H. Jennings	Mercury	116.152, 1st. alt.
49		Willets	J. Macy Willets, Jr.	Miller	
51		Clemons	F. E. Clemons	Clemons	
56		Marks	Joe Marks	Offy	
57	Bill Lipscomb	Greene	Donald J. Greene	Miller	

1946

NO.	DRIVER	CAR	ENTRANT	ENGINE	REMARKS
9	Al Miller	Blue Crown Spark Plug	Joe Lencki	Lencki	
27	T. Bettenhausen	Marchese	Carl Marchese	Miller*	Qualified, withdrawn
28	Steve Truchan	Offenhauser	Jimmy Chai	Offy	
34	Tom Hinnershitz	Maserati	Milt Marion	Maserati*	
35	Louis Gerard	Alfa Romeo	Harry O'R. Schell	Alfa Romeo*	
36	Louis Gerard	Maserati-Schell	Harry O'R. Schell	Maserati	
37	Buddy Rush	Enlist in U.S. Army	Bud Bardowski	Studebaker	116.268, 1st. alt.
43	Wally Mitchell	Mitchell Corp.	H. Walter Mitchell	Brisko	
44	Rudi Caracciola	Thorne Engineering	Thorne Engineering Corp.	Sparks	Wrecked in practice
46	Harry Schell	Maserati	Harry O'R. Schell	Maserati	
49	Z. Arkus-Duntov	Talbot	Zora Arkus-Duntov	Talbot	
53	Achille Varzi	Maserati	Covorado Filippini	Maserati*	
55	Joe Langley	Clemons	Jack Dixon	Clemons	
56	Bruce Denslow	Greene-Holland	D. Greene & L. Holland	Plymouth	
57	R. Arbuthnot	Lagonda	Robert M. W. Arbuthnot	Lagonda	
58	Harold Bailey	Bee-Gee	B. F. Gregoric		
62	Chas. Van Acker	Singer	Charles E. Van Acker	Voelker	115.666, 2nd. alt.
65		Offenhauser	W. Frank Sharp	Offy	
67	A. Brunmeier	Offenhauser	G. Robson & C. Holland	Offy	
68	Jim Brubaker	Maserati	Jim Brubaker	Maserati	
69	Bud Rose	Purdy Offenhauser	Richard H. Purdy	Offy¢	
71	Freddy Winnai	Jewell	Lawrence Jewell	Hal	Didn't complete run
72	Rudi Caracciola	Caracciola Mercedes	Alice Caracciola Trobek	Mercedes*	Did not arrive
74		Maserati	Harry O'R. Schell	Maserati	

1947

NO.	DRIVER	CAR	ENTRANT	ENGINE	REMARKS
5	T. Hinnershitz	T. H. E.	Ted Horn	Offy	Did not arrive
6	Walt Ader	Olson	Norm Olson	Offy	
17		Schoof	William Schoof	Offy	
22	Red Byron	Pauley Ford	J. Edward Pauley	Ford V8	
23	Tommy Boggs / Louis Durant	Boggs	Tommy Boggs	Offy¢	
32	Duane Carter	Kuehl-Osborne	Kuehl & Osborne	Studebaker	
35	Henry Brooke	E. R. A.	Henry R. Brooke	E. R. A.*	
44	George Weaver / Louis Tomei	Miller	George B. Weaver	Miller*¢	
49	Z. Arkus-Duntov	Martin	Zora Arkus-Duntov	Talbot	
51			Sam Greco		

*Supercharged   ¢Front drive   4Four wheel drive   RRear Engine

1936   Overton Snell

1936   Dave Evans

1936   Al Putnam

1936   Henry Banks

1936   Roy Painter

1936   Luther Johnson

1936   Tony Gulotta

1937   Duke Nalon

1937   Joel Thorne

1937   Frank McGurk

1937   Henry Banks

1937   Zeke Meyer

1937   Ira Hall

1937   Woody Woodford

1937   Tommy Cosman

1937   Milt Marion

1937   Overton Phillips

1937   Vern Ornduff

1937   Lee Oldfield

1938   Ralph Hepburn

1938   Charles Crawford

1938   Doc Williams

1938   Charles Crawford

1938   Floyd Davis

NO.	DRIVER	CAR	ENTRANT	ENGINE	REMARKS
			1947 (Cont.)		
55	George Metzler	Dixon	Jack Dixon	Clemons	
57	Louis Tomei	Camco Motors Ford	Anthony Granatelli	Mercury	
64	Johnny Mauro	Phil Kraft	Johnny Mauro	Miller*	
67	Chas. Crawford	Murphy	W. D. Chambers	Duesenberg	
69	Norm Houser	Robert Allison	W. Allison & T. Houser	Ford V8	
86	Jim Brubaker	Jack Maurer	James O. Brubaker	Maserati	
	T. Bettenhausen	Thorne Engineering	Joel Thorne	Sparks*	
			1948		
10	Louis Tomei	Tom Sarafoff	Tom Sarafoff	Offy¢	
12	Ralph Hepburn	Novi Grooved Piston	W. C. Winfield	Novi*¢	Wrecked in practice
14	Jim Brubaker	Maserati	James O. Brubaker	Maserati	
15	Walt Ader	Peters	Fred Peters	Offy	Owner died
21	Eddie Zalucki	Automobile Shippers	Louis Rassey	Offy	
23	Milt Fankhouser	Milt Fankhouser	Milt Fankhouser	Offy	
24	Jackie Holmes	Indiana Plywood	Floyd H. Dreyer	Offy	
27	Art Hartsfield	Corley	Bill Corley	Offy	
28	Mel Hansen	Brady	Ray T. Brady	Sparks*	
29	Louis Durant	Automobile Shippers	Louis Rassey	Miller	117.666
32	Myron Fohr	Marchese	Marchese Bros. Eng. Co.	Offy	121.531, 2nd. alt.
37	Johnny Mauro	Miller	Johnny Mauro	Miller*	
38	Henry Banks	Federal Eng. Detroit	R. A. Cott	Offy¢	
39	Andy Granatelli	Grancor V8	J. & A. Granatelli	Mercury	
41	Ken Fowler	Don Lee	Don Lee Division	Alfa Romeo*	120.446, too slow
43	Red Byron	Parks-Vogt	Raymond D. Parks	Ford V8	
44	Bob Droeger	Baldwin	E. Baldwin & E. Hoovener	Duesenberg	
45	Cowboy O'Rourke / Walt Ader	Speedway Cocktail	Joe Lencki	Lencki	
46		Fageol	Lou Fageol	Ford V8	
47	George Metzler	Glessner Motors	Lee S. Glessner	Clemons	
48	J. Shakleford	Johnston Offy	Fred W. Johnston	Offy	121.745, 1st. alt.
49	Pete Romcevich	Norm Olson	Norm Olson Enterprises	Offy	
56	George Lynch	Lisher & Lynch	Lisher & Lynch		
57	Joel Thorne	Thorne Engineering	Thorne Eng. Co.	Sparks	
58	Mack Hellings / Mike Salay	Blue Crown Spark Plug	Lou & Howard Moore	Offy	
59	A. Granatelli	Grancor-Werner	Grancor Auto. Spec.	Mercury	Wrecked in practice
62	Joe Perkins	Kurtis-Kraft	Joe Perkins	Offy	
66	Al Miller	Preston Tucker	Tucker & Offutt	Miller* 4 R	
67	Lee Wallard	G. & M.	R. J. Pierson	Duesenberg	
68	R. Householder	Speedway Cocktail	Joe Lencki	Lencki	
69	Walt Brown	Werner-Grancor	Grancor Auto. Spec.	Maserati*	
71	Loral Tansy	Tansy	Loral R. Tansy	Offy	
72	Spider Webb	Anderson Offy	Clarence Anderson	Offy	121.421, too slow
73	Roland Free	Gustafson K. F. Motors	Tech. Air Service	Miller*¢	
78		Schoof	William Schoof	Offy	
79		R. E. C.	N. J. Rounds	Offy	Did not exist
83		Miller	Ralph S. Miller	R. Miller*	
84		Suttle Steamer	Lawrence D. Suttle	Steam¢	Car not finished
85	Cliff Bergere	Grancor-Werner	A. Granatelli	Offy	
87	Ralph Pratt	Lutes-Gdula-Pratt	W. J. Lutes	Offy	
88	Manuel Ayulo	Weidel	Conrad Weidel	Mercury	
89	Chas. Rogers	Jewell	Lawrence Jewell	Voelker	
92		Ardun	Zora Arkus-Duntov		Did not arrive
93	Jackie Holmes	Jimmy Chai	Jimmy Chai	Offy	
95	Mike Salay	Kuehl-Osborne	Paul B. Kuehl		
		Guthrie	Paul Guthrie		Did not arrive
			1949		
16	Johnny Mauro / T. Bettenhausen	Alfa Romeo	Johnny Mauro	Alfa Romeo*	125.156, too slow
21	Henry Banks	Federal Eng. Detroit	R. A. Cott	Offy	124.939, too slow
23	Hal Robson	Miller	Indianapolis Race Cars	Miller	
24	Frank Burany	Schoof	William Schoof	Offy	Wrecked in practice
28		Dayton Coil Spring	Ralph S. Miller	R. Miller*	
34	Ralph Pratt	Belanger Motors	Murrell Belanger	Offy	125.764, 1st. alt.

NO.	DRIVER	CAR	ENTRANT	ENGINE	REMARKS
35	Sam Hanks / Henry Banks	Federal Eng. Detroit	R. A. Cott	Maserati*	94.867, too slow
36	Bill Cantrell	Fageol Twin Coach	Lou Fageol	Fageol	125.022, too slow
39	Byron Horne	Grancor V8	Anthony Granatelli	Mercury	
42	Randall Bienke / Louis Tomei	Worline	Ray Worline	Offy¢	120.846, too slow
43	Pat Flaherty	Grancor V8	Anthony Granatelli	Mercury	
44	Mel Hansen	Bowes Seal Fast	Bowes Racing Inc.	Meyer-Offy*	
46	T. Bettenhausen	Flavell	Robert J. Flavell	Sparks*	125.764, 2nd. alt.
47	Ed Haddad	Page	Ross Page	Duray*	
48	Frank Brisko	Frank J. Lynch	Frank Brisko	Brisko*	
49	Mike Salay	Szalai	Virginia Szalai	Offy	
51	Bill Taylor	Rounds Rocket	N. J. Rounds	Offy R	
55	Kenny Eaton	Bowes Seal Fast	Bowes Racing Inc.	Offy	
56	Jimmy Daywalt	Bill & Bud Motor Sales	Steve Truchan	Offy	
58	Danny Kladis	Speedway Cocktail	Joe Lencki	Lencki	
59	Dick Frazier	Grancor	Grancor Auto. Spec.	Offy	
62		Koehnle-Smith	John F. Koehnle	G.M.C.	
63	Jim Rathmann	Grancor	Jim Rathmann	Offy	
65	Doc Williams	Sarafoff	Tom Sarafoff	Offy	125.161, too slow
66	Lindley Bothwell	Peugeot	Lindley Bothwell	Peugeot	
67	George Metzler	Glessner	Lee S. Glessner	Offy	
72	Ted Duncan	Lutes	W. J. Lutes	Offy	
73	Milt Fankhouser / Manuel Ayulo	Karl Hall	Karl Hall	Offy	120.490, too slow
75	Wally Stokes	Kupiec	Thomas Kupiec	Offy	
76		Gdula's	Edward Gdula	Offy	
78		Swanson	George E. Swanson	Offy¢	Did not arrive
79	Jim Brubaker	Brubaker	James O. Brubaker	Maserati	
81	Joel Thorne	Thorne Engineering	Thorne Eng. Corp.	Sparks	
			1950		
9	Andy Linden / Bud Rose	Bromme	Louis & Bruce Bromme	Offy	Didn't complete run
10	Bill Vukovich	I. R. C.	Indianapolis Race Cars	Maserati*	
16	Ted Duncan / Hal Cole	Pritchard	Charles Pritchard	Offy	Wrecked qualifying
19	Ralph Pratt / Kenny Eaton	Lutes	W. J. Lutes	Offy	Didn't complete run
25	Johnny Mauro	Alfa Romeo	Johnny Mauro	Alfa Romeo*	
26	George Fonder	Ray Brady	Ray T. Brady	Sparks*	127.918, 2nd. alt.
29	Chas. Van Acker	Redmer	Geneva Van Acker	Offy	
33	Joel Thorne	Thorne Engineering	Thorne Eng. Corp.	Sparks	
34	Johnny Fedricks	Kupiec	Thomas J. Kupiec	Offy	
36	George Lynch	Automobile Shippers	Louis Rassey	Offy	
38	Duke Nalon	Novi Mobil	Winfield Engineering	Novi*¢	
39	Danny Kladis	Federal Eng. Detroit	R. A. Cott	Maserati*	Didn't complete run
41	Milt Fankhouser	Karl Hall	Karl Hall	Offy	
43	Chet Miller	Novi Mobil	Winfield Eng., Inc.	Novi*¢	
44	Bill Cantrell	Bowes Seal Fast	Bowes Racing, Inc.	Meyer-Offy*	Didn't complete run
46	Nino Farina	Maserati	S. A. Officine A. Maserati	Maserati*	Did not arrive
47	Ralph Pratt	Gdula	Edward Gdula	Offy	
48	Franco Roll	Maserati	S. A. Officine A. Maserati	Maserati*	Did not arrive
51	Mark Light	Glessner	Lee S. Glessner	Offy	
52	Dick Frazier / Mark Light	Iddings	Henry Meyer	Offy	Didn't complete run
53		Swanson	George E. Swanson	Offy	Did not arrive
58	Billy DeVore	Scopa	Joe Scopa	Offy	Didn't complete run
63	Bob Gregg / Joe James	Esmeralda	Leo Dobry	Offy	127.438, too slow
64	Bob Sweikert	Carter	Ray W. Carter	Offy	
65	Marvin Burke / Norm Houser	Offenhauser	Ross Page	Duray*	Didn't complete run
66	Cliff Griffith	Sarafoff	Tom Sarafoff	Offy¢	129.014, 1st. alt.
74	Carl Forberg	Jewell	Lawrence Jewell	Offy¢	
78	Cy Marshall	Vulcan Tool	Ralph S. Miller	R. Miller*	
79	Chuck Leighton	Cantarano	Paul Cantarano	Wayne Chevy	121.065, too slow
82	Joe James	Bob Estes	Bob Estes	Ardun Merc.	124.176, too slow
83	Al Miller	Trainor Auto Parts	Charles P. Kennedy	Miller* 4 R	
84	Mike Burch	George Hoster, Inc.	Edward Shreve	Maserati	
85	Jim Rigsby / Manuel Ayulo	Coast Grain	Bob Weinberg	Offy	120.000, too slow

*Supercharged   ¢Front drive   4Four wheel drive   RRear Engine

1939 George Robson

1939 George Robson

1940 Louis Durant

1940 Harry McQuinn

1946 Tony Bettenhausen

1946 Steve Truchan

1946 Buddy Rush

1946 Wally Mitchell

1946 Harry Schell

1946 Achille Varzi

1946 Robert Arbuthnot

1946 Charles Van Acker

1946 Louis Girard

1947 Tommy Boggs

1947 George Metzler

1947 Jim Brubaker

1948 Myron Fohr

1948 Andy Granatelli

1948 Ken Fowler

1948 Johnny Shackelford

1948 Mack Hellings

1948 Spider Webb

1948 Jackie Holmes

1949 Ralph Pratt

NO.	DRIVER	CAR	ENTRANT	ENGINE	REMARKS

1950 (Cont.)

NO.	DRIVER	CAR	ENTRANT	ENGINE	REMARKS
87	Billy Vukovich	R. E. C.	N. J. Rounds	Offy R	
99	Kenny Eaton / Emil Andres	Belanger	Murrell Belanger	Offy*	Didn't complete run

1951

NO.	DRIVER	CAR	ENTRANT	ENGINE	REMARKS
7	Paul Russo	Kennedy Tank	Paul F. Russo	Offy	121.914, too slow
14	Jerry Hoyt	Pat Clancy	Pat Clancy	Offy	127.700, too slow
24	Jackie Holmes	Palmer	Fred L. Palmer	Offy	129.259, too slow
29	George Fonder	Ray Brady	Ray T. Brady	Sparks*	
31	Manuel Ayulo	Coast Grain	Bob Weinberg	Offy	131.128, 2nd. alt.
33	Jimmy Daywalt	Iddings	Henry Meyer	Offy	Wrecked in practice
34	Johnnie Tolan	Wales Trucking	M. Pete Wales	Offy	
36	George Lynch	Rassey	Louis Rassey	Offy	Didn't complete run
37	Bob Sweikert	Marion Engineering	Milt Marion	Offy	131.224, 1st. alt.
41	Mike Salay	Szalai Offy	Mike Szalai	Offy	Wrecked in practice
42	Bill Boyd	Gdula	Edward Gdula	Offy	Wrecked in practice
45	Jackie Holmes	C. R. C.	Cincinnati Race Cars	Offy	Didn't complete run
46	Bayliss Levrett	Hunt Magneto	Joseph B. Hunt	Offy	128.329, too slow
47	Jimmy Daywalt	Merkler Machine Works	Franklin Merkler	Meyer-Offy*	
49	Joe Barzda	Barzda	Joseph J. Barzda	Offy	Spun qualifying
51	Bud Sennett	Auto Accessories Co.	Joseph J. Barzda	Maserati*	Wrecked qualif., SW
53	George Fonder	Hancock Dome	W. J. Lutes	Offy	128.892, too slow
55		Maserati	Maserati Race Cars	Maserati*	Did not arrive
56	Myron Fohr	Shaheen	Evelyn Shaheen	Offy	Didn't complete run
58	Frank Armi	Scopa	Joseph P. Scopa	Offy	Didn't complete run
61	Norm Houser	Tom Sarafoff	Tom Sarafoff	Offy¢	Didn't complete run
62	Bill Cantrell	Motor Trends	John F. Koehnle	Wayne Chevy	
63	George Fonder	Ray Brady	Ray T. Brady	Offy	Didn't complete run
64	Frank Armi	Bardahl	Ross Page	Duray*	130.242, too slow
65	Frank Armi	Vulcan Tool	Ralph S. Miller	R. Miller*	
66	Kenny Eaton	Jeanie-Lee	Lee S. Glessner	Offy	Didn't complete run
67	Gordon Reid	Johnson-Herbert	Bill Johnson	Chevy	118.234, too slow
72	Jimmy Bryan	Viking Trailer	Douglas J. Caruthers	Offy	124.176, too slow
75	LeRoy Warriner	Heller	George F. Heller	Offy	Didn't complete run
77	Doc Shanebrook	Elgin Piston Pin	Walter Redmer	Offy	Didn't complete run
78	Ray Knepper	Bardahl of St. Louis	Fred Tomshe	Offy	
79	Bill Cantrell	Fullerton	Hart Fullerton	Offy*	Didn't complete run
82	Bob Scott	Bob Estes Mercury	Bob Estes	4 O. H. C. Merc.	
84		Sampson	Alden Sampson, II	Offy*	Wrecked en route
88	Joel Thorne	Thorne	Joel Thorne	Sparks	
89	Danny Kladis	Trainor Chicago	Tully Trainor	Miller* 4 R	Bkn. rod qualifying

1952

NO.	DRIVER	CAR	ENTRANT	ENGINE	REMARKS
3	Walt Faulkner	Sid Street Motors	Sid Street	Offy	
6	Johnnie Parsons	Grant Piston Ring	G. Grant & J. Bartlett	Ferrari	
10	Paul Russo	Lutes Offy	Francis Bardazon	Offy	
15	Bob Ball	Blakely Oil	John McDaniel	Offy	Wrecked in pract.
19	Danny Kladis	Tuffanelli-Derrico	Charles Pritchard	Offy¢	
23	Carl Forberg	Fadely & Anderson	R. A. Cott	Offy	
25	Walt Faulkner	Automobile Shippers	Eugene A. Casaroll	Offy	Didn't complete run
32	Allen Heath	Engle-Stanko	John T. Stanko	Offy	Wrecked qualif., NW
35	Johnny Mauro	Kennedy Tank	Johnny Mauro	Ferrari	
38	Bob Ball	Howard Keck	Howard Keck	Ferrari	
39	Jud Larson	Iddings Auto Parts	Howard Iddings	Offy	
41	Jackie Holmes	Speed	Speed Partners	Offy*	
44	Art Cross	Bowes Seal Fast	Ray T. Brady	Offy	
47	Bill Taylor	Blue Crown Spark Plug	Charlie Marant	Offy	Didn't complete run
51	Spider Webb	Blue Crown Spark Plug	Slick Racers, Inc.	Offy¢	132.660, too slow
52	Bob Sweikert / Bill Cantrell	Pat Clancy	Pat Clancy	Offy	Didn't complete run / 132.553, too slow
53	Joe Barzda	Calif. Speed Equipment	Joseph J. Barzda	Maserati*	
56	Frank Luptow	Bardahl	Karl Hall	Offy	
58	Buzz Barton	Wales Trucking	M. Pete Wales	Offy	
61	Jimmy Jackson	Automobile Shippers	Eugene A. Casaroll	Offy	133.824, 2nd. alt.
62		Ellen Atomic	Albert Scully	Offy	
63	Dick Frazier	Jeanie-Lee	Lee S. Glessner	Offy	
64	Jimmy Daywalt	Merkler Machine Works	Franklin Merkler	Meyer-Offy*	
66	Mike Nazaruk	John Zink	M. A. Walker	Offy	133.844, 1st. alt.
68	Duke Dinsmore	Vulcan Tool	Ralph S. Miller	R. Miller*	Didn't complete run
69	Bayliss Levrett	Brown Motor Co.	Brown Motor Co.	Offy	
71	Bob Sweikert	Marion Engineering	Milt Marion	Offy	
74	Peter J. Hahn	Helin Flyer	Charles Helin	Offy	
76	Doc Shanebrook	Parks Offy	L. E. Parks	Offy	
79		Gdula	Edward Gdula	Offy	
82	Johnny Fedricks	Cal Connell	Calvin C. Connell	Cadillac	Did not arrive
84	Otis Stine	B. & M.	B. & M. Racing Team	Offy	
88	Geo. Tichenor	Schmidt	Peter Schmidt	Offy	133.427, too slow
92	Chuck Weyant	Pipe Fitters	Martin & Richards	Offy	
96	Gene Force	Brown Motor Co.	Brown Motor Co.	Offy	133.789, too slow
97	Allen Heath	Agajanian	J. C. Agajanian	Studebaker	
99	T. Bettenhausen	Belanger Motors	Murrell Belanger	Offy	Wrecked in qualif.

1953

NO.	DRIVER	CAR	ENTRANT	ENGINE	REMARKS
6	Jim Rathmann	Wynn's Frict. Proofing	Lou Moore	Offy	
10	Henry Banks	Hopkins	Motor Racers, Inc.	Offy	
15	Chet Miller	Novi Governor	Jean Marcenac	Novi*¢	Wrecked in practice
17	Joe Sostillio	Belanger Motors	Murrell Belanger	Chrysler	
24	Cliff Griffith	Bardahl	Ed Walsh	Offy	Wrecked in practice
25	George Connor	Chrysler	Roger G. Wolcott	Chrysler	135.237, 1st. alt.
26	Eddie Johnson	City of Detroit	W. J. Lutes	Offy	
27		Ansted Rotary	Rotary Engineering Corp.	Offy	Did not arrive
28	Pat O'Connor	Slick Racers, Inc.	Slick Racers, Inc.	Offy¢	
31	Len Duncan	Caccia Motors	Ray T. Brady	Offy	133.487, too slow
33	Art Cross	Ray Brady Motor Co.	Ray T. Brady	Offy	
34	Eddie Sachs	Morris	L. D. Morris, M.D.	Offy	
35	Buzz Barton	Parks Motor Co.	L. E. Parks	Offy	
36	Potsy Goacher	Sid Street Motor Co.	Sid Street	Offy	134.620, too slow
39	Bill Taylor	Blue Crown Spark Plug	Charles Marant	Offy	
42	Willard Cantrell	Malloy	Emmett Malloy	Offy	
43	Roy Neuman	Maserati	Robert J. McManus	Maserati*	
44	LeRoy Warriner	Jim Robbins	Jim Robbins	Offy	
45		Ferrari	Howard Keck Co.	Ferrari	Did not arrive
46	John Fedricks	Dunn	Edward Gdula	Offy	
47	Johnny Mauro	Ferrari	Johnny Mauro	Ferrari	Did not arrive
52	Duke Dinsmore	Tom Sarafoff	Tom Sarafoff	Offy	
54		M. A. Walker Electric	M. A. Walker	Offy	Did not arrive
57	Hal Robson	Voelker	Stanley Olszewski	Voelker	
61	Bill Holland	Slick Racers, Inc.	Slick Racers, Inc.	Offy¢	134.439, too slow
63	Danny Oakes	Hopkins	Motor Racers, Inc.	Offy	
64	Pat O'Connor	Engle-Stanko	Rouge Motors, Inc.	Offy	133.571, too slow
65	Allen Heath	Commercial Motor Freight	Karl Hall	Offy	
66	Johnnie Tolan	Chrysler	Roger G. Wolcott	Chrysler	
67	Johnny Kay	Jeanie-Lee	Lee S. Glessner	Offy	
69	Joe Barzda	Calif. Speed & Sport	Joseph J. Barzda	Maserati*	121.918, too slow
71	Jackie Holmes	Merkler Machine Works	Franklin Merkler	Meyer-Offy*	
74	John Fitch / Pat O'Connor	Brown Motor Co.	Brown Motor Co.	Offy	134.363, too slow
75	Wayne Selser	Christy	Arco Corp.	Offy	
76	George Fonder	Leitenberger	George H. Leitenberger	Offy	133.457, too slow
78	Cal Niday	Storey-Ricketts	Storey & Ricketts	Offy	134.927, too slow
79	Frank Armi	Mel-Rae	Mel B. Wiggers	Offy	
81	Len Duncan	Central Excavating	Pete Salemi	Offy	
82	Johnny Roberts	Burns	William P. Burns	Offy	
84	Bill Homeier	Coast Grain	Bob & Danny Weinberg	Offy	
85	Johnnie Tolan	Blakely Oil	Hinkle & McDaniel	Offy	
86	Bill Boyd	Merz Engineering	Merz Engineering, Inc.	Offy	
87	Bill Homeier	Cal Connell	Calvin C. Connell	Cadillac	
89	Spider Webb	Fadely-Anderson	R. A. C. Motor Corp.	Offy	
91	Red Hamilton	Dillon	Clyde R. Dillon	Offy	
93	Al Herman	Traylor Engineering	Samuel W. Traylor, IV	Offy	
95	Jorge Daponte	Wayne	Sacco & Wilson	Wayne Chevy	
96	Jud Larson	Helin	Dr. John A. Hirsch	Offy	
97	Alberto Ascari	Ferrari	Scuderia Ferrari	Ferrari*	Did not arrive

*Supercharged   ¢Front drive   4Four wheel drive   RRear Engine

1949   Bill Cantrell

1949   Pat Flaherty

1949   Tony Bettenhausen

1949   Mike Salay

1949   Bill Taylor

1949   Kenny Eaton

1949   Doc Williams

1949   Lindley Bothwell

1950   Bill Vukovich

1950   Chet Miller

1950   Bill Cantrell

1950   Joe James

1950   Bob Sweikert

1950   Cliff Griffith

1950   Joe James

1950   Al Miller

1951   Paul Russo

1951   Jackie Holmes

1951   Manuel Ayulo

1951   Bob Sweikert

1951   Bayliss Levrett

1951   Jimmy Daywalt

1951   Joe Barzda

1951   Norm Houser

NO.	DRIVER	CAR	ENTRANT	ENGINE	REMARKS

1954

NO.	DRIVER	CAR	ENTRANT	ENGINE	REMARKS
3	Marshall Teague	Fullerton	Hart Fullerton	Offy	137.552, too slow
5	Paul Russo	Ansted Rotary	Hoosier Race Team, Inc.	Offy	
6	Art Cross	Springfield Welding	Bessie Lee Paoli	Offy	137.362, too slow
8	Duke Nalon	Novi	Novi Racing Corp., Inc.	Novi*¢	136.395, too slow
18	Bob Scott	Brady	Ray T. Brady	Offy	Didn't complete run
21	Bob Scott	Travelon Trailer	Ernest L. Ruiz	Offy	137.504, too slow
22	Cliff Griffith / Geo. Tichenor	Tom Saraloff	Tom Saraloff	Offy	Didn't complete run / Didn't complete run
23	Jerry Hoyt	Sumar	Chapman S. Root	Offy	
26	Henry Banks	Hopkins	Motor Racers, Inc.	Offy	
36	Al Herman / George Fonder	Ed Stone	Edgar H. Stone	Offy	/ Didn't complete run
37	Eddie Russo	Federal Eng. Detroit	Federal Auto. Assoc.	Offy	Didn't complete run
39	Pat Flaherty	Shouse Motors & Herbert	James F. Shouse	Chrysler	
41	Frank Mundy	McDaniel	John L. McDaniel	Offy	
44	Walt Faulkner	Schmidt	Peter Schmidt	Offy	137.065, too slow
46		Gdula	Edward Gdula	Offy	Did not arrive
47	Danny Oakes	Ferrari	Marian A. Chinetti	Ferrari	
48		Sumar	Chapman S. Root	Offy	
49	Danny Oakes	Micro-Nut	John C. Balch	Offy	137.237, too slow
52	Chuck Weyant	Parks Motor Co.	L. E. Parks	Offy	
53	Jim Davies	Pat Clancy	Pat Clancy	Offy	137.583, 2nd. alt.
54	Eddie Sachs	Marion Engineering	Milt Marion	Offy	
59	Jim Rathmann	Elgin Piston Pin	Elgin Piston Pin Co.	Offy	137.132, too slow
62	Duke Dinsmore	Comm'l. Motor Freight	Karl Hall	Offy	137.096, too slow
66	Bob Christie	Christie	Bob Christie	Offy	Didn't complete run
67	Potsy Goacher / Duke Dinsmore	D-A Lubricant	3-L Racing Team	Offy	Wrecked in practice / Didn't complete run
68	Ed Elisian	Wales Trucking	M. Pete Wales	Offy	136.581, too slow
69	Johnnie Tolan	W. P. T.	Hoosier Racing Team	Offy*	
71	Frank Armi	Martin Bros.	T. W. & W. T. Martin	Offy	
76		Leitenberger	George H. Leitenberger	Offy	
81		Central Excavating	Pete Salemi	Offy	
83	Eddie Johnson	McNamara	Lee Elkins	Offy	137.599, 1st. alt.
89	Pat Flaherty	Dunn Engineering	Harry Dunn	Offy	Didn't complete run
93	Billy DeVore	Youngstown White Truck	Roy McKay	Offy	
97	Walt Faulkner	Belanger	Murrell Belanger, Sr.	Offy*	

1955

NO.	DRIVER	CAR	ENTRANT	ENGINE	REMARKS
7	Bob Christie	Dean Van Lines	A. E. Dean	Dodge	Wrecked, warm-up
9	Spider Webb	Walsh	Ed Walsh	Offy	Didn't complete run
18	Troy Ruttman	Novi Air Conditioner	Novi Racing Corp.	Novi*¢	Didn't complete run
21	Paul Russo	Wolcott	Roger G. Wolcott	Offy*	Wrecked in practice
24	Len Duncan	Ray Brady	Ray T. Brady	Offy	133.245, 1st. alt.
25	Johnny Boyd	Lutes Truck Parts	Francis Bardazon Co.	Offy	
28	Gene Hartley	Comm'l. Motor Freight	Karl Hall	Offy	Didn't complete run
32	Jiggs Peters	Glessner	Lee S. Glessner	Offy	
36	Tony Bonadies	Donaldson	Duke Donaldson	Offy	
47		Ferrari-Bardahl	G. Geddes	Ferrari	Did not arrive
51		Sumar	Chapman S. Root	Offy	
55		Thorne Engineering	Thorne Eng. Corp.	Sparks	Car not built
61	Russ Klar	Brady	Ray T. Brady	Offy	131.301, too slow
64	LeRoy Warriner	Ansted Rotary	Rotary Engineering Corp.	Offy	
69	Ernie McCoy	LaVilla	Mrs. Henry S. Lammers	Offy	133.038, 2nd. alt.
72	Bill Homeier	Travelon Trailer	Ernest L. Ruiz	Offy	
73	Len Duncan	McNamara	Kalamazoo Sports, Inc.	Offy	Wrecked in practice
74	Elmer George	Walmotor	Walmotors, Inc.	Offy	Wrecked in practice
76	Johnny Kay	Leitenberger	F. L. Leitenberger	Offy	132.193, too slow
78	George Tichenor	Hopkins	Motor Racers, Inc.	Offy	
82		Planacircle	Walter F. Strader	Strader	Car not finished
88	Manual Ayulo	Schmidt	Peter Schmidt	Offy	Wrecked in practice
91		Walsh	Ed Walsh	Offy	Did not arrive
93	Danny Kladis	Roy McKay	Roy McKay	Offy	Didn't complete run

1956

NO.	DRIVER	CAR	ENTRANT	ENGINE	REMARKS
3	Marshall Teague	Dean Van Lines	Dean Van Lines	Offy	
9	Nino Farina	Bardahl-Ferrari	Bardahl Lubricants	Ferrari	
22	Dempsey Wilson	Martin Bros.	W. Thayer Martin	Offy	Didn't complete run
25	Tony Bonadies	Duke Donaldson	Duke Donaldson	Offy	
31	Jim Davies	Novi Air Conditioner	Novi Racing Corp., Inc.	Novi*	
32			Walter J. Travers		Did not arrive
33	Eddie Russo	Belond Miracle Power	So. Calif. Muffler Corp.	Offy	
35	Johnny Kay	Pete Wales	M. Pete Wales	Offy	
44		Schmidt	Peter Schmidt	Offy	
46	Shorty Templeman	Glessner	Lee S. Glessner	Offy	
47	Marshall Teague	Sumar	Chapman S. Root	Offy	
51	Len Duncan	Ray Brady	Ray T. Brady	Offy	
58	Eddie Sachs	Ray Brady	Ray T. Brady	Offy	137.373, 1st. alt.
62	Len Sutton	Wolcott	Roger G. Wolcott	Offy	
63		D-A Lubricant	Racing Associates	Offy	
74	Mike Magill	Chesty Foods	Henry S. Lammers	Offy	
75	Marvin Pifer	Comm'l. Motor Freight	Karl Hall	Offy	Wrecked in practice
77	Jim McWithey	Dayton Steel Foundry	George Walther, Jr.	Offy	
78		Hopkins	Motor Racers, Inc.	Offy	
79	Dempsey Wilson	Parks	L. E. Parks	Offy	
84	Bill Cheesbourg	H. B. T.	H. B. T. Co.	Offy	
85	Gig Stephens	Slick Airway	Otto & Adolph K. Stoye	Offy	
87	Dick Reese	McDonald	Cecil McDonald	Offy	
91	Johnny Baldwin	Bardahl-Ferrari	Mrs. Marian Chinetti	Ferrari	
92		McKay's Bulldog	Roy McKay	Offy	
93	LeRoy Warriner	McKay's Bulldog	Roy McKay	Offy	

1957

NO.	DRIVER	CAR	ENTRANT	ENGINE	REMARKS
4	George Amick	Federal Engineering	Federal Auto. Assoc.	Offy	139.443, 2nd. alt.
15	Tony Bonadies	Ray Brady	Ray T. Brady	Offy	
25	Jud Larson	John Zink	John Zink	Offy	139.061, too slow
32	Jim Davies	Trio Brass Foundry	Carl L. Anderson	Offy	138.462, too slow
33	Billy Garrett	Federal Engineering	Federal Auto. Assoc.	Offy	139.546, 1st. alt.
34	Jim McWithey	Federal Engineering	Federal Auto Assoc.	Offy	Wrk'd., warm-up, NE
35	Chuck Weyant	Jim Robbins	Jim Robbins	Offy	139.104, too slow
42	Dempsey Wilson	Martin Bros.	T. W. & W. T. Martin	Offy	139.109, too slow
45	Bill Cheesbourg	Las Vegas Club	Fred Gerhardt	Offy	138.878, too slow
49	Ray Crawford	Meguiar Mirror Glaze	Ray Crawford	Offy	139.093, too slow
56		Ed Walsh	Ed Walsh	Offy	
58	Andy Furci	Ray Brady	Ray T. Brady	Offy	Didn't complete run
59	Bud Clemons	Chiropractic	Bob Sorenson	Offy	
62	Keith Andrews	Farina	Giuseppe Farina	Offy	Wrecked in practice
64	Gene Force	Shannon Bros.	R. B. & E. W. Shannon	Offy	Didn't complete run
67	Don Edmunds	Braund Birch	Douglas J. Caruthers	Offy	136.400, too slow
71	John Fedricks	Gdula	Edward I. Gdula	Offy	
72	Danny Kladis	Morgan Engineering	Marguerite Morgan	Maserati*	124.412, too slow
81	Tony Bonadies	Central Excavating	Pete Salemi	Offy	Didn't complete run
84	Danny Kladis	Safety Auto Glass	Edward Shreve	Jaguar	
98	Johnnie Parsons	Agajanian	J. C. Agajanian	Offy	138.975, too slow

1958

NO.	DRIVER	CAR	ENTRANT	ENGINE	REMARKS
3		Hopkins	Lindsey Hopkins	Offy	
10	Rex Easton	Hoover Motor Express	John R. Wills	Offy	140.972, too slow
17	Jack Ensley / Art Bisch	Ansted Rotary	Jack R. Ensley	Offy	/ 141.376, too slow
18	Marshall Teague	Sumar	Chapman S. Root	Offy	Didn't complete run
24	Gene Hartley	Hoyt Machine	F. W. & R. F. Sommer	Offy	142.231, 1st. alt.
28	Elmer George	Ansted Rotary	William B. Ansted, Jr.	Offy	
48	Jerry Unser	Sumar	Chapman S. Root	Offy	
49	Ray Crawford	Meguiar Mirror Glaze	Ray Crawford	Offy	141.688, too slow
51	Jerry Unser	Duncan	H. Duncan & T. Capanna	De Soto	
55	Eddie Russo	Scalavi & Amos	Fred Sclavi	Offy	
56	Fred Agabashian	City of Memphis	Pat Clancy	Offy	142.135, 2nd. alt.
59	Van Johnson	Ray Brady Chiropractic	Ray T. Brady	Offy	Wrecked in practice
62	Joe Giba	Carl Anderson	Carl L. Anderson	Offy	
66	Jim McWithey	Federal Engineering	Federal Auto. Assoc.	Offy	
69	Jimmy Daywalt	Federal Engineering	Federal Auto. Assoc.	Offy	
71	Dempsey Wilson	Hall-Mar	W. Thayer Martin	Offy	142.029, too slow
72	Rex Easton	Wyandotte Tool	John Marco Pusilo	Offy	

*Supercharged ¢Front Drive

1951   Frank Armi

1951   Gordon Reid

1951   Jimmy Bryan

1952   Johnnie Parsons

1952   Johnny Mauro

1952   Bill Taylor

1952   Spider Webb

1952   Bob Sweikert

1952   Jimmy Jackson

1952   Jud Larson

1952   Peter J. Hahn

1952   Gene Force

1952   Tony Bettenhausen

1953   Jim Rathmann

1953   Joe Sostillio

1953   Cliff Griffith

1953   George Connor

1953   Eddie Johnson

1953   Len Duncan

1953   Potsy Goacher

1953   Roy Neuman

1953   Leroy Warriner

1953   Bill Holland

1953   Danny Oakes

NO.	DRIVER	CAR	ENTRANT	ENGINE	REMARKS
			1958 (Cont.)		
74	Bill Homeier	Kurtis-Kraft	Leonard G. Smith	Offy	
75	Al Herman / Fred Agabashian	D-A Lubricant	Racing Associates	Offy	141.011, too slow
82	Len Sutton / Jimmy Daywalt	Central Excavating	Pete Salemi	Offy	Didn't complete run
93	Bob Cortner	McKay Bulldog	Roy McKay	Offy	
95	LeRoy Warriner / Bill Homeier	Safety Auto Glass	James Edward Shreve	Offy	Didn't complete run
98	Troy Ruttman	Agajanian	J. C. Agajanian	Offy	
			1959		
1	T. Bettenhausen	Ansted Rotary	Ansted Rotary Corp. sold after accident to…	Offy	Wrecked in practice
	Eddie Russo	Turner	Harry Turner	Offy	
12	Ralph Liguori	El Dorado Italia	Scuderia El Dorado	Maserati	136.395, too slow
17	Johnny Kay	Safety Auto Glass	Shreve, Perkins, Griesemer	Offy	
21	Earl Motter	Dean Van Lines	Dean Van Lines, Racing	Offy	Wrecked in practice
25	Bill Cheesbourg	Hardwood Door	Ashley Wright	Offy	
34	Dempsey Wilson	Novi Diesel	Novi Racing Corp., Inc.	Novi*	Didn't complete run
35		City of Daytona	Smokey Yunick	Offy	
38	Paul Russo	Novi Diesel	Novi Racing Corp., Inc.	Novi*	
39	Rex Easton	Massaglia Hotels	Hart Fullerton	Offy	139.438, 1st. alt.
41	Ralph Liguori / Jim Davies	Sumar	Chapman S. Root	Offy	Didn't complete run
42	Bill Homeier	Go-Kart	Ollie Prather	Offy	Threw rod qualifying
43	Johnnie Tolan	Chapman	H. A. Chapman	Offy	Didn't complete run
51	Bob Cortner	Cornis Engineering	T. P. Cornis	Offy	Wrecked in practice
52	Jud Larson	Leader Card Duo	Leader Cards, Inc.	Offy	
54	Don Edmunds	Bill Forbes	Bill Forbes	Offy	
55	Jim Packard / Gene Force	Sclavi & Amos	Sclavi, Inc.	Offy	Wrecked in practice / Didn't complete run
57	Jerry Unser	Helse	H. H. Johnson	Offy	Wrecked in practice
62	Bill Homeier	Rusco Battery Cable	Osborn & Young	Offy	130.928, too slow
69	Shorty Templeman	Frank Arciero	Frank Arciero	Maserati	Didn't complete run
72	Chuck Arnold	Speed Enterprise	Leonard G. Smith	Offy	
76	Shorty Templeman	Braund Plywood	Braund Plywood Co.	Offy	139.023, 2nd. alt.
78	Bob Schroeder / Gene Force / Eddie Russo	Midwest Manufacturing	Carl Lee Gehlhausen	Offy	Didn't complete run / Didn't complete run
82	Chuck Rodee / Dempsey Wilson	Central Excavating	Pete Salemi	Offy	Didn't complete run
84		Zink Heater	John Zink Co.	Offy	
91	John Moorhouse	Binter	Joe Binter	Offy	Wrecked in practice
92	Jack Ensley	McKay	Roy McKay	Offy	
93	Eddie Russo	McKay	Roy McKay	Offy	
98	Chuck Daigh / Eddie Russo	Agajanian	J. C. Agajanian	Offy	Didn't complete run
			1960		
19		Hoover Motor Express	Hoover Motor Ex., Inc.	Offy	
21	Chuck Arnold	Gerhardt	Fred Gerhardt	Offy	Didn't complete run
24	Johnnie Tolan	Greenman-Casale	Lysle Greenman	Offy	
25	Jack Turner	Kelso Auto Dynamics	Kelso Auto Dynamics	Offy	Didn't complete run
29	Cliff Griffith	North Electric	William Tucker, Inc.	Offy	
31	Cotton Farmer	Bardahl	Fred Gerhardt	Offy	
34	Jim Davies	Turner	Harry Turner	Offy	
35	Al Keller	McKay	Roy McKay	Offy	138.264, too slow
36	Duke Dinsmore	McKay	Roy McKay	Offy	
41	Ebb Rose	Ellen Zink	Ebb Rose	Offy	138.153, too slow
42		Dean Van Lines	Dean Van Lines, Racing	Offy	
43	Chuck Hulse	Chapman	H. A. Chapman	Offy	Wrecked in practice
45	Bill Cheesbourg	Braund Plywood	Braund Plywood, Inc.	Offy	
47	Dempsey Wilson	Novi	Novi Racing Corp., Inc.	Novi*	
49	Paul Russo	Novi	Novi Racing Corp., Inc.	Novi*	
52	Jack Rounds	Fullerton	Hart Fullerton	Offy	Wrecked in practice
54		San Diego Steel Pdts.	Charles M. Chenowth	Chevy	
57	Al Keller	Helse	H. H. Johnson	Chevy	
58	Lee Drollinger	Brady	Ray T. Brady	Offy	Wrecked in practice
61	Bob Cleberg	Detroiter Mobil Homes	Braund Plywood, Inc.	Offy	Wrecked in practice

NO.	DRIVER	CAR	ENTRANT	ENGINE	REMARKS
62	Eddie Russo	Bob Jones	Myron E. Osborn	Offy	
67		Dowgard	Lindsey Hopkins	Offy	Did not arrive
68		Chapman Park	Ken-Paul, Inc.	Offy	Did not arrive
69	Chuck Hulse	Sorenson	Bob Sorenson	Offy	137.174, too slow
71	Jim Packard	Sclavi & Amos	Fred Sclavi	Offy	Didn't complete run
74		Bill Forbes	William P. Forbes	Offy	
77	Mike Magill	Dayton Steel Foundry	George Walther, Jr.	Offy	
79	Russ Congdon	Hall-Mar	Karl Hall	Offy	Didn't complete run
87	Chuck Weyant	Wheeler-Foutch	LeRoy E. Foutch, Jr.	Offy	
88	Chuck Weyant	Hardwood Door	Ashley I. Wright	Offy	
89	Chuck Rodee	Dunn Engineering	Harry Dunn	Offy	140.100, 1st. alt.
92	Norm Hall	Thompson Industries	Indianapolis Racing, Inc.	Offy	
95	Duke Dinsmore	Safety Auto Glass	Safety Auto Glass Co.	Offy	
			1961		
6	Bob Cleberg	Bell Lines Trucking	Fred Sclavi	Offy	143.672, 2nd. alt.
9	Lloyd Ruby	Kelso Auto Dynamics	Kelso Auto Dynamics	Offy	Didn't complete run
21	Paul Russo	Bryant Heating & Cooling	Your Bryant Dealer	Offy	143.983, 1st. alt.
23	Cotton Farmer / Bob Veith	Bardahl	Fred Gerhardt	Offy	Didn't complete run / 143.581, too slow
24	T. Bettenhausen	Stearly Motor Freight	Douglas Stearly	Offy	Wrecked in practice
25	Bob Veith	Shaler Rislone	Bignotti-Bowes Racing	Offy	143.062, too slow
27	Don Freeland	Chapman	H. A. Chapman	Offy	Didn't complete run
29	Jim McWithey	Fullerton	Hart Fullerton	Offy	Didn't complete run
36	Donald Schisler	Jerry Alderman Ford	Indiana Engine Exchange	Offy	Did not arrive
37	Chuck Hulse	Vatis Enterprises	Vatis Enterprises, Inc.	Offy	Wrecked in practice
43	Ronnie Duman	Ray Brady	Ray T. Brady	Offy	Didn't complete run
44	Jack Rounds / Bob Veith	Schmidt	Peter J. Schidt	Offy	Threw rod, spun SW / Didn't complete run
47	Dan Jones / Don Freeland	Joe Hunt Magneto	Joseph B. Hunt	Offy	Wrecked in practice / 141.476, too slow
53		Cooper-Climax	Cooper Car Co., Ltd.	Climax R	Did not arrive
54	Bud Tingelstad	Dean Van Lines	Dean Van Lines, Racing	Offy	Didn't complete run
59		Sarkes Tarzian	Robert Peterson	Chevy	
61	Duane Carter	Roy	Leonard A. Roy	Offy	
62	Chuck Arnold	Denver-Chicago Trucking	Myron E. Osborn	Offy	Didn't complete run
67		Rathmann Xterminator	Ken-Paul, Inc.	Offy	Did not arrive
68		Agajanian Willard Batt.	J. C. Agajanian	Offy	
69	Russ Congdon	Eelco Custom Shift	Sorenson & Childers	Offy	Didn't complete run
74		Bill Forbes Racing	William P. Forbes	Offy	
75	Dick Rathmann	Paxton Products	Paxton Products	Novi*	
77	Leon Clum	Dayton Steel Foundry	George Walther, Jr.	Offy	Didn't complete run
78		John Zink Trackburner	John Zink Co.	Offy R	
79	Bert Brooks	Hall-Mar	Karl Hall	Offy	143.415, too slow
82	Mike Magill	San Diego Steel Pdts.	Charles M. Chenowth	Chevy	Didn't complete run
84	Jack Ensley	Ansted-Thompson	Ansted-Thompson Racing	Offy	
85	Bob Veith / Don Davis	Federal Engineering	Federal Auto. Associates	Offy	Didn't complete run / Didn't complete run
87	Jack Rounds	M. P. C.	Harry Beck	Offy	
88	Chuck Weyant / Norm Hall	Drewry's	Ashley Wright	Offy	Didn't complete run / Didn't complete run
89	Chuck Rodee	Dunn Engineering	Harry Dunn	Offy	Didn't complete run
91	Vern Harriman	Honeymoon Express	Honeymoon Express, Inc.	Offy	Did not arrive
92	Norm Hall	Concannon Car Co. Flying	Joseph J. Concannon	Offy	141.861, too slow
94	Ray Crawford / Duane Carter	McCullough	Ray Crawford	Offy	Didn't complete run
95	Bill Randall	Safety Auto Glass	Perkins Griesemer Nicholas	Offy	Wrecked in practice
			1962		
6	Leon Clum	Sclavi	Sclavi, Inc.	Offy	Didn't complete run
10	Jim Rathmann	Simoniz	Smokey Yunick	Offy	
16	Chuck Stevenson	Tropicana	Novi	Novi*	
22	Bruce Jacobi	Frohde Mobil Homes	Joe Langley	Offy	144.939, too slow
23	Leon Clum / Chuck Arnold	Turtle Drilling	Turtle Drilling Co.	Offy	Didn't complete run / 145.366, too slow
24		Lencki	Joe Lencki	Lencki	
25	Norm Hall	Dean-Autolite	Dean Van Lines, Racing	Offy	Wrecked in practice
28	Ronnie Duman	Stearly Motor Freight	United Rentals, Inc.	Offy	145.908, 2nd. alt.

*Supercharged   ¢Front drive

1953   Pat O'Connor

1953   Joe Barzda

1953   Johnnie Tolan

1953   Al Herman

1954   Marshall Teague

1954   Duke Nalon

1954   Bob Scott

1954   Al Herman

1954   Walt Faulkner

1954   Danny Oakes

1954   Jim Davies

1954   Jim Rathmann

1954   Bob Christie

1954   Duke Dinsmore

1954   Ed Elisian

1954   Eddie Johnson

1954   Billy DeVore

1955   Troy Ruttman

1955   Len Duncan

1955   Jiggs Peters

1955   Russ Klar

1955   Ernie McCoy

1955   Bill Homeier

1955   Roy Neuman

NO.	DRIVER	CAR	ENTRANT	ENGINE	REMARKS

1962 (Cont.)

NO.	DRIVER	CAR	ENTRANT	ENGINE	REMARKS
31	Dempsey Wilson	Lysle Greenman	Lysle Greenman	Offy	146.086, 1st. alt.
33	Porky Rachwitz	Kimberly	James H. Kimberly	Buick R	
35	Chuck Daigh / Bill Cheesbourg	Harvey Aluminum	Mickey Thompson	Buick R	Didn't complete run
36	Don Freeland	Fullerton	Hart Fullerton	Offy	145.366, too slow
37	Ed Kostenuk / Chuck Arnold	Leader Card 500 Road.	Leader Cards, Inc.	Offy	Didn't complete run
41	Norm Hall	Bill Forbes Racing	William P. Forbes	Offy	Wrecked qualif., SW
43	Bob Mathouser	Ray Brady	Ray T. Brady	Offy	Wrecked in practice
46	Jimmy Daywalt / Mike McGreevy / Chuck Arnold	Goff Bros. Drumstick	Maurice F. Goff	Offy	Wrecked in practice / Didn't complete run / Didn't complete run
47	Chuck Arnold	Joe Hunt Magneto	Joseph B. Hunt	Offy	
52	Dan Gurney	John Zink Trackburner	John Zink	Gas Turbine R	
55	Roy Graham	Metzloff Jetfire	James E. Metzloff	Offy	
58	Tommy Copp	Sorenson	Bob Sorenson	Offy	
59	Bill Cheesbourg	Tropicana	Novi	Novi*	
61	Gig Stephens	Automatic Radio	Harry Turner	Offy	
62	Paul Russo	Denver-Chicago Trucking	Myron E. Osborn	Offy	
64	Al Miller	Federal Engineering	Federal Auto. Associates	Offy	Didn't complete run
65	Jim Hemmings	Kurtis-Kraft	Roy McKay	Offy	Didn't complete run
68	Ralph Liguori / Johnny Coy	White Spot	Joseph P. Scopa	Offy	Didn't complete run
69	Herb Hill	Grizzly Brake	Robert Peterson	Chevy	
72	Duane Carter	John Zink Trackburner	John Zink Co.	Offy	145.867, too slow
75		Tropicana	Novi	Novi*	
77	Chuck Arnold	Dayton Steel Foundry	George Walther, Jr.	Offy	
78	Jack Fairman	De Villiers	Pierre De Villiers	Alta	
82		Concannon Choice Car	Concannon Choice Car	Offy	
84	Cliff Griffith	Thompson Rocket	Ansted-Thompson Racing	Offy	
85		Hopkins	Lindsey Hopkins	Offy	
86	Ebb Rose	J. H. Rose Truck Line	Herb Porter	Offy	Wrecked in practice
89	Jack Conley	Chapman Rocker Panel	Jack D. Conley	Offy	
92	Johnny Coy	WRD	William R. Deakin	Offy	
94	Jim Hemmings	Speed Enterprise	Leonard G. Smith	Offy	
95	Jack Ensley	Safety Auto Glass	R. Perkins & L. Griesemer	Offy	
97		Agajanian Willard Bat.	J. C. Agajanian	Offy	
99	Jim Hurtubise	Demler	Norm Demler, Inc.	Offy	Wrecked qualif., SS
72	Cliff Griffith	Lencki	Joe Lencki	Lencki	Didn't complete run
73	Junior Johnson	Amer. Rubber & Plastics	John Chalik	Offy	
77	Chuck Engle	Dayton All Star	George Walther, Jr.	Offy	Wrecked in practice
81	Masten Gregory	Harvey Aluminum	Mickey Thompson	Chevy R	147.517, too slow
82	Bill Krause / Masten Gregory	Harvey Titanium	Mickey Thompson	Chevy R	Wrecked in practice / Didn't complete run
85	Bill Cheesbourg	Thompson Harcraft	Mickey Thompson	Chevy R	
89	Jack Conley	J. E. Engineering	Jack Conley	Offy	
91	Dan Gurney	Lotus powered by Ford	Lotus Indapls. Project	Ford R	Wrecked qualifying
94		Agajanian Willard Bat.	J. C. Agajanian	Offy	

1963

NO.	DRIVER	CAR	ENTRANT	ENGINE	REMARKS
3	Bob Mathouser / Ralph Liguori	Schulz Refueling Equip.	C. O. "Ollie" Prather	Offy	147.620, 2nd. alt.
7	Len Sutton	Leader Card 500 Road.	Leader Cards, Inc.	Offy	147.372, too slow
12	Curtis Turner	Fiberglas	Smokey Yunick	Offy	Wrecked in practice
15	Ronnie Duman / Bob Mathouser	Federal Engineering	Federal Auto. Associates	Offy	Wrecked in practice / Didn't complete run
18	Bud Tingelstad	Auto-Power	Charles M. Chenowth	Chevy	
19		Dean Van Lines	Dean Van Lines Racing	Offy	
24	Colby Scroggin	Amer. Rubber & Plastics	John Chalik	Offy	
25	Jimmy Daywalt / Chuck Rodee	Wynn's Friction Proof.	Joseph B. Hunt	Offy	Didn't complete run / Didn't complete run
27	John Rutherford / Bill Cheesbourg	U.S. Equipment	George Walther, Jr.	Offy	Didn't complete run
28	Bob Christie	Stearly Motor Freight	United Rentals, Inc.	Offy	
31	Bob Harkey	Amer. Rubber & Plastics	John Chalik	Offy	Wrecked in practice
38	Chuck Rodee	Konstant Hot	Bruce Homeyer	Offy	147.197, too slow
41	Dempsey Wilson	Lysle Greenman	Lysle Greenman	Offy	
43	Gig Stephens	Hook Lobster Co.	Edgar H. Stone	Offy	
44	Jack Turner	Precision Piston Ring	D. V. S. Inc.	Offy	Wrecked in practice
46	Ebb Rose	Racing Associates	Racing Associates	Offy	147.293, too slow
47	Ray Crawford / Len Sutton	Crawford	Ray Crawford	Offy	Didn't complete run / 147.620, 1st. alt.
48	Pedro Rodriguez	B. M. C. Aston-Martin	Kjell H. Qvale	Aston-Martin R	146.687, too slow
53	Paul Russo	Spirit of St. Louis	Walter Weir, Jr.	Offy	
55	Norm Hall	Demler	Norm Demler, Inc.	Offy	
61	Porky Rachwitz / Norm Hall	Federal Engineering	Federal Auto. Assoc.	Offy	Didn't complete run
62	Don Freeland	White Spot	Myron E. Osborn	Offy	Didn't complete run
63	Jim Davies	Kimberly	James H. Kimberly	Buick R	
64	Porky Rachwitz	Kimberly	James H. Kimberly	Buick R	

1964

NO.	DRIVER	CAR	ENTRANT	ENGINE	REMARKS
7	Chuck Rodee	Dean Van Lines	Dean Van Lines Racing	Offy	
8	Dempsey Wilson	Vita Fresh Orange Juice	Gordon Van Liew	Offy R	Wrecked qualifying
10	John Rutherford	Racing Associates	Racing Associates	Offy R	
17	Duane Carter	Hopkins	Lindsey Hopkins	Offy	
21	Elmer George / Paul Russo	Sarkes-Tarzian / Kemerly Chevy & Olds	Mari George sold to... / Richard Kemerly	Offy	Didn't complete run / 148.644, 1st. alt.
24	Dempsey Wilson	New England Speed Equip.	Edger H. Stone	Offy	
33	Bob Christie	Robbins Auto-Crat S. B.	J. M. Robbins	Offy	147.583, too slow
35	Cliff Griffith	Central Excavating	Pete Salemi	Offy	
36		Lotus Ford	Team Lotus Ltd.	Ford R	
37	Don Horvath	Dean Van Lines	Ed Kostenuk	Offy	
38	Ralph Liguori	Ollie Prather	C. O. Prather	Offy	
45	Jerry Grant	Bardahl	Fred Gerhardt	Offy R	
47	Bobby Johns	Hurst Floor Shift	S-C Corporation	Offy R	Wrecked qualifying
48	Pedro Rodriquez	MG Liquid Suspension	Kjell H. Qvale	Offy R	Wrecked in practice
55		Zink-Urschel Trackburner	Zink, Urschel, Slick, Inc.	Offy R	
61		Federal Engineering	Federal Auto Associates	Offy	
63	Gig Stephens	Hall-Fran Trucking	Frank Curtis	Offy	
65	Dee Jones	Travelon Trailer	Ernest L. Ruiz	Offy	Didn't complete run
67		Morcroft & Taylor	G. Morcroft & R. Taylor	Offy R	Did not arrive
71	Chuck Arnold	M. R. C.	M. R. C. Racing Team	Chevy R	Didn't complete run
75	Duane Carter	D. V. S.	D. V. S., Inc.	Offy R	
81	Chuck Rodee	Joe Hunt Magneto	Joseph B. Hunt	Offy	146.466, too slow
82	Masten Gregory	Thompson Sears Allstate	Mickey Thompson	Ford R	148.038 2nd. alt.
85	Jud Larson	Kaiser Aluminum	Leader Cards, Inc.	Offy	147.432, too slow
87	Chuck Rodee	Amer. Rubber & Plastic	John Chalik	Offy	
93	Al Miller	Gerhardt & DeOrian	Fred Gerhardt	Offy	147.227, too slow
94		Delta Int'l. Movers	Dean Van Lines Racing	Offy	
97	Parnelli Jones	Agajanian Bowes Seal Fast	J. C. Agajanian	Offy R	

1965

NO.	DRIVER	CAR	ENTRANT	ENGINE	REMARKS
2	Rodger Ward	Moog-St. Louis	Leader Cards, Inc.	Ford R	153.623, 1st. alt.
3		American Eagle Racing	David R. McManus	Ford	Did not arrive
6	Bobby Unser	STP Oil Treatment	STP Division Studebaker	Novi* 4	Wrecked in practice
8	Norm Hall	Pope-Hall	Pope-Hall Enterprises	Offy	153.407, too slow
10	Bob Harkey	Federal Engineering	Federal Auto. Associates	Offy R	
15	Jud Larson	Wynn	Leader Cards, Inc.	Offy R	Wrecked in practice
21	Paul Russo / Bob Christie	Kemerly Chevy & Olds	Richard D. Kemerly	Offy	153.472, too slow
27	Mel Kenyon	Federal Engineering	Federal Auto. Associates.	Offy	153.597, 2nd. alt.
28		All American Racers	All American Racers, Inc.	Ford R	Did not arrive
31		Wally Weir's Mobiloil	Walter Weir, Jr.	Offy	Did not arrive
33	Carl Williams	Dayton Steel Wheel	George Walther, Jr.	Offy	Didn't complete run
34	Bob Hurt	Jim Robbins	J. M. Robbins	Offy	
35		Hopkins	Lindsey Hopkins	Ford R	
36	Paul Goldsmith	Jack Adams Aircraft	Jack Adams	Offy R	Withdrawn
44	Dempsey Wilson	Vita-Fresh Orange Juice	Gordon Van Liew	Offy R	Wrecked in practice
46		Sheraton-Thompson	Ansted-Thompson, Inc.	Offy	
56	Jim Hurtubise	Tombstone Life	D.V.S., Inc.	Ford R	Wrecked in practice
62	Bill Cheesbourg	Wilbur Clark	Myron E. Osborn	Offy R	
63	Al Unser	Arciero Bros.	Frank Arciero	Maserati R	
64		Dean Van Lines	Auto Technics, Inc.	Offy	
67	Bob Wente / Art Malone	G. C. Murphy Stores	Gilbert E. Morcroft	Offy R	Didn't complete run
68		G. C. Murphy Stores	Gilbert E. Morcroft	Offy	Did not arrive

*Supercharged   4Four wheel drive   RRear Engine

1956 Giuseppe Farina

1956 Tony Bonadies

1956 Eddie Russo

1956 Bill Boyd

1956 Johnny Kay

1956 Shorty Templeman

1956 Eddie Sachs

1956 Dickie Reese

1957 George Amick

1957 Jud Larson

1957 Billy Garrett

1957 Chuck Weyant

1957 Bud Clemons

1957 Dempsey Wilson

1957 Bill Cheesbourg

1957 Don Edmunds

1957 Danny Kladis

1957 Johnnie Parsons

1958 Marshall Teague

1958 Gene Hartley

1958 Jerry Unser

1958 Jim McWithey

1958 Dempsey Wilson

1958 Rex Easton

NO.	DRIVER	CAR	ENTRANT	ENGINE	REMARKS
			1965 (Cont.)		
69	Gig Stephens	New Boston	Frank Curtis	Offy	
75		Jerry Alderman Ford	Jerry Alderman Ford Sales	Ford R	
77	Bob Mathouser	Dayton Disc Brake	George Walther, Jr.	Offy	
79	Ebb Rose	Racing Associates	Racing Associates	Offy R	Wrecked in practice
84		Lotus powered by Ford	Team Lotus (Overseas)	Ford R	
86	Ebb Rose	Racing Associates	Racing Associates	Offy	
	Bobby Grim				153.309, too slow
87	Bob Mathouser	M/T Challenger Wheel	Mickey Thompson	Chevy¢	Threw rod qualifying
91		Scopa	Joseph P. Scopa	Chevy R	
93	Skip Hudson	Harrison	J. Frank Harrison	Chevy R	
95	Bobby Grim	Leader Card	Leader Cards, Inc.	Ford	
96	Lee Roy Yarbrough	Harrison	J. Frank Harrison	Chevy R	
	Al Unser				Didn't complete run
97		Agajanian-Hurst	J. C. Agajanian	Ford R	
99	Ralph Liguori	Demler	Norm Demler, Inc.	Offy	Wrecked in practice
			1966		
5	Gordon Johncock	Weinberger Homes	W. & W. Enterprises	Ford R	
7	Chuck Stevenson	Vita-Fresh Orange Juice	Gordon Van Liew	Offy* R	
9	Jud Larson	Michner Petroleum	Michner Petroleum, Inc.	Ford R	
10	Jim Clark	STP Oil Treatment	STP Division Studebaker	BRM R	Did not arrive
15	Greg Weld	STP Oil Treatment	STP Division Studebaker	Novi* 4	Wreck. qual., wrm up
17	Ronnie Duman	Jim Robbins	Jim Robbins Co.	Ford R	Didn't complete run
	Bob Mathouser				Didn't complete run
23	Dave Paul	Paul Enterprise	David A. Paul	Offy R	
32	Art Malone	Wally Weir	Walter Weir, Jr.	Offy R	Wrecked in practice
35	Ralph Liguori	Flynn	Walter J. Flynn	Ford R	
36	Bob Hurt	Viking Racing	Viking Racing, Inc.	Offy* R	Didn't complete run
38	Sam Sessions	Federal Engineering	Federal Auto. Associates	Offy R	Didn't complete run
41	Bobby Johns	Prestone	Geo. R. Bryant Racing	Ford R	Didn't complete run
44	Art Pollard	Hegar & Compton	Hegar & R. Compton	Offy R	157.985, 2nd. alt.
45	A. J. Foyt	Sheraton-Thompson	Ansted-Thompson Racing	Ford R	Didn't complete run
46		Gerhardt Offy	Fred Gerhardt	Offy* R	
48	Bob Harkey	Prather	C. O. Prather	Offy R	
49	Hal Minyard	Ring Free-Ansen	Senter & Tipton	Offy R	
51	Dempsey Wilson	Greenman-Wilson	L. Greenman & D. Wilson	Chevy R	
52	Jim McElreath	Zink-Urschel-Slick	Zink-Urschel-Slick	Offy* R	
55	Ron Lux	Barnett Bros.	Joe G. Barnett	Offy	
	Bob Christie				Didn't complete run
57		Agajanian Rev 500	J. C. Agajanian	Ford R	Did not arrive
59		STP Gas Treatment	STP Division Studebaker	Novi* 4	Did not arrive
61	Bob Tattersall	McManus	David R. McManus	Offy R	
63	Bob Veith	MG Liquid Suspension	Kjell H. Qvale	Chevy R	
64	Mario Andretti	Dean Van Lines	Dean Racing Enterprises	Ford R	
65	Mike McGreevy	Travelon Trailer	Ernest L. Ruiz	Offy R	
	Bob Wente				Didn't complete run
67	Bob Veith	MG Liquid Suspension	Kjell H. Qvale	Offy* R	Didn't complete run
68	Bruce Jacobi	Western Racing Asscts.	George O. Reves	Chevy R	
	Ronnie Bucknum				Didn't complete run
69	Ronnie Bucknum	Arciero	Frank Arciero	Chevy R	
71	Gig Stephens	Fairchild Hiller	Karl Hall	Offy R	
74		Blum	Henry Blum	Rambler*	
76	Lee Roy Yarbrough	Pure Firebird 76	Jim Rathmann	Offy* R	Wrecked in practice
78	Masten Gregory	G. C. Murphy	Lindsey Hopkins	Ford R	Didn't complete run
79	Bill Cheesbourg	Stein Twin Porsche	Albert H. Stein	2 Porsch 4	
81	Bob Harkey	Central Excavating	Pete Salemi	Offy R	
84	Al Unser	STP Gas Treatment	STP Division Studebaker	BRM R	Did not arrive
85	Bob Wente	Caves Buick Offy	Caves Buick Co.	Offy* R	
	Bob Harkey				Didn't complete run
86	Chuck Hulse	Leader Card Racer	Leader Cards, Inc.	Ford R	
87	Red Reigel	Calif. Speed & Sport	Joseph J. Barzda	Offy R	Wrecked in practice
89	Jack Conley	Conley & McManus	J. Conley & D. McManus	Offy R	
91	Don Branson	Leader Card Racer	Leader Cards, Inc.	Ford R	
92	Chuck Rodee	Leader Card Racer	Leader Cards, Inc.	Ford R	Wrecked qualifying
93		Harrison	J. Frank Harrison	Chevy R	
97	Dick Atkins	Agajanian Rev 500	J. C. Agajanian	Offy* R	158.158, 1st. alt.
99	Bill Cheesbourg	Jack Adams Aircraft	Norm Demler, Inc.	Gas Turbine	

*Supercharged   ¢Front drive   4Four wheel drive   RRear Engine

1958 Bob Cortner

1958 Le Roy Warriner

1958 Troy Ruttman

1959 Tony Bettenhausen

1959 Ralph Liguori

1959 Dempsey Wilson

1959 Rex Easton

1959 Bob Cortner

1959 Jud Larson

1959 Jim Packard

1959 Jerry Unser

1959 Bill Homeier

1959 Shorty Templeman

1959 Bob Schroeder

1959 Van Johnson

1959 Chuck Daigh

1960 Ebb Rose

1960 Bill Cheesbourg

1960 Jack Rounds

1960 Chuck Hulse

1960 Chuck Rodee

1961 Bob Cleberg

1961 Paul Russo

1961 "Cotton" Farmer

1961   Bob Veith

1961   Jim McWithey

1961   Chuck Arnold

1961   Bert Brooks

1961   Norm Hall

1961   Duke Dinsmore

1962   Bruce Jacobi

1962   Chuck Arnold

1962   Ronnie Duman

1962   "Porky" Rachwitz

1962   Chuck Daigh

1962   Tommy Copp

1962   Al Miller

1962   Duane Carter

1963   Len Sutton

1963   Curtis Turner

1963   Ronnie Duman

1963   Chuck Rodee

1963   Ebb Rose

1963   Pedro Rodriguez

1963   Masten Gregory

1963   Jack Conley

1964   Chuck Rodee

1964   Johnny Rutherford

 1964 Paul Russo

 1964 Bob Christie

 1964 Don Horvath

 1964 Ralph Liguori

 1964 Bobby Johns

 1964 Pedro Rodriguez

 1964 Masten Gregory

 1964 Jud Larson

 1964 Al Miller

 1964 Parnelli Jones

 1965 Norm Hall

 1965 Bob Harkey

 1965 Bob Christie

 1965 Paul Goldsmith

 1965 Ronnie Duman

 1965 Al Unser

 1966 Greg Weld

 1966 Bob Hurt

 1966 Art Pollard

 1966 Dempsey Wilson

 1966 Bob Veith

 1966 Bill Cheesbourg

 1966 Bob Wente

 1966 Dick Atkins